Renaissances

EUROPEAN STUDIES SERIES

General Editors: Colin Jones, Richard Overy, Joe Bergin, John Breuilly and Patricia Clavin

Published

Robert Aldrich	*Greater France: A Short History of French Overseas Expansion*
Nigel Aston	*Religion and Revolution in France, 1780–1804*
Yves-Marie Bercé	*The Birth of Absolutism: A History of France, 1598–1661*
Christopher F. Black	*Church, Religion and Society in Early Modern Italy*
Susan K. Foley	*Women in France since 1789*
Janine Garrisson	*A History of Sixteenth-Century France, 1483–1589*
Gregory Hanlon	*Early Modern Italy, 1550–1800*
Michael Hughes	*Early Modern Germany, 1477–1806*
Matthew Jefferies	*Imperial Culture in Germany, 1871–1918*
Dieter Langewiesche	*Liberalism in Germany*
Martyn Lyons	*Napoleon Bonaparte and the Legacy of the French Revolution*
Richard Mackenney	*Renaissances: The Cultures of Italy, c.1300–c.1600*
Hugh McLeod	*The Secularisation of Western Europe, 1848–1914*
Robin Okey	*The Habsburg Monarchy, c.1765–1918*
Pamela M. Pilbeam	*Republicanism in Nineteenth-Century France, 1814–1871*
Helen Rawlings	*Church, Religion and Society in Early Modern Spain*
Tom Scott	*Society and Economy in Germany, 1300–1600*
Wolfram Siemann	*The German Revolution of 1848–49*
Richard Vinen	*France, 1934–1970*

Renaissances

The Cultures of Italy, *c.*1300–*c.*1600

RICHARD MACKENNEY

First published 2005 by
PALGRAVE MACMILLAN
Houndmills, Basingstoke, Hampshire RG21 6XS and
175 Fifth Avenue, New York, N.Y. 10010
Companies and representatives throughout the world

PALGRAVE MACMILLAN is the global academic imprint of the Palgrave Macmillan division of St. Martin's Press, LLC and of Palgrave Macmillan Ltd. Macmillan® is a registered trademark in the United States, United Kingdom and other countries. Palgrave is a registered trademark in the European Union and other countries.

ISBN 0–333–62904–3 hardback
ISBN 0–333–62905–1 paperback

This book is printed on paper suitable for recycling and made from fully managed and sustained forest sources.

A catalogue record for this book is available from the British Library.

A catalog record for this book is available from the Library of Congress.

10   9   8   7   6   5   4   3   2   1
14   13   12   11   10   09   08   07   06   05

Printed in China

For Margaret
Per celebrare la memoria di una grande donna

Contents

List of Illustrations

Figures

Plates

Acknowledgements

This book has been ten years in the making. In that time, I have accumulated one set of academic and intellectual debts to people whose patience and encouragement have brought the work to eventual fruition, and another set which are deeply personal to friends who have shored me up in difficult times. It is a wonderful comment on human magnanimity that many people come into both categories. All of these debts are much greater than those whom I acknowledge below can ever know, and certainly more than I can ever repay.

The Department and latterly the School of History in the University of Edinburgh have been immensely supportive in the long process of production. I am fortunate to work in an environment in which I count so many of my colleagues among my friends. The University's librarians have remained cheerful and helpful in tracing often very obscure references despite the appalling pressures upon them. The argument of this study of the recovery of pagan antiquity owes much to my struggles with Augustine in the neo-Gothic surroundings of New College Library in the School of Divinity.

For their extensive insights on the text in its various stages of development, and for all the improvements for which they are responsible, I thank Michael Angold, Rob and Nora Bartlett, Peter Burke, Owen Dudley Edwards, and Peter and Doreen Laven, Peter Brand (Chapter 8) and Mike Spiller (Chapter 9). All of them have been both kind and heroic. For publication, Brian Pullan and Joe Bergin made wise comments that helped pull the final version into shape. Terka Acton and Sonya Barker have been unfailingly patient. I am very grateful to Bruce Hunter for his deft handling of negotiations. Ben Angove's work on the illustrations was invaluable, as was the hospitality of his brother Greig. Katy Coutts was a sensitive and perceptive copy-editor. The remaining errors are mine.

For gentle friendship when the going was very tough, whether consistently or at key moments, I am forever indebted to some of the best people one could hope to know (and their children): Rosemary and Hugh Gentleman, Hattie and Martin Chick (Fred and Tom), David and Alex Howarth (Jessica, Naomi and Alice), Kate and Simon Dessain (Constanza, Amabella, Georgia Rose and Alexander), Maurice and Enid Larkin, Nick Phillipson, Jill and Steve Stephenson, Tricia Allerston and Patrick Elliot,

Chris and Elizabeth Black, Gary and Margaret Dickson, Caroline Cullen (Ryan and Bremner), Gloria Ketchin, Randall Stevenson and Sarah Carpenter, Dorothy Finnie, Paul and Wendy Hartle, Stephen Lees, Rob Wyke, John and Margaret Stephens (Lizzie, Mary and Joe), John Hall, and Mick Lewis and Alison Barnett (Jessica and William). For practical assistance in keeping me going, I very warmly thank Terry and Joan Cole, Jeremy Crang and Fiona Douglas, Jim and Lorraine Francis, Janette Rutherford, and Roger Paige. For reminding me of the sweetness of life, I thank Robert Anderson, Jim and Donatella McMillan, Ken and Anne Fowler, and Tony and Jackie Goodman. My son George has worked hard and thought hard to stay in touch, and I love him for it.

Undergraduate students in Edinburgh have contributed much to the book, as have the postgraduates whose research on the Renaissance I have been privileged to supervise: Alistair Millar, Stephen Bowd, James Shaw, Henry Knox, May-shine Lin, and William Landon and his wife Carla. The Thursday class in Continuing Education – all of them, but I single out Gay, Frank, Ian, John, Dorothy, and Tom – merits special mention for sitting through an entire draft in the autumn of 2001, as does my undergraduate class at Colgate in the fall of 2003. The warmth of my welcome to upstate New York introduced me to a delightful environment in which to put the very last touches to the project.

My final acknowledgements are intensely personal – and go way beyond what words can express. Jane and Roger Gouldstone, my sister and brother-in-law, have always found time for me and never lost faith in me – and more recently the same has been true of my friend Margaret Angove.

Richard Mackenney

Dutton Signet, a division of Penguin Group (USA) Inc., for *Great Dialogues of Plato* by Plato, translated by W.H.D. Rouse, © 1984 by J.C.G. Rouse.

Edimedia, for Leonardo, *Cloudburst*, Windsor, Royal Library, reproduced courtesy of Edimedia.

George Kay and Penguin Books for 'Cantico delle creature' by St Francis of Assisi; 'A Carnival Song' by Lorenzo de Medici and 'Hymn to Bacchus' by Andrea Poliziano from *The Penguin Book of Italian Verse* edited by George R. Kay (Penguin Books 1958, revised edition 1965) copyright © George Kay, 1958, 1965.

Metronome Recordings, Ltd, for permission to reproduce the sleeve notes to *Music and Art: Florence*, produced by Metronome Recordings, Ltd, in association with the National Gallery.

Metropolitan Museum of Art, New York, for Piero di Cosimo, *Human Life in the Stone Age: Hunting Scene* and Piero di Cosimo, *Human Life in the Stone Age: Return from the Hunt*. Both paintings a gift of Robert Gordon, 1875. All rights reserved, The Metropolitan Museum of Art.

National Gallery of Art, Washington, DC, for Giovanni Bellini, *The Feast of the Gods*, Widener Collection, image © Board of Trustees, National Gallery of Art, Washington, DC.

National Gallery, London, for Piero di Cosimo, *The Fight between the Lapiths and the Centaurs*; Sassetta, *The Legend of the Wolf of Gubbio*; Titian, *Bacchus and Ariadne*; Ugolino di Nerio, *The Resurrection*; all images © National Gallery, London.

Princeton University Press for Piero della Francesca, 'Of the Perspective of Painting', in *A Documentary History of Art, Vol. 1: The Middle Ages and the Renaissance*, ed. Elizabeth Holt (1957), © 1987 by Princeton University Press.

Scala, Florence, for Uccello, Paolo (1397–1475), *Faceted Chalice*, Florence, Gabinetto dei Disegni e delle Stampe degli Uffizi © 1990, Photo Scala, Florence; Angelico, Fra (1387–1455), *Crucifixion with the Virgin and Saints Cosmas, John and Peter Martyr*, Florence, Museo di San Marco © 1995, Photo Scala, Florence – courtesy of the Ministero Beni e Att. Culturali; Orcagna, Andrea (14th cent.), *Triumph of Death* – detail showing the beggars,

Florence, Santa Croce (Museum) © 1990, Photo Scala, Florence – courtesy of the Ministero Beni e Att. Culturali; Titian (1477/89–1576), *Bacchanal*, Madrid, Prado © 1995, Photo Scala, Florence; Titian, *Offerings to Venus*, Madrid, Prado © 1996, Photo Scala, Florence; Giotto (1266–1336), *Last Judgment* – detail showing the damned, Padua, Scrovegni Chapel © 1990, Photo Scala, Florence.

Sarah Challis for Fig. 6, p. 37, in Ross King, *Brunelleschi's Dome: The Story of the Great Cathedral in Florence* (2001), © Sarah Challis.

Every effort has been made to trace the copyright holders but if any have been inadvertently overlooked the publishers will be pleased to make the necessary arrangement at the first opportunity.

A Note on Illustrations and Translations

Illustrations

The argument makes frequent reference to works of art. However, including all the works referred to in illustration proved neither practical nor desirable. Accordingly, I have limited illustration to works which are either less familiar than some of the more renowned images of the Renaissance, or which are not often seen in combination. Into the first category come the works of Piero di Cosimo, into the second the Camerino of the d'Este in Ferrara (memorably assembled in the National Gallery in London in 2003). These feature importantly in Chapter 7. However, I have also provided a list of works referred to which the reader may wish to pursue or examine at leisure. As appropriate, these are numbered in square brackets in the body of the text (as O.1, O.2, O.3, etc.), and their location in museum, gallery or collection is listed at the end of the book. They should prove readily accessible in books on the collections or on individual artists. Alternatively, it may well be fruitful for some readers to view these works from web sites on the Internet.

Translations

Wherever possible, I have made my own translation from the original Latin or Italian. I have then referred the reader to another modern translation – probably both smoother and more accessible – in the endnotes. Translations from the Greek are acknowledged as those of other scholars, and in one or two instances where I could not track down an original, I have used a standard translation. I am grateful for permission to cite the published work of others in these cases.

Map of the Italian peninsula showing places mentioned in the text, and principal political divisions, *c.*1494. 'For I do not really know whether Italy's not coming under a monarchy has been fortunate or unfortunate for this land' – Francesco Guicciardini.

Ugolino di Nerio, *Resurrection*. From Santa Croce altarpiece, *c.*1324–5. London, National Gallery.

Forewords

Another book on the Italian Renaissance? The very question reeks of the weariness and terror that an author feels when confronting the vast, varied and venerable literature on this endlessly fascinating and enduringly enigmatic subject. There is no condescension in the term 'venerable'. On the contrary, it retains connotations of work that has stood the test of time and is deserving of the highest respect. Jacob Burckhardt's extraordinary meditations on Italy from the mid-nineteenth century remain the essential starting point; John Hale's masterpiece from the late twentieth, movingly brought to fruition by his wife Sheila and by David Chambers, extends and completes the picture for Europe as a whole.[1] Those works remain the essential bookends for this study. One contemplates with joy and awe the extraordinarily rich shelf of literature that comes between them. For the purposes of manageability and accessibility for a general audience, the works referred to in this book are largely available in English. Even with that confinement, the list of significant scholarship is very long indeed. On the Renaissance itself, there are John Addington Symonds's seven monumental volumes (the first of which was published long ago, in 1875). Other general interpretations are of widely different character: Denys Hay's many pioneering aperçus, Peter Burke's inquisitive vitality, the raw challenge of Lauro Martines, the meditative connection of antiquity and its revival in the work of John Stephens. Brilliant insights from an older generation present themselves in the essays of Walter Pater and Johan Huizinga. In assessing the arts, one turns to the towering scholarship of Erwin Panofsky, Ernst Gombrich, Edgar Wind, and – though it is elegantly disguised – of Kenneth Clark. One feeds off the rich understanding of the history of Italy in the work of John Larner, Brian Pullan, Peter Laven. That distinguished list says nothing of work on specific places and themes: Gene Brucker, Marvin Becker, George Holmes, Nicolai Rubinstein on Florence; Hans Baron, Eugenio Garin, Paul Kristeller and a host of others on humanism; Frances Yates, Peter Burke (again) and, most recently, Stephen Greenblatt on the European connections. In the works in other languages, passing mention does no justice to the contributions of André Chastel in French, Federico Chabod, Eugenio Garin or Vettore Branca in Italian. Such a list is arbitrary, almost whimsical, and one can only apologise to those scholars

1

not mentioned in it, though they are included, I hope, in the Bibliography, which remains only a hint of what there is to read and learn from.

Then, as the sense of one's ignorance burgeons, one trembles at the prospect of saying anything new about the giants who populated the place and the period: Giotto, Dante, Petrarch, Donatello, Brunelleschi, Botticelli, Leonardo, Raphael, Michelangelo, Titian, Machiavelli, Monteverdi, Galileo. Overall, one feels trapped between two unsatisfactory mental processes: the first that synthesises everybody else's syntheses, the second that summarises a lifetime of scholarship in a few glib lines.

This book seeks to make a virtue of necessity by combining both approaches. It is intended for the general reader who knows little of the detail of the Renaissance, but the generalities are illustrated with specific case histories drawn as often as possible from primary sources, and this may be of interest to some specialist readers. The title emphasises the plurality of achievement in the Renaissance and the diversities of Italy. The central paradox – some would say tragedy – of the Italian experience is that the regional identities that made possible the Renaissance made impossible the unification of Italy. Put another way, what set Italy in the vanguard of cultural achievement also made it lag behind other parts of Europe in political development.[2] In order to take account of scholarship on the centres and regions, the title and chapter headings preserve a deliberate plurality: there is no unitary phenomenon called 'the Renaissance' in this book. With deference to one of the formative influences on what the book contains, perhaps one might suggest that the plurality that the great Erwin Panofsky applied to preceding classical revivals or 'renascences' might be applied to 'the Renaissance' itself. After all, one of Panofsky's 'renascences' occurred in the twelfth century, and medievalists had already begun to see it as a fully fledged 'Renaissance' in its own right.[3]

Fear and despair have certainly figured prominently in the writing of this book. What, if anything, might make it worth reading? After many years of unsatisfactory writing (and some of not writing at all), I hope that the finished product may have certain features to recommend it. The first and foremost of these is clarity of scope and organisation. In this, my model in style and method has been Aldous Huxley, whose writings on cultural history seem to me sadly neglected. Some enlargement is necessary here, since I do not intend to tie myself in methodological knots over what constitutes 'cultural history'. Under 'culture', the *Oxford English Dictionary* quotes Matthew Arnold: 'the acquainting ourselves with the best that has been known or said in the world'. Huxley's credentials as a historian of culture so defined assert themselves most expansively in his remarkable studies of the Baroque: *The Devils of Loudon* (1952) and, less famously, but no less worthy of note, _Grey Eminence (1941)_. Though neither book is based on primary sources, both explore the attitudes and mindsets of the Baroque, and particularly the relationship between religion and politics, in brave new ways. More specifically in relation to the Renaissance, Huxley wrote a string of superlatively witty essays that suggest the coincidence of his views with those of Arnold. In particular, one refers to 'Conxolus' on fashionable mediocrity, and to the majestic piece entitled, unashamedly, 'The Best Picture' – meaning 'best in the world', by the way, which in Huxley's view is Piero della Francesca's _Resurrection_ in Borgo San Sepolcro. It helps to define a central theme of this book, depicting as it does the solemn triumph of Christ over the ancient Romans. There was no snobbery in Huxley's aesthetics, and he had an acute sensitivity to the rhythms of popular culture (see below, Chapter 8).[4]

There are two matters that connect Huxley to the themes and preoccupations of the chapters that follow. The first is his acute sensitivity to matters of perception and sight, partly despite his own near blindness, partly because of it. Through what gauzes we might see reality, and how its outlines might prove distorted, is the subject of _Doors of Perception_ (1954). Second, the very last essay that Huxley wrote, 'Shakespeare and Religion', is precocious in Anglophone writing as an exploration of historical mentalities.[5] In many ways it might be said to foreshadow the ideas of the celebrated modern Shakespearean scholar Stephen Greenblatt. As a tribute to both Huxley and Greenblatt, the last chapter of this book is unashamedly devoted to Shakespeare and his connections with the Renaissance (see below, Chapter 9). Huxley had just completed the essay when he died, on 22 November 1963. He passed away as news came through of the assassination of President John F. Kennedy, and one wonders whether that event rather put posthumous assessments of Huxley's importance in the shade.[6]

With regard to the limited amount that my own thinking has brought to the text, here are some of the intentions. As a chronological narrative, the story begins with the building of the chapel that Giotto di Bondone (1266/7–1337) was to decorate in Padua for the merchant-usurer Enrico Scrovegni in 1300. Within the Italian peninsula, it ends with a sketch of the new developments in science associated with the trial of the astronomer and mathematician Galileo Galilei by the Roman Inquisition in 1632 and in music with the first recognisable opera, Monteverdi's _Orfeo,_ first performed in 1643 (Chapter 8). Thus, the book spans three centuries of development in Italy: the _Trecento_ (fourteenth century), the _Quattrocento_ (fifteenth) and the _Cinquecento_ (sixteenth). The Italian Renaissance may be seen as an exploration of new dimensions (Chapters 6 and 7), and it is very tempting to define the chronological span as stretching from Giotto to Galileo, both of whom have given their names to space probes.

However, that is too neat. The temptation to see the trial of Galileo as the end of free inquiry becomes too strong, and too formulaic. Music and science in an important sense open a new era in which cultural explorations seek to escape from an ecclesiological framework. Significantly, the latest work of art discussed in any detail is Gianlorenzo Bernini's sculpture of the *Ecstasy of Santa Teresa* from 1650, marking, as it does, the triumph – ambiguous but perhaps necessary – of Christian over classical values (Chapter 7). However, the Renaissance that began in Italy was to find its culminating expression beyond the peninsula. The very last chapter suggests that the story of the Italian Renaissance finishes a little earlier, with Shakespeare's *The Tempest* in 1613 and, symbolically, with the destruction of the Globe Theatre by fire in the same year. The unifying continuum of the discussion is an exploration of how shadows of puppets before Plato's captive audience in the cave in the world of ancient Greece become the creations of Renaissance artists and finally the illusions of Shakespeare's Prospero.

Chiaroscuro: the management of shadows

Conventionally enough, the book addresses the Renaissance in Italy as a revival of interest in the cultures of antiquity and the questions that arose from that interest with regard to the Christian centuries that came to be known as the 'Middle Ages'. In an effort to dispel some of the ho-hum sameness that surrounds such an approach, I have focused discussion in particular on one representative of the ancient world, the Greek philosopher Plato (*c*.427–347 BC), and one representative of the Middle Ages, the theologian St Augustine (AD 354–430). Neither is a monolithic figure representing the two conflicting traditions of 'ancient paganism' and 'medieval Christianity', as though either of those phenomena were simple, static and unitary. Plato, in his quest for the sublime, can seem to be a precursor of some of the fundamental principles of Christianity. Augustine's interest in the classical philosophy of Plato was both passionate and dispassionate, and he can seem a forerunner of the humanists of the Renaissance rather than the originator of 'medieval' Christianity. While respecting those ambiguities – which existed throughout the Middle Ages and the Renaissance – both figures are symbolically representative. The Platonic quest for the sublime was to be achieved through the cultivation of the soul. This dispensed with the need for a priestly intermediary, which was, at least by implication, a threat to the machinery of salvation provided by the medieval Christian Church. Augustine, meanwhile, was the most formidable of the great Christian philosophers who stood between Renaissance humanists and the classical past that they sought to explore. He had already censored much of the culture of pagan antiquity and synthesised it with Christian principles before that culture was 'rediscovered' in the Renaissance.

Yet the ambiguities remain, and are caught under the subheading 'Chiaroscuro'. Much of what follows is a discussion of the relationship between paganism and Christianity. But there is a still larger question of the relationship between reason and faith, between reality and illusion. The Renaissance marked one of the most significant changes in the way human beings viewed the world around them and their place within it. New modes of perception prompted new ways of representation. That in turn intensified experimentation with different intensities of light and shade applied to all the colours of the spectrum. The protagonists in succeeding chapters are engaged in the management of shadows, the technical definition of the term *chiaroscuro*. Plato argues that shadows can be more comforting than realities, Augustine insists on black-and-white certainties, humanists conversed with the ghosts of antiquity, artists represented reality through the management of all the tonalities of light and shade. The possibilities that faith might be a surer guide to reality than reason, and that reality without faith might take reason away, are the psychological double helix at the centre of the argument.

The book takes as the most representative – and the most elusive – passage of Plato's writings part of the philosopher's cave sequence from *The Republic* (see pp. 6–11). This deals with illusion and reality and the problem of distinguishing the one from the other. As a starting point for a book on the Renaissance, the juxtaposition of light and dark seems appropriate both for its significance as an artistic technique, and in the idea that the humanists 'brought to light' the culture of antiquity by rescuing it from the 'Dark Ages'. The relevant passage is reproduced in full at the end of this introduction. St Augustine, on the other hand, was immersed in Platonic as well as Christian learning. He appears as an unsurpassable and insurmountable censor of the culture of the ancient world in Chapters 6, 7 and briefly in Chapter 8, a censor whom Renaissance humanists and artists could neither get round nor climb over.

This leads to consideration of the book's organisation. The first five chapters pick out what appear to be the most significant features of the social and political contexts in which the Renaissance unfolded. Chapter 1 tries to ditch some of the more cloying aspects of the existing historiography as a prelude to piecing together the salient features of an appropriate chronology (which includes the 'Middle Ages') in Chapter 2. The urban and courtly milieux form the subjects of Chapters 3 and 4 respectively, while Chapter 5 concentrates specifically on the question of patronage.

There is no necessary or determinist connection between the first five chapters and the last four. To try to understand the social context of artistic creativity is not to deny the autonomy of that creativity itself. Chapter 6 deals with the nature of humanism and its relationship, via Augustine, with the ancient world, Chapter 7 replicates the exercise for the visual arts. Both suggest ways in which the study of the ancient world raised some fundamental questions about traditional Christian cosmology. Chapter 8 examines the sound world of the Italian Renaissance, the role of language and literature and, latterly, of music and science in the development of Renaissance culture. The book finishes with some examples of how the discoveries and rediscoveries of the Renaissance in Italy reached a broader Anglophone audience – including us – in the plays of Shakespeare.

This is, of necessity, a selective rather than an encyclopaedic exercise. Its unifying theme is *chiaroscuro,* formally defined in Renaissance art as 'the management of shadows', more expansively used here as the exploration of the delights and dangers of creating illusions, managing appearances and fashioning the self. Plato's dialogue on shadows and realities provides a philosophical model for the scholars and artists whose endeavours have given us our notions of the Italian Renaissance. That is also the source of the tremendous tension that existed between the lay, secularising cultures of the Renaissance and the authority (variously and sometimes conflictingly asserted) of the Christian Church and its teachings. The former was the property of a tiny social elite, the latter felt a duty to protect what it saw as the spiritual well-being of the much larger community of souls within its care. The Church's arguments were perhaps stronger and more reasoned than is usually assumed, the activities of the secular and lay elites more introverted and self-indulgent. Neither side in the cultural debate promoted the cause of Italy as a whole, the one intensifying attachment to regions, the other to universals. Persons on both sides sometimes changed sides. While the discussion retains a forward momentum, I have found myself returning to the same topics: the detachment of princely courts from society at large in the later fifteenth century, the impact of the Italian Wars (1494–1530) on the disunited peninsula, the centrality of the Sistine Chapel, Julius II (pope 1503–13) and Michelangelo (1475–1564). Rather than this being mere turgid repetition, I hope that the approach will always be from different angles, my own tiny planet circling a central source of light in the quest for illumination.

In Book VII of *The Republic*, Plato sets out a 'parable of education and ignorance as a picture of the condition of our nature'. It is expressed through the mouth of Socrates recalling his own discourses, with brief assents from Glaucon. While the quest for the sublime remains apparently elevating and enlightening, it has a darker political potentiality. How many humans are to see the light? And does that give them power over those who remain in darkness? Who controls what the illusions are – or seem to be?

'Imagine mankind as dwelling in an underground cave with a long entrance open to the light across the whole width of the cave; in this they have been from childhood, with necks and legs fettered, so they have to stay where they are [Figure 1]. They cannot move their heads round because of the fetters, and they can only look forward, but light comes to them from fire burning behind them higher up at a distance. Between the fire and the prisoners is a road above their level, and along it imagine a low wall has been built, as puppet showmen have screens in front of their people over which they work their puppets.'

'I see,' he said.

'See, then, bearers carrying along this wall all sorts of articles which they hold projecting above the wall, statues of men and other living things, made of stone or wood and all kinds of stuff, some of the bearers speaking and some silent, as you might expect.'

'What a remarkable image,' he said, 'and what remarkable prisoners!'

'Just like ourselves,' I said. 'For, first of all, tell me this: What do you think such people would have seen of themselves and each other except their shadows, which the fire cast on the opposite wall of the cave?'

'I don't see how they could see anything else,' said he, 'if they were compelled to keep their heads unmoving all their lives!'

'Very well, what of the things being carried along? Would not this be the same?'

'Of course it would.'

'Suppose the prisoners were able to talk together, don't you think that when they named the shadows which they saw passing they would believe they were naming real things?'

'Necessarily.'

'Then if their prison had an echo from the opposite wall, whenever one of the passing bearers uttered a sound, would they not suppose that the passing shadow must be making the sound? Don't you think so?'

'Indeed I do,' he said.

'If so,' said I, 'such persons would certainly believe there were no realities except those shadows of handmade things.'

'So it must be,' said he.

Figure 1 Plato's cave[7]

'Now consider,' said I, 'what their release would be like, and their cure from these fetters and their folly; let us imagine whether it might naturally be something like this. One might be released, and compelled suddenly to stand up and turn his neck round, and to walk and look towards the firelight; all this would hurt him, and he would be too much dazzled to see distinctly those things whose shadows he had seen before. What do you think he would say, if someone told him that what he saw before was foolery, but now he saw more rightly, being a bit nearer reality and turned towards what was a little more real? What if he were shown each of the passing things, and compelled by questions to answer what each one was? Don't you think he would be puzzled, and believe what he saw before was more true than what was shown to him now?'

'Far more,' he said.

'Then suppose he were compelled to look towards the real light, it would hurt his eyes, and he would escape by turning them away to the things which he was able to look at, and these he would believe to be clearer than what was being shown to him.'

'Just so,' said he.

'Suppose, now,' said I, 'that someone should drag him thence by force, up the rough ascent, the steep way up, and never stop until he could drag him out into the light of the sun, would he not be distressed and furious at being dragged; and when he came into the light, the brilliance would fill his eyes and he would not be able to see even one of the things now called real?'

'That he would not,' said he, 'all of a sudden'.

(Plato continues with this strange and painful initiation into understanding until it eventually brings enlightenment. But who would choose the initiates? How many are there to be? And what of those who remain in the dark?)

'He would have to get used to it, surely, I think, if he is to see the things above. First he would most easily look at shadows, after that images of mankind and the rest in water, lastly the things themselves. After this he would find it easier to survey by night the heavens themselves and all that is in them, gazing at the light of the stars and moon, rather than by day at the sun and the sun's light.'

'Of course.'

'Last of all, I suppose, the sun; he could look on the sun itself by itself in its own place, and see what it is like, not reflections of it in water or as it appears in some alien setting.'

'Necessarily,' said he.

'And only after all this he might reason about it, how this is he who provides seasons and years, and is set over all there is in the visible region, and he is in a manner the cause of all things which they saw.'

'Yes, it is clear,' said he, 'that after all that, he would come to this last.'

'Very good. Let him be reminded of his first habitation, and what was wisdom in that place, and of his fellow-prisoners there; don't you think he would bless himself for the change, and pity them?'

'Yes, indeed.'

'And if there were honours and praises among them and prizes for the one who saw the passing things most sharply and remembered best which of them used to come before and which after and which together, and from these was best able to prophesy accordingly what was going to come – do you believe he would set his desire on that, and envy those who were honoured men or potentates among them? Would he not feel as Homer says, and heartily desire rather to be serf of some landless man on earth and to endure anything in the world, rather than to opine as they did and to live in that way?'

'Yes, indeed,' said he, 'he would rather accept anything than live like that.'

'Then again,' I said, 'just consider: if such a one should go down again and sit on his old seat, would he not get his eyes full of darkness coming in suddenly out of the sun?'

'Very much so,' said he.

'And if he should have to compete with those who had been always prisoners, by laying down the law about those shadows while he was blinking before his eyes were settled down – and it would take a good long time to get used to things – wouldn't they all laugh at him and say he had spoiled his eyesight by going up there, and it was not worth-while so much as to try to go up? And would they not kill anyone who tried to release them and take them up, if they could somehow lay hands on him and kill him?'

'That they would!' said he.

'Then we must apply this image, my dear Glaucon,' said I, 'to all we have been saying. The world of our sight is like the habitation in prison, the firelight there to the sunlight here, the ascent and the view of the upper world is the rising of the soul into the world of mind; put it so and you will not be far from my own surmise, since that is what you want; but God knows if it is really true. At least, what appears to me is, that in the world of the known, last of all, is the idea of the good, and with what toil to be seen! And seen, this must be inferred to be the cause of all right and beautiful things for all, which gives birth to light and the king of light in the world of sight, and, in the world of mind, herself the queen produces truth and reason; and she must be seen by one who is to act with reason publicly or privately.'[8]

A closely similar exploration of the relationship between reality and illusion was central to the art of the Renaissance. What made possible a systematic reordering of the relationship was linear perspective. The first artist to apply these rules in a rigorously scientific fashion was a Florentine architect, the engineer of the vast cupola on the Duomo, Filippo Brunelleschi (1377–1446). According to his biographer, Antonio Manetti, he devised an experiment that set onlookers the task of distinguishing between the illusion that he had created and its real surroundings. Brunelleschi was not trained in humanism, and there is no suggestion that he had Plato in mind when he conducted the exercise. The impulse to make people think hard about the reproduction of reality as an amazing and original feat is symptomatic of the extraordinary confidence that characterised the cultures of Italy. That same confidence led Brunelleschi to place his representation of reality in situ with reality itself and is a precise illustration of the parallels one can draw between classical Athens and Renaissance Florence, between the ancient world and its revival. Brunelleschi painted a picture of the Baptistery in Florence from a specific point inside the main door of the Cathedral of Santa Maria del Fiore [Figure 2]. The viewer was then challenged to look, from exactly the same position, through the back of the painted panel at a reflection of the picture in the exact location of the Baptistery that it represented [Figure 3].

To blur the edges of the panel, 'he put burnished silver, so that the air and natural skies might be reflected in it; and thus also the clouds, which are seen in that silver, are moved by the wind when it blows':

... he had made a hole in the panel on which there was this painting, which came to be situated in the part of the church of San Giovanni, where the eye struck, directly opposite anyone who looked out from that place inside the central door of Santa Maria del Fiore, where he would have been positioned if he had portrayed it. This hole was as small as a lentil on the side of the painting, and on the back it opened out pyramidally, as does a woman's straw hat, as much as would be the size of a ducat or a little more. And he wished the eye to be placed at the back, where it was large, by whoever had it to see, and with the one hand bringing it close to the eye, and with the other holding a plain

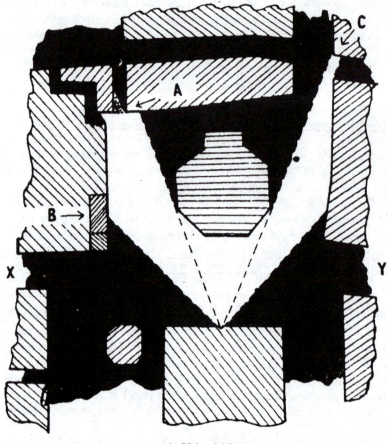

A. Volta dei Pecori
B. Misericordia
C. Canto alla Paglia
X. Via de' Calzaioli
Y. Via de' Martelli

Figure 2 Brunelleschi's illusion (1): the Baptistery seen from Santa Maria del Fiore[9]

mirror opposite, which came to reflect back the painting; and the distance of the mirror in the other hand, came to be about the distance in small braccia as that in true braccia, from the place where he showed that he had been to paint it, as far as the church of San

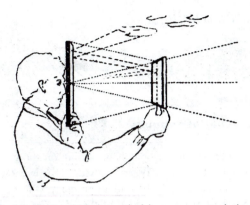

Figure 3 Brunelleschi's illusion (2): the optical instrument – painting to the left, mirror to the right[10]

Giovanni, which on looking at it, with the other circumstances already mentioned of the burnished silver and of the piazza and so on and of the hole, it seemed as if one saw the real thing ['pareva che si vedessi 'l proprio vero']: and I have had it in my hand and seen it several times in my life, and I can give testimony of it.[11]

1 Deconstructions

The temptations of antiquity

There are certain abiding problems in writing on the Renaissance which continue to generate debate. When studying what is known as the Italian Renaissance, one needs to be careful about defining terms. In this chapter discussion revolves around the idea of the 'Renaissance' itself. However, that may imply a break with the past, a break that, since Burckhardt, has raised questions about how far the dawn of 'modernity' is marked by 'individualism'. That in turn may give rise to a dangerously monolithic and unitary idea of the preceding 'Middle Ages'. With regard to 'modernity', the relationship between 'art' and 'science' in the Renaissance was very different from the one that exists in our own times. Then again, how far changes in culture were the property of a social elite and how far they were generally shared raises questions which render very stark the contrast between Renaissance sensibilities and our own.

We might use as our starting point, however, something unexceptionable and generally agreed: the Renaissance was a rebirth of interest in the culture of antiquity. Among the writers and artists of Italy in the period after 1300, there developed a striking determination to recreate the culture of the ancient world, to piece together the fragments, to imagine the original on the basis of its ruins. In 1430, for instance, the Florentine humanist Poggio Bracciolini (1380–1459) at once lamented the decay of Rome and tried to picture its former grandeur:

> Indeed this city is to be mourned, which once gave birth to so many illustrious men and emperors, so many leaders in war, which was the nurse of so many excellent rulers, the parent of so many virtues and such great ones, the creator of so many fine skills, from which flowed discipline in military matters, sanctified morals, the sanctions of the law in life, the models of all the virtues, and the reason for living well. Once mistress of the world, she is now, by the iniquity of fortune, which overturns all things, not only despoiled of her empire and her majesty, but given over to the vilest servitude, deformed and abject, showing forth her former dignity and greatness only in her ruins.[1]

14

This is an extract from a traditionally Christian literary genre 'On the misery of the human tradition'. The cardinal deacon Lotario, who became Pope Innocent III (1198–1216), had written a dogmatic essay on the same subject. Despite the traditions of the genre, Poggio's digression on Rome makes no reference to a Christian framework of explanation. He does not argue that Rome was to give way to a new and morally superior Christian world that has lasted down to his own time. He does not suggest that Rome's ruin was part of the providential scheme of his own God. Instead, he points to the fragile relationship between human virtue and the mercilessness of Fortune. Virtue and Fortune, *virtù* and *fortuna*, were to become sensationally familiar as the result of their revolutionary deployment in the works of Niccolò Machiavelli (1469–1527). However, Machiavelli, too, felt that there were lessons to be learned from ancient Rome: and not only learned, but applied. At the beginning of his *Discourses* on the Roman historian Titus Livius (Livy, 50 BC–AD 17), he too mused on fragments. While a piece of ancient sculpture might be expensive to its purchaser, and a subject of diligent imitation by artists, the deeds of the ancients did not inspire contemporaries:

> the most virtuous enterprises that the histories show us to have been carried out in ancient kingdoms and republics by kings, military leaders, citizens, lawgivers and others who have exhausted their energies for the land of their fathers are admired rather than imitated, indeed are avoided by everyone in the slightest detail, to the extent that no trace of that ancient virtue has remained to us . . .[2]

In neither of these quotations is there any evidence of a Rome that could somehow be fitted into a Christian scheme of divine providence. That does not necessarily mean that the authors were 'secular' or even 'pagan'. However, it indicates a most important consideration: that the humanists' journey back to the ancient world involved stripping away what had accumulated in the course of the centuries which separated their own world from the classical past. This was an attempt – in the Western tradition perhaps the first detailed attempt – to understand a past culture on its own terms.[3] While the identification of the Renaissance with modernity is an idea to be used, if at all, with caution, such an enterprise marked the beginning – albeit uncertain – of an historical purpose and method with which we can identify. The process of clearing a path from the present to the classical world was not a task that could easily be stopped, as Giovanni Boccaccio (1313–75), humanist and author of *The Decameron*, makes clear in his assessment of Petrarch (Francesco Petrarca, 1304–74), whom he greatly admired. Petrarch, he wrote, 'began to follow the ancient path', and by clearing away the brambles and thickets with which the negligence of mortals had blocked the path, and piling up in a solid heap the half-eroded rocks which had descended in an avalanche, he opened the way for himself and for those who wished to ascend after.[4]

Here is *homo viator*, man on a journey, but he is not on an unswerving pilgrimage to the city of God as a medieval Christian would have been. In Boccaccio's paean, Petrarch returned from Parnassus to Rome and 'forced the rusted hinges of the Capitol to turn in the opposite direction'. He is on a journey from one age to another, not shuffling through the vale of tears which is this world before moving to the paradise of the next.[5] This was the humanist enterprise: the return to accurate ancient sources uncluttered by the detritus of intervening centuries. Humanists were technicians who sought the original model, who wanted to learn from the design and from the patterns of thought that had created it.

In our turn, in order to understand the freshness and excitement of these humanist exercises, we might usefully perform one of our own in removing or at least questioning some of the accumulated historiography, some of the intervening misconceptions, which distort or obscure the original. In so doing, Renaissance artists and writers made great leaps of the imagination across vast tracts of time and found themselves in something infinitely larger and more complicated than they had ever dreamed. The more they explored the classical world, the larger it became. We might do the same in getting back to the world of the Renaissance, but our work of restoration is complicated by the need to be selective in what we strip away. Put another way, it is impossible to dismiss all that lies between us and the Renaissance, as some Renaissance writers and artists sometimes dismissed all that lay between them and their beloved antiquity. In some ways, ours is a less strenuous exercise. The purpose of this book is to characterise cultural change in a single geographical region over three centuries in the light of some of the work that has been done in the last four hundred years. By 1500, Renaissance artists and writers had leapt a thousand years and discovered another thousand. While they created 'dark ages' which lay between them and the classical past, there is much still to learn and enjoy from the scholarship that has enriched the study of the Italian Renaissance. Put another way, if we are to understand the phenomenon of the Renaissance more precisely, then we need to explain it rather than merely celebrate it. This involves being aware that the Italian Renaissance had a dark and painful side. The breakthrough to the classical past was incomplete, as Petrarch and Boccaccio were soon to discover. For the value systems that the humanists rediscovered and admired in pagan antiquity were to clash with the value systems of the Christian centuries that followed the fall of Rome (see below, Chapters 6 and 7).

That is the first instance of the delicacy of recreating a vivid picture of the Renaissance. Generations of scholars have asserted the essential Christianity of Renaissance scholars and artists. Is that quite the case? Were there not significant ways in which the study of the ancient world involved some contradiction of the Christian message? The purpose of this introductory chapter is to indicate further areas of study where cleaning materials might usefully be applied, often because some assumptions have become almost unshiftably crusty. The remainder of this chapter identifies and discusses some of the more significant problems that the existing literature has yet to resolve.

'Italian Renaissance'/'Renaissance Italy'

First there is the problem of the frame. What contains the Italian Renaissance? Renaissance Italy. What contains Renaissance Italy? The Italian Renaissance. Two valuable books published in successive years by the same house carried the respective titles *Italy in the Age of the Renaissance, 1380–1530* and *The Italian Renaissance: The Origins of Intellectual and Artistic Change before the Reformation*. After an introduction, the first book – admittedly part of a series – deals with 'Society, the state and the Church', 'Political histories', and finally 'Learning, the arts and music'. The second book groups its chapters under three main headings: 'Humanism', 'The artist, the patron, and the sources of artistic change', and 'The achievement of the Italian Renaissance'. The three authors trained at the same university, and two of them were colleagues in the same university department. Both books have enriched this one, their authors my friends.[6] Yet in one book the Renaissance is the context of Italy, in the other, Italy is the context of the Renaissance. Obviously, one book gives priority to Italy, the other to the Renaissance that took place there, but the inquiring reader might sometimes wonder whether they are books about the same phenomenon in the same place. 'The Italian Renaissance' which the viewer might have thought was represented by the *Man in a Circle and Square* by Leonardo has suddenly become a staircase by Moritz Escher. [O.1; O.2]

A unitary idea of Italy gives a misleading idea of the Renaissance, and a unitary idea of the Renaissance gives a misleading idea of Italy. The Renaissance was not a single phenomenon common to an entire region. Rather, the manifestations of cultural change – or the lack of it – took different forms in different places. At the same time, there is a unifying theme.

The Renaissance developed a new view of the world through the manipulation, recreation and imitation of realities. While this was frequently a source of joy in new understanding, disquiet and disillusion were never far away.

Moreover, the deliberate caution in linking the contexts discussed in the first five chapters of this book with the artistic developments of the last four derives from reservations about characterising a period in relation to its cultural achievements – or achievers: 'Italy in the age of the Renaissance', 'Italy in the age of Dante and Petrarch'.[7] The concept has been brilliantly extended to 'Baroque personae', but no one yet writes about 'Rococo diplomacy', and do we perceive our own times in such terms?[8] Would an academic historian of the twenty-first century write a book on 'Europe in the age of modernism', or 'The Mediterranean in the age of Picasso and Dalí'? (The answer could, perhaps should, be 'Yes'.) This problem is further complicated by the fact that the humanists of the Renaissance invented a title for the period that preceded them and called it 'the Middle Ages'.

'Medieval' and 'modern'

In Rome, in 1341, musing on 'the walls of the shattered city . . . the fragments of the ruins', Petrarch looked forward to a revival of antiquity, but saw his own age as an *aevum in medium*: 'There was a more fortunate age and probably there will be one again; in the middle, in our time, you see the confluence of wretches and ignominy.'[9] There is a sense, then, of a 'middle age' that has somehow lost contact with antiquity. According to a view that sees this text of Petrarch as prophetic, the Renaissance was to return to the classical past and derive from it patterns of thought at odds with those of the 'middle age'. That is certainly what Petrarch wanted posterity to think, and it is what some later humanists believed they had done.

Here are two other texts that – at least in translation – might seem to be expressions of 'new ways of thinking' that the Renaissance encouraged. Within the increasingly secular mentality of the Renaissance, political power became identified with the prince as head of a secular state. This is readily identified with Machiavelli. The apparently anti-Christian sentiments that he expressed were inadmissible, and in order to accommodate them, the absolutism of the *princeps* came to be officially sanctioned by the 'divine right' bestowed by the Christian God.

Thus, the prince is raised to the heights and is splendid with as many privileges, and as great, as he believes necessary to himself. Indeed, this is right, because to the people nothing is more useful than that which is necessary to the prince be fulfilled, since it cannot be that his will be found adverse to justice. Therefore, as many define it, the prince is the public power, and a certain image on earth of the divine majesty. Beyond doubt a large share of the divine virtue is shown to be in princes, while men, at their nod, submit their necks and for the most part offer their heads to the axe to be struck off, and as by a divine impulse, anyone who is supposed to be afraid of him fears him.

Yet, as Machiavelli was to point out, human affairs were ruled by fortune, the vagaries of which, once again, had to be reconciled – albeit with some room for irony – with what was directed by the will of God:

What can we say about fortune? This man's lands were situated between those of two great enemy princes. He held some very strong places and he had four hundred well-paid men-at-arms whom he could enrol and muster as he pleased. He had already controlled them for twelve years. He was a very wise, valiant and experienced knight. He had a large store of ready cash. Yet he found himself in this predicament lacking courage and any means of escape! It could well be said that fickle fortune had turned against him. But to put it more accurately, we must reply that such strange mysteries do not proceed from Fortune and that Fortune is nothing but a poetic fiction; rather it must have been God who abandoned him . . .

The first extract is from *Policraticus: The Statesman's Book* of John of Salisbury, Bishop of Chartres (*d.* 1180). He was the disciple of Thomas à Becket, murdered on the orders of his king, Henry II. The second is taken from the *Memoirs* of Philippe de Commynes, who was writing on the reign of Louis XI of France (*r.* 1461–83). Denys Hay once observed that Machiavelli would have had little to teach Commynes. John of Salisbury's anatomy of tyranny in some ways looks beyond Machiavelli to the theories of the right of political resistance put forward in the aftermath of the Reformation.[10]

Both of those 'medieval' thinkers were from the 'Gothic' north – a rural world dominated by the feudal vision of a society imagined as consisting of three orders: *oratores, bellatores, laboratores*, the clergy, the nobility and the peasantry, those who pray, those who fight, those who work.[11] Yet that world too produced its own 'medieval humanism' – as several formidable medievalists have pointed out. For Walter Ullmann, Renaissance humanism had its roots in the secularisation of government in the twelfth and thirteenth centuries, which culminated in the emergence of the *civis* or citizen and the questioning of the status of the subject or *subditus*. For Ullmann, the idea of the Renaissance as a 'break' with the Middle Ages is 'not tenable'.[12] His notion of 'rebirth' as a phenomenon closely linked to Christian baptism, which follows the views of Johan Huizinga, is also illustrated in the career of Cola di Rienzo (?1313–54), who rose to power in Rome in the mid-four-teenth century. This self-conscious reviver of ancient Rome, who took the title of 'tribune', was also 'the Immaculate Knight of the Holy Ghost' following a ritual immersion in rose water.[13] Richard Southern's work was built around the characteristically elegant and provocative idea of 'medieval humanism' as a phenomenon in its own right, not as a prelude to something later.[14] As in the case of Renaissance specialists, so too for medievalists, the term 'humanism' is complicated and many-sided. The debt that the 'humanism' of the Middle Ages and the Renaissance owed to Byzantium – that vast historical continuum between the classical and Christian worlds in the East – was considerable.[15] In some ways, scholars from either period who studied the ancient world had more in common with each other than with us. Virtually without exception, both 'medieval' and 'Renaissance' humanists would have declared themselves to be devout Christians. In our time, a 'humanist' funeral service is one without religious overtones, and many who describe themselves as 'humanists' are also athe-ists. This is an indispensable reminder of the dangers of juxtaposing 'medieval' and 'modern' history and the need to avoid identifying 'relevant' history as modern. As another medievalist, Geoffrey Barraclough, once put it in an aside, 'all history which means anything is contemporary history'. He was examining the origins of the term 'Middle Ages'. While Renaissance humanists provide a congeries of casual references, in the seventeenth century 'Middle Ages' became a formal term of academic peri-odization in the work of a mediocre German scholar called Keller or Cellarius.[16]

The greatest specialists on the Renaissance have avoided the exaggera-tion of its novelty. One of the leading authorities on Renaissance human-ism, Paul O. Kristeller, has argued that 'Renaissance humanism' owed a considerable debt to the 'medieval scholasticism' of St Thomas Aquinas (1224/5–74). Even so revolutionary a figure as the philologist Lorenzo Valla (1407–57) thought highly of Aquinas and said so.[17] All in all, it is now difficult to speak of a 'revival of learning' in the Renaissance as though there had been no learning in the Middle Ages.[18] Indeed, as a teacher of classi-cal literature, the humanist was closely connected to the 'scholastic' system. It was only around 1500 that the rather narrower identification of the humanist as a student of classical learning (and not necessarily a teacher) began to emerge.[19]

It must be stressed that if we are to characterise cultural change in Italy after 1300, then caricature of the Gothic north is to be avoided. The next chapter will discuss the distinctive features of the Middle Ages in Italy. Perhaps it is worth asking whether 'dark age' institutions such as the monastery at Monte Cassino ensured the preservation as well as the corruption of ancient texts. Poggio was said to be looking for manuscripts there in the early fifteenth century. Niccolò Niccoli (1364–1437), the avid Florentine collector (who wrote virtually nothing), asked cardinals travelling to France and Germany to seek out manuscripts that were to be found preserved in Gothic surroundings at centres such as the monasteries of Hersfeld and Fulda.[20] And in order to open the fault line between the Renaissance and 'modernity', one might point out that 'medieval' values of chivalry and courtesy had their part to play in Baldassare Castiglione's *The Courtier* (published in 1528) and in the exotic literary flowering in Ferrara (see below, Chapter 8).[21]

The invention of the 'dark ages', which by the seventeenth century had become a 'middle age', was in fact the work of Renaissance humanists. Even now, the term refers not to a relationship between a particular period in the past and our own time, but to the period that separates antiquity from its revival. That Renaissance characterisation of the period that preceded it can still seem indispensable. When Denys Hay wrote a book called *From Roman Empire to Renaissance Europe*, stockists and purchasers were confused as to its subject matter, and the second edition was re-titled *The Medieval Centuries*.[22] Much more recently, in discussing political development, Trevor Dean has concluded that 'we should not assume that certain "modern" features were present in the seventeenth century and absent in the thirteenth'.[23]

In literary terms, the revival was one of the language and form of classical Latin (and, later, Greek), as the ancients themselves had recorded it, in the pursuit of eloquence. Among the concerns of the humanists were the subjects of the *studia humanitatis*: grammar and poetry, because they wanted to imitate the elegance of the Latin language, and moral philosophy as a system of ancient virtue. Grammar, with its highest refinement, philology, was necessary because scholars needed to be sure of the accuracy of their own imitations, philosophy because they wanted to absorb the wisdom of the ancients, and history since the documents with which they worked were products of the past.[24]

But for the modern historian, perhaps the most perplexing of the skills that the humanists self-consciously revived was in some ways the most prosaic, in that it was the tool of a profession: rhetoric. Rhetoric is the skill of the orator, the manipulation of language to argue a case. The most important model to imitate was the Roman author Marcus Tullius Cicero

(106–43 BC) – who was an orator who delivered speeches that made either a case for his clients (*Pro Milone*), or a case against his opponents (*In Verrem*) in law courts, as well as more explicitly political orations in the Senate (*In Catalinam*). To plead a case is often to exaggerate, sometimes to distort, occasionally to mislead. The humanists mastered the techniques of rhetoric, and when they presented their opinion about the time that separated them from antiquity, they were often pleading a case in favour of their own originality – which is often exaggerated, sometimes distorting, occasionally misleading. Petrarch put distance between himself and his great poetic predecessor Dante Alighieri (1265–1321). Yet, in the next generation of humanists, the Florentine chancellor Leonardo Bruni (1370–1444) admired Dante for his active political life, something that Petrarch had rejected in favour of contemplation.[25] Bruni himself exaggerated the uniqueness of the Florentines. He made a rhetorical distinction in asserting 'aliud est laudatio, aliud historia' ('panegyric is one thing, history another') as though he always observed the distinction. Yet his *History of the Florentine People* has also been described as a 'panegyric to republicanism'. Petrarch himself had asked the rhetorical question 'Quid est enim aliud omnis historia quam Romana laus?' ('What else, then, is all history, if not the praise of Rome?'). There is a species of double-talk here of which the reader should be wary. Just as the humanists made a case for whoever employed them as speechmakers, so they made their own case in trumpeting the differences between their own times and the ages that preceded them.[26]

Yet in many ways the humanists remain persuasive in the case they make for their own break with the past. They have even persuaded some recent historians that they began modernity, or that modernity – whatever that is – begins with them. This is despite the caution that Johan Huizinga expressed many years ago, emphasising the theme of 'renewal' in a 'medieval' author such as Dante, and stressing the way in which romanticism had distorted the view of the Middle Ages. Even so, for William Manchester, a reputable popular historian of modern times, in a book published in 1993, 'medieval men' were 'crippled by ten centuries of immobility', and it took figures such as Leonardo da Vinci to break out of 'the dense, overarching, suffocating medieval night'.[27]

For those generations when Marxism was fashionable and the dialectic explained everything, the novelty of the Renaissance lay in the 'bourgeois' character of its society. The attachment of Renaissance to modernity has proved doggedly persistent. The adhesive gluing the one to the other can be, however, a monocausal variant on the Marxist interpretation. In an arresting book covering the same period as this one attempts to, Richard Goldthwaite has argued that changes in patterns of material demand developed a consumer culture that in turn created a 'demand for art'. He is careful to acknowledge, however, that he is exploring a neglected dimension of Renaissance culture rather than that culture *tout court*.[28] The inflation of the concept can have disastrous consequences.[29]

In short, when assessing the relationship between the Renaissance and 'modernity', we should be careful not to think that artists and writers in Italy from the fourteenth century were scrambling to be where we are now. Revealingly, although Burckhardt himself identified the Renaissance with modernity, he also expressed serious doubts about where modernity might be heading.[30] One particular aspect of our 'modern' culture that would certainly have puzzled Brunelleschi or Leonardo is the distinction that we draw between 'art' and 'science'.

'Art' and 'science'

During the Renaissance, the status of some artists – not very many – changed from that of craftsman to individual genius.[31] However, after the Dominican puritan Girolamo Savonarola (1452–98) began preaching against worldliness and consigning works of art to his 'bonfires of the vanities' there were new constraints on artistic freedom. Pope Paul IV (*r.* 1555–9) hired a hack (Daniele da Volterra) to cover the nakedness of the figures in Michelangelo's fresco *The Last Judgment* behind the high altar of the Sistine Chapel, and some churchmen would have preferred to destroy the painting completely. Michelangelo's work was mentioned during the trial of the painter Paolo Veronese before the Holy Office in Venice in 1575. Asked why he had depicted soldiers and dwarfs at the Last Supper, Veronese replied that this was 'a licence permitted to poets and madmen'. This was spirited stuff, but Veronese was still in front of the Inquisition and he still had to change the title of the picture. (It became the *Banquet in the House of Levi* – which might even make better sense than the original title.)[32]

The romantic notion of the artist as defiant social commentator and the scientist as mechanical conformist crystallises in the nineteenth century (for example, in Gericault's portrait of an artist or in Dickens's *Hard Times*). Curiously, that development reverses the meaning of the original Latin terms, and in a book that deals with humanist cultures one must be careful to be accurate in the use of the original Latin. We cannot read back to the Renaissance the absurd separation of 'art' and 'science' that prevails in modern educational institutions. In Latin, *ars* refers to handicraft skill, *scientia* to abstract knowledge. One of the genuinely exciting aspects of the cultures of Italy in the Renaissance is 'the creative tension between . . . the essentially practical application of manual skills and the abstract intellectual processes of learning and the dissemination of knowledge'.[33] Yet one recent interpretation of the Renaissance firmly excludes the discussion of science, while another interprets its visual culture as part of a wider 'science of art'.[34] The celebrated Florentine architect Brunelleschi was also a great mathematician and engineer (and a formidable site manager). It is important to remember that the *ingegno* at the root of the term *ingegnere* was the 'talent' or 'ingenuity' that was a mark of 'genius'. Brunelleschi was also probably the individual who formulated and applied the rules of linear perspective. The learning and application of these rules underpinned every art school education until the end of the Second World War. Yet the full implications of perspective can now be realised in the three-dimensional graphics of

Plate 1   Uccello, *Faceted Chalice*, *c.*1430–40. Florence, Gabinetto dei Disegni e delle Stampe degli Uffizi.

computers – the product of modern 'science' – which can achieve something approaching Uccello's extraordinary drawing of a chalice at the touch
of a key. [Plate 1] Another example of the lack of barriers between art and
science is provided by Leonardo, not only because of his endless curiosity
about how the world worked, but also because he provided illustrations for
Luca Pacioli's mathematical treatise (see below, Chapter 7). Extending the
parallel with Brunelleschi, the machines that Leonardo designed for the
fanciful 'Festa del Paradiso' in Milan in 1490 were also described as *ingegni*,
or what we might call 'the products of genius'.[35] [O.3] What must be
acknowledged is that the achievements of Brunelleschi or Leonardo or
Uccello are expressive of an extraordinarily close relationship of mind and
hand through which the ideas formed in one found exact visual realisation
through the other.

All those examples are Florentines. It was another Florentine who was to
provide us with our notion of the 'visual arts'.

'Italian' or 'Florentine'?

Giorgio Vasari (1511–74), a painter of some talent, though not of the first
rank, was the first art historian. He produced an enormous work with the
title *Le vite dei più eccellenti architetti, pittori e scultori*, which was first published
in 1550. Despite some apocryphal material – Leonardo did not die in the
arms of Francis I, as Vasari records[36] – it remains an indispensable source
for biographical detail and for contemporary perceptions of artistic quality.
Yet the reader should also be aware that Vasari provided a clear but rigid
template of what constitutes art history, and he emphasised that all the best
artists were from his adopted city, Florence (he himself was a native of
Arezzo).

Vasari's vision of his subject was driven by a teleology that culminated
in his own time. While his work is a series of *vite* or 'lives', there is also a
fairly clear overall interpretative schema organised around three great
bursts of creativity. The first occurred around 1300. The greatest sculptors
of this time were the Pisani, Nicola (active *c.*1258–78) and his son Giovanni
(active *c.*1265–*c.*1314) – as Pisan natives exceptional in Vasari's Florentine
pantheon. The greatest painter was Giotto di Bondone (*b.* 1267 or 1277, *d.*
1337), who was also the greatest architect. The next great advance was
around 1400, very specifically in Florence, when Masaccio (*c.*1401–28) in
painting, Donatello (1386–1466) in sculpture and Brunelleschi in architecture were the leaders of the avant-garde. The sequence culminated in
Vasari's own time around 1550 with Michelangelo (1475–1564), 'il divino',

the greatest painter, the greatest sculptor, the greatest architect, the greatest of them all. He was rivalled by the Venetian Titian (mid-1480s?–1576)
as a painter, but ultimately Titian's skills as a colourist had to bow to
Michelangelo's supremacy as a draughtsman. Venetian *colore* did not quite
match Florentine *disegno*.[37]

Ever since Vasari's lifetime, Florentine achievements in painting, sculpture and architecture have set a pattern for everyone else. Other artists in
other places either fit, or are left behind, or try to catch up. Artistic merit is
judged by pictures, buildings and sculptures which can be attributed to
individual artists. Library and slide collections are organised according to
named artists, indexed individually and alphabetically, divided among
painters, sculptors and architects. Such a classification is standard, and
obviously has its own rationale. But both Vasari's teleology and the system
of classification within it may be questioned. First, one might argue that the
relationship between Vasari's successive phases is neither as clear nor as
developmental as he suggests. The Giottesque movement was, according to
some, cut short by the Black Death; the age of Masaccio, Donatello and
Brunelleschi is separated from Michelangelo by the complex allusiveness of
allegory and Neoplatonism in the later fifteenth century. Might the earlier
fifteenth century be seen as distinctive because of the particularly close relationship of the visual arts to humanist literature within the matrix of the
Florentine Republic? Indeed, is that culture distinctive in being so squarely
based in Florence? After all, Giotto's most revolutionary work was in the
Arena Chapel in Padua, and Michelangelo's career cannot be separated
from papal Rome (see below, Chapter 5). Given what the 'Florentine' tradition in painting owed to Roman frescoes and mosaics, and to the Sienese,
and what its sculpture owed to natives of Pisa, is there a sense in which we
might speak of a plurality of cultures even in the single centre of Florence,
with the most original 'Florentine' work being in architecture?[38]

If it is legitimate to pose that last question, then maybe one might ask
whether Vasari's schema is appropriate to other cities and states. In the
Trecento, 'the absence of Paduan or Sienese interpretations of their own
histories at this time created something of a cultural power vacuum', since
Vasari wrote little about these places, and similarly little on the courts of the
later fifteenth century.[39] Venice will often appear in this book as a place the
author knows something about, as an antidote and as an alternative: not
better, merely different. The Venetians experienced a 'rebirth' later, from
the late fifteenth century onwards, and their 'Renaissance' acquired a
sudden momentum through the systematic refashioning of Venice as a new
Rome under Doge Andrea Gritti (r. 1523–38). While one can point to a
string of painters, and while Jacopo Sansovino (1486–1570) and Andrea

Palladio (1508–80) rank with the best in architecture, the culture of Venice is incomprehensible without reference to music. There is no sculptor to rank with Donatello, yet this is curious since in Venice itself one is struck by the extraordinary abundance of carved decoration – exterior as well as interior – in wood and in stone throughout the city. Indeed, visitors are sometimes disappointed by the main picture gallery, the Accademia, because of its presentation of great masterpieces on bare walls in the manner of the Uffizi in Florence. One completes a tour of the galleries by confronting Titian's *Presentation of the Virgin* beneath the richly gilded ceiling commissioned by the religious confraternity called the Scuola Grande della Carità. This is the only picture in the collection that remains in its original location. [O.4] Similarly, the extraordinary series of works by Jacopo Tintoretto (1518–94) in the hall of the charitable confraternity, the Scuola Grande di San Rocco, would lose much of its impact if removed from the rich decoration and ornate carving of the Scuola itself which was added in the seventeenth century by Francesco Pianta, scarcely a household name. The same is true of the subject matter of the cycle and its relationship to the *scuola* as a social institution devoted to good works relieving the hungry, the thirsty and the sick.[40]

All these are examples of how collections of works of art in galleries and museums have decreased our understanding of them by a 'veiling' of their original functions. Perhaps it is no accident that among the greatest devotees of Venetian culture was one of the sternest critics of the 'Renaissance'. The Victorian writer John Ruskin (1819–1900) was more concerned with how the stones of Venice were shaped and put together – an approach vindicated in important recent work on palace building in Venice – than he was in the attribution of the work to a particular individual.[41] But Ruskin escaped the Renaissance by immersing himself in the Gothic. Perhaps the time has come to apply Ruskin's suspicions of individualism and attribution to the Renaissance itself.

'Individualism' and attribution

Part II of Burckhardt's magisterial work is entitled 'The development of the individual' through its manifestations in 'personality', 'glory', 'ridicule and wit'. The headings are symptomatic of the towering originality of what Burckhardt wrote. The sense of individual creativeness finds obvious examples in Vasari's work, and has persisted in modern times in very different ways.

One of these is the fascination with attribution that marked out the 'true' connoisseur. This is a subject that shows how easily contemporary preoccupations can altogether replace historical ones – especially when money is involved. One of the most significant and talented of modern critics, Bernard Berenson (1865–1960), is acknowledged as 'the standard bearer of a coherent set of values and the most sensitive precision instrument that has ever been applied to the study of Italian art'.[42] From around 1895, Berenson gave certificates of authentication to make money for himself and for his clients, the owners of the work, while writing to friends 'at bottom I no longer care a brass farthing who painted anything'. In an astute – and acerbic – comparison, Kenneth Clark observed that 'the nearest parallel is the authentication of relics in the late Middle Ages'.[43] What is arguably Berenson's finest work is on an artist who has never attained the recognition he deserves, the Venetian master Lorenzo Lotto (c.1480–1556). Perhaps it is Berenson's subconscious expression of atonement.

All that reminds us that consumerism is the product of relatively recent circumstances and should not necessarily be read back to the Renaissance. Consumerism relates to general – even 'mass' – patterns of demand. More readily applicable to the Renaissance is the concept of 'conspicuous consumption' – the expenditure of resources on costly luxuries by the social elite.[44] It was within that elite that patrons were to be found. The role of the patron was that of an active supplier, rather than merely a source of demand. As Mary Hollingsworth has emphatically demonstrated:

> We might talk about Filippo Lippi's *Coronation of the Virgin*, but the picture itself tells another story. The praying figure, indicating a scroll that reads 'he carried out the work', is a portrait of Maringhi [the patron], not Lippi.

Perhaps we should regard the Medici family rather than Brunelleschi as the real 'architects' of the church of San Lorenzo.[45]

The perspective on Renaissance individualism has changed dramatically in recent writing thanks to Stephen Greenblatt's deployment of the concept of 'self-fashioning', in many ways a development of the history of mentalities first explored by scholars such as Marc Bloch and Lucien Febvre. This has altogether changed the historian's perspective on self-perception, awareness and identities, emphasising a 'psychic mobility' that enabled some people to construct an identity at once profound and superficial. In a clash of value systems, this development promoted pride – a capital sin in the Middle Ages – and, looking forward to our own times, amounted to what we might call the discovery of the ego. Baldassare Castiglione (1478–1529) and Machiavelli wrote handbooks on the subject, and the contemporary guessing game of who is acting, what is real and what is illusion finds its supreme expression in the plays of Shakespeare.[46]

There remains the danger that the discovery of the individual or of the ego can become self-fulfilling.[47] Within an interpretative schema that celebrates the birth of individualism, it is easy to lose sight of the importance of the collective. In everyday life this might run across a spectrum such as family, household, workshop, guild, neighbourhood, city and region, and it is supplemented in religious life by parish and confraternity.[48] One of the most obvious examples of the 'universal man' of the fifteenth century, Leon Battista Alberti (1404–72), wrote an important treatise on the family, while Machiavelli addressed what may have been his last work to a penitential confraternity.

It may be that 'in the course of the fourteenth century the individual found his political bonds of loyalty to the family, as those to guild and other communal corporations, slowly loosened and finally dissolved'. At the same time, it might be said that 'the individual emerged from the corporate world of the late Middle Ages bereft of traditional supports'.[49] These are not necessarily contradictory statements. Taken together, they make the point that the 'discovery of the individual' could be an anxious quest for identity as well as an assertion of confidence in the self. More concretely, the 'individual' artists of the Renaissance trained in the workshops of the corporate guilds. A 'masterpiece' was, after all, a piece of work that qualified a trainee as a master. Both Brunelleschi and his rival Lorenzo Ghiberti (1378–1455) were trained as goldsmiths in this way. Moreover, any number of great 'Renaissance' projects depended on the skills and organisational flexibility of traditional corporations.[50] One of the problems that this poses is to what extent society at large – people in workshops and guilds, people in the streets observing new monuments – participated in the cultural change and identified with the Renaissance.

Whose Renaissance?

To whom did the Renaissance belong? Burckhardt's vision was, as he was aware, limited to the social elite. Peter Burke defined a creative elite of 600 people for the period 1420–1540, divided among artisans and the upper class. Only seven of these 600 did he identify as 'unconventional'. It may be symptomatic of the noise that the humanists made as rhetoricians that Lauro Martines was able to reduce the quantitative dimensions of their social world in the period 1390–1460 to just 11 individuals who were 'almost the only Florentine humanists of the period'. As types, 'touchy, ambitious, erratic', they 'never exhibit vital contacts with any sector of the lower classes', and they looked after their friends.[51] In another work, Professor Martines reminds us still more forcefully that

In surveying the age, historians constantly suppose, like the humanists themselves, that the heroic vision spoke for all men. Not at all. It spoke for an elite, and to ignore this is both to get the Renaissance wrong and to show that we do not see the forces and social interests that lie behind our own values.[52]

When we consider the still more concentrated and refined cultures of the princely courts, their detachment from society at large is even more striking.

Even in republican Florence, the Renaissance touched relatively few people, and in places like Urbino and Mantua it was practically confined to the court. This is contrary to our modern sense of equality, but one can't help wondering how far civilisation would have evolved if it had been entirely dependent on the popular will.

W. B. Yeats used the example of Urbino in his poem 'To a Wealthy Man who promised a Second Subscription to the Dublin Municipal Gallery if it were proved that the People wanted Pictures':

> And Guidobaldo, when he made
> That grammar school of courtesies
> Where wit and beauty learned their trade
> Upon Urbino's windy hill,
> Had sent no runners to and from
> That he might learn the shepherds' will.

The above is based on the text of Kenneth Clark's episode on the Renaissance in his 1969 television series *Civilisation*. Yet he evidently remained slightly troubled by the courts, and one cannot help but feel that the cultures of Italy lost something when they were stashed away from general view. In the television programme, Clark went on to remark that 'in the last quarter of the [fifteenth] century, the Renaissance owed as much to the small courts of northern Italy' as it did to republican Florence. In the published text, it owed 'almost as much', a significant qualification.[53] Without wishing to lapse into caricature, there are times when Castiglione's *The Courtier* – the 'grammar school' referred to in Yeats's poem – can be profoundly irritating because it can seem no more than a bunch of wealthy dilettanti at their charades.

For there was indeed a weakness in the structures – and in the number – of the princely courts, and it went beyond modern suspicions of elitism. The courtly culture of the later fifteenth century lacked solid social foundations, and that was to prove politically disastrous. Surprisingly in a culture that was ordering the experience of the world in time and space, there was a notable lack of a sense of proportion in politics. Federigo Gonzaga's living in the style of the 'king of Italy' as marquis of puny Mantua – a city of maybe 25,000 people, which he ruled from 1519 to 1540 – is a case in point.[54] Remote from the everyday life of small populations, the delicate but tiny worlds of the princely courts were to be overwhelmed in the early sixteenth century by the human and material resources of France and the Habsburg monarchy in an experience so shattering that the cultivated delights of the court look like playful escapism. As Castiglione recognised, 'knowledge of letters' was no compensation for 'lack of valour on the battlefield'. At the same time, Machiavelli was lamenting the political and military weakness of the Italian states and their failure to develop a united national consciousness in *The Prince*. He was unheeded. In 1526, the continued 'independence' of Ferrara was ensured only by the duke's desertion of the defeated French and his joining the victorious imperial cause.[55]

While the courts were exclusive in social terms, they were relaxed in their inclusion of women. Was there a 'Renaissance woman' to counterpoise 'Renaissance man'? The question of what role women played in Renaissance societies has a long history. Castiglione devoted one book of *The Courtier* to the social role of women; Burckhardt discussed the matter in terms of 'perfect equality', with emancipation 'a matter of course'.[56] However, the growth of interest in women's history has led to a prolific expansion of the historiography in recent years. Much of the work has increased our understanding of the social context in which the cultures of Italy took shape.[57] However, the stridency of some feminist writing may, one fears, tell subsequent generations more about our preoccupations than about women in the cultures of the Renaissance. Women, it has been argued, were marginalised, subordinated, ignored, used as chattels in infinitely complicated marital strategies. They were excluded from the male-dominated cultures, they were expected to show modesty and submission in the private domestic sphere. This thinking presents both danger and irony. The danger is that the gender struggle is replacing the class struggle as the measure of historical change. In much the same way as feudalism was always in a transition to capitalism, so women were always in a condition of submission prior to their eventual liberation. There are only three women among the 600 names of Peter Burke's creative elite. There are a few examples of women humanists, such as Isotta Nogarola (1414–66), Cecilia Gonzaga (1426–51), Laura Ceretta (*d.* 1499) and the influential Vittoria Colonna (1492–1547). There were a few women artists, such as Tintoretto's daughter Marietta (*c.*1552–90) and Sophonisba Anguissola (*c.*1532–1625). Some women were important patrons, including the d'Este sisters Isabella (1474–1539) and Beatrice (1475–97) and Caterina Sforza

(1462–1509). Some others were undoubtedly influential in politics –
Lucrezia Borgia (1480–1519), for instance, and, in France, Catherine de'
Medici (*d.* 1589).[58] The irony, however, is that despite historians' now
much wider social vision, as yet very little attention has been paid to women
who were not members of the social elite.

In that upper stratum, women could be enormously influential within
the household, particularly when the household was a court. Outside the
elite it may well be the case that there were many social outlets for women
that competed with the family and domesticity. In Venetian confraternities,
regulations for women are not listed separately from those for men 'in order
not to multiply too many words'. The masculine terminology is not exclusively male but reflects a humdrum grammatical fact: the male plural in
Italian often refers to women and men collectively. There is evidence, too,
of women's economic independence within the structures of guilds. There
was certainly much more to the strategies of Venetian women than
marriage, the nunnery or prostitution.[59]

There are at least two other preoccupations that might suggest that
women were not mere banished witnesses of cultural change. They are
contemporary preoccupations, not our own, but they should not be ignored
if we are seeking to understand the *outillage mentale* of Renaissance society.
In the specific context of the cultures under scrutiny, the role of woman was
central both to antiquity and to Christianity. The one prized the ideal of
feminine beauty, the other that of the Virgin Mary, and the one often
blended into the other. Both of them commanded the devotion of men.
[O.5; O.6] Loren Partridge has emphasised the importance of the 'female
principle' in the High Renaissance and particularly in the art of
Michelangelo. In the *Pietà* of 1499, for instance, the sculptor depicted a very
young mother, who also seems to be the bride of the Church and, while
grieving for her dead son, also presents him to the worshipper. The position
of her knees is reminiscent of the act of giving birth, the tension in her torso
perhaps recalls her feeding Christ as a baby at her breast.[60] [O.7]

In the culminating section of the Sistine ceiling, the *Separation of Light from
Darkness*, 'Michelangelo here conceived of God as embodying both the
dynamism of youth and the wisdom of age, the strength of a male and, as
signalled by the developed breasts, the fecundity of a female'.[61] [O.8] In the
Last Judgment:

> To the extreme left in the zone of the elect, in front of a group composed
> mostly of women, a bare-bosomed personification of the church chari-
> tably shelters a genuflecting woman who embraces her fecund body,
> signifying the potential of regeneration through the church.[62] [O.9]

We should add the observation that at the centre of the Sistine ceiling is the *Creation of Eve* – not the much more familiar *Creation of Adam*. As fallen man lies asleep, it is the first woman who intercedes on his behalf as Mother Church with God the Father. [O.10]

Nowadays, there is little inherent attractiveness in an historical phenomenon that can so readily become the preserve of a male-dominated social elite. Some readers may wish to finish here. However, for those who continue, perhaps we should now ask what have been the influences on our own vision of the Renaissance and its significance? The evolving historiography carries the marks of the preoccupations of successive periods. Vasari's notion of *rinascita* helped to crystallise Christoph Keller's notion of the 'Middle Ages' in the seventeenth century. The neo-classicism of the eighteenth century that Voltaire (1694–1778) exemplifies placed the achievements of Medicean Florence in a line of succession that culminated in the age of Louis XIV. The Romantic reaction against classical values produced a 'rehabilitation' of the Middle Ages that took concrete form in the Gothic revival. Burckhardt's Renaissance was influenced by the 'modernity' of nationalism and state-building that were such striking features of the world in which he lived.[63]

As in the general, so in the particular, successive generations have made their own Renaissances. The view that we have of Leonardo da Vinci (1452–1519) began with Vasari's invention of him in his *Life*. Even here there are variants. Leonardo was a non-believer in the 1550 edition, but, perhaps with an eye to what the Council of Trent had set down, he became a good Christian in the edition of 1568. French academicians of the seventeenth century interpreted Leonardo's significance differently, and he was reinvented yet again, this time as the precocious scientist, in the nineteenth century. More recently, he has been seen as the supreme naturalist. The historical fortunes of Castiglione's book *The Courtier* might incorporate a 'renaissance of the Renaissance'.[64]

The foregoing are intended as words of caution. By the same token, cultural changes in various parts of Italy in the three centuries under scrutiny do not have to be seen as completely haphazard.

2 Reconstructions

Chronologies

Having identified some of the more persistent problems in studying the Italian Renaissance, we may now establish some patterns. The panorama of the Renaissance is enormous and covers an extended period. Should it be seen as a natural extension of the Italian Middle Ages? Or was it a complicated response to a sudden catastrophe, in particular the Black Death of the mid-fourteenth century? No simple answer is satisfactory, since the forces that formed the context of cultural change, and sometimes influenced its course, were tremendously varied. They could be economic, social, political or religious: singly, jointly, or totally. This makes it impossible to establish a unitary and linear direction in which the Renaissance headed. Given the range and diversity of context, can we define the historical subdivisions within which the Renaissance took shape? Those subdivisions are loose and overlapping, and apply in different ways to different areas of Italy. South of the Papal States, the peninsula was the setting for an extraordinary cultural amalgam. Central and northern regions nurtured a precocious urban life, and produced two figures at once unique and representative in St Francis and Dante. The extended absence of the papacy from Italy during the fourteenth century needs consideration, as does the Black Death; Florence seizes the attention in the early fifteenth century, but must not eclipse the evolution of the princely courts and their contrasting politics and cultures. The variety and complexity of the states and regions of Italy, sadly, sustained one truly 'Italian' experience: the wars that devastated the peninsula between 1494 and 1530 and left nearly all of it under foreign domination. The new mood of spiritual seriousness after those horrendous upheavals is often rather turgidly stereotyped as the 'Counter Reformation'. Yet the whole span of the three centuries under discussion here witnessed a number of significant religious revivals that we should also address. Spiritual disquiet is an abiding theme that runs all the way from Petrarch to Galileo. Were religious revivals part of the Renaissance itself, or were they part of a contrasting and critical culture, wary of flirtations with the ancient pagan world? The first stereotype that we need to address is the exaggerated difference between the Renaissance and the preceding era.

The humanist chorus of rejection of the 'Middle Ages' neglected the dependent connection of the Renaissance itself to the centuries that had gone before.

Medieval Italies, *c*.1000–*c*.1350

Following the disasters of the ninth and tenth centuries associated with the incursions of Vikings, Magyars and Saracens, yet for reasons that remain obscure, European life stabilised somewhat about the year 1000. Indeed, with a characteristically mischievous disregard for convention, Robert Lopez once went so far as to suggest that the Renaissance itself began around that time, with the emergence of 'Europe' and the beginnings of a 'commercial revolution'.[1] As Richard Southern and more recently Robert Bartlett have shown in remarkable books, the latter part of the tenth century opened a new epoch in medieval history.[2] North of the Alps, the vision of a feudal society with ties of dependence between its three orders began to take shape, first in the minds of churchmen, and then in the world at large. By the twelfth century, the feudal order had been harnessed to the Church in a mission of holy violence called the crusade.[3]

Paradoxically, although the central government of the Church that imagined and enlisted the feudal north was based in Rome, some Italian societies were on a rather different path of development. The feudal vision was highly influential in the shaping of several regions of medieval Italy. While the 'Italian Renaissance' is often presented as a strictly 'urban' phenomenon, the whole peninsula was not heavily urbanised, and there was no single type of 'town'. This is especially the case in the southern half of the peninsula occupied by the Kingdom of Naples and the Papal States. These regions were heavily influenced by northern Europe and in particular by the presence of feudal armies from Normandy, from the German Empire and from Anjou.

About the year 1000, Italy south of the Papal States was still under direct rule from Constantinople, though the island of Sicily was under Arab domination. The Normans appeared as mercenaries in 1017 or thereabouts, and established themselves in fiefs that were united under Roger II – who received Sicily as a fief from Pope Innocent II in 1138. Norman rule in Sicily was subsumed by the German Empire when Henry VI inherited Naples and Sicily from his Norman mother in 1194.

The struggles of the popes with their Hohenstaufen neighbours dominated much of the thirteenth century. The most notable, and the most enigmatic, of these was the emperor Frederick II (1194–1250), the first individual ruler to figure prominently in Burckhardt's study. His rule illustrates clearly the problems of defining the origins of the Renaissance. An emperor from the feudal north, he drew on Byzantine traditions in establishing autocratic rule and a sumptuous court, having inherited Naples and Sicily in infancy (in 1198) 18 years before his election as Holy Roman Emperor.

The contradiction between Byzantine-style autocracy and the independent feudal baronage was to prove too great – and in a way is still proving so. Yet in this 'feudal' and 'medieval' complex there were overt imitations of Roman tradition. In seeking to quell feudal and ecclesiastical power, Frederick issued his *Liber augustalis,* in direct imitation of the first Roman emperor, Augustus, in 1231. After his victory over the Milanese at Corte Nuova in 1237 he celebrated with a triumphal procession through the streets of Rome itself. After his death in 1250, the papacy grew increasingly hostile to Hohenstaufen rule, which came to an end with the death of Frederick's bastard son Manfred in 1266. That was achieved through a papal alliance with the house of Anjou, and Charles, brother of the king of France, became king of Sicily on Manfred's defeat and death. The uprising known as the Sicilian Vespers ousted the Angevins from Sicily in 1282. The rebels invited Peter III of Aragon – who was married to Manfred's daughter – to be their king. Thus, southern Italy was torn between Angevin and Aragonese influences. The former – retaining Naples – tended to favour the empowerment of the baronage and the consequent stunting of urban life, the latter brought to Sicily the political vitality of the Catalan tradition. Even when Alfonso the Magnanimous united the two territories (after much dynastic havering) in 1443, the 'Two Sicilies' had no link apart from the sovereign.[4]

Those Catalan and Angevin connections help to explain why it was armies from France and Spain that brought an end to the independence of the states of Italy after 1494. However, the deep-rootedness of the conflict was also intimately connected to the efforts of the popes to maintain their own state in central Italy. In this area, too, social relations were feudal in character, and there is no evidence of the flourishing urban life to which the Renaissance is said to have owed so much. Indeed, as John Larner has courageously remarked, 'to many kinds of temperament the quality of life in the little towns must have been inexpressibly boring'. Any excitement must often have been of a most unwelcome kind. The Romagna region was 'an uneasy amalgam of armed camps of hostile nobles whose interests were irreconcilable', there was almost constant 'senseless and treacherous conflict', and papal control of the province remained 'ineffectual until the advent of Cesare Borgia and Julius II' in the early sixteenth century.[5]

Professor Larner anatomises the unrelieved anarchy of the region that Cesare Borgia was to bring to order with the actions that so impressed Machiavelli. The communes that represented the urban base of the Renaissance coexisted with the despotisms that gave birth to the princely courts (see below, Chapters 3 and 4) in different parts of Italy.[6] The rural areas of the Romagna were conspicuously not under the control of the towns. The reverse applied in Lombardy and in Tuscany, where the 'medieval' experience was different.

By the middle of the twelfth century, many of the towns of northern Italy had grown rich through trade, and this attracted the attention of their German overlord, the Holy Roman Emperor Frederick I (Barbarossa, c.1123–90). In 1154, he made his first attempt to assert his power in pursuit of the cities' wealth through demanding imperial taxes or *regalia*. When he arrived with his feudal army to collect them, he was accompanied by his uncle, Bishop Otto of Freising. He was astonished by what he saw in Lombardy:

> But [the Lombards] having put aside the barbarous rancour of ferocity, perhaps from having joined with the natives in marriage, their sons from maternal blood and from the land and its character, inherited something of Roman gentleness and retain sagacity and the elegance of the Latin language and the urbanity of their customs. Moreover, in the management of the cities and in the preservation of their republics, they still imitate the cleverness of the ancient Romans. Finally, they so love liberty that, avoiding the insolence of power, they are governed by the will of consuls rather than commanders. There are three orders among them: captains, vavasors and commoners. And in order to suppress pride, the consuls are chosen not from one but from each of the aforesaid orders. And lest they should break out in lust for power, they are changed almost every year. Hence it is that, since almost the whole of that country is divided among cities, each of them compels its bishops to stay with them, and scarcely any noble or great man can be found in all that territory who does not follow the command of his city. But they are accustomed to force together all the single territories of individuals and by this power of command call it their *contado*. Also, that they may not want for the means of subduing their neighbours, they do not disdain to bestow the girdle of knighthood or the grades of dignity on young men of inferior condition and even some workers of the contemptible mechanical arts, whom other peoples force away like the pest from the more honest and free positions. From this it has resulted that they surpass other cities of the world in riches and in power.[7]

This passage surely suggests that the Roman past had scarcely been forgotten or neglected. The survivals of antiquity are refinement, elegance and wisdom, a political system that prizes liberty. There is also a distinctiveness in the pattern of evolution since the Lombard invasions, most notably a process of urbanisation subordinating bishops and nobles to the civic authorities and engendering a measure of social mobility while generating wealth and power. Otto's incomprehension of the importance of merchants in this pattern of life made his tripartite social classification vague.[8] All this in the middle of the twelfth century.

The distinctiveness of Lombardy and Tuscany in 'medieval' Italy was either ignored by many of the humanists or hidden from them.[9] The wealth and power that the medieval cities had accumulated enabled their alliance to defeat Barbarossa at the battle of Legnano in 1176. The rallying cry in diplomatic exchanges was 'liberty', foreshadowing – and on a rather larger political scale – the rhetoric of the civic humanists of the fifteenth century. The passage from Otto of Freising gives some indication of what 'liberty' meant to the communes. The towns are city-states (in Latin *civitates*), and some adult males (*cives*) express their cities' independence of any internally or externally imposed overlord in their regular elections of consuls.[10]

When the emperor came to terms with the pope, he did so through the mediation of the city of Venice. In 1204, the feudal crusaders had to pay off their debt to the Venetians for transportation by sacking Constantinople, a distasteful illustration of the power that a single commercial city could exert.[11] The commercial activity of cities in Italy certainly marked a break with the traditions of the ancient world, but scarcely a descent into 'dark ages'. It is a curious thought, and a measure of what the humanists neglected about the post-classical era, that the rhetoric of liberty in the fifteenth century did not see the economic and social life of the medieval town as a progression from ancient economies based upon slavery.

The commune had a large number of features – liberty, consuls, elections and rotation of office – that imitated the ancient city-state.[12] However, communal society was emphatically different from that of the *polis* of antiquity. There were some slaves, but the economy was not based upon the institution of slavery. One must not create another rhetorical construct here. The condition of slaves in antiquity was varied: some enjoyed a comfortable life, despite their un-free status. But there was an assumption that an apparently inexhaustible supply of un-free labour would sustain the pattern of everyday life. Imperial expansion – Spartan, Athenian or Roman – would ensure that the supply continued. The commercial laity whose culture in many ways made possible the Renaissance was a feature of urban life that developed in the post-Roman world. As John Larner has argued, the conquest of distance between markets and the determination to conclude transactions whatever the obstacles of time depended upon the measurement and control of the visible world. This is of vital importance in creating a connection between cultural output and its social matrix. As will be discussed later (see below, Chapters 6 and 7), it is precisely in the humanists' approach to time and the artists' approach to space that innovation is so marked. Made up of bricks and mortar, streets, shops, churches and communal palaces, the urban space was an expression of urban cultures, and 'in some ways it could be argued that the greatest works of art in thirteenth- and fourteenth-century Italy were the cities themselves'.[13]

Yet we might usefully remember that the clearing of space for new projects was often due to the alternate destructions of one faction's property by another. This may help to account for the imagination and realisation of so many buildings for the work of the communal government. When the Ghibelline imperial supporters returned victorious to Florence after the battle of Montaperti in 1260 they turned on their Guelph opponents (supporters of the pope) and destroyed 103 palaces, 580 houses and 85 towers. In Rome in 1257, 140 towers were lowered or destroyed. In Bologna, by contrast, literally cramping the style of the Renaissance, there were at least 194 towers acting as family strongholds. The dominant family there, the Bentivoglio, built another for themselves as late as the 1490s.[14]

One of the most important contributions of urban commercial life to Renaissance culture was its secularisation of the passage of time. According to the Church, time belonged to God as part of His eternity. In the Middle Ages, even the prominence of the Wheel of Fortune (as in the poem from the *Carmina Burana*, 'Fortuna mundi imperatrix') could never dislodge a vision of time that was linear and direct, and linked this world to the next. It relied upon 'a magical mentality which turned the past into the present, because the web of history was eternity. Appropriate to the tripartite social vision, time was rural, seigneurial and clerical – not urban.'[15] To charge interest on loans that accumulated over time was to appropriate what belonged to God. That was an expression of pride, the sin of Lucifer. The love of money, *avaritia*, was another mortal sin. Thus it was that 'homo mercator vix aut numquam potest Deo placere' ('man the merchant can hardly ever or never be pleasing to God').[16] The commercial life of the towns of medieval Italy had institutionalised two capital sins in direct affront to God. Christianity's efforts to come to terms with the commercial ethos, and the new assertiveness of the culture of lay people, are represented in two figures of revolutionary genius.

St Francis and Dante

The ecclesiological framework of medieval society was strained and perplexed by urban life. The Church's efforts to accommodate the urban culture are concentrated in the life of St Francis, a layman who founded a religious order, and the fundamental incompatibility of ecclesiastical and urban values is embodied in Dante as the self-assured literate layman. St Francis of Assisi (1182–1226) was particularly influential in emphasising through his own life the humanity of Christ as in itself something divine. In keeping with the love of nature expressed in the poetry of St Francis himself (see below, Chapter 8), the religious order that he founded used its patronage of the arts to celebrate the 'beauty of the created world' and thereby foster 'naturalism'. Of central significance to this study is that St Francis rejected the Augustinian distinction between the city of God and the city of man. In an important way, that links him to Petrarch, and, still more important, makes him more 'modern' in his rejection of a preceding era than Petrarch and succeeding generations of humanists (see below, Chapter 6). In that sense, Franciscanism and its revivals were part of the Renaissance itself.[17]

St Francis and the Franciscan order were to play a profound part in cultural development before the Black Death and again in the fifteenth century with the Franciscan revival associated with San Bernardino of Siena (1380–1444). He was the exact contemporary of those Florentine 'civic humanists' who seemed so self-consciously committed to the imitation of the Roman Republic.[18] While the Franciscan order was often factious and divided – even over how to portray itself to posterity – the ideals of St Francis, especially the rejection of worldly goods, were to be the inspiration of other religious organisations, known as 'mendicants' because they lived by begging. The rejection of material prosperity was certainly a critique of the urban world to which the Renaissance owed so much. Even so, the relationship between mendicant spirituality and commercial activity was one of wary interdependence. One mendicant order was founded in Florence in the 1230s or 1240s, as the Servants of Mary or 'Servites'. The relationship between mendicancy and the urban milieu is neatly conveyed by an early fourteenth-century account of the order's formation. The seven original brothers had been 'involved in this earthly business and exchange', and became instead 'dealers in celestial goods'.[19] Thus, the renunciation of urban life helped to define it. While the Franciscans and others like them embraced material poverty and rejected a life devoted to material gain, both types of existence were the product of the urban milieu and each came to shadow the other. In a cycle on the life of St Francis, the fifteenth-century artist Sassetta (Stefano di Giovanni, *c.*1392–1450) included the saint's placating the wolf of Gubbio. He persuades the animal to stop eating the citizens in return for regular supplies of food. Charmingly, this fanciful scene shows St Francis having the agreement formally registered by a notary; legal contract bears witness to legend. [Plate 2]

Significant numbers of people sought to follow a devout life as 'tertiaries', members of a third order which was half secular and half spiritual. There were regular collective expressions of lay piety through organisations such as confraternities, and their penitence often took the form of almsgiving to ease the plight of the poor. The religious confraternity was an expression of Franciscan-style 'brotherhood'.[20] The Company of Orsanmichele in Florence may have given as much as 85 per cent of its income in charity in the 1320s – which probably amounted to six times what the commune of Florence spent on poor relief. At moments of crisis such as the first half of 1357, that company alone gave alms to about 10 per cent of the city's population.[21] Vice versa, mendicant life was influenced by the material culture of the towns. The Basilica of St Francis at Assisi surely

Plate 2   Sassetta, *St Francis and the Wolf of Gubbio*, 1437–44. London, National Gallery.

speaks of wealth, status and power rather than of humility and poverty. [O.11]

The discussions of literate laymen may often have turned to 'renewal'. The second of our defining figures, Dante Alighieri (1265–1321), may himself have been involved in such exchanges. He was to write a work, *De vita nova*, literally *On the New Life*, the themes of which were taken up in the *Comedy*.[22] Dante was the contemporary of the painter Giotto and acknowledged the latter's revolutionary impact in his own masterpiece. The context in which he did so was a reflection on the rise and fall of the Wheel of Fortune, not an exercise in art history, but in the *Purgatorio*:

> . . . In painting, Cimabue thought
> to lead the field; and now the cry is Giotto and Cimabue's
> fame is overshadowed. (XI.94–5)

As for Dante himself, 'no other individual writer can have done so much to mould and elevate the languages of both poetry and prose and at the same time to create a sense of native literary tradition'.[23] Curiously, however, Dante was not to be the founder of a 'school' or 'movement' in his own century. Petrarch and Boccaccio in the fourteenth century and Salutati and Bruni in the fifteenth were to assert the dominance and superiority of Latin over Italian (see below, Chapter 8). Such developments narrowed the social appeal of literature, but they were also symptomatic of a new way of looking at the classical past and its languages. Dante wrote in what he thought was the Italian vernacular, and he did so within a Christian schema. However difficult the problem, and however painful in expression, the intellectual giants of antiquity had to stay in hell. Dante acknowledged that it was scarcely their fault that they had not known Christ, and he sought to protect them from the worst infernal torments, but his classical world bowed to his Christian beliefs. This may provide insight into some of the fundamental differences between medieval and Renaissance humanism – however strong their similarities (see above, Chapter 1). As his guide, the Latin poet Vergil, gloomily informs him as early as Canto IV of the *Inferno*:

> I want you to know, before you go further
> That these did not sin, and whatever their merits,
> They are insufficient, since they did not receive baptism,
> Which is the gateway to the faith that you believe in.
> If they lived before Christianity,
> They did not worship God appropriately;
> And among such as these am I myself.
> For such defects, for no other sin,
> We are lost. (IV.33–41)

At the very edge of hell

> I spied the master of those who know,
> Seated amid the family of philosophers.
> All admire him, all do him honour.
> There I saw Socrates and Plato,
> Who ahead of all the others stand closest to him,
> Democritus, who sets the world at chance,
> Diogenes, Anaxagoras and Thales,
> Empedocles, Heraclitus and Zeno;
> And I saw the good collector of qualities,
> Dioscorides I mean; and I saw Orpheus,
> And Cicero and Livy and Seneca the moralist;
> Euclid the geometer and Ptolemy,
> Hippocrates, Avicenna and Galen,
> Averroes, who made the great commentary. (IV.131–144)

Perhaps the incomparable richness of Dante's writing derives at least in part from his standing athwart two traditions, the one that of the scholastics, the other that of the humanists. 'The master of those who know' is Aristotle, whom St Thomas Aquinas (1224/5–74) had firmly reconciled with Christianity. In the *Comedy*, it is as though one tradition can pass peacefully yet in the full resplendence of its expression, knowing that what is to come is full of hope and vitality. We do not need to classify Dante as a 'medieval' or as a 'Renaissance' author: he was neither and both. Perhaps his writings are the supreme example of how artificial it is to see the Renaissance as a 'break' with the Middle Ages. Yet Dante was a representative of the culture of a literate laity with an interest in the wisdom of the ancients. How significant was it that the chief institution of the Christian Church was in disarray and only intermittently present in the peninsula as that culture emerged?

The absent papacy, 1305–1420

The history of the papacy in the fourteenth century is immensely complicated. After the move to Avignon in 1305, the validity of papal elections remained in some doubt until the Great Schism of 1378 when there were three separate claimants to be the legitimate heir of St Peter. The definitive return to Rome occurred only with Martin V in 1420. The point one seeks to make is that when the papacy moved to Avignon, much of what stood between the Italian humanists and ancient Rome went with it.[24] Much else

stayed behind to obscure the contours of the ancient world: Byzantine influence in the visual arts, and strong Provençaux traditions in poetry. And it
should be firmly stated that there is no question that somehow or other the
papacy had to be 'out of the way' before the Renaissance 'proper' could
begin. The papal court at Avignon proved to be an important source of
patronage for key figures in the 'Italian' Renaissance such as Petrarch and
the Sienese painter Simone Martini (see below, Chapter 4). However, the
decline in the papacy's moral authority, of which, before the Great Schism
of 1378, the move to Avignon seemed the disastrous depths, may have
removed certain constraints on social and political behaviour. While there
are signs that the 'laicisation of spirituality' may have continued, there was
an intensification of the violent tenor of life – much of it fostered at a
distance by the popes themselves.[25] Petrarch, who urged the popes to
return to Rome, suggested in a letter to Cola di Rienzo that opinion in
Avignon favoured keeping Italy divided:

> Recently a doubt arose and a question was discussed here: would it be
> to the advantage of the world that Rome and the rest of Italy should be
> united and at peace . . .? After many arguments on both sides the
> speaker who has the highest reputation for wisdom reached a venomous
> decision, and declared amidst unanimous applause that it would not be
> advantageous.[26]

The states of Italy were not only divided against each other but also divided
within themselves. The *consorterie* of Florence were sources of disorder, and
peace associations were no substitute for the enforcement of law. The *vita
civile* in Florence was already under severe threat in the 1290s from an
apparently endless cycle of *vendette*.[27]

Nevertheless, the absence of the papacy from Rome seems to have
increased the cultural autonomy of the mercantile laity, even though the
manifestations of that autonomy were often violent. The Church regarded
usury as a crime against divine law. Lending for a return on the loan above
its initial value without risk to the lender defied the Scriptures. In the book
of Luke (6:35), Christ Himself in the Sermon on the Mount urged people to
'lend, hoping for nothing again; and your reward shall be great'.[28] But
usury was open in Florence, and Church doctrine on the matter received
no more than lip service. More positively, it is possible to identify the emergence of a genuine 'civic spirit' in Siena. It is also worth reflecting that the
great banking houses of Siena and Florence disposed of far greater
resources in the early fourteenth century than did banks after the crashes of
1343 and 1346 and the economic depression that followed the Black Death.
Such wealth made possible projects such as the Palazzo Pubblico in Siena,

the Arena Chapel in Padua, and the Bardi and Peruzzi chapels at Santa Croce in Florence. These projects lack something of the self-conscious advertisement that the rhetoric of civic humanism was to provide in early fifteenth-century Florence. Put another way, the imagery of the civic ideal was not at this stage complemented by similar tendencies in the world of letters.[29] However, such projects as those listed above may suggest a link between economic life and cultural development. Deploying resources in patronage may have begun to become one way of compensating for the *avaritia* involved in making money in the first place (see below, Chapter 5).

With increasing momentum from the 1340s onwards, there occurred a string of catastrophes which were to destroy existing economic structures and disorientate intellectual attitudes. This certainly changed the way people viewed the world. There were signs of strain in economic life in the 1340s, the most notable being the collapse of the Bardi and Peruzzi banks when Edward III of England reneged on his debts (incurred for the early stages of the Hundred Years War) in 1346.[30] However, the recurrent disasters that followed the initial onset of plague in 1348 were to create a new atmosphere of crisis and recession. The very intensity of the shared experience seems to have generated preoccupations which helped to give the visual arts and literature a complementarity that had beforehand been lacking or tentative.

The Black Death

The relationship between the plague and cultural change remains a controversial subject. This may seem rather surprising since visitation of disease so obviously disrupted the regular patterns of life that one would assume major cultural consequences to have been inevitable. The sudden disappearance of perhaps as many as one person in three immeasurably increased life's uncertainties, even though it left more goods available to those who survived. Many artists died in the epidemics – such as the Lorenzetti brothers, who had created the frescoes in the Palazzo Pubblico in Siena. Major enterprises such as the building of the cathedral in Siena had to be abandoned because of the acute shortage of labour.[31]

Controversy, however, persists surrounding the influence of the plague on the style and content of painting. Millard Meiss set out his brilliant thesis in *Painting in Florence and Siena after the Black Death* (1951), arguing that in the aftermath of the plague of 1348, painters tended to forsake the Giottesque breakthrough and instead went back to an old-fashioned style. In particular, Meiss identified a reversion to depictions of Christ as a stern judge and a return to a hierarchical perspective in which the most important figures were the largest, wherever they were located. There was a corresponding weakening of the impulse to further the developments made by Giotto and his followers in the mathematical organisation of space.[32]

The dating of certain works central to Meiss's thesis, particularly two depictions of the Triumph of Death, one in Florence by Andrea Orcagna (active *c*.1343, *d.* 1368), and one in Pisa now attributed to Buffalmacco (whose precise dates are unknown), diminish the case for the Black Death of 1348 as the key moment in the redefinition of artistic sensibilities. Orcagna may have been projecting his own perceptions of reality, of a grim, retributive divinity before which human beings were small and helpless, as early as 1339. But then, what could be more immediately realistic than Orcagna's riveting depictions of the resentful faces of beggars, crippled and blind, in the *Triumph of Death* – whatever its date – in Florence's Santa Croce? [Plate 3]

However, the plague surely deepened the sense of impending apocalypse. On the basis of testamentary dispositions, Samuel Cohn has argued persuasively that it was the repeated experience of plague in 1361–2 that marked the watershed.[33] Precisely when the change took place remains a

Plate 3 Orcagna, beggars, det. from *Triumph of Death*, *c*.1360? Florence, Santa Croce.

matter for argument, but its nature is clear. To the artist's eye, Death, which for St Francis had been a sweet prelude to paradise, was now something to dread. Whatever the date, it seems that 'the *Triumph of Death* was the new generation's answer to that hope in the temporal state which had sustained their fathers and which had been illustrated in Lorenzetti's allegory of justice'.[34]

Painters themselves may have sensed a change, which they, like Millard Meiss, interpreted as decline. Whatever the inadequacies of its spatial representation, what could better depict the dislocation and violence of a plague-stricken world than Giovanni del Biondo's *Scenes from the Life of St Sebastian*? [O.12] In 1390, a group of painters and other artisans working at San Miniato al Monte in Florence discussed precisely what had happened:

> After feasting and drinking royally with the abbot, they set to considering certain questions. The following question was put by one of their number, a certain Orcagna, who was capomaestro of the splendid oratory of Our Lady of Orsanmichele: 'Who is the best master of painting we have had, after Giotto?' Some said Cimabue and some said Stefano, Bernardo or Buffalmacco, some gave this name and some advanced that one. Taddeo Gaddi was in the group, and he replied: 'Certainly there have been many skilled painters, and they have painted in a way that can never be equalled by anyone, but such art is of the past now, and each day it becomes worse.'[35]

The pessimism of painters was – very strikingly – shared by men of letters. These common changes in perception suggest that historians should follow Professor Larner's heading 'The Age of Orcagna and Petrarch'. Among the plague's victims was Petrarch's beloved Laura:

> Will posterity believe that there was a time without flood, without fire, in heaven or earth, without wars or visible catastrophe, in which not this area or these lands, but almost the whole world remained without an inhabitant? When was such disaster seen or heard of? In what annals has it ever been read that homes were empty, cities deserted, the countryside fouled, heaped with dead bodies and a horrible and vast solitude in all the world?

Petrarch was prepared to push the implications of his thoughts to their limits, in what seem anguished lamentations rather than rhetorical exercises. Why should God have judged this generation so much more harshly than any other?

Or is it perhaps more the case, as many great minds have suspected, that God does not care for mortal things? (*An illud fortasse verius, quod magna quedam ingenia suspicata sunt, Deum mortalia non curare?*)[36]

Petrarch's sense of the fragility of human arrangements became much more than a traditional idea of the transience of earthly life:

> Look. I had come to this point in my letter, and thinking about what more I should say, or what I should not say, among other things, as is my custom, I was tapping the blank sheet with the end of my pen. This very action brought me a subject, for I was thinking in that brief spell I was flowing, and in the meanwhile, going away, becoming deficient, and as I should say rightly, dying. We are dying continually, I while I write, you while you read, others while they listen or do not listen. I shall die as you read this, you will die as I write this, we both are dying, we are all dying, we are always dying, we never live while we exist.[37]

To add to this confluence of changing sensibilities, the stories – some hilarious, some macabre – which make up Boccaccio's *Decameron* were related over ten days by seven ladies and three young men who had assembled in a villa outside Florence in an attempt to escape the pestilence of 1348. According to Boccaccio, any contact seemed deadly. Some shunned company altogether, others decided 'to drink plenty, to enjoy themselves, and go around singing and seeking solace in the satisfaction of every possible appetite, to laugh and joke about what was happening as the most certain medicine for such ill'.[38] The terrifying and the hilarious went hand in hand. Here is the chronicler Marchionne di Coppo Stefani's description of the overflowing mass graves:

> In the morning they [the citizens] always found many of them [dead bodies] in the common grave, and they took earth and threw it down on top of the dead; and then other bodies were placed on top of them, and then more earth was placed on them, in the same way as they put cheese when they prepare lasagne.[39]

The immediate impact of the tidal wave of plague in the wake of a succession of calamities may, therefore, be measured fairly straightforwardly. Altogether more difficult to explain is the extraordinary burst of creative activity in the early fifteenth century. Perhaps the Florentine humanism of that period was papering over some alarming cracks in the social structure that seemed to replicate fractures in the collective psyche.

Civic culture in Florence, 1378–1434

The economic dislocation in the wake of the plague caused social unrest on a massive scale, in Florence and elsewhere. The collapse of demand for manufactures put many out of work. Most vulnerable were the unenfranchised workers not permitted to form guilds. Such conditions were once widely thought to be particularly dangerous in the woollen cloth industry. More recent research has undermined any simple connection between a single industry and the disturbances across Italy. The most famous of these took place in Florence in 1378. The Revolt of the Ciompi sought to establish new guilds for unenfranchised workers.[40] It failed, and the oligarchy rapidly re-established its grip. Yet within barely 20 years of this rebellion, Florence radiated a 'civic humanism' which, in embracing the active life in the service of the state rather than the contemplative life of the philosopher, sought to emulate the 'republican liberty' of ancient Rome (see below, Chapter 6).

Hans Baron argued that the suddenness of the transformation was itself an expression of the towering external threat to Florence from the armies of Gian Galeazzo Visconti, the duke of Milan, around 1400.[41] Yet random but obvious personal connections can be made between the Revolt of the Ciompi and the emergence of civic humanism. The public life of the humanist Coluccio Salutati (1331–1406), one of whose letters, according to Visconti himself, was worth 'a troop of horse', spans the period in question as head of the Florentine Chancery from 1375 to 1406.[42] The chief magistrate in 1378 was one Salvestro de' Medici, and Donatello's father had been one of the rebels. Moreover, the Republic that the humanists staffed and praised proved fleeting and insecure, and was superseded by the Medicean ascendancy.[43]

Nevertheless, the cultural achievements of the Florentines in this period are unique and unsurpassed. They are characterised by the close association of 'civic humanism' with the visual arts, perhaps begun in the time of Orcagna and Petrarch. Simultaneously, Brunelleschi's discovery of the laws of linear perspective made possible the systematic ordering of objects in space in order to represent scientifically three dimensions on two (see below, Chapter 7). Masaccio and Donatello produced works without precedents that demonstrated a commitment to a new conception of the freedom and dignity of the human person.

But were painters 'deeply committed' to the survival of the Florentine Republic against either Gian Galeazzo or Ladislas of Naples in 1424?[44] As John Larner has pointed out, 'artists and writers passed from the world of the communes to that of the tyrants and back again without changing their styles or ideals'.[45] Even with that qualification, the culture of this phase in this place was distinguished by the dynamic interaction of the visual arts and the world of letters. The 'universal man', Leon Battista Alberti (1404–72), set out the theory of artistic practice in treatises in Latin, the sculptor Lorenzo Ghiberti (1378–1455) tried to do the same. Leonardo Bruni (1370–1444) wrote in the vernacular for Brunelleschi to read, and artists and writers shared a set of humane values.[46]

The political limitations of Florentine civic culture were exposed in the process that resulted in the Medicean ascendancy. A republic built around guild structures gave way to an oligarchy divided by family factions, and from that oligarchy the Medici emerged, exercising control through a network of clientage that expanded to the increasing isolation of any possible opposition. The hopes of the humanists of an ideal republic almost within their grasp were delusions: their flight to a contemplative literary world was a source of melancholy, even for the ebullient Alberti.[47] As the Florentine Republic gave way to the rule of the Medici, so the city's civic culture began to fall into line with that of the princely courts.

Courtly culture in the later fifteenth century

Family faction tore apart the Florentine Republic (which again makes the words of the civic humanists seem all the more strained). For a time, the Albizzi family was in the ascendant. The Medici opposed them and Cosimo was exiled because of his opposition in 1433. He returned the following year when the Albizzi were discredited and his own position vindicated. The Republic's divisions were thereafter suppressed for a period of 60 years. The informal control that the Medici exercised (they hardly ever held office in Florence) dispensed with people who wrote fanfare speeches in praise of republican liberty. The return of scholars to the ideal of the contemplative life, which the works of Plato encouraged, suited the Medici admirably, and they were pleased to nurture Neoplatonism (see below, Chapter 6).

The 1420s and 1430s were in many ways a period of intense creativity. Cosimo's assumption of power marked no obviously decisive break with the past, but we can focus on the Council of the Church that met in Florence in 1439 as an important instance of something quite new: the culture of the ancient Greeks studied in its own right for its own sake and not mediated by scholasticism. The Council, which had had to move from Ferrara because of an outbreak of plague, brought Greek scholars and Greek manuscripts westward in quantity, and Medicean patronage of a Platonic

Academy elevated contemplation above action. In so doing, that patronage took the politics out of humanism and the humanists out of politics. George Holmes does not connect the change in the character of humanism to the change of regime in Florence, emphasising instead new ecclesiastical constraints, particularly the vigorous episcopate of Sant'Antonino (1389–1459) and the firm re-establishment of the papacy in Rome in 1420. However, he records that Giannozzo Manetti, the last of the 'civic' generation, was exiled for opposing Cosimo in 1453, which is at least symbolic of the altered climate.[48]

The increasingly princely style of the Medici's exercise of power might seem to be symbolised by Lorenzo's title, 'the Magnificent'. In fact, this was a title of anyone who was politically powerful, though not of princely blood. Nevertheless, 'magnificence' was a quality that princes cultivated in order to set themselves above their subjects. While princes did not create a unitary courtly 'style' in the works of art that they commissioned, they all aimed to exalt their own position. With the establishment of a Medici court, the Renaissance of the later fifteenth century was almost completely centred in the households of princes (the Venetian Republic remains an important exception).[49] While the Renaissance is so often characterised as an urban phenomenon, in the later fifteenth century single dynasties in states that were not very large made a disproportionate contribution to cultural change. The Montefeltro in Urbino, the Gonzaga in Mantua, the d'Este in Ferrara all come into this category. The court was also the centre of gravity in larger states such as Milan, where the Sforza had come to power in 1450, and in Rome, to which the papal court had returned definitively in 1420 (see below, Chapter 4).

These centres of grace and delicacy (at least in appearance) danced and played in the peaceful decades that followed the Peace of Lodi of 1454, which established a balance of power between the major states of the peninsula. After 1494, that period seemed a golden age, an age of prosperity and stability identified with Lorenzo 'il Magnifico'. The comfortable and enclosed world of the Renaissance courts was like an agreeable interior, impeccably furnished but lacking firm foundations; those living in it complacent about their self-sufficiency. It was a world that delighted in its own effortless superiority, unaware of changes in the balance of power beyond Italy itself – and it was untested by wind and weather. In 1494 the storm broke.

The Italian Wars, 1494–1530

The early part of the sixteenth century is closely associated with the so-called 'High Renaissance', which found its most notable expression in papal Rome. This was the age of Leonardo (1452–1519), the supreme 'universal man', of Raphael (1483–1520), whose grace as a painter perfectly complemented the *sprezzatura* of Castiglione's courtier, of Michelangelo (1475–1564), the greatest artist the Renaissance produced. This is a culture of full maturity and of apparently boundless confidence in the potentialities of human beings. In strictly cultural terms, it seems the natural extension of the previous period – until we reflect that Italy was engulfed by what were probably the most frighteningly destructive wars that Europe had seen since the fall of the Roman Empire. It bears repetition that the shocking experience of war in this period was perhaps all that was a genuinely 'Italian' experience during the Italian Renaissance.

The international background is roughly as follows. In the later fifteenth century, the French monarchy had consolidated its domestic power following the end of the Hundred Years War and the collapse of England into the Wars of the Roses. The Catholic monarchs of Spain, Ferdinand of Aragon and Isabella of Castile, completed the Reconquest of the Iberian peninsula by taking the last Muslim stronghold, Granada, in 1492. The French had an ancient claim through the Angevin line to the Kingdom of Naples (see above, Chapter 1). Naples had been in the hands of the Aragonese since 1435. The duke of Milan, Lodovico Sforza, known as 'il Moro', had taken the ducal title in 1479 in defiance of the claims of his nephew Gian Galeazzo, whose wife Isabella was the daughter of the king of Naples. In order to offset the threat of Neapolitan intervention, Lodovico allied with the French. This set in train a whole series of invasions in the course of which the Italian states lost control of their own affairs. The complex narrative of events – changing alliances, decisive battles and so on – may be followed elsewhere, notably in Machiavelli's *The Prince* and Francesco Guicciardini's *History of Italy* (first published in 1561). Of critical importance is the social and cultural impact that these wars were to have.

The 'Military Revolution' was a process of change in the character of warfare that took place throughout the period 1500–1800.[50] There is a strong case for saying that its principal features are focused sharply and suddenly in the Italian Wars. There were three fundamental changes. First, infantry superseded cavalry as the principal body of fighting men. When Charles VIII of France invaded in 1494, half his army of 18,000 men was made up of horsemen. In 1515, Francis I's cavalry accounted for only a fifth of a force of 45,000. Second, developments in the design of fortifications, perfected in Italy, made for longer sieges: low, thick walls absorbed cannon fire, and projecting towers covered any wall vulnerable to frontal assault. Some of the most vivid designs of such fortifications are to be found in the

drawings of Leonardo and Michelangelo. Finally, both on the battlefield
and in sieges, gunfire itself – from both cannon and handguns – made its
first decisive contribution to the outcome of a campaign. Much larger
armies involved in longer campaigns made for much more destructive wars.
Moreover, these were conflicts that needed the consolidated human and
material resources of states such as France and the Spanish monarchy. The
new style of war makes the battles of the *condottieri,* or mercenary commanders, of the fifteenth century seem both petty and refined. Compared with
the murderous lines of crossfire that the bastion provided, Uccello's pranc-
ing horses seem as harmless as a Disney cartoon.[51] [O.13; O.14]

The new destructiveness was awesome. Mercenary captains had traditionally manoeuvred to avoid the needless waste of manpower that was
their capital asset; the Italian Wars seemed to promote the absorption of
losses to gunfire or push of pike in a macabre species of sales drive. The
Swiss lost 3000 men at Bicocca in 1522 – the equivalent of one-third of the
entire population of Zurich. At Ravenna in 1512, the Spaniards lost 9000
men, the French 4000. More than 12,000 died at Marignano in 1515.
While the wars culminated in the sack of Rome in 1527, Ravenna, Brescia,
Prato (all 1512), Fabiano (1519), Como (1521), Genoa (1522) and Pavia
(1525) had all suffered a similar fate.

The horrors of war and the sense of divine retribution for sinfulness – of
which Savonarola's prophetic puritanism was the first symptom (see below,
Chapter 6) – became generalised. There was a palpable change in religiosity. In Lombardy, for example, many were killed in the fighting and it was
a Christian duty to see that they were buried. So great was the task that it
produced new religious orders such as the Somaschi and the Barnabites,
often wrongly seen as part of a reaction to the Reformation rather than the
product of circumstances in Italy. Even so, the new religiosity cannot be
isolated from the earlier history of the Renaissance itself.[52]

Religious renewals

The relationship between the Italian Wars and the religious life of the High
Renaissance remains a neglected area of study.[53] The shattering effects of
the sack of Rome by unpaid imperial troops, many of them Lutherans,
marked the climax of the wars, and is sometimes thought to have brought
the Italian Renaissance to an end. The danger of this interpretation is that
the Catholic revival thereafter is presented as a benighted authoritarianism
squeezing the life out of the Renaissance in Italy. That is the conclusion, for
example, of an important book by Lauro Martines. After the wars, Italy

was, he argues, afflicted with 'narrowing religious orthodoxy, frozen ruling classes, and an economy dipping yet once more into prolonged stagnation'. 'After the conclusion of the Council of Trent', he goes on, 'Italy was enmeshed in the tightening web of religious and political orthodoxy.' He compiles a startling list of examples from Renaissance literature which appeared on the *Index of Forbidden Books*: works by Dante, Boccaccio, Petrarch, Valla, Machiavelli, Castiglione, Ariosto, Aretino. 'Any and all criticism of the clergy', he says, 'was considered an affront to the Roman Church; anticlericalism became tantamount to heresy', which in turn would be rooted out by the Inquisition.[54]

It is tempting to speculate on what Galileo might have achieved had he been a refugee in seventeenth-century Amsterdam rather than the prisoner of the Holy Office (but see below, Chapter 8). This book emphasises the contrasts and conflicts between the value systems of Christianity and the ancient world. However, during the Renaissance Christian subjects dominated the visual arts, and while alternative cosmologies that challenged Christianity could, as we shall see, take shape, they were by no means common and still less were they typical. Whatever the whispers of secularisation within the social elite, there were certainly signs of vitality in the Church throughout the Renaissance, and they were to make a succession of impacts upon the populace at large. Many of them drew strength from the mendicant orders. In this regard, we might cite the influential careers of the Franciscan San Bernardino of Siena (1380–1444) and the Dominicans Sant'Antonino (1389–1459) and Girolamo Savonarola (1452–98). Robert Lopez once wrote that 'between Counter-Renaissance and Renaissance, the preaching of Girolamo Savonarola built temporarily a fiery bridge'.[55] This is a point well worth pursuing, since it dispenses with the term 'Counter Reformation' and enables us to ask whether mainstream piety remained largely unbroken.

There are two main arguments in favour of that step. First, there is plenty of evidence of spiritual disquiet, and, sometimes, even anguish, in the Renaissance itself. Second, the religious revival of the sixteenth century was to set down social roots that went far deeper than those of the Renaissance. Both of these points will be dealt with more expansively in later chapters, but each merits a brief mention here. If we concentrate for a moment on the High Renaissance, we find a sincere Christian piety at work in seeking to reconcile Christianity with ancient wisdom. It seems certain that Michelangelo painted the Sistine ceiling in accordance with a Neoplatonic scheme which may owe something to the ideas of Egidio da Viterbo (1469–1532), the head of the Augustinian order. Raphael's evocation of ancient learning, the *School of Athens*, is balanced on the opposite wall by a depiction of the debate over the Holy Sacrament, the *Disputa* (see below, Chapter 7). If we shift the focus from Rome to Venice, we find in the work of the three great masters of the sixteenth century, Titian, Veronese and Tintoretto, not only classical subjects, but any number of celebrations of saints' lives, Last Suppers and Crucifixions that celebrate the truth of the Christian religion – and this in a city that was resistant to influence from Rome. While the mysteries of Neoplatonism may have been lost on simple believers, they understood well enough the cult of the saints, above all the Virgin. As we shall see, there were reasons far more complicated than bigotry and authoritarianism why the Church would wish to protect the faithful from some of the more troubling aspects of Renaissance culture (see below, Chapters 6 and 7).

With the transfer of cultural energies in the seventeenth century to centres such as London and Amsterdam, the history of the Renaissance in Italy may be seen to come to an end – though not, perhaps, a definitive one. We should remember, however, what the Renaissance in Italy and Europe owed to the cities in which it was originally embedded.

3   Contexts I: Cities

The dangers of determinism

The achievements of Renaissance artists and writers are inseparable from the urban contexts that nurtured them. But not every city was a centre of the Renaissance. There is no unitary 'urban culture' magnetising contributions from particular towns in ways that can be reduced to a simple formula. This book, of considerable scope but limited scale, neither can nor would give detailed attention to every potential setting for major cultural achievements. In essence, this chapter is a tale of three cities that exemplify the relationship of the Renaissance to earlier periods, and it investigates the historical location of three different places: Rome, Florence, and Venice. Rome, with all its ancient associations, was also the centre of the Christian Middle Ages as the seat of the papacy. Florence recreated the ancient world and applied its values to a medieval commercial city. Venice, the quintessential commercial city of the Middle Ages, was home to a distinctive Gothic tradition and a late and luxuriant flowering that retained the distinctiveness of its setting. However, Siena also draws attention as a place in which a 'medieval' civic culture foreshadows fifteenth-century developments in Florence.

However localised a 'tradition' may seem, these cities were not culturally self-contained, but influenced each other and, to a lesser extent, other places. What follows focuses on a few specific but differing cities and queries the conditions that prevailed in them. Less expansive treatment than that of Bram Kempers, it owes much to the dynamics that he identifies. Professor Kempers provides a mobile picture of cultural change and its identification with different centres that the reader may wish to relate to the chronological patterns sketched out in the preceding chapter. In painting, Professor Kempers stresses an overlapping periodisation identified with different centres: Rome, Pisa and Assisi from 1200 to 1320, Siena from 1296 to 1340, Florence from 1270 to 1490, Urbino and Mantua from 1470 to 1500, Rome from 1500 to 1520, Florence once more from 1550 to 1580.[1] This chapter is concerned with the general historical significance of various cities, not with painting alone. Of Professor Kempers's list, Rome, Siena and Florence are discussed below, and Venice, which he omits, is added. Mantua and Urbino follow in the next chapter, which deals with courts.

In its conclusion, this survey notices cities exhibiting characteristics that feature here yet do not seem to be part of 'the Renaissance' at all. There is no necessary connection between commercial prosperity or recession, social tranquillity or unrest, political stability or instability, and cultural achievement. This is demonstrated by the experience of some of the great cities of the Italian Middle Ages. The exercise focuses attention on two further questions. First, why do cities with great university traditions, such as Padua and Bologna, not figure prominently in accounts of the Renaissance? Second, is there a case for saying that the 'investment in culture' that funded many artistic projects was the product of 'hard times' rather than the surplus wealth of a prosperous era? One city, however, was to be inseparable from cultural change, both as a physical entity and as an idea.

Rome: place and idea

Rome the place was to become the centre of the High Renaissance.[2] In an important sense, that was when the culture of the Renaissance came home. For in many ways the idea of Rome (rather than Rome itself) had proved still more influential in shaping the perceptions and priorities of writers and artists who applied their minds to the classical past. 'Rome' represented not just a city but a world – 'urbs et orbis' – a world of order. It was governed by laws, enforced by invincible armies whose roads held together an empire stretching from Scotland to Syria, from Germany to Libya, and made the Mediterranean a 'Roman lake'. Within that political order, the arts thrived. To equal such an achievement was the humanist dream.

The idea of Rome remains one of the chief unifying forces in the Western historical experience, providing at once a measure of change and an extraordinary continuity. Western civilisation since the fall of the western Roman Empire can be seen as a series of revivals of interest in the classical world in its Romanised form, with recovery and the restoration of order linked to a revival of the idea of Rome.[3] Thus, the coronation of Charlemagne in 800 established a 'Holy Roman Empire' that was the basis of a 'Carolingian Renaissance'. Then, the defeat of the Magyars by Otto the Great at the battle of the Lech in 955 preceded his taking the same imperial title in 962 and the so-called 'Ottonian Renaissance'. In the twelfth century there was to be a 'Renaissance' in the sense of a revival of interest in classical learning among Roman churchmen. Even after the 'Italian Renaissance' (as conventionally understood) there were further revivals. The classicism of the Enlightenment reinvented ideas and institutions familiar from ancient Rome in the 'New World'.[4] The term 'candidate' refers to the togas

specially whitened with chalk that marked a man out as standing for office
(*candidatus*). Americans vote for a Senate, their representatives assemble at
the Capitol. In reflecting on how the West refers to its past and at the same
time celebrates advances away from it, the historian is drawn to reflect on
all the tension and anxiety – not to mention the delusion – that the attempt
to discern the difference between continuity and change can generate.
Western culture is fundamentally historical – and the historical pattern of
'ancient', 'medieval' and 'modern' periods is the legacy of the rediscovery
of an alien culture in the remote past during what is known as the
Renaissance.

Rome is central to the historicising tendencies of Western culture, and in
the much more limited scope of this chapter, what needs to be grasped is
that Rome's very fabric as a place was the inspiration of Rome the idea, and
the idea inspired the re-creation of the place. In the city, the links with the
Roman past were often physical, layer upon layer 'like a huge compost
heap of human hopes and ambitions'.[5] This is embodied in buildings such
as the church of San Clemente with its successive strata of foundations from
the Roman Republic, pagan sarcophagus, a temple to Mithras, fourth-
century basilica, early Christian frescoes, Christian mosaics that place the
saviour in a triumphal arch – all in the same building as Renaissance frescoes by Masaccio and Masolino. [O.15] The lower church there was not
discovered until the eighteenth century, but there were plenty of obvious
classical remains elsewhere in the city. Medieval Rome contained the
'church of the Holy Saviour of the arch of Trajan'. The temple of
Antoninus and Faustina dating from AD 141 had become the church of
San Lorenzo in Miranda by the twelfth century. It is perhaps no surprise
that Frederick II imitated an imperial triumph after his victory at Corte
Nuova over the Milanese in 1237.[6]

There were some surprisingly early developments in Rome that suggest
the first stirrings of the Renaissance itself. This is particularly so in the late
work of the painter Pietro Cavallini (active 1273–1308) – such as his *Last
Judgment* in Santa Cecilia – which prefigures that of Cimabue in Assisi and
even Giotto in Padua.[7] [O.16] Cavallini worked with the Florentine master
Arnolfo di Cambio (*d. c.*1302), who had been trained in sculpture by Nicola
Pisano and who was to be the architect of the cathedral in Florence.[8]

Constantly as an idea but intermittently as a place, Rome was to prove
enormously influential in shaping the cultures of Italy with which we are
concerned. As already noted (see above, Chapter 1), the absence of the
papacy in Avignon during the fourteenth century may have been a stimulus to innovation in places such as Florence and Siena. During that absence,
Rome was a city of about 17,000 people, substantially smaller than

Florence (about 90,000 people) or Venice (perhaps 100,000). The muddy, ruined, overgrown city, torn apart by family faction, was something akin to Lorenzetti's *Allegory of Bad Government*. It was to be the setting for a tragi-comic episode that is nevertheless revealing of the political inspiration that ancient Rome continued to offer. In 1342 – a year after Petrarch had received the laurel crown as poet in the city – a popular revolt against the papal governor demanding more power for the guilds brought to prominence a self-taught nobody called Cola di Rienzo (1313?–54). In an act of supreme opportunism, he offered to represent the new regime as 'notary of the people' at the papal court in Avignon (where he met Petrarch and developed a friendship with him). He returned with papal approval for a vigorous defence of the new republican regime. In May 1347 he assembled 100 followers at Santa Sabina, and the following day, with a further 100 mercenaries, set off for the Capitol. There, he urged the crowd to acclaim him as 'Tribune', and, having received his acclamation, assumed dictatorial powers, demanding the submission of the nobles and dealing out summary justice. After various failures of nerve partly induced by military fiasco in the *contado*, the rural area surrounding the city, he was brought to heel by the pope's vicar-general, Bertrand de Deux. He submitted to all papal requirements, resigning his office and living incognito as a Franciscan tertiary. He sought imperial support but was imprisoned in Bohemia for his pains prior to being sent back to Avignon for further investigation. Here, he benefited from the death of Clement VI and the election of Innocent VI in 1352, and as anarchy took hold in Rome was despatched as Innocent's 'ally and envoy' to restore order. Amid the factional struggles of the Savelli and the Colonna, the mob turned on him and butchered him.[9]

It is a rather seamy tale, but revealing all the same. First, Rienzo appears to have been the first Renaissance rhetorician who 'talked his way to the top', perhaps on the basis of an evident knowledge of works by classical authors such as Livy, Sallust, Seneca and Cicero. Second, he literally sought to remove the 'Middle Ages', trying to take the imperial title away from Germany, retracting every renunciation of rights since the Roman Republic and reassuming its full sovereign power. His friendship with Petrarch at least suggests a complementarity of aspiration between humanism and politics as well as a tension between the active life and the contemplative. He believed in the prophetic future associated with Joachim of Fiore (*d.* 1202) in which, after the ages of the Father and of the Son, the age of the Spirit would bring Paradise to earth. Such beliefs show that he never entirely escaped his own times, but the very mixture may have intensified a species of political fantasy that is disturbingly modern. Yes, one can, for once, use the term 'modern' with some accuracy, since Rienzo played at least a coincidental role in the shaping of twentieth-century dictatorship. Both the Soviet Union and the Nazi regime used Richard Wagner's overture to his opera *Rienzi* (first performed in 1842) to celebrate the tribune's memory, the Soviets as a hero of the people, the Nazis as the man of the people who was ultimately let down by the people and brought his regime crashing down with him. It is sometimes said that the original manuscript of the opera perished in Hitler's bunker in Berlin. To complete the obscene trilogy, Rienzo's fate brings to mind the corpse of Mussolini hanging upside down from a lamppost. Perhaps all of that is a modernity that Renaissance scholars would not choose for their subject. For the purposes of this book, Rienzo's importance lies in his precocious linkage of rhetoric and republican liberty, the demonstration in his career that tyranny was never far away – and in the fact that Petrarch appears to have taken him seriously. Perhaps it is indicative of the violent anarchy of *Trecento* Italy that any form of order was worth trying – which may say something about the 'rise of the signori'.[10]

While Rienzo's rhetoric may have evoked the idea of Rome, the physical remains of the city were of more importance. It was to Rome that Brunelleschi travelled in order to draw motifs from the ruins, motifs which he could incorporate into his own work. It is worth speculating whether he could have designed the Pazzi Chapel at Santa Croce in Florence without having seen the Pantheon in Rome, built at the behest of Augustus's admiral, Marcus Agrippa, in the early first century AD. The Pantheon itself when drawn by Raphael can look like a 'Renaissance' building. [O.17] The ruins of the Basilica of Constantine and Maxentius resemble an engraving that seems to be of another ruin. In fact it is a view of the new St Peter's under construction. [O.18]

The papacy returned definitively to Rome with Martin V in 1420. Thereafter one perceives – much more clearly than in any other place – the problems of reconciling pagan antiquity and the medieval Christian era. Yet as a conscious work of construction from then on, Rome remains much more obviously a piece of urban planning along classical lines than any other city in Italy. It was in Rome that the principles of axiality, symmetry, focus, hierarchy and unity noted by Loren Partridge were established – and still stand in stark contrast to the higgledy-piggledy roofs and dark, narrow streets of Florence or Venice.[11] Moreover, after the sack of 1527, there were 2800 curial positions for a population of 55,000, so one person in 20 might be a papal employee. The sheer size and physical presence of the clerical establishment was formidable, but whether there was any glaring contradiction between the Rome of the ancient world and the Rome of the Christian centuries is debatable. The medieval papacy had institutionalised a compromise between antique paganism and medieval Christianity. The pope held the title of a magistrate in ancient Rome, 'pontifex maximus', and the papacy's exercise of power chiefly depended for its justification much less on the Scriptures than on the Roman law.[12]

Within this unusual urban environment, the sources of patronage were mainly courtly. The papal court itself (see below, Chapter 4) was supplemented by the courtly households of cardinals (at least 20 of them in the early sixteenth century), and by wealthy laymen such as the Sienese banker Agostino Chigi (1465–1520), whose Villa Farnesina is graced with the frescoes of Raphael. That the layman was exceptional in what are often seen as the cultures of the urban laity is another specifically Roman feature. It was hard to be a layman and a humanist when the sources of employment were identified with the Church. Very few humanists became bishops or cardinals – the popes Nicholas V (r. 1447–55) and Pius II (r. 1458–64) were exceptions – which made the men of letters all the more dependent on employment by senior ecclesiastics.[13]

In certain respects, the Roman humanists were extraordinarily successful in reinventing the compromise of antiquity and Christianity: identifying the Roman Emperor with the Roman pope, the Roman Empire with the Roman Church, senators with cardinals, the forum with the curia. There was plenty of work for Latin scholars, since Latin remained the official language of the papal secretariat. Roman imitation of Cicero was often more committed than that of even the Florentines, even though it was Cicero as supreme stylist, not Cicero as champion of republicanism, on whom they modelled themselves. As late as 1587, Pope Sixtus V capped the columns of the Emperors Trajan (AD 47–117) and Marcus Aurelius (AD 129–90) with statues of Saint Peter (martyred AD 64) and Saint Paul (AD 67), physically putting together ancient Rome and Christianity.[14]

Europe was by then fiercely divided by the Reformation, itself apparently a reaction to the sheer worldliness of the Roman Church. One might argue that ultimately, the inherent contradictions between the culture of antiquity and that of the Christian era were most evident in Rome, though, paradoxically, one might also see the Reformation as a protest against Catholicism's compromises with paganism since the time of the Emperor Constantine. While Luther's protest was the most dramatic and strident statement of this position, it was also more tentatively inherent in some of the work of writers and artists in the Renaissance itself (see below, Chapters 6 and 7).[15] The worldliness of Renaissance Rome was certainly undisguised. Virginity was acknowledged as impractical, venality of office was taken for granted, and violence was common. In 1493, the poet Jacopo Corsi was foolish enough to recite some satirical verses about Cardinal della

Rovere (later Julius II), who, when he heard of the matter, simply hired three hit men and had the comedian stabbed to death. When the body of the duke of Bisceglie was found in the Tiber in 1500, suspicion of the murder fell upon his brother-in-law, Cesare Borgia, who, like his sister Lucrezia, was the child of the reigning pope, Alexander VI. This book challenges the idea that a worldly and corrupt 'Renaissance' papacy was transformed into a spiritually austere and authoritarian institution by protest in the north of Europe. On the contrary, there is plenty of evidence of a propensity for being 'reform-minded' from St Francis onwards. However, in Rome itself there were perhaps just too many vested interests within the establishment to make reform likely. On this interpretation the syntheses that the High Renaissance achieved between pagan Neoplatonism and Christianity were ultimately illusory, as observers such as Erasmus and Luther perceived them to be.[16]

There was a strand of ecclesiastical reform throughout the Renaissance, though it became more emphatic in grandeur and seriousness after the sack of Rome in 1527. Between 1527 and 1590, more than fifty new churches were built in Rome. St Peter's itself embodies the majesty of reformed Catholicism:

> This compact solidity was surely intended as a metaphor for Christ the cornerstone and Peter the rock, and its unity the oneness of the body of Christ and Christianity – precisely at the moment when the impossibility of reconciliation with the Protestants became clear.[17]

There were clear continuities between the Rome of the High Renaissance and the Rome of the 'Counter Reformation', both in terms of the preoccupations of ecclesiastics and in terms of artistic style. One must reiterate, however, that – whatever its importance as an idea – in the fourteenth century, Rome as a place was a city of fewer than 20,000 people, lacking the presence of its most important source of patronage as well as its political *raison d'être*. The early stages of the Renaissance are identified not with the city of Rome, but with other centres.

Siena: late medieval or early Renaissance?

It is perhaps indicative of the problems involved in characterising Sienese culture that a book on the city as a 'medieval Italian commune' and a book on 'early Renaissance Italy' have, apart from the titles and the authors' names, identical dust jackets (even on the spines). Both use Ambrogio Lorenzetti's *Allegory of Good Government* from the Palazzo Pubblico.[18] Perhaps one should be easy with the apparent contradiction and acknowledge that Siena is to be understood as a medieval city that produced some of the most notable works of art of the early Renaissance. Before the Black Death, the city itself may have had a population of around 40,000 and the *contado* that surrounded the city to a radius of about 50 kilometres may have contained a further 60,000 souls. Siena's economic life exemplified the commercial vitality of the medieval communes of Italy, and its bankers were active on a broad international scale. Its wealthiest families – the Tolomei, the Piccolomini, the Salimbeni, the Gallerani and the Malavolti – tended to be 'landowner-financiers'.[19] The city lacked a notable manufacturing sector, which meant that the guilds had little political clout, but the oligarchical rule of a council known as 'the Nine' gave the city political stability.

It is within a matrix of commercial prosperity and political stability that we find a culture that gave early expression to the 'civic spirit'. Siena was 'the City of the Virgin' and the religious life of Siena was an integral part of social and political life. Religion was itself a civic phenomenon.[20] In 1260, the Sienese had been victorious at the battle of Montaperti, thanks, they believed, to an image of the Virgin Mary kept in the cathedral. In 1308, a new version was commissioned from Duccio di Buoninsegna (1255/60–1315/18), already a master of advancing years. The chronicler Agnolo di Tura recorded that when Duccio completed the work in 1311 there was public rejoicing, and a procession bore the 'beautiful and rich painting' from the painter's workshop to the cathedral:

And the Sienese bore the said picture to the cathedral on Wednesday, the ninth day of June, with great devotions and processions; with the bishop of Siena, Messer Rugeri da Casole, with all of the cathedral clergy, and with all of the religious of Siena, and the lords [of the Signory] with the officials of the city, *podestà* and capitano [of the people], and all of the most worthy citizens in order, with lighted lamps in their hands. Afterwards the women and children with much devotion went in procession through Siena around the Campo, all the bells sounding a Gloria. And throughout the day the shops were closed for devotion, and throughout Siena many alms were given to the poor, with many orations and prayers to God and to his Mother, Madonna always Virgin Mary, that she might aid, conserve and increase the city of Siena and its rule in peace and in good condition, as the advocate and protectress of this city.[21]

The sense of general accessibility and involvement, the sense of a common interest, the sense of pride and localised patriotism in the civic identity were thus all associated with a work of art. [O.19] In 1315, another great Sienese master, Simone Martini (*c*.1284–1344), produced another version of the *Maestà* in the Palazzo Pubblico which intensified the political identification of the commune with the Virgin. On the opposite wall is the lone figure of Guidoriccio dei Fogliani on horseback, symbolising the state's military power. [O.20] In the Palazzo, the city's magistrates took their decisions beneath the *Allegory of Good Government* in both town and countryside, which occupied two walls, the *Bad Government* on a third. Ambrogio Lorenzetti painted these between 1337 and 1340, and they spell out the importance of justice and the common good and contrast them with the dangers of tyranny.[22] [O.21]

Sienese art from this period is also notable for its setting down of some significant stylistic landmarks. In Duccio's *Maestà*, 'the harmony of the decorative surface is never disturbed', yet there is a naturalism in the spatial representation of landscape that in some ways surpasses the more austere natural surroundings of Giotto. The Sienese masters' empathy with the beauty of the natural world is confirmed in the depiction of the effects of good government in the countryside, for this marked the momentous discovery of pure landscape. Lorenzetti 'has not only achieved verisimilitude; he has also translated the city statutes, hardly a lively series of texts, into an evocative pictorial form'.[23] There were livelier texts to work from, however, and a precocious intersection of the worlds of painting and letters ensued. In 1335, 'Cieco, master of grammar' translated the life of San Savino into the vernacular for Pietro Lorenzetti 'that it might be illustrated on a panel'. The attention that Simone Martini paid to the position of the spectator looked forward to the kind of unity of pictorial composition that is associated with the revolutionary developments of the early fifteenth century in Florence. The control of pictorial space that Ambrogio Lorenzetti demonstrates in his *Purification of the Virgin* (1342) seems close to the discovery of linear perspective.[24] [O.22]

However, within a few years of the Black Death, the Nine were overthrown and great civic projects abruptly ceased. The extension of the cathedral, never completed, symbolises the sense of overstretch that marks the economic and political ambitions of Italian cities in the earlier part of the fourteenth century. As William Bowsky has remarked, 'For a town of its limited strength, size and wealth to have housed the greatest church in western Christendom would have been anomalous'.[25] Siena's political history in the fifteenth century has not attracted much attention, but its cultural contribution was significant, promoting a curious mix of the so-called 'International Gothic' style and a sharp-edged realism more readily associated with the Florentines. This is particularly marked in the work of the painter Stefano di Giovanni Sassetta (*c*.1392–1450) but also in that of the sculptor Vecchietta (1412–80), and of the fortress builder Francesco di Giorgio (1439–1501/2).[26] Moreover, San Bernardino was to launch from Siena a Franciscan revival that took in much of northern Italy. That revival was to prove an emphatic reminder of the relationship between mendicant spirituality and cultural change. San Bernardino's attacks on greed, worldliness and vanity resonate with those of Savonarola, and they prompt caution in the assessment of Renaissance 'secularism'. The sermons of San Bernardino were part of a reforming impulse that predates by generations the Reformation (see below, Chapter 8). That in itself should make historians wary of seeing change in the Roman Church in the sixteenth century as a simple reaction to Protestantism.

In the early sixteenth century, Sienese artists such as the architect Baldassare Peruzzi (1481–1537), who designed the Villa Farnesina for Agostino Chigi, and the painter Il Sodoma (Giovanni Antonio Bazzi, 1477–1549) worked in Rome. But by then any civic spirit in Siena itself was virtually extinct. In 1502, Bernardino Pintoricchio (c.1454–1513) produced an anti-republican series of paintings on the life of the Sienese pope, Pius II, and in 1506, Pandolfo Petrucci felt either so secure or so insecure in his despotism that he had Duccio's *Maestà* removed from the cathedral. The Sienese state itself is an important example of a petty Italian entity overtaken by the 'military revolution' unleashed in the Italian Wars (see above, Chapter 2). Siena was absorbed into the empire of Charles V because it could not afford to build and maintain the sort of defences that might have preserved its independence.[27]

Siena's chief importance in this book is exemplified in the precocity and sure-footedness of a culture that celebrated political ideals in the earlier fourteenth century. That should be borne in mind as we turn to Siena's more famous neighbour 50 kilometres to the north.

Florence: city of movement

The contribution of the Florentines to the cultures of Italy throughout the period was extraordinary both in originality and in pervasiveness. We could begin the story of the Renaissance with the Florentine Giotto in Padua and end it with the Florentine Michelangelo in Rome and still not feel slavish in following Vasari's schema (see above, Chapter 1). Burckhardt's judgement that Florence was 'the city of incessant movement, which has left us a record of the thoughts and aspirations of each and all who, for three centuries, took part in this movement' retains a remarkable freshness.[28] This short section attempts to sketch the social and political context in which artists thrived. Since there is ample opportunity to discuss the achievements of the Florentines outside of Florence in other chapters, here we concentrate on the early fifteenth century as the period when cultural creativity in the city itself was most notable.[29]

In the early part of the fourteenth century, the city's population may have been as many as 90,000 people, making it one of the largest in Europe.[30] Like the Sienese, the Florentines prospered through banking – notably the companies of the Bardi, Peruzzi, and Acciaiuoli – which acted for the popes, and for monarchs such as Edward III of England. International commercial networks proved fruitful for the expansion of manufactures, most notably woollen cloth. As Hidetoshi Hoshino has demonstrated, the networks enabled the Florentines to discover the source of the best raw materials and the best production processes, then buy up the raw materials, install the appropriate machines in Florence, and – crucially – produce the goods more cheaply than could their competitors.[31] As in the case of Siena, recession struck in the 1340s and was deepened by the Black Death and its recurrent visitations. The later part of the century witnessed the Revolt of the Ciompi, and as the fifteenth century opened, the city was faced with the threat of conquest by the duchy of Milan (see above, Chapter 2). The Republic survived the external threat and for some of its citizens acquired a new sense of its own identity in so doing. Since much attention has focused on the relationship between 'humanism' and 'republicanism', it is desirable to give some idea of how the republican constitution was designed to work.

The *catasto* – a species of census or survey – of 1427 suggests a population in the city itself of about 40,000. The political population consisted of those adult males (over 30 years of age) who were members of the city's 7 Major Guilds and 14 Minor Guilds, the former representing merchants and financiers, the latter craftsmen and shopkeepers. Potentially, the electoral process might have involved 5000–6000 men. From among them, elections were made to the city's main offices. These were eight priors who, with the Gonfaloniere di Giustizia, formed the Signoria. In order to become law, their decisions needed the approval of 12 'good men', the 'buoni uomini', 16 standard bearers and two large general councils of over 500 members each. Apart from these offices, there were various ad hoc committees such as the Dieci di Balía and the Otto di Guardia. The significance of the constitution's committees is that it reveals how narrow was the gulf between 'republics' and 'despots'. Since the committees were called for specific purposes, they could be used to suspend the regular functions of the other organs of government. These committees, then, were vulnerable to manipulation, especially since the other offices tended to rotate after as little as six months and often after as little as two. The speed of rotation of office had the effect of institutionalising inexperience and therefore making the intervention of an 'emergency' agency all the more attractive. The people who chose the members of the ad hoc committees, the *accoppiatori,* were therefore key figures. They were in a position to pack the committees with members of their own faction – and they frequently did so. As Francesco Guicciardini, writing in retirement after 1537, observed in his *History of Florence*:

> Cosimo [de' Medici] bound together the state by having a number of citizens given *balía* [special powers] for five years. And he had new scrutiny lists made for all magistracies in the city and outside. None the less, because the authority that the *balía* had was so great, the Lords [Priors] were hardly ever chosen by lot, but were elected instead by the *accoppiatori* according to Cosimo's wishes. When the five-year term of the *balía* was up, he simply had their powers extended for another five years.[32]

Professor Nicolai Rubinstein's painstaking and groundbreaking research on office holding suggests that the political population, which stood as high as 6000 in theory, was reduced in practice to a circle of about 75 men.[33] Unsurprisingly, therefore, the Republic's politics were in the hands of a shadowy group of 'men of influence' at one remove. The fact that the city's institutions were not the locations of real power says much about Florence's troubled political history.

While the Florentine humanists were to compare their city with Rome, it is more accurate, perhaps, to find an ancient parallel with Athens.[34] Athens seems more appropriate both in terms of its political scale (and instability), and because of the intensity of its cultural activity. The arts and letters of the period also illustrate the Florentine political experience, and in this regard the fascination of the Roman experience was inescapable. In studying ancient Rome, the humanists concluded that – with the exception of Christ's coming to earth – the key change in all human history had been the process by which the Roman republic had become a principate that might be ruled by a tyrant. In studying Roman history one could therefore learn how to avoid that degeneration. In the event, the Florentine political experience was to replicate in miniature that of ancient Rome, and the Medici managed the transition. Their exercise of an increasingly princely power while maintaining the façade of republican institutions was highly influential in shaping Machiavelli's vision of politics, with its cultivation of appearances in order to mask the sordid realities of power.

In the early part of the fifteenth century, Florence was the scene of the unique interaction of the humanists' new sense of time and the artists' new sense of space. There had been nothing comparable in Siena a hundred years earlier. Since subsequent chapters (see below, Chapters 6 and 7) deal with developments in humanism and the visual arts separately, this is the place to emphasise the dynamism of their interaction. Even though his suggestion was ignored, the humanist and Florentine chancellor, Leonardo Bruni, was quite clear about what the 20 Old Testament stories for the bronze doors of the Baptistery of San Giovanni needed, and was characteristically vain in the precision of what he thought best in a letter of 1426:

> I have chosen according to my judgement twenty stories, which I am sending to you noted on paper. It will be necessary that he who has to design them be well instructed about each story, so that he can place well both the persons and the actions which occur, and that he has a gentleness so that he knows how to adorn them well. In addition to the twenty stories, I have made a note of eight prophets, as you will see on the paper. Now I do not doubt that this work, as I have designed it for you, will succeed most excellently. But I would very much like to be close to whoever will have the designing to do, to make him take on every significance that the story conveys.[35]

It is significant that Bruni makes no mention of the importance of a narrative clarity that would make the Bible stories easy to follow. The idea that the work should delight the eye is an important expression of the emergence of new aesthetic and philosophical values (see below, Chapter 6). Yet the city itself should also offer the eye delight, as Bruni makes clear in his ringing rhetorical acclamation of Florence's clean streets. While this may seem slightly absurd as an exercise in speechmaking, it also offers a concrete example of the importance of looking after the earthly city – without necessarily looking to the celestial one. And there is more pleasure for the senses:

> Indeed, we see that Florence is so clean and neat that nowhere else could be found cleaner. This city is indeed unique and in all the world singular, in which there is nothing that is foul to the eye, nothing offensive to the nose, nothing dirty under foot. By the utmost diligence of its inhabitants all things are taken care of and provided for so that all filth is taken far away, so you encounter that which may bring delight and joy to the senses. Thus, in its splendour Florence perhaps surpasses all cities that now exist, and also, in its splendour and elegance there is no argument it surpasses all the cities that exist and all that ever will be.[36]

There was a clear aspiration to improve and embellish the material fabric of the city. This is not only an aim that modern municipal authorities might

consider. The rhetoric may for once reflect the fact that conditions elsewhere were inferior: in 1433 Ambrogio Traversari grumbled in a letter to
Cosimo de' Medici that Ravenna was simply impossible to cross on foot.[37]
As in the case of Siena, there is an awakening idea that the city of man
might be fashioned into an agreeable shape. The city of God was, after all,
for the dead enjoying eternal life. It was in extolling the potential of the
earthly city that Florentine 'civic humanism' challenged the Augustinian
vision of the 'Civitas Dei' (see below, Chapter 6). A couple of appropriately
rhetorical questions underline the point. Where but in Florence could one
see a Foundling Hospital so obviously geared to providing a comfortable
environment for vulnerable children? Where else but in Florence would
there be such competition among patrons seeking to outdo each other in
civic monuments? The Opera del Duomo advertised a general competition
for the completion of the dome of the cathedral; each of the guilds wanted
the best statue for its niche in the exterior wall at Orsanmichele (see below,
Chapter 5).

The Florence of the early fifteenth century was not a 'democracy', and
its culture was not 'popular' in the way in which we would use those terms.
Yet it is possible to avoid anachronism in acknowledging that perhaps the
most exhilarating feature of the 'Florentine Enlightenment' was that it was
accessible. The Medici were to change that (see below, Chapter 5). When
Cosimo was buried in San Lorenzo in 1464, he was commemorated with
the same title that the Emperor Augustus had held in ancient Rome: *pater
patriae*, 'father of the fatherland'. It is as though the state had become a
family business. It was to remain so until 1494, when Lorenzo's son Piero
made a fatal error in handing over the keys to the Republic's fortresses to
the invading Charles VIII of France. Charles entered the city with his lance
on his thigh, which signified conquest, and Cosimo's title was removed
from his memorial as inappropriate. Piero's departure opened the way for
Savonarola's godly republic. When, after four years, the Dominican died at
the hands of the hangman, the Republic staggered on until 1512 – at which
point the Medici returned to power. The Medicean regime gave way to the
last Florentine Republic in 1527. In 1530, the Medici firmly established
themselves as a ducal dynasty and became grand dukes of Tuscany by
imperial order when the Duchy absorbed Siena in 1569.[38]

The garish marbles and gigantic statuary of the Medici Chapel at San
Lorenzo come as a shock after a visit to the church designed by Brunelleschi
and decorated with sculpture by Donatello. Yet even that troubling experience is expressive of the pace of cultural and political change. Republics
and civic values tumbled before princes and Neoplatonism in a breathtaking whirligig that left political observers of the sixteenth century uncertain

as to which regime they should favour – and whether it made any difference which one they chose to support.[39] Such a history contrasts sharply with the history of a city that had a reputation for stability: the Most Serene Republic.

Venice: *La Serenissima*

Despite the contrast between movement and stability, there were, nevertheless, some important similarities between the Venetian and the Florentine contexts. Both were republics, Venice continually, Florence intermittently at least in name. Somewhat surprisingly, neither had a particularly strong connection with ancient Rome. Florence was 'not very rich in Roman remains', while in Venice there were none at all.[40] Certainly, the approaches to antiquity in general and Rome in particular were vastly different. In Florence, humanists and artists looked to the ancient world with a view to its eager absorption. Bruni pored over classical texts in order to learn the lessons of ancient history, Brunelleschi sketched motifs among the ruins of Rome and incorporated them in his own original designs. In Venice, there existed a political culture acutely wary of excitement of this kind. Even though the government promoted Venice as 'nova Roma' in the aftermath of the sack of Rome in 1527 (see below, Chapter 5), the Venetians did not develop a civic myth linking the foundation of the city to Rome. The founders of the city were said to be refugees from Attila the Hun's invasions in the mid-fifth century AD. The government fostered a myth of the independence of the city and the interdependence of prosperity and stability, the one reinforcing the other.

There was some historical justification for this in the city's amphibious history. After the initial foundation (in reality in the late seventh century), the inhabitants looked landward and traded fish and salt for corn. By the eleventh century, they could afford to look east, to the sea, and there opened an age of trade and crusade which gave the Venetians such commercial power that they brokered a peace between the pope and the emperor in 1177. Shortly afterwards, crusading armies from the feudal north sacked the city of Zara in order to pay the Venetians what they owed in transportation costs. The profits of plunder proved so pleasing that they went on to sack Constantinople itself. These episodes were to provide some of the most frequently addressed subjects of the art that the state sponsored. The thirteenth and fourteenth centuries were dominated by wars with Genoa culminating in the War of Chioggia (1378–81), when, startlingly, a Genoese fleet entered the lagoon, but only to be crushingly defeated.

Thereafter the Republic's Mediterranean interests were under constant and often severe threat from the advance of the Ottoman Turks. There was a momentous turn back to the land, and in the course of the fifteenth century the Venetians consolidated a formidable territorial state in one of the most heavily urbanised areas of Europe, stretching from the lagoon to Crema, which is close to Milan. Defeat by the Turks at Zonchio in 1499 and by the League of Cambrai at Agnadello in 1509 left the Venetians nowhere to turn.[41]

Prizing their status as an independent republic and pointing to the historical deep-rootedness of that tradition, the Venetians had little need of humanist noises about the danger of the slide from republic to tyranny: that would be to suggest that it might happen. The identification of Venice with Rome came after Rome itself had been sacked in 1527. The refashioning of the city's political and commercial centres at San Marco and Rialto took place through the patronage of Jacopo Sansovino (1486–1570) by Doge Andrea Gritti (see below, Chapter 5). Along with the scurrilous author Pietro Aretino (1492–1556), Sansovino was a refugee from Rome. The accentuation of Venice's identity as a safe haven was emphatic but forced. Only the divisions among the victors prevented the city from falling to its enemies after the catastrophic defeat at Agnadello in 1509.[42]

By the early sixteenth century, the city's economy was overtly challenged by the opening of the Atlantic, and beyond that the Indian Ocean and the markets of the East. There was even talk of cutting a canal at Suez in order to compete for the spice trade with the Portuguese. By an admirable process of adaptation, the Venetians transformed their economy, and this was to safeguard their prosperity for most of the sixteenth century. Maritime enterprise and colonial exploitation were the hallmarks of the Venetian Empire in the fourteenth century.[43] From the fifteenth on, a metropolitan economy with a significant textiles sector expanded enormously in the city itself. Put another way, in the earlier period Venetians went overseas to trade, from the fifteenth century onwards foreigners came to buy in Venice. Some of them bought printed books, of which the city was Europe's leading producer. The metropolitan centre of the Mediterranean economy was devastated by pestilence in 1575–7, yet it made a remarkable recovery – at least in terms of its population. From the plague of 1630 there was to be no such recovery: the city of Venice recouped its losses, but only at the expense of the cities and regions of the mainland.[44]

However, the city's myth survived its fading glory: generations of Europeans in a continent torn apart by religious war looked to Venice as a model for political stability. Yet was not this singular city typical in its singularity?

Absentees?

This short survey has so far taken in four obvious and famous centres. The historian needs to take a very different approach in each case. Rome was an idea as well as a place. As a place its significance varied. The absence of the papacy for most of the fourteenth century may have liberated cultural energies elsewhere. After its return in the fifteenth, increasing imperial grandeur in imitation of ancient Rome was essential to religious revival, but it heightened concerns about the Church's worldliness and apparent paganism. The achievements of the Sienese in the early fourteenth century were extraordinary, particularly in the way in which they foreshadowed developments in Florence at the beginning of the fifteenth, yet they were strictly limited in time and space. Florence itself remains dominant in historical writing. The speed of change in politics and culture is exhausting. There is probably no precise relationship to identify, merely an instability that swung between republicanism and princely rule amid a growing realisation that the swing did not cover a very large arc – a view that finds its supreme expression in the works of Machiavelli. Of Venetian history, one can take an expansive view since the Republic's constitutional position remained fixed and stable throughout the period, though its cultural activity is generally late and shows marked dissimilarities to Florence – and anywhere else.

That summary is a restatement of 'the dangers of determinism'. There is no direct causal link that runs 'city–commercial prosperity–Renaissance', and can be applied to any case history. Yet it is important to play up the positive aspects of the reluctance of the Renaissance to become an Italian synthesis. While brief surveys of obvious places do not provide a unitary view of 'the Italian Renaissance', they demonstrate the extraordinary richness and diversity of cultural achievement within a relatively small geographical space. That complex of achievements becomes all the more extraordinary when one reflects that those cities were not insulated against each other. Many of the Florentine humanists worked in Rome at some stage, and Sienese masters painted in Florence. Any number of painters went to Assisi because of the Franciscan project, not because of its commercial prosperity or Roman ruins.

Padua had both prosperity and Roman ruins, as well as one of Europe's great centres of learning, the university. However, there is no continuous 'Renaissance' tradition there, despite the city's boasting several extraordinary landmarks, such as Giotto's cycle in the Scrovegni Chapel from the very early fourteenth century (see below, Chapter 5) and Donatello's equestrian statue of the mercenary Gattamelata (the sculptor was in the city from

1444 to 1453). The glittering culture of the Carrara court is a subject for the next chapter. Of civic projects, Vasari says that the city authorities pleaded with Donatello to stay in the city after completing the statue. He also reports Donatello's reason for leaving:

> saying that if he had stayed there any longer he would have forgotten all he knew, being so much praised there by everyone, and that he was returning willingly to his homeland, because there he would be constantly reproved and such reproof would give him reason for study, and consequently for greater glory.[45]

Donatello was notoriously eccentric, but does his reasoning suggest he needed the competition between artists (and patrons) that only Florence could offer?

Even if that speculation could be substantiated, it should not lead commentators to denigrate what Padua nurtured. In many ways, the city exemplifies the plurality of the urban experience in 'medieval' Italy. It set down a pattern of development quite different from that of the Florentines. Marsilius of Padua (c.1290–1343) was a great Aristotelian scholastic – and in that sense a 'medieval' figure. Yet he formulated a thorough political justification for the subordination of the Church to the state, 'and in so doing he achieved a renaissance of the secular spirit of antiquity more radical than anything yet dreamed of by students of literature'.[46] 'It should be clearly apparent to all', wrote Marsilius in the *Defensor pacis* (1324),

> that both in word and in deed Christ excluded and wished to exclude himself from all worldly rulership or governance, judgement or coercive power, and that he wished to be subject to the secular rulers and powers in coercive jurisdiction.[47]

A number of observations about Marsilius make his originality matter-of-fact. 'Marsilius was the first authority to deny the church its own autonomy as an institution, the early disciples had always "rendered unto Caesar"', and there was 'no papal primacy'. Yet Marsilius can be associated (in a marvellous book) with 'the dissolution of the medieval outlook' as easily as with a 'proto-Renaissance'.[48]

Perhaps the relatively slight impact of another famous university city, Bologna, may shed further light on the problem. Was the culture of the visual arts and literature more likely to flourish away from formal and traditional centres of learning? But as George Holmes has emphasised, no Italian university had a faculty of theology, and one might therefore have expected them to foster a 'new learning' for the independent layman. Again, the question of patronage in relation to artistic endeavour raises itself. The Bentivoglio, who ruled Bologna from 1443 to 1506, were not among the more resplendent of the princely dynasties.

However, both the Bentivoglio and the papacy maintained generous support for the University of Bologna. It remained a centre of international renown, its most famous scholar in the sixteenth century being the great astronomer Nikolaus Copernicus (1470–1543). Under the rule of the Venetian Republic (which incorporated Padua in 1405) the University of Padua enjoyed a true golden age, distinguished by figures ranging from the humanist Pietro Pomponazzi (1462–1525) in the late fifteenth century (he went on to Bologna) to Galileo in the early seventeenth.

Elsewhere, humanists might become professors of rhetoric. Francesco Filelfo (1398–1481) took up such an appointment in Florence in 1429 (before he quarrelled with Cosimo de' Medici and went off to Milan), and Angelo Poliziano (1454–94) became professor of Greek at the *studio* in 1480. However, humanists do not seem either to have boycotted universities or to have revolutionised them. This may tell us two things. First, it reinforces the idea that the originality of humanist scholarship was in many ways the product of their own rhetoric (see above, Chapter 1). Second, it suggests that the Renaissance never became an institutionalised phenomenon, which makes the task of connecting culture and society all the more complicated.

Such problems become still more perplexing when one thinks of the cases of the four great maritime republics of medieval Italy: Amalfi, Genoa, Pisa – and Venice. Of these great and precocious centres of commercial prosperity and political independence, Venice is the odd one out precisely because it is so readily identified with the Renaissance. Why did the other three not develop 'Renaissance' cultures? Pisa thrived as a medieval commune. The spatial and architectural combination of baptistery, cathedral and tower remains breathtaking. In the Pisani, the city produced the first great sculptors of the new art, and the Campo Santo displays frescoes from the fourteenth century to match those of Orcagna in Florence. It is also an inconvenient case history for those inclined to believe in the rhetoric of republican liberty. True, Pisa became part of the territorial state of Gian Galeazzo Visconti, but when he died in 1402, his natural son simply sold the city to Florence for some 200,000 florins, and Florentine (republican) rule throughout the fifteenth century was often very harsh indeed. It would seem that the Pisans had little to celebrate as the subjects of either princely magnificence or a humanist republic.[49]

Genoa was the place that combined the maritime commercial enterprise of Venice with the political instability of Florence. Its population around 1500 stood at about 85,000. Its entrepreneurial tradition proved at least as adaptable as those of either the Venetians or the Florentines. Its bankers were unrivalled. The city also had an intensely networked religious life, including many confraternities which were, potentially at least, patrons of the arts. Yet its cultural achievements were slight. In the fifteenth century this may be explained by almost continual political upheaval. There was greater stability in the sixteenth, but Doge Andrea Doria's patronage of Perino del Vaga scarcely compares with Andrea Gritti's patronage of Sansovino and Titian in Venice. Mary Hollingsworth's major study points to a 'building boom' in sixteenth-century Genoa, but the section does not merit a single plate.[50] Perhaps fashion will change and projects in Pisa and Genoa will receive reappraisal both artistic and historical. Equally, perhaps it is no accident that it took an expert on Genoa, Robert Lopez, to question whether there was a necessary link between commercial prosperity and artistic or literary output. Indeed, Lopez went so far as to argue that the reverse might be true. 'Hard times' produced 'investment in culture' because investing in a villa or a palace might be safer than risking money in other business enterprises. In the case of Florence, there may even have been incentives for the embellishment of private houses because this did not attract taxation.[51]

The example of Amalfi is perhaps the most revealing in its paradoxes. Its situation, deep in the south of the peninsula, on sheer cliffs which drop precipitously into the sea, does not appear less impregnable than that of Venice. Its inhabitants were trading with Byzantium and fighting Saracens when the Venetians were huddling in huts in the marsh. Civic pride insists that one of its citizens, the twelfth-century merchant-navigator Flavio Gioia, be celebrated as the inventor of the compass.[52] In imitation of Venice, Amalfi's head of state was a doge, and the city had its own arsenal. Like Venice, it was an apostolic city: its magnificent cathedral houses the body of St Andrew. Indeed, the saint's remains were looted from Constantinople in the sack of 1204. The basilica also has the first of the great bronze doors of Italy, the creation of Simon of Syria in 1066 under the patronage of the Pantaleone or Mauro family. The 'Cloister of Paradise' is evocative of a mosque garden, and peacefully conducive to meditation and prayer. Yet Amalfi suffered military defeat at the hands of the Pisans, and conquest by the Normans. Given the city's apparently impregnable location, one is drawn to reflect on the good fortune of the Venetians in avoiding a similar fate in the dark days after Agnadello in 1509. Amalfi's best days were over, staggeringly, by the early twelfth century, though even in 1300 the population was said to be around 80,000.[53] Yet in 1343, the city literally disappeared from view in storm and earthquake.

Amalfi was not an urban oddity in the rural south. Boccaccio praised the beauty of the cities of the Amalfi coast in one of the stories in *The Decameron* (II.iv). 'The coast of Amalfi is full of little cities, of gardens and fountains, and of men as rich and enterprising in the business of trade as any others.' In Ravello, 'just as today there are rich men, there was one who surpassed them all . . .'. This was a member of the Rufolo family, Landolfo. The cathedral city of Ravello, perched even higher than Amalfi on the cliffs, boasted 30,000 inhabitants in its prime. The Rufolo family had acquired wealth through banking, and status as bankers to the Angevins. The agreeable sophistication of their lifestyle is still evoked in the Moorish cloister and exquisite gardens of their villa, built around 1200. In civic pride and political independence, in commercial enterprise and prosperity, and in the cultivation of a civilised lifestyle, Amalfi and Ravello can seem to anticipate the Renaissance by some three hundred years, the Mauro and the Rufolo precocious forebears of the Medici. While rather neglected in modern historiography, the region was an artistic inspiration. Amalfi is the setting for John Webster's dark and bloody revenge tragedy, *The Duchess of Malfi*, first performed in 1614 (by Shakespeare's company, the King's Men), a year or so after *The Tempest.*[54]

The examples cited in this chapter, both the case histories of cultural dynamism and those cities that do not appear to have been centres of the Renaissance, suggest that creative achievements in the arts were perhaps due to the coincidental clustering of competitive talents in particular places at particular times. As Burckhardt makes clear by beginning his discussion of courts with that of Frederick II (see above, Chapter 1), this was a phenomenon not necessarily confined to the period 1300–1600. What has already become plain is the importance of initiative on the part of the patron or patrons in commissioning a project. Cities that became centres of an identifiably 'Renaissance' culture were, in many ways, few and far between. Often, and especially by the latter part of the fifteenth century, patrons were more likely to be found in courts.

4   Contexts II: Courts

Communes–*Signori*–Princes

> Is there in fact such a thing as Haematomania, Blood-madness? But if
> we answer this question in the affirmative, we shall have to place how
> many Visconti, Sforzeschi, Malatesti, Borgias, Farnesi, and princes of
> the houses of Anjou and Aragon in the list of these maniacs?[1]

John Addington Symonds's lurid characterisation of the tyrants of
Renaissance Italy leaves little doubt as to the degree of their political
corruption and wickedness. This is the 'cruelty used badly' – the indulgence
of an enjoyment of killing – that Machiavelli condemns in Chapter VIII of
The Prince. However, just as not all cities were homes of a 'civic' culture, so
too not all princes were bloodthirsty tyrants. The presentation here in
successive chapters of the cultures of cities and the cultures of courts is a
matter of historical logic, not necessarily of typological distinction. In some
cases, courts were located in cities. The early manifestations of cultural
change were associated with certain cities and in their full maturity found
expression in the Florence of the early fifteenth century, but by its end
princely courts proved the nurseries of cultural ambition.

It is easy but misleading to see cities and courts in stark ideological
juxtaposition. The emergence of the courts as cultural centres was closely
connected with the triumph of *signori* or 'lords', but that does not mean that
'republics' had somehow degraded into despotisms. There were princely
palaces in Urbino, Mantua, Ferrara, Milan, and, of course, Rome. It might
therefore be argued that the contrast drawn between this chapter and the
previous one is between republics and princes. The cultures that princes
sponsored were symptomatic of objectively definable political weaknesses
(see above, Chapter 1), but there were weaknesses too in the communes that
they superseded. The most important of the shared characteristics is that
both cities and courts fostered politics that were localised. This encouraged
impressive cultural diversity, but it also ensured the continuing disunity of
Italy as a whole. Symonds himself raised doubts about his own characterisation, and at the same time confirmed the astuteness of many of his historical judgements, by identifying no fewer than six types of signory. A

summary of his analysis shows that while there is no doubt of the political triumph of the *signori*, only a few of them were to make a significant difference to cultural life.

Symonds's categories and examples are as follows. First, there were hereditary dynasties, such as those of Monferrat and Savoy, the marquises of Ferrara, the princes of Urbino. Second were holders of imperial vicariates such as the della Scala in Verona and the Visconti in Milan. Third were those nobles who held judicial power as *capitani* or *podestà* such as the Carrara at Padua, the Gonzaga in Mantua, the Rossi and Corregi in Parma, the Torrenti and Visconti in Milan, the Scotti of Piacenza. These 'used their authority to enslave the cities they were chosen to administer'.[2] The fourth type were the *condottieri*, 'who made a prey of cities at their pleasure' – like Castruccio Castracane, who came to power with an imperial vicariate in Lucca but extended his rule to Pisa and Pistoia, the Malatesta in Rimini and the Montefeltro in Urbino. The fifth category was made up of nephews or sons of popes of less well-connected families, of whom the most notorious is Cesare Borgia. Finally, there were prominent citizen families who 'gradually tended to tyranny'.[3] These included most famously the Medici, but also the Bentivoglio of Bologna, the Vitelli of Città di Castello and the Gambacorti of Pisa. Given the acknowledged overlap between these categories and the obvious importance of local tradition and circumstance, it is somewhat surprising that Symonds's overall characterisation of 'blood-madness' was so incautiously monolithic.

Modern scholarship has demolished the ideological underpinnings of the distinction between 'republics' and 'tyrants'. As long ago as 1965, John Larner decisively concluded his study of the lordships of the Romagna with this fundamental critical judgement:

> For too long the slow transition from commune to *signoria* has been popularly portrayed as a process in which a free and democratic society, represented, as in Carducci's poetry, by virtuous men of heroic stature, was replaced by an evil form of government whose representative was the *signore*, symbol of wickedness, albeit of cultivated wickedness.[4]

In a seminal article published in the same year, Philip Jones emphasised that the differences between 'communes' and 'despots' have often been exaggerated. 'City-states' had never been unified, and the resemblances between them and the 'despots' were as striking as the differences. Dr Jones has now elaborated his thesis in a study that brings out in full the complexity of regional diversity within the peninsula in the Middle Ages.[5] Brian Pullan's measured synthesis of 1973 drained the ideological juice from the general problem and reduced it to the proportions of 'monarchs and oligarchs', concluding, memorably, that 'there was little to choose between the corporate authoritarianism of a dominant city and the personal absolutism of a monarchic ruler – save that the first was more enduring'.[6] Though one must be wary of generalisation, the emergence of the signory was a development of the commune rather than its replacement. The communes themselves lacked legitimacy, since their independence was a challenge to their imperial or papal overlords. What often made the *signori* 'legitimate' was that the communes volunteered to accept them in the interests of order.[7] The process recalls Plato's discussion of appearances and realities, and their political manifestations: the philosopher-king was the ideal ruler, the despot the worst, and democracy too could erode into despotism – but which was which?

It remains a curious thought that the Renaissance is seen to be an urban phenomenon, and yet by 1300 – the starting point for this book – the *signori* had already triumphed over the communes. The chief distinction to be made among the *signorie*, or lordships, themselves is whether the *signore* had emerged supreme from internal factional rivalries or imposed his rule from outside.[8] In the Romagna, the *contado* – or, rather, the power networks in rural localities – controlled the town, and regional power was associated with the great feudatories: the da Polenta in Ravenna, the Alidosi in Imola, the Manfredi in Faenza, the Ordelaffi in Forlì, the Malatesta in Rimini. These were not so much 'despots' as the families that ruled, and the rule of a single family was 'infinitely preferable to intermittent anarchy'. What had happened was that a 'small feudal oligarchy' had become the dominion of one man.[9] An analogous process brought the Medici to pre-eminence in Florence.

To drive the point home, there are many important instances when the differences between 'republics' and 'despotisms' could disappear for practical purposes. As early as 1260, the republic of Siena denounced the republic of Florence as the tyrannical dragon that St George had slain, and Milan was a dragon for fifteenth-century Florentines. 'Despotisms' could squabble over which of them controlled 'communes': in 1318, Robert of Anjou defeated the Visconti to establish his lordship over Genoa. While characterised and perhaps caricatured as despots by Florentine humanists, the Visconti could also be seen as bringers of peace and order rather than tyranny. The Malatesta tyrants in Rimini were responsible for the installation of a 'popular' regime in Siena in 1368. Then there is the awkward concept of republican ideology as applied to Florence itself. We are accustomed to see at least a measure of attachment to 'republican liberty' in Florence's struggle against Milan in the early *Quattrocento*. Yet in the War of the Eight Saints between Florence and the Avignon papacy (1375–8), it is pertinent to recall that the Florentines sought the protective mediation of its future enemies, the Visconti, 'and amidst the hypocritical clamour of its humanists, praising the benefits of "freedom", restored the Ordelaffi and Manfredi tyrants to power'. By 1392, Florence had lined up with the Gonzaga and the Malatesta against the Visconti. The Republic, as we have seen, was quick to buy Pisa from the heir of the despot (see above, Chapter 3). Throughout the period, Coluccio Salutati – often identified with the 'republican liberty' of 'civic humanism' – was head of the Florentine chancery.[10]

As Philip Jones has remarked, 'communal Italy was not Florence, Venice, Genoa or even Milan', and there was nothing typical in a single region such as the Romagna. If we turn our attention to the major republics, then we find tendencies similar to those observable in the *signorie*. While Florence remained in appearance a republic, the style of government under the Medici after 1434 was increasingly princely, especially under Lorenzo. While Venice was never subject to a prince, all references to the 'commune of the Venetians' disappeared mysteriously from official documents in 1423, and the state was referred to instead as the 'Signoria'. Moreover, at around the same time, the custom of presenting the newly elected doge for popular acclamation underwent significant modification. The announcement 'This is your doge and it please you' became 'This is your doge' *tout court*. Any hint of popular assent was thereby removed. Even tyrants sought the approval of the crowd.[11]

The political matrices of courtly culture were as varied as the characters of princes themselves. As Kenneth Clark put it:

> In one state was Federigo Montefeltro, the God-fearing father of his people; in the neighbouring state was Sigismondo Malatesta, the wolf of Rimini, who did things that even the most advanced theatrical producer would hesitate to put on stage [i.e. in the late 1960s]. And yet both of them employed Alberti and were painted by Piero della Francesca.[12]

That variability is an important prelude to the rest of the chapter, which sketches a catalogue of certain of the lordships that became princely courts, of the political fortunes of those courts, and what projects of princely magnificence those courts promoted.

While there is no identifiable 'courtly style' that characterises the art of all courtly centres, some generalisations, all of them qualified, remain helpful in establishing an overall picture. In most cases, the ostentation of princely magnificence was proportionate to the insecurity of the regime's foundations. *De facto* assumption of power set a model for usurpation, sometimes by assassination. One is frequently dealing with bastards. Legitimacy

– the political variety frequently weakened further by the personal – was rarely obvious, and the attempts to compensate for that in display often produced exaggeration and overstatement. The thinner the claim, the more emphatically it had to be made. All the material available for such programmes was put to use, and the petty princes of Italy liked to see themselves ranked with European royalty. They could achieve this through the purchase of titles and exchanges of favours. In cultural terms, it often involved imitation of foreign styles. The distinctiveness of the Florentines in the 'civic' phase of the early fifteenth century is that they relied on their own Tuscan traditions and were less open to outside influence. The courts absorbed French, Flemish and Spanish influences much more freely. Courts also used spectacle as a theatre of power both in public and in private. What was on display was often ephemeral and rarely survives.

As a reminder of the varieties of culture that courtly centres spawned, it is appropriate to begin with the most famous dynasty of the Renaissance, the dynasty that illustrates most clearly the ease with which a republic could become a princely state.

The Medici

The history of the Medicean 'court' has two main phases, the first running from 1434 to 1494 (and characterised by an increasingly princely style of rule exercised from behind a republican façade), the second from 1530 onwards, when the state and its culture became crushingly absolutist. Their 'court', like any other such institution, was, at bottom, their household, though this was reinforced beyond its confines by their vast clientage network. Thus it was that Cosimo's son, Piero, often bedridden with gout, could deal with the business of government from his bedchamber, even though he did not hold formal office.[13]

Cosimo de' Medici's return from exile in Venice to power in Florence in 1434 began a period of exactly 30 years of his own personal dominion, exactly 60 of his family's enjoyment of political ascendancy. The durability needs to be emphasised because Medicean rule provided a political stability that Florence had not previously enjoyed. Through skilful manipulation, Cosimo (r. 1434–64), his son Piero (r. 1464–9) and grandson Lorenzo (r. 1469–92) resolved the chronic constitutional problem that had ensured the prevalence of private interests over the public good. The realities of political life were a world away from the rhetorical constructs of the civic humanists earlier in the fifteenth century. Cosimo recognised this, and it was reflected in the style of his exercise of power.

The historian Francesco Guicciardini (1483–1540), friend of Machiavelli, writing in 1508–9, gives a sense of Cosimo's political *maniera*, and communicates the political equivalent of what Vasari might have written about an artist. Indeed, the following extract persuasively illustrates Burckhardt's idea of the state as 'a work of art' – Guicciardini examines Cosimo's style of government and makes a significant attribution. In Guicciardini's account, Cosimo is in control of the shadows. 'The citizens had more authority and made dispositions as they chose: much more so than they did afterwards at the time of Lorenzo.' However, Cosimo kept careful and unquestionable control of real power, in the Signoria, the city's main council, and in matters of taxation. And, like Prospero's usurping brother in Shakespeare's *The Tempest*, he knew 'who t'advance and who to trash for overtopping'. He was, for instance, well aware of the capabilities of one Neri di Gino, and entrusted him with important missions. He balanced such promotion with his patronage of Lucca Pitti, 'who was not a very able man, but lively, generous, spirited, and more devoted to his friends than anyone else in Florence'. He did not have the brains to be dangerous. Cosimo rigged debates to ensure that Lucca would advocate the exact opposite of Neri's proposals – and receive the backing of the majority. Cosimo even pre-empted any possible threat that Neri might translate his isolation into military opposition:

> There was at that time a captain of infantry named Baldaccio d'Anghiari, a man of great spirit, worthy in his profession, and held in great respect by the soldiers, a very close confidant of Neri. Fearing this friendship, and wishing to remove from Neri this instrument so suited to innovation, Cosimo waited until Neri was away from Florence as ambassador or commissioner, he had messer Bartolomeo Orlandini, the Gonfalonier of Justice, send for Baldaccio to come to the palace. When he got him in the chamber, he suddenly had Baldaccio thrown out of the window to the ground by people ordered there for the purpose.[14]

Making the control seem remote was one of the managerial successes of the regime. The early Medici did not need to hold office because they were acknowledged as supreme by the leading men of the city. Lorenzo's description of his coming to power upon the death of his father, Piero, in 1469 is highly revealing:

> Although I, Lorenzo, was very young, being twenty years of age, the principal men of the city and of the regime came to us to condole with us on our loss and to encourage me to take charge of the city and the regime as my grandfather and father had done. This I did, though on

account of my youth and the great peril and responsibility arising there-from, with great reluctance, solely for the safety of our friends and of our possessions. For it is ill living in Florence for the rich unless they rule.[15]

Thus, the private interests of the Medici were identified with the public good, and, vice versa, the public good came to be identified with the inter-ests of the Medici. We noticed Cosimo's commemoration as *pater patriae* (above, Chapter 3). Another revealing symptom of the identification appears in the work of the humanist Angelo Poliziano (1454–94). In 1478, the Pazzi conspiracy, in which the papacy was involved, attempted the assassination of Lorenzo and his brother Giuliano while they were at Mass in the Duomo. Giuliano was killed, but Lorenzo survived. In a shamelessly pro-Medicean account which owes a great deal to the classical model of Sallust's *Bellum Cataline* (published in 42–41 BC), Poliziano records the scene he witnessed (or imagined he witnessed, or would have liked to have witnessed) in the Medici palace in the aftermath of the killing:

> The whole house was full of armed men and full of cries in favour of the Medici, which resounded off the roof in a great din. It was something to see: boys, old men, young men, priests and laymen seizing arms to defend the Medici house as though it were the public safety.[16]

Again, the rhetoric masquerading as history sets a tone of high-mindedness and high principle completely at odds with the ruthless exercise of power. Lorenzo's rule became increasingly princely in character. Opponents such as the Pazzi received no mercy. One of the conspirators, Bernardo di Bandino de' Baroncelli, was hunted down as far away as Constantinople. He was unceremoniously hanged in the courtyard of the Bargello on 28 December 1479. The young Leonardo sketched his dangling corpse, and made notes in his mirror-writing detailing the colours of the dead man's exotic oriental clothes. [O.23]

The degree of political expertise that Cosimo, Piero and Lorenzo all demonstrated is revealed by the speed of the regime's collapse within two years of Lorenzo's death in 1492 owing to the political blunders of his son Piero (see above, Chapter 2). The distinctive features of the early Medicean regime with regard to the cultural expression of its power are subtlety and understatement, self-assured irony: qualities in keeping with their control of the political system from behind the scenes. The 'court' seemed to defer – with a species of *sprezzatura*, or effortlessness – to the Republic. The signifi-cance of the early Medici as patrons of the arts is a matter of some contro-versy: the strident self-advertisement of other princes is lacking.[17] Vasari asserts that Cosimo rejected Brunelleschi's design for a Medici palace as being too ostentatious for a mere private citizen (see below, Chapter 5). However, the Medici presided over and fostered significant changes in Florentine culture. They squeezed the life out of the civic spirit while apparently promoting the virtues of Neoplatonism. Civic projects faded, and private commissions, not for general display, came to predominate. As A. Richard Turner has pointed out:

> A republic was giving way to an imperium under Medici domination, accompanied by a cultural shift toward an elite literary and philosophical culture that had less and less to do with the religious beliefs and behaviour of ordinary people.[18]

Donatello's sculptures of tyrannicides – David with Goliath's head, Judith and Holofernes – kept up an appearance of ideological commitment to liberty and patriotism (and there is no suggestion that Donatello ever 'sold out' to a regime of any hue). However, the artistic transformation manifests itself in the commissioning of works of art more suitable for the mighty to savour privately than for the populace at large to admire. In what might be characterised as both a return to the 'international Gothic' style and a 'refeudalisation' of the imagination, the ideal life is to be found in countryside and court, not in the republican city. The Medici palace is unostentatious compared with, say, Palazzo Pitti: it is possible to walk past without noticing it. Yet the inner courtyard compares stylistically with that of the princely palace at Urbino. [O.24; O.25] Inside, the chapel is decorated with the delicate delights of Benozzo Gozzoli's frescoes of *The Journey of the Magi* (*c*.1459). It seems symptomatic of how new projects were now shut away from private view that there is barely room for a dozen people to stand in the chapel, and it is impossible to see a general view of this narrow place of worship without the distortion of a specially curved lens.

The frescoes themselves show a cavalcade of lords, knights and squires with all the chivalric connotations of pilgrimage, joust and hawking. The depiction of the Byzantine emperor John VIII Paleologus (*r*. 1425–48) is a topical reference to the General Council of the Church in Florence – which fleetingly achieved the reunification of the Orthodox Church with the Roman in 1439. The Medici themselves appear on the walls. The figure of the young Lorenzo (if it is he) with his crown and sumptuous fur-lined doublet, his jewels and caparison, his elegant attendants, evokes an image of a duke of Burgundy. [O.26]

In keeping with the rural setting of the frescoes, Lorenzo himself was happier to be in the countryside than in the city – and took little interest in the management of the family bank, which foundered disastrously under his delegate, Francesco Sassetti. As though to confound all attempts to typify a courtly culture, the Medici palace in the city was not the nucleus of a court, however courtly its trappings. Lorenzo's circle would gather in a villa such as Poggio a Caiano and discuss the Neoplatonic humanism which the Medici sponsored and which celebrated the delights of the contemplative life in the works of Marsilio Ficino (1433–99) and Poliziano (see below, Chapter 6).

The brisk ousting of the Medici in 1494 brought a sudden end to the early phase of their dominion. When they returned as princes, their use of the arts to celebrate their power was anything but subtle. The first duke, Alessandro (assassinated in 1537), who appears to have been almost universally loathed, began work on the great bastion or Fortezza da Basso that marked out the city as the capital of an absolutist state. Cosimo I (duke, 1537–74, grand duke from 1569) stressed the imperial theme in his construction of an overtly authoritarian regime. The court transferred to the grand surroundings of the Palazzo Pitti. In what became known as the Palazzo Vecchio, Vasari was the creator of the imperial image in 42 paintings and six huge frescoes. The *Apotheosis* that he produced comes close to vulgarity, but sets a pattern for overblown images of the absolute prince in Europe as a whole. Vasari was also the duke's creature, flattering his master in paint, in words and in the dedication of his *Vite*.[19] While the Medici had to invent the continuity of their rule and its culmination in the grand duchy, traditions of princely rule elsewhere had deeper roots.[20]

The d'Este of Ferrara

After Lorenzo de' Medici died, Ercole d'Este (who ruled as duke from 1471 to 1505) became the most powerful and prominent prince in Italy. The family was the oldest of the princely dynasties, having established its lordly dominion as early as 1209. Their hereditary dominance received the acknowledgement of the rest of the nobility in 1332 – another illustration of the developmental aspect of the *signoria*, as a monarchy emerging from oligarchy. At around the same time, the d'Este cemented their authority with a grant of the papal vicariate and seem to have ceased to ask the commune for a title. The d'Este held Modena from the emperor from 1354, and were dukes there from 1452. The ducal title to Ferrara was granted to Ercole in 1471.[21]

'The ideal of courtly recreation in all its diverse forms – intellectual, physical, theatrical, musical – lies at the very heart of Este patronage.'[22] Alison Cole's point is beautifully made. There is a marvellous shifting, shimmering quality to the culture of the Estensi. The seductiveness of escapism – for all its dire political consequences for Italy – is borne out by the names of their palaces: Belvedere ('beautiful view'), Belfiore ('beautiful flower'), and especially Schiffanoia ('escape nuisance'). It is very difficult to work out exactly when the Estensi got down to the business of government. As in the case of Naples, many of the great commissions in Ferrara are now lost. What survives is vigorous and distinctive, particularly in its fruitful blending of the chivalric and the classical. This may owe something to the relative lack of influence from Florence. Instead, Ferrara was the scene of a mutually deferential amalgam of Franco-Burgundian and classical influences. What could be more celebratory of the delights of the hunt than Pisanello's *Vision of St Eustace*? His observations of animals and birds show the same sensitivity to nature as Leonardo. [O.27; O.28] This was perfectly at home – quite literally – with classically inspired palaces, gardens and a theatre that saw the first performances of some of the works of the Roman playwrights Plautus (writing between about 205 and 184 BC) and Terence (160s BC) since ancient times. The plays and other entertainments were accompanied by sweet music. The d'Este court received Josquin des Près (*c*.1440–1521), the acknowledged master of new musical style, who wrote a Mass for Ercole in 1503. While Adriaan Willaert became famous as Maestro di Capella at San Marco in Venice after 1527, he was among the chapel musicians in Ferrara before that, in 1520.[23]

Those characteristics do not sit easily with the Florentine model of arts and humanism, but Ferrara was also home to some notable painters and men of letters, even though much of their work was dynastic propaganda. Pisanello (Antonio Pisano, 1395?–1455/6) struck bronze medallions for Leonello d'Este (*r*. 1441–50) and signed them 'pictor', which we would naturally translate as 'painter'. Perhaps Pisanello was describing his principal field of expertise. Yet the relief work of the medals is a reminder of the moulding of verisimilitude, the imitation of reality, a reminder that the 'pictor' is someone who 'depicts' in whatever form he chooses, and a reminder that the depiction expresses an impulse for earthly memory, a sort of secular immortality (see below, Chapter 6). Leonello's brother Borso (*r*. 1450–71) had the painter Francesco del Cossa (1435/6–77) decorate a room devoted to the months of the year in the Schiffanoia palace, again reflecting a delight in the works of nature. But the greatest native painter in Ferrara was Cosimo Tura (*c*.1431–95). He was strongly influenced by the Flemish style. Leonello owned a *Deposition* by Rogier van der Weyden (1399/1400–1464), and the Flemish master also designed costly tapestries for him. Tura's seated *Euterpe* follows the oil painting technique of van der Weyden, who may even have instructed him. Since the importation of oils to Italy is sometimes said to have been via Antonello da Messina (*c*.1430–79), who took them to Venice, it may have made the work of Venetian masters all the more attractive in Ferrara. For the Camerino that celebrated the delights of love and wine, Alfonso I (1505–34) acquired Giovanni Bellini's *Feast of the Gods* (1514), and later commissioned from Titian a strictly programmed *Offerings to Venus* (1518/19), though he seems to have allowed the artist much greater freedom for his *Bacchus and Ariadne* (1520–3; see below, Chapter 7).

The influence of humanism in Ferrara is difficult to chart. Certainly, notable figures gravitated to the Estense court. Angelo Candido Decembrio set out the delight of the antique in his dialogue *De politia letteraria* of 1462. Guarino da Verona (1374–1460), one of the pioneers of the revival of Greek learning, left Florence to become tutor to the children of Niccolo III (1393–1441) in 1429. But looking for Florentine 'types' of humanist – 'Petrarchan', 'civic' or 'Neoplatonic' – in Ferrara can be fruitless and tends also to divert attention from the extraordinary literary flowering from the late fifteenth century onwards in the work of Matteo Maria Boiardo, Lodovico Ariosto and Torquato Tasso (see below, Chapter 8).

For all that they spent their time in their self-contained palaces, the Estensi made some considerable impact on the city of Ferrara itself. Ferrara had a distinctive religious life in which sacred drama played an important part. So, a tradition of Christian drama coexisted with an intense interest in the classics, just as Shakespeare worked with the traditions of the morality play as well as those of classical tragedy (see below, Chapters 8 and 9). The architectural projects of Ercole included the enormous Palazzo dei Diamanti (begun in 1493, but only completed in 1567), and a vast extension of the city, the Addizione Ercolanea, that, unusually, drew inspiration from a Florentine model, Palazzo Strozzi. It was a project that drew a paean from the humanist Giovanni Sabadino degli Arienti in 1497:

> Just as Augustus found Rome in brick and left it in marble, so too will your celsitude, by virtue of your magnificence, be recognised by posterity with very great glory. For you found a Ferrara of painted brick, and you have left it . . . carved in adamite marble, as a result of which one can already make this judgement: that this your city, gleaming more than oriental lapillo, will be among the most wondrous cities of the World.[24]

As noted so often in this book, the lack of a sense of scale is breathtaking: in 1497, it was surely clear from the experience of invasion that Ferrara and its 30,000 people were not a reinvention of the Roman Empire. The way in which the Italian Wars generated cultural change by destroying existing sources of patronage was manifest in other centres in other ways. But one part of the story is the same: cultural self-indulgence gave way to a desperate struggle for political survival.

Urbino: the Montefeltro

The Montefeltro were the rulers of Urbino from 1255 until 1508. However, as though to emphasise the significance of the individual patron, for some time there was no sign of an emergent culture sprouting from the court. The eventual flowering was due to the exploits and endeavours of Federigo da Montefeltro in the period of his rule, 1444–74. It was Federigo who cemented the family fortune through his career as a successful mercenary captain. At the time of his death he was under contract to various employers for 165,000 ducats. The biographer Vespasiano da Bisticci likened him to the Roman general and dictator Quintus Fabius Maximus Cunctator, 'the delayer' who had outmanoeuvred Hannibal, praising him for the avoidance of pitched battle in campaigns in Italy in the early third century BC. The *condottiere* way of war was less strategic, and the intention was to preserve the band of soldiers with minimum losses (see above, Chapter 2). Yet again, a comparison with the ancient Romans is almost certainly misplaced.[25]

Federigo's rise to power was tainted with violence and intrigue, and not inspired by a patriotic ideal. He came to power through the murder, perhaps with his own connivance, of his half-brother Oddantonio. But although arms were his profession, he combined fighting and letters. He had grown up in Mantua and had studied under the humanist Vittorino da Feltre (1378–1446). Federigo's life as scholar and man of action – the ideal that Shakespeare's Prospero failed to attain (see below, Chapter 9) – is celebrated in the famous portrait in which he sits reading in full armour, his international status discreetly vaunted by the garter he wears as a knight of its Order. This image is representative of the cohesive style of life that Federigo sought to achieve. He used the money he had earned from soldiering to build a magnificent palace, employing the skills of the architects Luciano Laurana (1420/5–79) and Francesco di Giorgio (1439–1502). He was an avid collector of codices and owned 1100 of them, more beautiful than textually accurate, and he enjoyed them as works of art. It is indicative of the blending of foreign influences in the court of Urbino that the painter of his portrait may have been either the Flemish master Justus of Ghent (active 1460–after 1475) or the Spaniard Pedro Berruguete (*c.*1453–1503/4). As in Ferrara, it was a Flemish painter (in this case Justus) who introduced oil paints to Urbino. [O.29] Yet Federigo's tastes were broad in range, and he also commissioned work from Melozzo da Forlì (1438–94) and Piero della Francesca (1410/20–92). Piero's work for Federigo included the well-known portrait of him and his wife Battista Sforza in profile (Federigo had lost an eye and was too disfigured to be painted full face), and the enigmatic *Flagellation* (both of 1474).[26] [O.30; 0.31]

The celebrated intarsia work that decorated Federigo's *studiolo* or 'little study' shows again that what one needs to imagine about Urbino is not a mere catalogue of masterpieces, but the style of life that the surroundings both nurtured and enhanced. This is what Castiglione's *Courtier* commemorates, with a melancholy wistfulness – like that of the chivalrous fantasies of Ferrara – for an age that has gone. Celebrating Federigo's military virtues, Castiglione compares his subject with the ancients. Of Federigo's Urbino, he wrote:

> This, among his other laudable achievements: he built on the rugged site of Urbino a palace, according to the opinion held by many, which is the most beautiful to be found in all Italy; and he furnished it so well with everything appropriate, that it seemed not a palace, but rather a city in the form of a palace. And his ornaments were not only what is usual, such as silver vases, tapestries of the richest cloth of gold, silk and the like, but also an infinity of antique statues of marble and bronze, the most singular pictures, every kind of musical instrument; nor did he want anything there that was not most rare and excellent. In addition, at great cost, he brought together a large number of the finest and rarest books, Greek, Latin and Hebrew, all of which he decorated with gold and silver, judging that this was the supreme excellence of his great palace.[27]

Thus, the illegitimate mercenary commander and possible fratricide for power was the equal of Cosimo de' Medici as a patron of the arts and learning. His military success and independence are a stark contrast with his sixteenth-century successors, the della Rovere, for the political context of artistic patronage had altered irrevocably. After the change of dynasty, Francesco della Rovere (*r.* 1508–16) survived as duke only by abandoning France for the imperial cause. The Gonzaga of Mantua showed an even greater determination for political survival.

The Gonzaga of Mantua

The Gonzaga ruled Mantua – which had a unique link to the classical past as the birthplace of the supreme Roman poet, Vergil (70–19 BC) – for three centuries from 1328. However, the focus of attention should be from 1433, when the Emperor Sigismund granted Gianfrancesco Gonzaga the title of marquis. Like the Montefeltro and the Sforza, the Gonzaga came to prominence through mercenary soldiering. Their military record was, however, undistinguished. They provide yet another example of the failure of Italian commanders to keep up with developments elsewhere in Europe, and Mantua's interests too came to be dictated by the fortunes of the invaders.

As in the case of Urbino under the della Rovere, the patronage of the victorious emperor proved all-important, and in 1530 Charles V rewarded Federigo Gonzaga's loyalty with the title of duke. That was only part of the elaborate network of links that the dynasty built up with northern Europe. While the Montefeltro held the Order of the Garter from the English monarchy, Henry IV or Henry V granted the Gonzaga the right to wear the livery of the house of Lancaster, probably between 1408 and 1411, and there were marriage links not only with the Malatesta, the Montefeltro and the Estensi in Italy, but later and further afield with the Hohenzollerns, the Wittelsbachs and the Habsburgs. That last connection conveys how the Italian princes lost their states. The Gonzaga male line died out in 1627, and the Emperor Ferdinand II, who was married to Eleonora Gonzaga, sent an army to occupy the duchy two years later. So Mantua became caught up in the Thirty Years War. When the *studiolo* of Isabella was broken up in 1627, it contained around 2000 paintings, many of which became the foundation of the English Royal Collection under Charles I.[28]

The dynasty provided many patrons, but few intellectuals. In the heyday of the Gonzaga in the fifteenth century both Pisanello and Lorenzo Costa (c.1460–1535) enjoyed their sponsorship. But far and away the most important artist to work for the Gonzaga was Andrea Mantegna (c.1431–1506). The works he executed for his employers were highly significant for different reasons. The *Triumph of Caesar* (c.1486–94) is an extraordinary exercise in classical archaeology, in every detail. Chariot, standards, inscriptions, amphorae, the equipment of the legionaries, right down to the straps of their sandals: all of this is recreated with a virtually microscopic precision worthy of the philological accuracy of the scholarship of Lorenzo Valla (see below, Chapter 6). No one before Mantegna had so wholeheartedly identified the ancient world so uncompromisingly on its own terms. Earlier masters had usually depicted the military equipment of their bearded contemporaries. [O.32]

Mantegna's contemporaries recognised his special qualities, and Ludovico Gonzaga spared no pains in hiring him. Yet Ludovico wanted him for more than a specific project. From 1458, he offered several inducements to the artist – who may have been reluctant to commit himself to

Mantua, a small and rather unhealthy place with malaria in the surrounding swamps. Ludovico persisted, offering a retainer of 180 ducats a year along with a house, food (for six people) and other benefits. Mantegna eventually accepted, which marks his appointment as the first court painter of the Renaissance. That in turn marked a dramatic change in the status of the artist. To be part of a princely household was very different from being a hired craftsman in a workshop. Perhaps it was that elevation that was to give such naturalism to Mantegna's superlative depiction of the Gonzaga household in the Camera degli Sposi, a decoration that he finished in 1474. The scenes of the family in their domestic life are portraits without formal grouping and they appear to the spectator as an extension of the room itself. The ceiling, in perfect perspective, shows figures looking down from beneath an open sky. As Mary Hollingsworth has said, this is 'a masterpiece of illusion in every way'. The spectator feels as though he or she is being granted an audience, and surely all the figures on the wall leave the room for bed when night draws in.[29] [O.33]

The sense of *trompe l'oeil*, what can fool the eye, is in this instance a delight. But some of the illusions of pictures were false comforts. Mantegna's *Madonna della Vittoria* (1495) comes into this category. The 'victory' that the picture celebrates is the battle of Fornovo, when an Italian alliance of 30,000 troops commanded by Francesco Gonzaga allowed a French army of a third of that number, which had marched the length of Italy, to cut its way to safety.

Yet, somehow, the Gonzaga were to hang on to their princely status from the age of Vittorino da Feltre in the fifteenth century to the age of Monteverdi in the seventeenth. The far more powerful state of Milan had its cultural life truncated by the experience of war at the end of the fifteenth century.

Milan: the Visconti and the Sforza

As in the case of Florence, Milan was a big city which became home to a princely court. The Visconti took control of the city when Matteo, great-nephew of the archbishop, Ottone, was proclaimed 'Captain of the People' in 1287. The grant of an imperial vicariate in 1311 cemented his power. In 1349, the commune conferred the *signoria* on the Visconti in perpetuity, and in 1395, the Emperor Wenceslas granted the ducal title to Gian Galeazzo. By that time, the ambitions of the Visconti seemed to extend to the monarchy of all Italy, but those same ambitions dissolved after Gian Galeazzo's death in 1402. The first half of the *Quattrocento* was turbulent, and culminated in a brief republican revival (the so-called 'Ambrosian Republic') of 1447–50. But in the latter year, the *condottiere* Francesco Sforza (1401–66), who had married Bianca Visconti, seized power, and his family was to remain in control until the end of the century. The new dynasty was obsessed with legitimising its power, and ran up huge debts in trying to do so, owing around 180,000 ducats to the Medici bank by 1467. The problems intensified with Lodovico 'il Moro' (1451–1508), second son of Francesco, because of suspicions that he had supplanted his own nephew. Through a gift of 400,000 ducats and 100,000 ducats' worth of other presents, Lodovico persuaded the Emperor Maximilian to marry his niece – and confer on him a ducal title.[30]

As in the cases of Ferrara, Mantua and Naples, our understanding of the contribution of the Milanese court to Renaissance cultures is much diminished by what has been lost or destroyed. The life of the court oscillated between the Certosa, the 'court monastery' at Pavia, and Milan itself. Sforza patronage of the arts included architectural projects involving Donato Bramante (1444–1514) as designer and Antonio Filarete (1400–69) as site manager. Leonardo spent – some would say 'wasted' – six years at the Sforza court, from 1483 to 1489. Yet the court of the Sforza in many ways embodies the idea of a space that could be as small or as large as suited the prince's wish of the moment, and therefore illustrates the essentially personal character of princely rule. The court of Galeazzo Maria Sforza (he was assassinated in 1476) could vary from 20 members to 20,000.[31]

While the 'civic humanists' of *quattrocento* Florence tended to drown out the opposition, the tyrants of Milan had their scholar apologists: Antonio Loschi (1368–1441), for the Visconti, Pier Candido Decembrio (1392–1477) and Francesco Filelfo (1398–1481) for the Sforza. Filelfo was an expert in Greek who, like Guarino, fared poorly in Florence and had to flee when Cosimo returned in 1434. Having settled in Milan, he waged a continuous literary war against his Florentine enemies.

There was to be no escape for the Sforza. The state, the dynasty and the court were all ruined by the Italian Wars. Milan's obliteration as a cultural centre at the end of the fifteenth century was as sudden as that of Siena had been in the middle of the fourteenth (see above, Chapter 3). The imposing Castello Sforzesco surrendered to the French without a fight. Lodovico, having fled to the emperor, was captured by the French in 1500 and died in prison eight years later.

That sad, trivial case history provides a tellingly bitter example of how the fantastic claims of princely magnificence belied the fragility of princely power, of how ludicrous princely ambition now seems. Leonardo's never-realised project of a bronze equestrian statue to rival that of the Roman emperor Marcus Aurelius, ruler of most of the known world, only got as far as a clay model – which the conquering French used for target practice. [O.34] The copper for the project became a cannon for Duke Ercole d'Este of Ferrara. Did Lodovico ever see Leonardo's designs for weapons of war, and assume that if manufactured they would make him invincible? [O.35] In the event, the case of the Sforza shows that some princely regimes lacked any social foundation.[32] The duchy of Milan, which had once aspired to the monarchy of Italy, became the chief object of dispute between Francis I of France and the Emperor Charles V, for a time was occupied by masterless Swiss mercenaries, and eventually came under Spanish dominion. Spanish dominion in Italy had begun in the south.

The court of Naples

The kingdom of Naples that Alfonso the Magnanimous ruled from 1443 to 1458 was historically and culturally a curious amalgam. Greek and Arab influences from antiquity and the early Middle Ages mingled with Norman and German customs, particularly at the court of Frederick II (see above, Chapter 2). The Angevin–French contribution exercised a particular attraction for the Sienese master Simone Martini (c.1284–1344), thus making his final years in Avignon something of a home from home. Aragonese, and especially Catalan, traditions of constitutionalism – which were very different from those of Castile – meant that the court, in contrast with other examples, was not the basis of government. This took the form of a council and a representative assembly. The court itself was itinerant. Perhaps the failure of the princely household to identify itself with the sovereignty of the state is the distinguishing feature that set a pattern of 'modern' statehood that other territories in the peninsula failed to achieve.[33]

As in the case of Ferrara and Milan, the cultural life of the court cannot be reconstructed from surviving materials: too much has been destroyed. It is clear, however, that, like many other courts, Naples absorbed many outside influences, French, Flemish and Spanish as well as from other parts of Italy. They came together in projects such as the Castelnuovo. Pope Pius II praised the Neapolitan court for its splendour. Alfonso was not a learned man of action in the way that Federigo da Montefeltro appears to have been – he seems to have spent as much time as possible hunting. Yet, according to Vespasiano da Bisticci, he rivalled Cosimo de' Medici in the copying of texts, and he was active in discussions with the humanists of the courtly circle. These included two highly controversial figures, Lorenzo

Valla (1407–57), whom Alfonso rescued from a trial for heresy, and the risqué Antonio Beccadelli, 'il Panormita' (1394–1471), who had written a scandalously lewd poem called *Hermaphroditus* in 1425. Bartolomeo Fazio was in Alfonso's employ from 1444 and wrote a history of the king's reign.[34] Masuccio of Salerno (?1410–?1475) wrote 50 stories, very much in the tradition of Boccaccio, collected as the *Novellino*. Though he worked as a secretary for Prince Roberto Sanseverino of Salerno, each of the tales is addressed to a member of the Aragonese court. There are five groups of ten tales corresponding to the five days of story-telling, each day with a speci-fied theme: criticism of the clergy, practical jokes, the lasciviousness of women, an alternation of tragic and comic tales, and virtuous acts. The career of another secretary, Giovanni Pontano (1422–1503), also attracts attention. Pontano served Alfonso I in Tuscany, and went on to become the leading light of the Naples Academy. As a man who was prepared to push the implications of classical revival to their limits, he bears comparison with Valla. His erotic poetry and his preoccupation with astrology comple-mented an overt indifference to Christian values illustrative of and encour-aging more general tendencies (see below, Chapter 6). However, he also pursued an active political life. In the fateful conflict with Lodovico Sforza (see above, Chapter 2) he strove to avoid the involvement of the French, arguing that a French invasion would bring about disaster not just for Milan or Naples, but for the whole of Italy – as was to prove the case in 1494.[35]

Thus, however 'modern' Alfonso's state may have been, it could not withstand the baronial opposition that shook his illegitimate son Ferrante (*r.* 1458–94) with open revolt in 1485. Once again, as in the case of the rival of Naples, Sforza Milan, it is a measure of the impact of the wars that began in 1494 that the Italian state was swiftly incorporated by King Ferdinand of Aragon's dominion through direct Spanish rule in 1503. A rather earlier case history is a reminder, however, that the destruction of a particular courtly centre was not always linked to the disasters that began in 1494.

The Carrara of Padua

The city of Padua is notable for two extraordinary landmarks in the history of art – not just Renaissance art, but the whole Western tradition. The first is the Scrovegni Chapel. Its decoration in the years after 1300 is the one work that we can certainly attribute to Giotto. It marks a new spatial and psychological realism in the pictorial representation of human beings (see below, Chapter 5). The second is Donatello's equestrian statue of the mercenary captain Gattamelata – the first of this type since Roman times. [O.36] Nothing much survives for the period between Giotto's work in the early fourteenth century and Donatello's departure after ten years in the city in 1453 – and Donatello's reason for leaving may suggest that the city was culturally a bit lifeless (see above, Chapter 2). As in the cases of Naples and Milan, although 'nothing much survives', painstaking research has pieced together from fragments a tantalising picture of a flourishing culture under the Carrara dynasty that controlled the city from 1337 to 1388 and again from 1402 to 1405. Padua under the Carrara provides a rather inconvenient case history for any work of synthesis, which demonstrates very clearly the particularity of local experience in the peninsula throughout the period from the beginning of the fourteenth century to the end of the sixteenth.[36]

Padua had an early experience of tyranny under Ezzelino da Romano in the mid-thirteenth century – which Symonds vividly evokes:

> Thus by his absolute contempt of law, his inordinate cruelty, his prolonged massacres and his infliction of plagues upon whole peoples, Ezzelino established the ideal in Italy of a tyrant marching to his end by any means whatever . . . It laid a deep hold upon the Italian imagination, and, by the glamour of loathing that has strength to fascinate, proved in the end contagious . . . Ezzelino was indeed the first of a long and horrible procession, the most terror-striking because the earliest, prefiguring all the rest.

When he died – according to Symonds, 'in silence like a boar at bay, rending from his wounds the dressings that his foes had placed to keep him alive' – the despotism became a commune, only to turn again, under pressure from a war with the della Scala of Verona, to a *signore*, Jacopo da Carrara, in 1318.[37] Gian Galeazzo Visconti (in alliance with the Republic of Venice) absorbed Padua into his state in 1388. In terms of 'republics' and 'despotisms', there is a very curious tale to tell from the point of Gian Galeazzo's death in 1402. The Carrara returned, but after three years the Republic of Venice annexed Padua and murdered Francesco Novello and his sons. Who is the tyrant? And what is liberty? At all events, this is a world away from the ideological struggle that the Florentine humanists inform us they were waging at exactly this time.

Under Francesco I 'il Vecchio' (r. 1350–88), Carrara dominance began to acquire a princely style, and by 1362 'a household government of kinsmen and favourites' exercised political control.[38] The Carrara proved to be significant patrons, and like other dynasties strained to emphasise the legitimacy of their regime. The fourteenth-century masters Guariento and

Altichiero both worked for them, though the full magnificence of the Reggia Palace is only vaguely imaginable since the building is largely destroyed. We do know that the inspiration of the decoration was classical. There were separate chambers for Thebes, Camillus, Hercules, Nero and Lucretia, as well as a 'Hall of Illustrious Men'. This last took its inspiration from Petrarch's work of that title, and Petrarch himself was permanently resident in the city from 1367. He may have felt the influence of Lovato Lovati (1237–1309) and Alberto Mussato (1261–1329), a poet and historian who was, intriguingly, leading an active political life in the early fourteenth century. Both were experts in antiquity, and in particular on the work of Livy, Padua's most famous ancient son. In Giovanni Dondi dall'Orologio (1318–89), Padua under the Carrara boasted another 'civic' humanist before such figures had come to prominence in Florence:

> An ease with a variety of disciplines and an accompanying sense of civic responsibility has long been the hallmark of the humanist. Giovanni Dondi dall'Orologio is a Paduan paradigm: he was creator of the planetarium; lecturer in medicine, astrology, philosophy and logic at the Studium [University]; possessor of a library rich in classical texts (as well as in recent Paduan 'classics' by Alberto Mussato); friend of Petrarch, ambassador for Francesco il Vecchio; and protoarchaeologist in Rome, where in 1375 he made his famous annotations and measurements.[39]

Other humanists variously active in the city do not seem to have gravitated towards the court. These included Petrarch's secretary Lombardo della Seta, Giovanni Conversini, who was head of the princely chancery from 1393 to 1404, and Pier Paolo Vergerio (1370–1444), the first major educational theorist of humanism. Vittorino da Feltre (1378–1446) took up the chair of rhetoric in the university – which had also benefited from Carrara patronage – in 1421. The past perfect tense is important, however. By 1421, Padua had been under Venetian dominion for over 15 years. Like Milan, like Naples, like Urbino, the end of the dynasty brought about a decisive change. The murder of the Carrara by the Venetians 'finishes the tragedy of our chronicle'.[40] There may be other stories to tell. That of the Carrara remains singular. What would our view of the early Renaissance be had bombs in the Second World War destroyed the Scrovegni Chapel and had the Palazzo Reggia survived?

Malatesta? Bentivoglio? Della Scala?

The foregoing has by no means exhausted the dynasties of Italy, merely sampled them. There should be mention of the Malatesta of Rimini, the opportunist *signori* of the fourteenth and fifteenth centuries. The Tempio Malatestiano that Alberti began to build in 1450, but never finished, for the notorious Sigismondo (1417–68) provides an important symbol of cultural change since the age of Dante. In Dante, however strenuously, the Christian framework contains the classical world (see above, Chapter 2). In Alberti's design, a classical temple literally encases a Christian church. [O.37]

However, as in the case of cities, so too in that of courts, there are some famous examples that appear to have made little cultural impact, as reference to Symonds's typology of tyrants reminds us. The Rossi and Corregi in Parma, the Torrenti in Milan, the Scotti in Piacenza, the Vitelli in Città di Castello, the Gambacorti in Pisa: none of these springs to mind in formulating a thesis on the development of the Renaissance. Bologna, as mentioned above, did not spawn a notably civic culture; the Bentivoglio clan – full of illegitimacy in both senses – did not establish a princely court, perhaps in part because of their unsteady dominance of this violent city in the fifteenth century. In that regard, they were unlike the usurping Sforza, who did seek to cover their illegitimate tracks, but similar to the early Medici in not holding formal office. In Verona, Cangrande I della Scala is commemorated by an equestrian statue dating from the early part of the fourteenth century (he ruled from 1308 to 1329). His family continued to predominate until 1387, but there are no particular signs of a flourishing culture – despite the presence in the city of an enormous Roman amphitheatre, which in some ways gave Verona a more obvious classical connection than had either Florence or Venice.

In the case of secular princes, as in the case of civic projects, the initiative for the commissioning, design and activation of a project would appear to have lain with the patron. That idea can be tested over the full span of the period in the case of the most important princes of the Church.

The popes in Avignon and Rome

The papacy was in many ways the most advanced and sophisticated patron of the arts. The papal curia appropriated the mendicant message and used it for propaganda purposes in the great project of Assisi and in numerous Dominican commissions. With regard to political identities, the papacy was also a source of confusion, sometimes denouncing tyranny, sometimes damning republicanism as heresy – it all depended on whether the lord or town concerned favoured the cause of the emperor or the pope.[41]

The papal court was, throughout the period from 1300, one of the chief centres of power and patronage, not just in Italy, but in Europe as a whole. After 1300, its history unfolds in four principal phases that define the general history of the papacy in the period. Since so much of this book is devoted to an examination of the tensions that existed between Christianity and pagan antiquity, the history of Western Christendom's chief institution merits treatment in expansive terms. Such an approach may seem odd compared with the study of a single room in a palace in Mantua or Ferrara, but too often and too easily the popes of the period are seen only as secular rulers in Italy, and this is misleading with regard to the works of art that they commissioned.[42] Moreover, one suspects that such a view is the product of the same interpretation of religious development to which we have often referred, the one that sees the Renaissance papacy as worldly and corrupt, the Reformation as protest against that corruption, and subsequent changes in the character of Catholicism as a response to that protest. What follows is an attempt to contextualise the artistic ventures of the papal curia as the spiritual centre of Christendom as well as the centre of a secular state in Italy – and a particularly quarrelsome one at that.

The first of the four periods is that of papal residency in Avignon from almost the start of the chronological span under review until the papacy's return to Rome in 1420. The second phase extends from that date until 1502. During this time, the political and spiritual fortunes of the papacy were varied, and the fashioning of its identity as expressed in cultural projects was never entirely certain. The third phase opens with the milestone pontificate of Julius II (r. 1503–13), which proved decisive in resolving that identity crisis and is expressed in the full maturity of the High Renaissance. The final phase, which can be conveniently dated to the period after the sack of Rome in 1527, and emphatically not from the German Reformation, is characterised by the reassertion of the authority of the Catholic faith in moral terms and its communication to the world. The sack of 1527 made necessary an enormous programme of rebuilding, but in other ways the final phase that opened in that year was an extension of the third.

Indeed, there is also a thematic unity to the period as a whole. This is provided by a deep and often bitter conflict over the location of sovereignty in the Church. It prompts what may seem to be something of an excursus. However, the subject is central to an understanding of the Renaissance. It shows how the temporary loosening of spiritual authority played a part in unleashing the speculative energies that, through contemplation of pagan antiquity, developed a new, daring and dangerous cosmology (see below, Chapters 6 and 7).

The conflict within the Church was as old as the Church itself and as modern as the present day. It involved the clash of two imagined visions of the transmission of power from heaven to earth. Protagonists of the papal monarchy saw authority descending from God to the Vicar of Christ. This vision was most potently formulated during the Investiture Contest that had begun in the late eleventh century and ended in triumph for the papacy over the Hohenstaufen in the middle of the thirteenth. It still found powerful expression as our period opens, in the bull *Unam Sanctam* (1302) of Boniface VIII, who declared that it was 'necessary for salvation for all creatures to be subject to the Roman pontiff'. But once Boniface had been mugged by the henchmen of the king of France at Anagni, and the papacy had removed to Avignon, such claims appeared at once overarching and flimsy. Throughout the fifteenth and sixteenth centuries, secular rulers eroded papal authority: in Bohemia, France and Spain, and eventually in Germany and England – and there was always the danger that the same could happen in Italy itself.[43]

All of this made attractive an alternative ascending vision of ecclesiastical power. According to this view, God vested power in the whole body of believers (the *ecclesia*) who, through their representatives, the bishops, chose a college of cardinals who in turn elected a pope. In simple terms, this was to be the basis of what is known as 'conciliarism', that is to say, a view going back to the days of the early Church and the councils of Nicaea in 325 and Chalcedon in 451, that the representative bishops who convened in a General Council were superior to the pope, and could, if necessary, therefore depose him. The ascending thesis had to be addressed in the later phases of the Great Schism of 1378, when three popes claimed to be head of the Church. Only a council could decide between them.

The first council that gathered to sort out the mess met in Pisa in 1409, but the council that ended the Schism eventually convened at Constance in 1415 and elected Martin V. There were further meetings at Basel in 1431, and then at Ferrara and Florence in 1439. As well as weakening papal authority in Europe generally, conciliarism imposed constraints on papal relations with other Italian states. However, religion and politics were never clearly separate, and it is distorting to see the papacy as concerned only with 'worldly' affairs.[44] The Fifth Lateran Council of 1512 is usually but inconsiderately dismissed as a papal ruse to buy off opposition, but it forms an important link between the councils of the fifteenth century and the intermittent gatherings of the Council of Trent between 1545 and 1563. In an important sense, Trent marked the climax of conciliarism and resolved the question of sovereignty by formulating decrees for reform of the Church, which the popes then issued in their own names. This is worthy of emphasis in order to avoid the idea that the spiritual revival of the 'Counter Reformation' papacy had somehow 'disowned' the 'worldliness' of the 'Renaissance' papacy.

A previous chapter suggested that the emergence of new cultural expressions in the fourteenth century owed much to the absence of the papacy from Rome (see above, Chapter 2). One should remember, however, that 'the papacy of Avignon in no way relaxed its interest in Italy'.[45] Moreover, the flow of interest and exchange operated in both directions. Petrarch's father, exiled from Florence, had a post in the papal curia. Petrarch himself studied at the University of Montpellier: it was there that he acquired his love of classical literature, also absorbing Provençaux lyrics. It was in Avignon, too, that he was to set eyes on his beloved Laura in 1327. He composed the sonnets – yes, the Petrarchan sonnets – that celebrate his love for Laura in his villa at Vaucluse. At some point – obscured thanks to his own contrivance – he climbed Mount Ventoux, and there he pondered the relation of earth and heaven, of the world and the spirit (see below, Chapter 6).

Simone Martini (active *c*.1315, *d.* 1344) absorbed French influence early in his career in the Angevin court of Naples, as was evident in his scenes from the life of St Martin in Assisi. His greatest work, the *Annunciation*, is based upon line and pattern and has not the remotest similarity to the work of Giotto. [O.38] Perhaps his previous contact with French culture, particularly its aristocratic elegance, was what attracted him to Avignon in 1340 or 1341. Here he met Petrarch and grew friendly with him, illustrating a manuscript of Vergil for him, and here he died in 1344.[46]

Thus, the 'Babylonish captivity' of the papacy in Avignon may be seen as a critical period for the development of forms and styles that were by no means exclusively 'Italian'. Petrarch's cultivation of his love of Latin in France, and Simone's delicate and luxuriant *maniera*, show how difficult it is to talk about an 'Italian Renaissance' in any narrow sense.[47]

Once reinstalled in Rome, the popes began, tentatively at first, to reinvent their image. Martin V's successor, Eugenius IV (*r.* 1431–47), was short of money, and his powers as pope were limited by the decrees of the Council of Basel, which he tried, unsuccessfully, to dissolve in 1431. At one point, according to Vespasiano, he was forced to flee Rome in an open boat disguised as a Franciscan friar.[48] Among the most significant developments in this period was the move to the Vatican Palace as the official papal residence under Nicholas V (*r.* 1447–55). His building schemes set the tone and scale of papal ambitions – in the name of the Church – that are more readily associated with the mid-sixteenth century. His biographer, Giannozzo Manetti (1396–1459), compared him to Solomon, and Rome to Jerusalem.

Christianity, of course, made the pope and Rome superior to the Judaic examples. The humanist studies that Nicholas encouraged added classical antiquity to scholasticism and the study of the Church Fathers. At his death the Vatican Library contained about 1200 texts. Pius II (r. 1454–64) was a most unusual pope since he was also a trained and avid humanist scholar. However, that appears to have made him the companion of men of letters rather than their patron. As an envoy to the Council of Basel, he had developed an anti-papal stance, which he subsequently abandoned. His main project was to rename and rebuild his birthplace between 1459 and 1464. In that time, Corsignano became 'Pienza', and the pope gave orders for the new town to the architect Bernardo Rosellino (1409–64). Of Sixtus IV (r. 1471–84), one might observe that his notorious nepotism and his Franciscan habit embody the contradiction at the heart of the Renaissance Church, a contradiction that was to persist beyond the Reformation. Indeed, Sixtus can be seen as a 'Counter Reformation' pope *avant la lettre*, encouraging the cult of the Virgin and commissioning works such as the frescoes in the Ospedale Santo Spirito that were designed for general appeal rather than aesthetic quality. Momentously, it was he who gave his name to the Sistine Chapel, which he built to replace one from the thirteenth century. That building provides physical linkage between the 'Renaissance papacy' and that of the 'Counter Reformation'. The interior decoration was strictly orthodox in character and included Botticelli's *Temptation of Christ* and Perugino's *Christ's Charge to Peter*. The combination is significant as a reminder respectively of the need to resist the temptation of worldly power and the only justification in Scripture of the supremacy of the bishop of Rome. [O.39; O.40] By the end of the fifteenth century, the papacy appeared only too easily tempted by worldly delights, and the work of humanist authors, most notably Lorenzo Valla (see below, Chapter 6), had exposed the dubiety of the evidence that supported papal claims to secular supremacy. The conflict became a stand-off between the puritanical Savonarola in Florence and the notoriously worldly Pope Alexander VI (1492–1503).[49]

Involvement in the affairs of this world has dogged the reputation of Alexander's successor, Julius II (r. 1503–13). As a 'warrior pope', allegedly modelling himself on Julius Caesar, he apparently sought to consolidate a secular state and to promote his own glory, aims quite incompatible with the principles embodied in the paintings just mentioned.[50] So it appeared to contemporaries, and Erasmus is the likeliest author of a satire, *Julius Exclusus*, in which St Peter refuses the pope admission to heaven. Within the city, Julius added the Via Giulia (modestly) and the Via Lungara. His planned rebuilding of St Peter's was to be a long process and had consumed over 70,000 ducats by the time he died. Much of that money was raised through the sale of indulgences in Germany, a practice that was to inspire Luther's initial protest and bring about the Reformation.

Was Julius's vision mere personal vainglory? In some ways, the paintings he commissioned, and the project for St Peter's, look forward to the age of the Catholic revival. More than that, those projects might be seen as beginning that revival. When Julius convoked the Fifth Lateran Council he was under threat from the French king, and schism was in the making. The combination was eerily reminiscent of the fourteenth century, and might have dragged the Church back to that unhappy era. This Julius managed to avoid, and he was not to know that Christendom would soon experience a still more dramatic upheaval.

For all the accusations of worldliness, there are manifestations in what Julius planned and commissioned of deep religious feeling. Raphael's frescoes in the Vatican Stanze juxtapose classical themes with the central tenets of Christian belief, most notably the Eucharist that embodies the human God. The *Disputa* that faces *The School of Athens* may be a depiction of a council of the Church meeting to discuss the nature of the most holy sacrament. Julius himself is depicted kneeling in prayer before the miraculous Host at Bolsena. The *Expulsion of Heliodorus* – which also includes a depiction of Julius – emphasises the 'liturgical, fiscal, military and diplomatic aspects of the papacy' and makes the point that the pope cannot avoid the affairs of this world. The liberation of Peter from his chains (a reference to Julius's titular church, San Pietro in Vincoli) may be read as the freeing of Italy from the bonds of foreign domination. Leo X (r. 1513–21) was to take this further when he commissioned Raphael to produce a fresco in which the pope's namesake Leo I is shown persuading Attila the Hun and his barbarian horde to withdraw. Such themes are surprisingly similar to those of *The Prince*. [O.41–O.46] Returning to Julius himself, he carried the Eucharist in all his triumphs, and after the expulsion of the French in 1512, the procession also included a chariot representing the Fifth Lateran. Rather than dismissing Julius as 'worldly', it might be appropriate to credit him with mobilising the Church Militant with a view to seeing the Church Triumphant.[51] His new St Peter's was the embodiment of that vision. In his pontificate, is it possible to identify 'the splendour of holiness', universal glory and intimate faith? Can we discern in Julius's achievements the characteristics that were to endure when, as we have seen, the worlds of secular princes and their courts proved so fanciful – and so fleeting?

Perhaps that notion becomes more persuasive when one reflects on what did *not* change about the papacy. What is consistently demonstrated is that the papal office *was* superior to the character of its incumbents – just as the

Roman law had stated.[52] Paul III (r. 1534–49) was a reformist who commissioned Michelangelo's vision of the end, *The Last Judgment*, yet he appointed his teenage grandsons as cardinals within weeks of his election. What a crafty old fox he looks in Titian's memorable painting of him with his grandsons! [O.47] The austere Franciscan and former inquisitor Sixtus V (r. 1585–90) replanned the city on a gigantic scale, with an aqueduct, a new road system, the embellishment of the Quirinal, the Lateran and Santa Maria Maggiore. When the French humanist Michel de Montaigne visited Rome in 1580, he was surprised by the lack of classical and pagan imagery. Was that perhaps because papal Rome had by then reasserted itself as the natural heir of ancient Rome?

Of necessity, discussion of the popes in general terms makes them much more than mere Italian princelings. Once again, the focus has narrowed to the question of the compatibility or otherwise of the cultures of the ancient world with Christianity. The investigation continues through particular projects that may be examined in detail.

5   *Sponsors*

Patronage: profane and sacred

As discussed in the opening chapter, one of the concepts that scholars have sought to define more specifically in the context of the Renaissance is 'individualism'. It was suggested that this in turn relates to the tradition of attribution in the field of art history (see above, Chapter 1). On the one hand, there is now much greater scholarly awareness of the role of the workshop, suggesting that the completed item was the product of a collaborative effort. Thus, the painter Giotto might have put his name to a work in order to authenticate it as completed under his supervision. There is no documentation to confirm that even the Arena Chapel in Padua, which we can definitely 'attribute' to him, is 'all his own work' (see below). The impulse to attribute 'relies on notions of individuality and originality that do not necessarily correspond to the values of Giotto's own times'.[1] Obvious certainties of attribution have dissolved. Some critics, for instance, contend that the painting of the military commander Guidoriccio da Fogliani, discussed above (in Chapter 3) as a fourteenth-century masterpiece by Simone Martini, may not be by Simone Martini and may not be from the fourteenth century. The Crucifixion in Cosimo de' Medici's cell in the monastery at San Marco in Florence can be attributed without question to either Fra Angelico or Benozzo Gozzoli (see below). More generally, as Bram Kempers concluded:

> Individual innovation in art has been elevated in our times to the status of an unquestioned aim, without reference to any network of patrons. This view has been projected on to the past. What this means is that our view of art history is dominated by artistic geniuses; we tend to regard them as having mapped out their own careers and having been guided solely by a set of ideals set above mundane social reality.[2]

Critical here are not just the role patrons played in commissioning works of art, but the functions of the works of art themselves. Renaissance artists did not produce work for exhibition in galleries. Kempers makes the arresting comment that 'tourists milling round churches are occasionally pulled up short by the celebration of the Mass, without for a moment being confronted with the role once played in that Mass by the paintings they have been admiring'.[3] In prayer, stained-glass windows behind the altar and statues, especially the crucifix above the altar, play an inspirational role rather than an aesthetic one.

Thus, the subjects of patronage and function have operated to give a more effective historical and social context for 'works of art'. When Peter Burke published the first version of his work on the Italian Renaissance in 1972, he asked the then daring question of 'whether the arts flourished because of the patrons, or in spite of them'. He concluded that the question was unanswerable 'because one does not know what the same artists would have created in different circumstances'.[4] Three decades or so later, we might not be so categorical, or at least we might acknowledge that it is unanswerable for different reasons. This clarification is due to a series of studies of patronage, of which Professor Burke's was a pioneering example. However, E.H. Gombrich had already made the point that 'the work of art is the donor's', and that Cosimo de' Medici had his own style or *maniera*. The fact that we can see a similar style in his control of political patronage is in itself significant (see above, Chapter 4). Even though Giovanni di Bicci de' Medici commissioned Brunelleschi to design and build a sacristy at San Lorenzo in 1419, it is now doubtful whether we should see Brunelleschi as 'the architect' of the church, given the interventions of Giovanni's sons, Cosimo and Lorenzo. Two generations later, Lorenzo the Magnificent (1449–92) submitted a design in the competition for the contract to put a façade on the Duomo (but died before a decision could be made, saving the judges embarrassment). We need not confine the examples to Florence. Ercole d'Este set his own stamp on Ferrara (which he ruled from 1471 to 1505) through the artists he hired.[5]

Sometimes, the artist had very little say. The painter Benozzo Gozzoli (*c.*1421–97) was left in no doubt as to what Piero de' Medici required in the frescoes for the Medici chapel:

10 July 1459

This morning I had a letter from Your Magnificence through Roberto Martelli [Piero's agent]; and I learnt that it seems to you the seraphs that I have done are not appropriate. I did one of them on one side among some clouds, and of this you see only the tips of the wings; it is hidden and the clouds cover it in such a way that it is not disfiguring in any way at all but rather gives beauty, and it is beside the column. I did another of them on the other side of the altar, but hidden in the same way.

Roberto Martelli saw them and said it was not something to make an
issue of. Nevertheless I will do as you command, two little clouds will
take them away.[6]

Through the assessment of transaction, requirements and contractual
obligation, patronage has become an excitingly concrete way for historians
to link art to society. However, as John Stephens has pointed out, the
demands of the patron do not explain the 'quality and form' of the work
of art itself. The work of Fra Angelico (c.1400–55) at the Dominican
convent of San Marco in Florence further illustrates the point. The
convent had stood at Fiesole but moved to Florence under the patronage
of Cosimo de' Medici. As we shall see, Cosimo most definitely set his stamp
on the decoration of San Marco, but the 40 or so frescoes reflect both the
devotional commitment of the painter and a nuance of communication for
different audiences both clerical and lay.[7] The relationship between
patron, artist and completed work prompts the use of the word 'sponsors'
as the title for this chapter. In an important sense, the patron is not a
'customer'. Rather, it is the artist who is the client. In the *Oxford English
Dictionary*, 'sponsor' is one of the definitions of 'godfather', a term that has
traditional overtones of a religious relationship, and modern overtones of
gangster clientage. Moreover, as we understand it, sponsorship is a
phenomenon that has its limits in the determination of results. The sponsors of a particular team hope to gain a great deal in publicity, but whether
their financial support improves the quality of a game is not something
that we can determine in any simple, direct or immediate way.

However, with that qualification in mind, it is now clear that the
commissioning of works of art was part of a broader social and political
process of networking and the establishment of power relations. There is
an important linguistic point to make here. The Italian language distin-
guishes between patronage of the arts, *mecenatismo*, after Maecenas, a sort
of minister for the arts of the Roman emperor Augustus (r. 31 BC–AD 14),
and political patronage or *clientelismo*, which reflects the notion of a
patron–client relationship. English does not make such a distinction, which
in one way is revealing, but in another dangerous.[8] Wary of the dangers of
terminological looseness, this chapter nevertheless addresses the ways in
which the power relationships of *clientelismo* found expression also in *mecenatismo* of the arts. At the same time, we must acknowledge that a work of
art can have more to say than the self-advertising message of its sponsor.

It may be useful at this point to remember that patronage cannot be
understood in terms of the relationship between 'the patron' and 'the
artist' as though each represents a clearly identifiable type. The unitary

aspect of that characterisation is misleading. There were numerous types of patronage. Among the most important were civic and courtly sources, which have already figured prominently in the previous two chapters. In this one, there will be fuller discussion of ecclesiastical patronage, and beyond that to the religious elements of patronage. A further distinction is required between the sponsorship provided by groups, which might best be described as 'corporate', and that of individuals. Guilds and confraternities are especially significant in this area. In Florence, the cloth merchants were responsible for the commissioning and oversight of the work on the great bronze doors of the Florentine Baptistery. With regard to the calibre of the end result, we might remember that Michelangelo referred to the doors, which Lorenzo Ghiberti worked on from 1403 to 1452, as 'the gates of paradise'. Ten more guilds sponsored a niche apiece at the church of Orsanmichele. The orphanage, the Ospedale degli Innocenti, was the responsibility of the silk merchants. The wool merchants became responsible for the completion of the dome on the cathedral. In the sixteenth century, the principal confraternities of Venice, the Scuole Grandi, fiercely sought to outdo each other in the construction and decoration of their halls.[9]

None of the distinctions between types of patron and types of patronage should be portrayed as rigid. Religion was inseparable from the 'civic' projects in Siena in the *Trecento*. A group of laymen in a confraternity almost invariably commissioned objects of devotion. By a strange and ironic contrast, individual cardinals in Renaissance Rome commissioned a large number of entirely pagan subjects. With regard to the classification of 'corporate' and 'individual' patronage, a prominent individual might drive a corporate project (as Enrico Scrovegni is said to have done in Padua from 1300 onwards), a prince might take counsel from a coterie of advisers. Corporate family projects could yet embellish the city in such a way as to promote the civic ideal – as private palaces did along the Grand Canal in Venice – and so on.

With regard to the motivation of patrons, then, it is important to observe the interaction of prestige, pleasure and piety. As we have seen with particular reference to Urbino, princely magnificence in the court was often supplemented by the enjoyment of a library, and a pious motivation can rarely be ruled out entirely. Even Sigismondo Malatesta (1417–68), the notoriously immoral lord of Rimini, had Piero della Francesca paint him kneeling before his namesake saint. [O.48] Such interaction and overlap are important because they generated competition. We have already noted this in the cases of Florence and Venice. Isabella d'Este (1474–1539) was determined to obtain for her collection works by the Venetian painter Giovanni Bellini (*c*.1430–1516) and by Leonardo, whoever else they might be committed to working for. In 1401, Brunelleschi and Ghiberti competed for the commission to design and cast the bronze doors of the Baptistery in Florence; Domenico Veneziano (active *c*.1438–61), to whom Piero della Francesca was an assistant, offered his services to Cosimo de' Medici on the grounds that he could equal the work of other masters such as Fra Angelico and Filippo Lippi.[10]

In order to give some steadiness to this diffuse subject, it is useful to remember a number of general points about what patrons controlled – however subtly artists managed to elude their constraints.

First, patrons determined the nature and scale of the project. It is important in this regard to avoid over-concentration on painting, because painting – especially fresco – was relatively inexpensive. Masaccio's epoch-making *Trinity* in Santa Maria Novella (*c*.1425–8), a fresco which displayed a new mastery of pictorial space, probably cost about 30 florins. That compares with the 5000 florins that Galeazzo Maria Sforza, duke of Milan (*d.* 1476), set aside as the annual budget for his kennels, or the 5274 *lire* that Duke Ercole d'Este spent every year on salaries for the staff of his stables in Ferrara.[11] Marble and mosaic were much more expensive than pictures. Most prestigious of all was bronze for commemorative purposes since it was likely to cost ten times as much as marble. This helps to explain the significance of projects such as the Baptistery Doors in Florence, and Leonardo's projected equestrian monument for Francesco Sforza, duke of Milan, in the 1470s.[12] Building was the most expensive pursuit of all – and therefore the most prestigious – for the city, the family and the Church. In the course of the fourteenth century, civic halls were erected in Volterra, Gubbio, Piacenza, Todi, Orvieto, Como and Bergamo, and in Venice work began on the Ducal Palace.[13] *Opere* – or 'boards of works' – for the construction of ecclesiastical monuments existed in Florence, Siena and Padua. Stately palaces advertised the magnificence of the respective ruling dynasties in Padua, Urbino, Ferrara and Mantua. Aside from the Medici, other Florentine families such as the Ruccellai, the Strozzi and the Pitti commissioned huge palaces in the *Quattrocento*.[14]

Second, while great building projects and bronze statues seemed to offer the best chance of long-lasting fame for those who commissioned them, much of what patrons called for was ephemeral. The bronze statue of Julius II, which the pope set up to commemorate his conquest of Bologna in 1506, was enormous – some 20 feet high. Yet the victorious French melted it down and recast it as a cannon, which they mockingly called 'La Giulia'. Work in precious metals might also be recast. The reputation of Benvenuto Cellini (1500–71) is well served by his boastful autobiography, but his work as a goldsmith survives only in the extraordinary salt cellar that he presented to Francis I of France.[15] We know a lot less than is desirable about the interior decorations for works of art. Tapestries, for instance, were much more expensive than paintings, and also more functional in keeping out the cold. The theatrical properties for court spectacle or religious drama did not survive, which immediately gives pause for thought about the relationship between the requirements of the patron and the reputation of the artist. We asked earlier whether we would see Leonardo as quite such a slowcoach in the completion of projects if we were able to see his sets and costumes for the Festa del Paradiso in tangible form rather than in a few miscellaneous sketches (see above, Chapter 1). We might fantasise that if, by some miracle, the performance had been recorded live for posterity, the reputation of Leonardo might have been far higher. After all, it seems unlikely that even Michelangelo would ever have completed the 40 life-size figures of the projected tomb of Julius II. If that same patron had not insisted that Michelangelo work – against his wishes – as a painter (see below), perhaps his reputation might be far lower.

Finally, and following on from that speculation, all types of project were subject to controls that patrons imposed, usually by the conditions of a contract. These specified the subject, the materials that the artist was to work with, the cost – including or excluding materials – and often a deadline for completion. Again, it must be emphasised that the aesthetic assessment of the work of a single master can distract from an understanding of the production process and the function of the finished work. One calculation suggests that between 1285 and 1537, the wooden structure of the frame for a picture accounted, on average, for one-fifth of the overall cost, gold leaf for between a third and a half.[16] The commissioning individual or body would also specify a date for completion, invoking what we now call a 'penalty clause' in the event of delay.

Time, money, materials: such matters seem the subject of more or less realistic bargaining between hard-nosed people operating in an emphatically secular world of business. Scholars working on patronage either in a specialist field relating to a single project or in synthetic studies of the subject have added a vital dimension to our understanding of cultural change in the Renaissance. The extraordinary variety of projects, and of the aspirations, motivations, desires and dreams that pressed them forward, is among the most persuasive reasons for retaining the notion of individualism as a key feature of the Renaissance. Moreover, this is accentuated in the *Quattrocento* as princely courts moved into the ascendant as patrons, replacing the corporate solidarities of guilds, neighbourhoods and fraternities. This point is worth developing as a concrete and quotidian example of the imitation of the classical world. With the collapse of the 'medieval' solidarities just listed, the individual sought security in social and political life through attachment to a patron. One might even argue that the gradual change in the status of some artists was a reflection of the same tendencies. Indeed, with regard to the 'Renaissance' as a 'rebirth' of classical values, it is an attractive speculation that, in Italian cities, a style of *clientela* such as existed in ancient Rome came to replace the corporatism of the Middle Ages.[17]

The clientage network of the Medici provides the most striking example of such a process that may be studied in detail. With the failure of the corporatist structures of the guild-based republic, attachment to the Medicean network of clients and supporters became of paramount importance in political life. Lauro Martines has argued persuasively that the extent of their clientage system made opposition all but impossible. In this light, the award to Cosimo of the title *pater patriae* in the tradition of Augustus, the first Roman emperor, is by no means a rhetorical construct but is the natural and culminating expression of a return to the political relationships of ancient Rome.[18]

The suggestion of individualism and the secularisation of political life in direct imitation of ancient Rome, with the Medici providing the critical case history, reinforces some familiar features of the Renaissance. Moreover, it may be further supplemented by the pattern of Medicean ecclesiastical patronage. The political messages that Cosimo contrived to send out by his patronage of the monastery of San Marco form a discrete study in this chapter (see below). However, the grip that Cosimo's family came to hold on the liturgical life of their local church of San Lorenzo is scarcely less remarkable. The new church, with which Brunelleschi's name is associated, involved 'new chapels with new dedications to new saints' and a dramatic alteration in the calendar of feast days. Thus, Cosimo's father, Giovanni di Bicci de' Medici (*d.* 1429), appropriated the chapel of San Giovanni Evangelista, along with the chapel to Saints Cosmas and Damian (the patron saints of doctors – or 'Medici'). When Cosimo died in 1464, he was buried beneath the centre of the dome directly in front of the high altar. Lorenzo promoted 'anniversary offices' for his late brother Giuliano, who had been murdered in 1478, and for his mother who had died in 1473, and he increased the festivities in celebration of his name saint, San Lorenzo. True, there had been some resistance to Cosimo's encroachments from the bishop of Florence, Antonino (*r.* 1446–59). Yet even this sincere reformer (who was canonised in 1523) was to some extent compromised by his attachment to the Medicean clientage network. He had been prior of San Marco, and Cosimo had funded its foundation in 1436.[19]

What cuts across this picture of authentic classical revival and the subordination of the Church is the historical significance of ecclesiastical patronage and Christian religiosity in launching and sustaining some of the most significant projects associated with cultural revival. The role of St Francis as the imitator of Christ can hardly be exaggerated, nor can the importance of the collaboration between Florentine and Sienese masters in the Basilica at Assisi in the fourteenth century. However, at this point we should turn our attention to the other mendicants, the Dominicans. They were especially committed to the cult of the Virgin Mary, and there is a strong case for saying that the Virgin was the supreme patron – or matron – of the arts. She interceded between heaven and earth, promoting the interests of her earthly clients. Everyone sought her favour. With regard to the subject matter of art, she provides the supreme continuity between 1300 and 1600, her influence was pervasive, and she inspired some of the transcendent expressions of faith that took the visual arts beyond the reach of politically motivated iconography. She was the Guardian of Siena, the Duomo in Florence was dedicated to her, and its construction began on the feast of her purification. She was the universal object of veneration in Venice, and she was far and away the most significant patroness of confraternities there. She was to sustain the iconography of the sixteenth century as the audience for it broadened during the religious revival. She was the patron of the Arena Chapel in Padua, and of the Sistine Chapel in Rome, and her influence on the iconography of the Dominican monastery of San Marco in Florence was everywhere. Her patronage – or matronage – and that of all the patron saints ranged with her was to exercise an extraordinary influence on developments in the visual arts.[20]

The Christian themes that the mendicants promoted, together with the significance of continuing religious preoccupations, are a reminder to avoid overemphasising the secularising tendencies of the age. Two features of mendicant influence attract attention. The first was an awareness of the need to reach an audience broader than the social elite. The arrangement and choice of subject matter at San Marco in Florence, for instance, depended heavily on the degree of religious education that could be expected in the audience. Among the religious, friars would have greater understanding than novices, while many images were not visible at all to lay brethren. What they were permitted to see was simpler to interpret.[21] The other was the continuing religious response to the mercantile life that had developed in medieval cities. Suspicion of usury became what we might call a 'tempering of magnificence'. This emerges strongly in the case histories of the Arena Chapel in Padua and, again, San Marco in Florence.

One of the chief influences of the mendicants was to provide a nagging reminder to merchants that making money for its own sake was sinful. Scholastic analysis had produced complicated regulations concerning the restitution of unlawful profit. That complexity itself reflected the contortions of merchants as they tried to evade the constraints of canon law, using a 'multiplicity of practices'. Philanthropy and the glorification of God through artistic patronage became ways in which merchants could avoid restoring to their victims what they had unjustly taken from them.[22]

At the risk of oversimplification, however, one or two generalisations are possible. Usurious gain could imperil a man's soul through pride and avarice. These were chief among the Seven Capital Sins, from which the others stemmed (see below, Chapter 6). The dangers of money-making form a constant theme in the teaching of St Francis and St Dominic (1170–1221), and of their spiritual heirs in the *Quattrocento*, San Bernardino (1380–1444) and Sant'Antonino (1389–1459). This is not to say that making a donation to the Church was merely a question of refunding illicit gains (which were otherwise unreturnable) or easing a bad conscience, though such impulses probably played their part. Rather, in the identification with mendicant poverty, such an act countered pride with humility, and avarice with liberality. This involved a Christianisation of magnificence. Vespasiano da Bisticci (1421–98), who ran a manuscript copying business and wrote a lively series of character sketches of famous contemporaries, informs us that Cosimo spent 40,000 florins at San Marco, 60,000 at San Lorenzo, and 70,000 at the Badía in Fiesole. The merchant Felice Brancacci, notorious for his sharp business practice, may have paid for the frescoes in the family chapel at Santa Maria dei Carmini – painted by Masolino (1383/4–1447) and then Masaccio (1401–28) from 1425 onwards – in similar spirit. It is striking that Vespasiano frequently – and even formulaically – praises his subjects for their liberality: 'Cosimo was liberal in all respects', 'Cosimo was liberal to all good men of worth', 'Cosimo was always liberal, especially to men of merit'.[23] Intriguingly, Leon Battista Alberti, that 'universal man' of the Renaissance, in building the palace of Giovanni Ruccellai (1403–81), made self-glorification a duty. In one way, of course, this is a direct imitation of an ancient model, deriving from Cicero's *De Officiis*.[24] However, such a principle also makes a significant distinction between 'luxury' and 'magnificence', so the latter was free of any taint of the sin of *luxuria* – 'excess' – of which lechery was part. Such abiding Christian moral influences should be borne in mind as we address a series of specific projects in various centres, although those same Christian influences in some respects faced compromise and subversion.

The Scrovegni Chapel: the motives of a patron

A justification for beginning a study of the cultural changes known as the Renaissance in the year 1300 is provided by a document of 6 February of that year. It was on that day that a wealthy merchant of Padua, Enrico Scrovegni, purchased a plot of land in the city from the Dalesmanini family. This marked the beginning of a project that was to link mercantile wealth to the work of the Church through the sponsorship of a work of art of revolutionary originality. The plot included the site of a Roman arena, so the physical link with the ancient past was clear. The decoration of the chapel that Scrovegni ordered to be built there is the certain work of Giotto and is one of the great landmarks in Western art. What particularly concerns us here is what the project might tell us about the reasons why a patron should launch a project of this scale and scope. The scheme is a concrete example of the relationship between commercial profit made in an urban environment and patronage of the arts. It is also an example of the way in which a layman turned his secular profits to religious purposes. More important still are the signs of strain between the life and work of a merchant and the traditional moral framework of Christianity, strain that is evident in the very effort to reconcile the two. Enrico's father, Reginaldo Scrovegni, was a notorious profiteer. Dante placed him in the seventh circle of the *Inferno*, and clearly identified him through the family coat of arms, which for some reason was a blue pregnant sow. Reginaldo is the only one of the usurers who speaks to the poet:

> And one, who had drawn a great blue pig
> On his white satchel, said to me:
> 'What are you doing in this pit?
> Go away now; and since you are still alive,
> Know that my neighbour Vitaliano
> Shall sit on my left side.
> Among these Florentines, I am a Paduan.
> Many times they thunder in my ears,
> Shouting: "Let there come that supreme knight,
> The one who will bring the pouch with three beaks." '
> At this point he distorted his mouth and stuck his tongue out
> Like an ox that licks its nose. (*Inferno*, canto xvii, lines 64–74)

Enrico's project was very closely associated with the cult of the Virgin, both Annunciate and as the Lady of Charity.[25] Crudely put, there is a strong suggestion that ill-gotten gains were returning to the Church as conscience money. Writing in the mid-sixteenth century, Bernardino

Scardeone included in his study of the antiquities of Padua the inscription on Enrico Scrovegni's tomb (the inscription was subsequently lost). It includes the following:

> Those who led a life of luxury in happy times,
> Having lost their wealth, are no longer even spoken of,
> But Enrico Scrovegni, the knight,
> Saves his honest soul; he respectfully makes for them a feast.
> For he solemnly dedicated the temple to the Mother of God,
> So that he would be blessed with eternal grace.
> Divine virtue replaced the profane vices
> The heavenly joys which are superior replaced earthly ones.

Scardeone himself commented that 'Enrico Scrovegni, pious lord, in order to redeem his father's soul from the punishment of purgatory and to expiate his sins, built a most beautiful temple in the Arena'.[26]

The theme of expiation for usury is prominent in the decoration. It is a grim scriptural fact: Judas betrayed Jesus for financial profit – for 30 pieces of silver. The plot against Christ, according to Saint Mark, was directly linked to his cleansing the temple in Jerusalem of the moneychangers who had set up shop there:

> And they came to Jerusalem: and Jesus went into the temple, and began to cast out them that sold and bought in the temple, and overthrew the tables of the moneychangers, and the seats of them that sold doves: And would not suffer that any man should carry any vessel through the temple. And he taught, saying unto them, Is it not written, My house shall be called of all nations the house of prayer? But ye have made it a den of thieves. And the scribes and chief priests heard it, and sought how they might destroy him: for they feared him, because all the people was astonished at his doctrine. (Mark 11:15–18 KJV)[27]

After the betrayal, Judas was filled with remorse, as recorded in Matthew 27:3–5:

> Then Judas, which had betrayed him, when he saw that he was condemned, repented himself, and brought again the thirty pieces of silver to the chief priests and elders. Saying, I have sinned in that I have betrayed innocent blood. And they said, What is that to us? See thou to that. And he cast down the pieces of silver in the temple, and departed, and went and hanged himself.

According to Acts 1:18–19, Judas killed himself in a different manner:

Plate 4 Giotto, The damned, from *Last Judgment*, *c.*1306. Padua, Scrovegni Chapel.

Now this man purchased a field with the reward of iniquity, and falling headlong, he burst asunder in the midst, and all his bowels gushed out. And it was known unto all the dwellers at Jerusalem; in so much as that field is called in their proper tongue, Aceldama, that is to say, The field of blood.

Moreover, his gains imperilled not only his salvation, but also his worldly goods:

For it is written in the book of Psalms, let his habitation be desolate, and let no man dwell therein; and his bishoprick let another take. (Acts 1:20)

The first version of Judas's death provided at least two themes to trouble the merchant conscience. The first was that the betrayal of Our Lord – the supreme betrayal – brought financial profit to the perpetrator; the second was that Judas polluted the temple with that profit. [O.49] This was the temple that Christ himself had cleansed. The second version in Acts provides an even more graphic account of Judas's death. In Giotto's *Last Judgment*, the artist combines the two versions to show Judas as the supreme usurer. He is included in an unusual way in that he has hanged himself and his entrails are also gushing forth. [Plate 4] Other usurers, having failed to heed the dangers of the profit motive, are hanging by their own purse strings. There is a real urgency about the patron's expiation for his ill-gotten gains. The usurer Scrovegni himself is literally on the edge – his gift of the chapel and its acceptance by the Virgin at the foot of the cross are all that separate him from hell. [O.50] His *avaritia* has in a sense been expiated by his liberality.[28] If that comment is accurate, then the medieval merchant of the civic community has adopted the magnificence that came to be extolled so fervently by Alberti, and embraced so willingly by princes. Thus, urban and courtly contexts, apparently so wide apart in political terms, were part of the same cultural world. In some cases, however, commissions for works of art did not apologise for wealth, but instead celebrated it.

Florentine competitions: patrons, artists and messages

The Scrovegni Chapel was firmly attached to a context of urban money-making that religious influences sought to rein in. By contrast, the commissioning of statues for the niches on the outside of the church of Orsanmichele in Florence might – unself-consciously and without anachronism – be characterised as competition among corporate sponsors. Orsanmichele had been a corn market and housed the magnificent sculpted tabernacle by Orcagna (1359). The exterior decoration was the responsibility of the city's guilds, each of which was to provide a statue of its patron saint for one of the niches. Progress was slow until 1406, when a communal directive ordered completion of the project within ten years. The project generated rivalry between the guilds as to which of them would acquire the greatest prestige. This in turn produced competition among sculptors, especially Ghiberti and Donatello. In at least one case Ghiberti was commissioned by one guild to produce a statue that would equal or surpass his previous work for another of the niches. In 1418, the moneychangers chose Ghiberti to cast the 'new figure of St Matthew, which they want to be made of brass and bronze in the niche newly acquired by the said Guild'. For his part, Ghiberti agreed 'to do the said figure of St Matthew in fine bronze at least as large as the present figure of St John the Baptist of the Guild of Merchants, or larger if it seems better'. [O.51] Yet in 1427 the Wool Guild charged him to make a St Stephen for their niche which 'exceeds or at least equals in beauty and adornment the more beautiful of the others'.[29] [O.52] Donatello produced a St Mark (1411–13) for the Linen Workers' Guild, St George (*c*.1416–20) for the Armourers. [O.53; O.54] The artists were by no means the slaves of their sponsors: rather, they competed and learned from one another. The result was 'radically new sculpture' that 'unequivocally constitutes the point of departure for a new art in Florence'.[30] Such competition was replicated in that between Ghiberti and Brunelleschi. Both made competition pieces – which have survived – for the doors of the Baptistery in 1403, when neither was much over 20 years of age. We do not know whether stylistic considerations weighed with the commissioners in allotting the commission to Ghiberti. It may be that his design was both cheaper and more weatherproof. [O.55] But in 1418, the Opera del Duomo put both Brunelleschi and Ghiberti under contract to place the cupola on the cathedral, even though the work came to be regarded as Brunelleschi's triumph.[31]

Such examples illustrate the problems of classifying particular projects in any strictly defined way. The decoration of the niches at Orsanmichele was the work of laymen who engaged in competition for worldly admiration at a religious monument. The decoration of the cloister of San Marco illustrates the ways in which the worldly requirements of the patron could harmonise with the spirituality of the mendicants. Vespasiano da Bisticci – who was involved in at least one of Cosimo de' Medici's projects – leaves his readers in no doubt as to where the roots of Cosimo's patronage lay:

> Since Cosimo had attended himself to the temporal affairs of his city, it could not be but that he had not put into them sufficient conscience, as do most of those who govern states, and who wish to take precedence over others. Knowing this, and he wished that God might have mercy upon him, and keep him in these temporal advantages, it was necessary for him to turn to pious matters, otherwise he knew that those advantages could not last without this means. For this reason, whence it came I do not know, it seemed to him that he had money that was not well-gotten. In order to remove this weight from his shoulders, since Pope Eugenius was in Florence, he conferred with his Sanctity about what lay on his conscience.[32]

In a project that Cosimo financed, Fra Angelico (*c*.1400–1455) was to produce in the 1440s around fifty compositions in tempera and fresco for a community of between 15 and 34 religious – including novices and lay brethren. Cosimo himself was a member of that community and the decorative work was 'a sacramental activity'. The Dominican painter conveyed an unmistakably Dominican message that reminded the onlooker of the unique position of the Virgin as the abbess of all the order's convents. The nine ways of prayer, the encouragement of brethren to imitate the founders of the order – the subtlety of the Dominican message may have been beyond Cosimo. Or it may be that he did not receive it because he was too busy putting out a message of his own.[33]

It was Cosimo who insisted on bringing the Dominican community into the city from Fiesole. He then lavished 36,000 florins on the convent between 1436 and 1453. The carpets were bordered with *palle*, the Medicean coat of arms. Cosimo's chapel was a consecrated space that included a representation of the Three Magi and a tabernacle for the sacrament, attributes normally reserved for crowned rulers.[34]

Most striking of all in this simple and delicate setting that exudes both religiosity and humanity is the decoration of Cosimo's own suite. The apartment reserved for Cosimo does not compromise with the contemplative humility of the setting. There are two rooms, not one cell. The scene at the entrance is a crucifixion with Christ speaking the words 'Woman, behold thy son. Behold thy son'. [Plate 5] This is a variation – with an interesting new emphasis – on Christ's words as spoken in John 19:26–7. These are 'Woman, behold your son' addressed to the Virgin and then 'Behold thy mother' addressed to St John. In Cosimo's cell, the spoken words are painted in a direct line leading to the Virgin. Next to her is the kneeling figure of St Cosmas – Cosimo's name saint and, along with St Damian, the patron saint of the Medici. Damian is left out of the composition and visually there is a clear implication that Cosimo's name saint is taking the place of the Son of God. Professor Hood's hushed conclusion that the painting 'was specifically designed with Cosimo's occupancy in mind' seems something of an understatement.[35] Indeed, an obedience to the Medicean message that borders on the slavish makes the attribution of this painting to Benozzo Gozzoli (*c*.1421–97) rather than Fra Angelico persuasive. We know that Gozzoli did as he was told in the decoration of the Medici chapel in the Medici palace (see above), and that included making the Medici the equals of the Magi.[36]

Cosimo's munificence also funded the great library at San Marco. The scale and ambition of such a project in the years before printing began the communications revolution were remarkable. Vespasiano makes that point in describing his own involvement in assembling the library at the

Plate 5   Fra Angelico/Gozzoli, *Crucifixion*, *c.*1436. Florence, San Marco, cell 38.

Medici church of San Lorenzo. In that instance, the collection of existing volumes was impossible because of their scarcity:

> I said it would be necessary to have the books transcribed. He asked whether I wanted to take responsibility for it . . . Once the library was

begun, because it was his wish that work proceeded with all possible speed, and that there should be no shortage of money, in rapid time I took on forty-five scribes and completed two hundred volumes in twenty-two months.

As executor of the will of the humanist Niccolò Niccolì, who died in 1437, Cosimo managed the transfer of the testator's remarkable collection of manuscripts to San Marco in accordance with the terms of the will.[37] Vespasiano depicts Niccolì as both scholar and patron of the arts:

> One might say, that Nicolao was the one who revived Latin and Greek letters in Florence, which had for a very long time lain buried; and although Petrarch, Dante and Boccaccio had revived them somewhat, they were not at the level that they were thanks to Nicolao, for various reasons. First, because he inspired innumerable people of his time to letters, and because he was the reason why any learned man – from Italy or elsewhere – came to Florence to study. . . . Nicolao, taking an interest in painting, sculpture, and architecture, was noted by all and gave them very great favour in their work: Pippo di Ser Brunelleschi, Donatello, Lucca della Robbia, Lorenzo di Bartolaccio, he was a very close friend to them all.

Interestingly, the texts at San Marco were there for anyone of studious inclination, or, in Vespasiano's words, 'common to everyone'. It appears, then, that the lay/religious divide between the texts was not as pronounced as it was in Fra Angelico's paintings. The collection of classical authors was extensive. Among the Greeks were the histories of Thucydides (c.460–404 BC), some of the plays of Aeschylus (525–456 BC), Sophocles (496–405/6 BC), Euripides (480s–406 BC) and Aristophanes (c.450–c.385 BC), while some of the Latin authors were Cicero (106–43 BC) and the poets Horace (65–8 BC), Ovid (43 BC–AD 16/17), Juvenal (active AD 115–130) and Lucan (AD 39–65).

In terms of a 'rediscovery' of antiquity, it is worth reflecting that the earliest and latest of those dates – 525 BC and AD 130 – span six centuries, roughly what separates the author and readers of this book from the competition to design the Baptistery Doors in Florence.[38] That may, however, have been difficult to absorb, since the manuscripts themselves dated from the 'Middle Ages', which were supposed to have obscured them! From detailed research on the holdings, two general points emerge that are crucial to our purposes. First, no one was working with 'originals'. The four hundred texts were the work of scribes in the 'dark ages' that the humanists so liked to deride. Of the Greek manuscripts, only 16 predated

AD 1100. As an illustration of the dependence of scholars in the *Quattrocento* on preceding revivals of interest in antiquity, 102 of the Latin manuscripts were from the twelfth century, which according to medievalists had a 'renaissance' of its own (see above, Chapter 1).[39] Second, however strong the interest in pagan antiquity, the foremost author in the collection was the man who took late antiquity into the Christian Middle Ages: St Augustine. We must soon ask whether – if at all – Renaissance humanism escaped his shadow (see below, Chapter 6). Indeed, in the design of the programme for perhaps the most famous and celebrated of Renaissance monuments, the Sistine ceiling, Egidio da Viterbo (1469–1532), confidant of Julius II, Neoplatonist and head of the Augustinian order, was to play a vital part. Egidio himself stands in the shadow of giants.

Michelangelo, Julius II – and Paul III

One of the strongest arguments for the Renaissance as promoter of individualism is the improvement that came about in the status of the artist. Gradually, painters, sculptors and architects came to be seen as free-standing creative beings who were not held back by the status of 'craftsman' or hemmed in by the regulations of guilds.[40] The 'rise of the artist' did not, however, emancipate even the most exalted genius from contractual obligations to a patron. Michelangelo, 'il divino', generally acknowledged as a celebrity in his own time, is an emphatic example of this point. Even he did not, as it were, go his own way, and the day when an artist would exhibit a corpus of work for sale to the *cognoscenti* was still some way off. Indeed, Michelangelo's tempestuous relationship with Pope Julius II shows how the supreme achievements of Renaissance art followed two-way contractual obligations.

Julius's unshakeable will turned Michelangelo to painting despite his own preference for sculpture. He undertook the painting of the ceiling of the Sistine Chapel under duress and under protest, signing a contract in 1508. The following year, he wrote to his father that work had been going badly: 'This is the trouble with this work; it's still not my true profession, and I waste my time.'[41] He even went so far as to describe the deforming physical discomfort of the work in a poem to Giovanni da Pistoia:

> In all this cramping I've given myself a goiter
> as water does to cats in Lombardy
> or indeed in whatever country it might be
> there's a force that sticks my belly under my chin.

My beard to heaven, I feel my memory
in the hump on my back, I'm acquiring the chest of a Harpy;
and the brush above my face the whole time
dripping turns it into a fine floor.
    My loins have gone into my guts,
I make my arse the rump of a beast of burden as a counterweight,
I take steps uselessly and sightlessly.
    In front of me my skin stretches
and bunches up behind in order to fold itself,
and I bend like a Syrian bow.
    But flawed and unfamiliar
grows the judgement that my mind bears;
you shoot askew through a bent barrel.
    My dead painting
Defend all the same, Giovanni, and my honour;
since I'm not in a good place, and I'm no painter.[42]

Julius's motives were as egotistically self-advertising as those of Cosimo de' Medici. The Sistine Chapel took its name from Sixtus IV (pope, 1471–84), Julius's uncle. Julius's project for the decoration of the ceiling was to complement what Sixtus had commissioned for the walls (see above, Chapter 4).[43] The grandiosity of the project was reflected in what Michelangelo was to be paid: 6000 ducats. However, the artist's letters are full of complaints about the pope's failure to pay up – yet another illustration of the power that the patron wielded.

It is also indicative of the complex interactive quality of artistic creativity with the demands of the patron that the 'authorship' of the schema for the ceiling as a whole remains obscure. That Neoplatonic philosophy animates the narrative is clear. There are strong grounds for arguing that the unifying power of oppositional forces that take the narrative from spiritual to fleshly, and the philosophical progression from flesh to spirit, was the inspiration of Egidio da Viterbo (1469–1532). [O.56] What is surprising, given the pope's authoritarian treatment of Michelangelo, is that Julius does not appear to have intruded much on the content of the composition. His influence may have accorded with Michelangelo's own religious sentiments.[44]

The ceiling was complete in 1512. Subsequently, Michelangelo returned to Florence to work for the Medici, sculpting their tombs at San Lorenzo. His extraordinarily long career was to connect again with the papacy, and this new phase in his own work manifests the changed preoccupations of a new age. Pope Paul III (r. 1534–49) was a less explosive character than Julius, and probably more discerning. He was also a worldly 'Renaissance pope', descendant of a family of *condottieri*, ascendant on the ladder of Borgia patronage. Yet it was Pope Paul who commissioned from Michelangelo *The Last Judgment* (1534–41), also for the Sistine Chapel. [O.57] The pope left the composition to the artist. In fact, the patron had to defer in at least one important detail. Michelangelo refused to include his family (Farnese) coat of arms, saying that the device did not fit with the arms of the della Rovere (Sixtus's or Julius's). As a product of Michelangelo's *ingegno*, what a contrast in mood with what appears on the ceiling! The purposeful, confident and exuberant programme of the earlier paintings gives way to the grim uncertainties of the Day of Doom, the artist's self-portrait appearing on St Bartholomew's flayed skin. [O.58] There is another self-portrait in the Pauline Chapel. Michelangelo depicts himself as St Paul, blind and grovelling on the road to Damascus. [O.59] The blind Gloucester's admission in *King Lear* comes to mind: 'I stumbled when I saw'. This painting, finished in about 1550, shows, as Kenneth Clark put it, that 'something very drastic has happened to the imagination of Christendom'.[45] The 'something' was emphatically not the Reformation. Probably the most important event in the Italian peninsula between Michelangelo's two periods of papal patronage was the sack of Rome in 1527. A new Rome emerged thereafter, and Michelangelo's designs for the church of St Peter are its epitome, but the sack itself had prompted the reinvention of another apostolic city, that of St Mark, a reinvention that was to continue throughout the remainder of the sixteenth century.

The Venetian state and the fashioning of history

Like Rome, the Venetian Republic was to experience a crisis of unprecedented proportions during the Italian Wars. This was at its most uncertain point in 1509 when the League of Cambrai (which Julius II had helped to engineer) inflicted a comprehensive defeat on the armies of the Republic at Agnadello. The Venetians lost their possessions on the Italian mainland. Imperial armies reached the gates of Padua. The city in the lagoon was itself under threat. However, unlike Rome, there was to be no sack. The Republic's subsequent recovery of its territories came to appear the most natural thing in the world. In fact, that recovery was due to divisions among the victors of Agnadello. The Venetian state was to make a lucky escape look like a triumph. The first trick of the light in this process was in large part due to the collaboration of patron and artist: Doge Andrea Gritti

(r. 1523–38) and the architect Jacopo Sansovino (1486–1570).[46] Their partnership has never achieved the same celebrity as that of Pope Julius and Michelangelo, yet it was the principal axis of Gritti's mighty scheme of urban renewal, or *rinovatio urbis*.

Gritti had been commander of the besieged garrison in Padua in 1509, and had good reason to know that the Republic had retained its independence by the skin of its teeth. Gritti was not a popular man, but he became doge in 1523. As Titian's magnificent portrait captures, he had all the leonine energy of Julius II. [O.60] Significantly, Sansovino was a refugee from Rome following the sack in 1527, after which Venice, as the last independent Italian state, began to be reshaped as the new Rome. In the later 1530s, in accordance with Gritti's wishes, Sansovino remodelled Piazza San Marco, the political and religious heart of the city. [O.61] The everyday business of government became a monument in the offices that he built to house the servants of the state, the Procuratie Nuove. Where once had stood shanty stalls of cheesemongers, there arose the Mint and the Library. Even today, the Zecca impresses upon the visitor the wealth of the state, while the Libreria (now the Biblioteca Marciana) is a reminder that the city was Europe's leading producer of books, technologically the most sophisticated wares of the age. [O.62] Indeed, the two buildings prompt the reflection that coins and books were the only items 'mass-produced' as identical in the pre-industrial era, and here they are in Venice housed at the centre of the city. Even political bargaining donned the mask of art, for Sansovino, in scenes redolent of the virtues of the Republic, embellished the Loggetta at the foot of the bell tower – where votes were bought and sold in the *broglio*.

Sansovino's friend Pietro Aretino (1492–1556) was another refugee from Rome. This scurrilous author, the self-styled 'scourge of princes', left Gritti in no doubt as to the uniqueness of the Republic, and of its superiority to Rome, in a letter of 1530:

O universal fatherland! O freedom common to all! O refuge of displaced peoples! How much greater would be the woes of Italy, if your goodness were less! Here is the refuge of all Italy's peoples, and the stronghold of its riches; here its honour is salvaged. Venice embraces Italy when others despise her, and upholds her when others abase her; feeds her when others starve her; she welcomes her when others hunt her, and in cheering her again in her tribulations, she keeps her in charity and in love. So let Italy kneel before Venice, and give prayer to God for her, whose majesty, by means of her altars and sacrifices, wishes Venice to share the eternity of the world, that world which is astonished

that Nature should have miraculously made place for her rise in the
most impossible location, and that Heaven should have been so generous in its gifts that in nobility, in magnificence and in dominion, in
buildings, temples, pious houses, in councils, in benignity, in customs,
virtues, riches, fame and glory. And let Rome be silent, for here there
are no minds that can or would tyrannise over her liberty, which in
Rome has been servile by spirits of its own.[47]

This manifesto for Venice as the 'new Rome' depended on the qualities of
stability and prosperity. The one seemed to reinforce the other as obviously and concretely as their reification in the Mint and the Ducal Palace.
As for the Grand Canal:

Never do I take myself to the windows but that I see a thousand people
and as many gondolas at market time. Before my eyes to the right stand
the Meat Market and the Fish Market, to the left the Bridge and the
Fondaco dei Tedeschi [a warehouse and lodging place for German
merchants]; at the meeting point of both views I have the Rialto,
swarming with businessmen. I have grapes in the barges, game and
game birds in the shops, garden produce in the open space. I do not
bother about streams irrigating fields when at dawn I admire the water
covered with every type of thing that finds itself in season.[48]

Aretino was a great admirer of the painter Titian (c.1487/90–1576), and
indeed posed for him. The writer, the architect and the painter formed a
powerful business syndicate when it came to cornering commissions and
running down the competition. The praise heaped on Michelangelo (which
included a contribution from Aretino) is probably the most famous example of 'the rise of the artist'. However, what the network of Aretino,
Sansovino and Titian achieved is scarcely less striking – though it was at the
expense of the reputation of so great a master as Lorenzo Lotto
(c.1480–1556), whom Aretino wickedly damned with faint praise. Bernard
Berenson cites a letter that Aretino wrote to Lotto in 1548 in 'a curious
mixture of good criticism, stabs in the back, and the usual log-rolling in
Titian's favour' – and Berenson knew a thing or two about 'log-rolling':

Envy is not in your breast. Rather do you delight to see in other artists
certain qualities which you do not find in your own brush, although it
performs those miracles which do not come easy to many who yet feel very
happy over their technical skill. But holding the second place in art is nothing compared to holding the first place in the duties of religion, for heaven
will recompense you with a glory that passes the praise of this world.[49]

The letter was in Titian's name, and came from Augsburg. This was exceptional. Titian did not have to leave Venice for work. Instead, patrons usually came to him. He was in Augsburg in the entourage of Charles V (1500–58, emperor 1519–56), and there is a story that the emperor, ruler of half the world, once stooped to retrieve a brush of his from the floor, the prince thus bowing to the painter.[50]

Like Michelangelo, Titian lived to a great age. He died of the plague in 1576. The following year, fire destroyed the interior of the Ducal Palace. The message of the replacement pictorial decoration is unmistakable. The Venetians rewrote their history. Even in the hands of painters such as Tintoretto (1518–94) and Veronese (c.1528–88), as Wolfgang Wolters reminds us, the pictures are 'not in the first place works of art'.[51] In the Hall of the Greater Council, the schema reaches its glorious articulation of history and myth. One of the two long side walls celebrates the events of 1177. That was the year in which the two major powers in Western Christendom, Pope Alexander III and the Emperor Frederick Barbarossa, made their peace in the city. The pope was there as a refugee, the emperor came to submit to him. The state thus asserts its sovereign independence acknowledged by both empire and papacy centuries before. The opposite wall depicts the events of 1204 that culminated in the sack of Constantinople by the armies of the Fourth Crusade. The grubby reality of Venetian demands for money from the crusaders is concealed in the emphatic pronouncement that since that time Venice had been independent of Byzantium in the East. The sack of 1204 was also a reminder to those who visited the palace that two Romes had fallen, and a fourth there would not be. Then, on the wall above the dais is the largest oil painting in the world, Tintoretto's *Paradiso*. [O.63] Christ crowns the Virgin amid 400 heavenly figures. Patricia Fortini Brown exactly summarises the political purpose behind the heavenly vision:

> In a supreme statement of the grandeur, power, and piety of one of the longest lasting republics in history, all the important decisions of state would be made under the auspices of Christ and the Virgin and with the inspiration of the heavenly hosts.[52]

The starry crown of the Virgin, whose name 'Miriam' means 'star of the sea', surely identifies the Mother of God with Venice herself. At least one observer confused Venice with the Virgin in Tintoretto's central panel in the ceiling. The *Paradiso* itself depicts the figures of St Theodore, St Mark, Moses and Christ in an arrangement that corresponds to the statue of San Teodoro, the Piazza San Marco, the church of San Moïsé and the church of San Salvador in the material fabric of the city.[53]

In the state-sponsored projects of sixteenth-century Venice, the city's rulers presented a myth that in a persistently reassuring way seemed to reflect the experience of the citizen in the street. The reinterpretation of the past for the purposes of the present is one of the ways in which developments in the visual arts and in the world of letters complemented and reinforced each other. However, it is now time to separate the two. While we might understand the art of the Renaissance as the exploration of space, humanist writers were engaged in the exploration of time.

6 Time Travellers

The clash of value systems

The last chapter discussed patronage as a key agency in the recasting of culture in Italy. We now turn to the letters, arts and music that we associate with the Renaissance. It must be underscored that there is no necessary causal connection between them and the wide range of subjects already examined. In history, ideas and their expression have a considerable measure of independence as variables, as unpredictable phenomena that are not the products of similar contextual patterns. A simple determinism driven by economic, social and political structures and circumstances cannot explain why ideas and works of art took the forms that they did. In the remaining chapters, there will be much reference to matters already discussed, but the relationship between an idea, expressed as a work of art, and the context in which someone thought or designed it may often seem fragile. The writers on whom the focus falls are often much more concerned with their predecessors than with their contemporaries. More than that, taking a lead from Dante, whose guide through Hell was the Roman poet Vergil (70–19 BC), we find that figures from the classical past, such as Socrates (469–399 BC) and Cicero (106–43 BC), *became* the imaginary contemporaries of the humanists: recipients of their letters, participants in their dialogues, partakers of their friendship. The novelty is not communication with the dead – Christians communed with dead saints – but communication with the pagan dead. Travelling back in time, the humanists collected ancient authors and brought them into their own times. If the text of the discussion hovers between the use of the past and present tenses, then this reflects the humanists' frequently electric sense of immediacy and intimacy of contact with people in the remote past.

As noted at the outset, it is vital not to take at face value the rhetorical juxtaposition of the Renaissance 'rediscovery of classical antiquity' with an intervening 'age of darkness' (see above, Chapter 1). The egotism of Renaissance writers, advertising how they had surpassed antiquity, can seem at once trivial and overblown when compared with the wise humility of some 'medieval' thinkers. Few Renaissance lyrics can match the musical poetry of Hildegard of Bingen (1098–1179), who described herself as 'a feather on the breath of God'. And when contemplating the advance of knowledge, who better acknowledges a debt to the ancients than John of Salisbury (*c*.1120–80), whose political acumen, as we have seen, sustains comparison with that of Machiavelli (see above, Chapter 1)? As he put it in the *Metalogicon*:

> Bernard of Chartres used to say that we are like dwarfs on the shoulders of giants, so that we can see more than they, and things at a greater distance, not by virtue of any sharpness of sight on our part, or any physical distinction, but because we are carried high and raised up by their giant size.[1]

Medieval culture had shown a surprising absorbency for pagan knowledge. As the humanists well knew, St Thomas Aquinas (1224/5–74) had achieved a remarkable synthesis of Aristotle's work with Christianity. But the works of Aristotle himself (384–322 BC) had survived thanks to Arabic scholarship: knowledge of paganism came via the infidel. What a contrast with the snooty dismissiveness of Petrarch, who wrote in a letter to Boccaccio in 1370, 'I will not be persuaded that any good can come from Arabia'.[2]

So much for the platitude that Renaissance humanists had discovered something sensationally novel that eclipsed the culture of the Christian centuries. Medieval churchmen had, however, established an ecclesiological framework which subordinated the wisdom of antiquity at the same time as allegedly superseding it. A re-examination of that framework in the light of a re-reading of classical texts by scholars who were laymen rather than clerics raised questions that had seismic implications. In general terms, perhaps the most gigantic of all was the clash of cosmologies. Did antiquity provide a non-Christian way of looking at the world? Of course it did. But did Christianity mark an advance on antiquity? The response to this became less assuredly positive. Filibustering rhetoric about ages of darkness and ignorance was sometimes grounded in technical demonstration of the fallibility of medieval scholarship.

At bottom, perhaps the most significant and specific question was the difference between what pagan authors and what Christian authors judged to be right and wrong. Probably the most familiar expression of what Christians were not supposed to do was the list of the 'Seven Deadly Sins': pride, avarice, gluttony, lechery, envy, sloth and anger. They were expunged in Purgatory, prior to the ascent to Paradise. That progression – that is to say, *Inferno–Purgatorio–Paradiso* – is the essential pattern of Dante's *Commedia*, which he started to write in 1302. Having left Hell, the poet has to ascend through seven terraces of Purgatory, where he is successively purged of each of the 'Deadly Sins' – though the order of the ascent from the worst sin to the least mortal is significant. Dante's experience of Purgatory shows a certain accommodation of avarice, the sin of the medieval merchant. Pride is still the basest of the sins, but the terraces that follow are in the order Envy, Anger, Sloth, Avarice, Gluttony and Lechery.[3]

It is ironic, given that humanists derided medieval scholars for distorting the words of classical antiquity, that the Seven Deadly Sins are a crude oversimplification of a sophisticated and lucid piece of scholastic exposition, yes, of medieval learning. Medieval culture could put a gloss on its own words. The attribution and authorship of the list of what qualities cause actions that can send you to hell remain obscure, perhaps suggesting that the list derives from popular preaching and its need to communicate a clear message to an unlettered audience. Nor should we be dismissive of this development. Communicating with a broad audience was something that never much bothered Renaissance humanists – and the consequences for Italy were disastrous. On the other hand, the solid vices of the medieval morality play (or Marlowe's *Doctor Faustus*) became in Shakespeare's hands a malleable commentary on the complexity and fragility of human arrangements (see below, Chapter 9).

A slightly unsteady list of eight sins appears in the work of Gregory the Great around AD 600. A much more precise formulation, carefully tested in logical questioning, appears in the *Summa Theologica* of St Thomas Aquinas (which he began in 1266).[4] The list of seven sins is not a dogmatic assertion, but evolves through reasoning that is both subtle and dynamic.

First, Aquinas discusses whether covetousness (*cupiditas*) is the root of all other sin. Against the proposition, he points out that its opposite is liberality, which is not the root of all virtue. Against this in turn, he cites St Paul (Timothy 6:10) and Ecclesiasticus (10:19). However, Aquinas observes that 'immoderate craving' is a component of all sin, while a craving for money is merely the means to an end, and an earthly end at that. For future reference (see below, Chapter 7) it is worth noting the overtones of erotic desire in the 'Cupid' element of *cupiditas*.

Second, Aquinas moves to pride as 'inordinate self love'. He identifies three types of pride: 'a disordered will for personal excellence', an 'explicit contempt for God', and a contempt for God deriving from man's fallen nature. He concludes that since the nature of moral evil begins in turning away from God, pride is sin's 'beginning'. In a persuasive synthesis, he argues that pride as 'the will to excel' is the 'capital' (he does not say 'deadly') sin of *intention*, while covetousness, in providing 'the opportunity to fulfil all sinful desires', is a sin of *execution*.

He goes on to consider whether there are any other 'capital' sins, but his terminology shifts to 'vices'. Surprisingly, he argues against Gregory the Great that there cannot be only four virtues to stand against seven vices. In an acknowledgement of individualism that should have made humanist commentators think twice, he reaches the humane conclusion that 'here there is no place for generalisation, since the individual characters of men are so varied'.

He then proceeds to a remarkable combination of simultaneous analysis and synthesis regarding the good, in relation first to the soul, then to the body, and finally to matters external to both. The prime threat to the good of the soul is pride ('vainglory' or *inanis gloria* – and how many humanists were prone to that?), to the body the threats are gluttony and lechery, and the threat to an external good derives from avarice. He extends the list. He defines sloth (with reference to pagan Aristotle) as a flight from personal good, and envy as sadness over the good of another, with anger as something that derives from passion and attacks someone else. Moreover, as an illustration of just how disturbing Machiavelli's observations were to be, Aquinas is careful to rule out the idea that the end justifies the means: 'evil should not be done that good may come of it'.

What is unmistakable is that the first two sins under discussion, pride and avarice, had been seriously compromised by merchant life in the medieval Italian city, as is apparent both from mercantile activity in pursuit of profit (see above, Chapter 2) and the desire to make amends for it in pious artistic projects (see above, Chapter 5). Thus, humility was a recompense for pride, liberality for avarice. How intriguing it is to note that the liberality on which patrons were so insistent was something that Aquinas had denied as the root of all virtue. In the courts of princes, liberality puffed itself into magnificence (see above, Chapter 4). Even in the late fourteenth century, in a painting that may have been for the guild of silk merchants, the Florentine painter Giovanni del Biondo placed the *inanis gloria* of the world alongside pride and avarice.[5] [O.64]

In some ways, the pride and avarice that usury embodied in the commercial life of the towns of medieval Italy were less compatible with Christianity than were some of the values of the ancient pagans. Neither Vergil nor Cicero would have disowned mercy or charity. Seneca's stoicism developed at the same time that the early Christian martyrs were resorting to 'patience' – both of them means of survival in the age of Nero's tyranny. Nevertheless, the other five 'capital vices' of the medieval scholastics were challenged by the celebration that those same vices enjoyed in classical literature. Put another way, the daily practices of the merchant in medieval Italy in an important sense paved the way for a broader questioning of Christian cosmology based on the study of ancient poets and philosophers.

A reading of classical literature went beyond abstract questions of right and wrong. What for Christians became 'sins' that put a believer in danger of hellfire had once been the qualities of the gods of Olympus. How often does Zeus succumb to lechery! And what jealousy this excites in his wife Hera! Gluttony is exalted in the rites of Bacchus, and sloth perforce follows the orgy. The most celebrated poem of ancient heroism, Homer's *Iliad*, begins with the line 'The wrath of Achilles is my theme'. That anger was unquestionably the cause of tragedy, but divine providence did not exact eternal torment, and Achilles was not denied the Elysian Fields forever.

There are other manifestations of pagan antiquity's celebration of values that the Christian Church had to condemn. Translations of the classics uncluttered by Victorian modesty or prudery are beginning to rediscover (that term again) more precisely how plain irreverent and obscene Aristophanes (*c.*450–385 BC) could be, how graphically and overtly sexual was much of the work of Catullus (*c.*84–54 BC) or Ovid (43 BC–AD 16/17).[6]

Along with the revelations of different standards of personal conduct and different patterns of behaviour came the idea that the gods endowed with such characteristics were relentlessly cruel. Why had Troy fallen? The Latin sequel to the tales of Troy, Vergil's *Aeneid*, unfinished at the poet's death in 19 BC, suggests that the city's fortune was the product of the 'mercilessness of the gods'. The Latin is 'divum inclementia, divum', thus emphasising that the gods are without pity (Book II, l. 602). The goddess Venus reveals to her own son that the gods themselves are destroying the city's walls, and that resistance is pointless. The appalling prospect that Providence itself might be malevolent rather than benign is to find its supremely pessimistic expression in *Macbeth* (see below, Chapter 9).

In sum, the two principal vices in the Christian value system, pride and avarice, were facts of life in Italian towns. Merchants used time to make money. The use of time was a manifestation of pride in that it appropriated what belonged to God. The merchant's lust for gain over time was avarice. The other five vices of Christian teaching were, in the thought of antiquity, far removed from the realm of moral absolutes. In many ways, this is the most palpable connection between the urban life of medieval Italy and the classical revival of the Renaissance, between the pride and avarice of the merchant and the gluttony, lechery, sloth, envy and anger of classical literature.

In that fundamental area of how people should and should not behave, there could seem a stark contrast between what Christianity had elaborated and what one could find in the works of the ancients. In celebrating their rediscoveries of the latter, humanists often caricatured scholastic learning.

The walls of the city of God, however, did not come tumbling down. In the humanists' quest to explore pagan antiquity, there was one figure who would not let them pass, or even allow them to sit upon his shoulders to see further.

The shadow of Augustine

Augustine of Hippo (AD 354–430) is one of the key figures in the shaping of the modern world. His shadow stretches from the fall of Rome to the present day. It is a shadow that the humanists of the Renaissance strove to escape – without much success. It is impossible to classify Augustine in any simple way because, gigantically, he bestrides the gulf between the pagan classical era and the Christian centuries. And we know an enormous amount about him thanks to his own extensive writings – far more than we know about Shakespeare, for instance. It may have been the sheer volume of his 117 books that made him so inescapable an obstacle between the humanists and the ancient past. Augustine's wild pagan youth gave way to sober Christian maturity, and he recorded the complexity of the transition in his *Confessions*. He saw a world pass away when he heard of the sack of Rome by barbarians in 411, and he recorded – in some ways presided over – the transition to a new era in which the next world obliterated this one. The rhetorical juxtaposition of a 'middle age' with 'classical antiquity' does not work in his case – not least because of his skills as a rhetorician.

Few converts have been so zealous – or so enduringly persuasive. Once the critical mass of intellectual and spiritual conviction had shifted in his personal experience, he expounded a reasoned belief that Christianity opened the way to a new and improved life, because that life was eternal. With the calm born of his conviction, he set out in his writings why Christianity is overwhelmingly right.

Augustine's knowledge of Platonism developed from a reading of the early Christian philosopher Plotinus (AD 205–70). The latter developed a new form of the ancient philosopher's ideas that became known as Neoplatonism. Confusingly, this is also the term applied to the Italian humanists of the later fifteenth century, and at the risk of conceptual awkwardness, this chapter plays down the novelty of Renaissance 'Neo-neoplatonism'. The Byzantine scholar George Gemistus Pletho (*c*.1355–1452/4) insisted on a Hellenic theology derived from Plato, but he was nevertheless an advisor to his emperor in the definition of orthodoxy at the Council of Florence in 1439, and came to be revered as Plotinus reborn. In the next generation, Marsilio Ficino (1433–99), who refined some of

Pletho's doctrines, never used Plato to challenge Augustine, but instead consistently deferred to Augustine's ideas.

Plotinus had used Plato to convey a sense of the fleeting quality of earthly life and the need to subordinate this to a higher good. This was a philosophical schema eminently compatible with Christianity's (and Augustine's) juxtaposition of a short journey through a vale of tears in pilgrimage to the eternal joy of the city of God. In seeking to understand the influence of Plato on Renaissance thought and the arts, we might well reflect on one of Plotinus's most telling axioms, which seems to come straight out of Plato's cave. Earthly passions are mere delusion:

> And if anyone does not know this experience, let him think of it in terms of our loves here below, and what it is like to attain what one is most in love with, and that earthly loves are mortal and harmful, and loves only of shadows, and that they change because it was not what is really and truly loved, nor our good, nor what we seek. But there is our true love, with whom also we can be united, having a part in him and truly possessing him, not embracing him in the flesh from outside.[7]

In an important sense, then, the great names of Renaissance 'Neo-neoplatonism' were tilting at windmills: the work of synthesising Platonic and Christian doctrine was already done. Perhaps that is what made the works of Augustine the chief influence on Luther and Calvin, and perhaps also the last 'classics' to be 'reborn'.

That said, for our purposes the legacy of Plato is twofold. First, he taught that the individual could aspire to the sublime through the progressive refinement of the soul. Second, he taught that individuals could think of their relationship with each other in society in ideal terms. It is precisely in these areas that Augustine parts company with him. Perhaps because Augustine knew his own self so well, he was wary of the kind of personal cultivation that Plato encouraged. The loss of individuality, rather than the elaboration of individuality, was the way to spiritual fulfilment. 'Hands off yourself', says Augustine. 'Try to build up yourself, and you build a ruin.' It is as though the 'discovery of the individual' would be to open the Pandora's box of the self. Moreover, unlike Plato, Augustine recognised no earthly politics other than ecclesiastical. The individual believer and sinner was on his own in this world, and could hope for solace only in the next. After his conversion in 386, Augustine wrote 117 books, but 'not a single one is devoted to political theory'. Earthly political debate was, for Augustine, 'the anxious questioning of a shadow'. Yet his *City of God against the Pagans* 'dominated the political thought of the Middle Ages' – and remains contemporary to us. As though it were the most natural thing in this world and the next, Augustine even transferred to the celestial city the mission that Vergil had given the Roman Empire, that is, 'to spare the lowly, and strike down the proud'. At the very start of the *City of God*, classical learning combines with the Scriptures, for Vergil's words confirm those of the book of Proverbs (3:34): 'Surely he scorneth the scorners: but he giveth grace unto the lowly.' Both the classics and the Bible combine against the proud.[8]

Readers can immerse themselves in Augustine, and enjoy the reassurance of his authority, because that authority is the wisdom of experience. At the same time, it is hard to talk to Augustine as an equal, and one can feel uneasy about the intimidating strength of his conviction that he knows what is good for everyone else. One cannot, however, scoff at him, or scorn what he has to say. The dynamics of humanism owe much to efforts to probe Augustine, to prise him open. For he is not monolithic: his thought connects contentiously with all the works of pagan antiquity that were available to him. He would not yield up his secrets, which were the secrets of Plato, and eventually the greatest of the humanists either bowed to his authority or thought dangerously without reference to him. Either way, Augustine knew what they would be up to. Three successive waves of humanism, represented by Petrarch in the fourteenth century and the 'civic humanists' and the 'Neo-neoplatonists' in the fifteenth, evaporated in spray when they crashed into Augustine's legacy. Another, which bore the ideas of Lorenzo Valla (1407–57) and Niccolò Machiavelli (1469–1527), worked prudently – or slyly – through other channels.

Petrarch

We have already encountered Petrarch (1304–74; see above, Chapter 1), a figure poised melancholically between two epochs, glorious antiquity and a golden age to come. His fame rests on his revival of ancient letters and his legacy to posterity. He was a scholar, a philosopher and a poet. We meet him as poet later (see below, Chapter 8). In his restlessness and his self-consciousness he displays characteristics that have led to his almost formulaic identification as the 'first modern man'.[9] If egotism is a mark of modernity, then Petrarch certainly fits the description: his is breathtaking. He is a writer who wants his readers to know everything about himself. His literary and philosophical career set down the pattern described at the beginning of this chapter. He is fierce in his rhetoric against scholasticism, and dismissive of Arabic learning. He yearns to know Greek. Most important of all, in his imaginary literary duel with Augustine, he acknowledges that he has met more than his match – even though, of course, he himself wrote the script of their dialogue.

It is revealing that in his assault on the scholastics, Petrarch is at pains to point out that it is their Christianity that is perverse and misleading, while classical authors can be party to a quest for Christian truth. This is particularly apparent in his work *On his own ignorance and that of many others*, which he probably wrote about 1366. There is a marvellous rhetorical sleight of voice in the way in which he admits his own ignorance with ironic humility while chiding the ignorance of scholastic critics. He derides the Aristotelian classification of nature, from which the scholastic says:

> Therefore many things about wild animals, about birds and fishes: how many hairs there are in a lion's mane; how many feathers in the tail of a hawk; with how many arms the cuttlefish binds a man overboard; that elephants couple from behind and are pregnant for two years; how the hunter deceives the tiger with a mirror, how the Arimasp attacks the griffin with a sword, that the bear has no shape at birth, that birth to a mule is rare, to the viper only once and then to its own unhappiness; that the mole is blind, the bee deaf, that the crocodile is the only animal that moves its upper jaw.[10]

He defends the paganism of the ancients as ignorance of Christ:

> For these ancient pagans, even though they may tell many fables about gods, yet they do not blaspheme; they have no knowledge of the true God, for they have not heard the name of Christ, and faith results from hearing.

The great ancients were dead when the apostles preached, and could not hear the words of the true faith: 'thus they are unhappy rather than guilty'.[11] For scholastics, there is no such excuse:

> So, God made the world by that Word which Epicurus and his followers could not know, and indeed our own [Aristotelian] philosophers do not deign to, and through that are more inexcusable than the ancients. Even a lynx cannot see in the dark: he who does not see with open eyes in the light is completely blind.[12]

In particular, it is proper to celebrate the qualities of Cicero and Plato – for these authors have the sanction of Augustine. In comparing Aristotle with Plato (to the former's disadvantage):

> In matters divine, Plato rose higher, as did the Platonists, though not one of them could reach the point toward which he was moving. But, as I

have said, Plato came closer. About this, no Christian, and above all no faithful reader of the books of Augustine will hesitate . . .[13]

Petrarch acknowledges that the pursuit of virtue needs Christ's help, and a draught from the waters of eternal life. 'However, to this very end those many learned authors of whom I was speaking gave much and were very helpful.' In support of this idea, he adds the example that 'from Cicero's *Hortensius*, specifically named, Augustine expresses his gratitude for what he learned'.[14]

Petrarch's admiration of Augustine is at its most concentrated and most effusive in three imaginary dialogues that probably belong to the 1340s: *The Secretum*, or *The Soul's Conflict with Passion*. In the first, Augustine, with insistent reminders of death ('this judge cannot be bribed'), answers in the affirmative Petrarch's question as to whether human misery is the product of free will.[15] In the second, Augustine successively convicts Petrarch of the seven capital vices. Augustine warns of the dangers of pride and then envy. Strikingly, Petrarch also has Augustine connect avarice with the abandonment of the contemplative life for the active life, linking the latter quite explicitly to the city:

> Ever since you began to tire of your leafy trees, and your simpler life, and living with country people came to disgust you, look, urged on by cupidity, you have relapsed into the tumultuous life of cities.[16]

Augustine's idea that urban life automatically corrupts was to be challenged by the ideas of the 'civic' humanists, and explicitly by Poggio Bracciolini (1380–1459), who suggested that avarice had its advantages (see below). However, that was in itself an expression of selfishness, and, in Petrarch's mind, Augustine indicts the fashioning of the self as illusory, a symbolically pre-emptive critique of both *The Prince* and *The Courtier*:

> . . . especially in the present day, men rise to high places; I mean the art of ingratiating yourself at the thresholds of the great, the flattering, deceiving, promising, lying, simulating, dissimulating.[17]

He also uses Plato to justify an abandonment of earthly things, for 'the soul must separate itself from the lusts of the body and eradicate its fantasies so that it can rise pure and free to the contemplation of the mysteries of the divine'.[18]

The third dialogue focuses still more sharply on the worthlessness of the mortal life and the rewards of life eternal. Love for a woman 'engenders forgetfulness of God'.[19] When Petrarch is rebuked (or rebukes himself) for his love of earthly glory he (himself) responds – albeit briefly – with contentious defiance:

For I do not think to become as God, or to grasp eternity, or to embrace heaven and earth. Human glory is enough for me. I sigh for that. Mortal myself, it is only mortal things that I desire.

Brushing aside Augustine's stern interjection 'then you are wholly earthly', Petrarch insists 'So will I follow after human fame in knowing that both myself and it are mortal'.[20] His principle, he continues, is that 'it is right for us to seek that glory while we are here below' and that 'mortal things are the first concern of mortals'.[21] However, when Augustine juxtaposes the 'brevity of human fame, the narrowness of time' with eternity, the chastened Petrarch thanks him for having dispersed 'the thick clouds of error'.[22]

Perhaps it was symptomatic of Petrarch's admiration for Augustine – as well as of his own vanity – that he appears to have seen himself as a figure of comparable stature, standing between two great historical epochs. In his *Ascent of Mount Ventoux*, Petrarch also seems to follow Augustine as a pilgrim poised somewhere between earth and heaven. At the summit, his mind turns to Greece and Rome, to the gods of Olympus, to Hannibal:

> First of all I stood as though amazed, overpowered by the unusual force of the air and the exhilarating spectacle. I looked around me: there were clouds under my feet, and Athos and Olympus became less incredible since what I had heard and read about them I now saw on a mountain of less renown. From there I turned the rays of my eyes in the direction of Italy, to which my spirit is still more inclined. The Alps were frozen and snow-covered, through which once passed that fierce enemy of the Roman name.

But he just happens to have a copy of Augustine's *Confessions* to hand (essential equipment for the mountain climber), and lo, where should it fall open, but . . .

> God be my witness, and my brother who was present: where first I fixed my eyes, it was written: 'And men go to wonder at high mountains, vast floods of the sea, the broad streams of rivers, the span of the ocean, and the revolutions of the stars – and relinquish themselves.' I was amazed, I admit. My brother was eager to hear more, but asking him not to vex me, I closed the book, angry with myself that even now I admired earthly things.[23]

Petrarch may have seen Augustine as the prophet of an age when the Church would be built on the ruins of the Roman Empire. One wonders whether he at least toyed with the idea that the revival in which he was engaged might one day rebuild an empire upon the ruins of the Church –

as Machiavelli came to advocate.[24] Surely, Petrarch's quest for immortality as expressed in fame in posterity challenges, at least implicitly, Augustine's idea that earthly life is a lonely pilgrimage to the heavenly city. For Petrarch – as he put it in *On the solitary life* – human beings were able 'through reflection and writing to leave our remembrance to posterity and so arrest the flight of the days and extend the all too brief duration of our life'.[25] However, in Petrarch's collection of books, neither Cicero, nor Seneca (4 BC/AD 1–AD 65), nor Vergil, nor Livy, could challenge Augustine's centrality.[26]

Those who followed Petrarch took a different tack in their quest to identify with the authentic ancient world. They set aside the contemplative life and enthusiastically embraced the active. In so doing, their challenge to what Augustine stood for was more direct. They sought to concentrate on the city of man rather than the city of God.

Civic humanism

Augustine's 'city of God' was, in the very title of his book, 'against the pagans'. It was a work which exalted the eternal peace of that city which would supersede earthly cares and strife. Belief in such a place necessitated the setting aside of pagan beliefs. A *paganus* in Latin was a 'civilian', a non-soldier. The early Christians were, in their own minds, soldiers, *milites*. In a fundamental sense the 'pagans' or 'civilians' dwelt in the city of man, where they followed the earthly ('civil') law, worked for earthly gain, for personal profit. All the ancient learning of the pagans, all their wisdom, could never carry them to the eternal city which would be the home of Christ's followers.[27] What has become known as the 'civic humanism' of the Italian Renaissance celebrated the city of man. In a fundamental sense, this was a challenge to the Augustinian city of God. Many of the cities of medieval Italy were embodiments of an impulse for worldly profit (see above, Chapter 3). Such an environment had nurtured 'civic humanism', and, often implicitly, and just occasionally quite explicitly, civic humanists could be accused of suggesting 'greed is good'.

It is that connection between the economic life of the medieval city and the values of civic humanism in the fifteenth century that this section attempts to explore. The significance of the urban life of medieval Italy as the fertile ground that nurtured the seeds of the Renaissance into flower is inescapable. There is a particularly strong connection to be made between the deep-rooted civic pride and patriotism of the age of the communes and the 'civic humanism' that was to develop in the generation after Petrarch.

As early as the eleventh century, the citizens of Pisa could find the glorious history of their commune compared in poetry to the deeds of the ancient Romans:

> Of the famous Pisans the history is to be written
> Of the ancient Romans I renew memory
> For Pisa only extends the admirable praise
> That once Rome received by conquering Carthage.[28]

That general consciousness of a Roman heritage was, as we have seen, instrumental in binding together the communes of Lombardy against the invasion of the Emperor Frederick Barbarossa in the mid- and later twelfth century (see above, Chapter 2). The subsequent conversion of Italian states into imitations of Rome was a long, complicated process in which local circumstances played a significant part (see above, Chapters 3 and 4). One of the grandest of such designs was the ambition of the Visconti rulers of Milan to create a territorial state in northern Italy in the late fourteenth and early fifteenth centuries on a scale unseen since Roman times. Famously, the Visconti 'tyranny' faltered in its failure to conquer 'republican' Florence. The 'civic humanism' that extolled the value of 'republican liberty' and warned of the dangers of 'tyranny' was the offspring of that particular struggle.[29] Yet one might argue that the civic humanists were drawing on the historical experience of the communal era as well as on the history of Rome. That may seem speculative at the general level, but there is also a particular and persuasive dimension to such an argument. The relations between the city-states of the Lombard League and the expression of their common cause in treaties depended on the notarial skills of those city officials trained in the *ars dictaminis* – fundamentally, the principles of letter-writing.[30]

While that is a reminder of the significance of the much-decried *medium aevum* or 'middle age' in the formation of civic consciousness, it has the character of a preliminary caveat rather than a reinterpretation. What we have to acknowledge is a shift – and a shift of profound importance – in the preoccupations of humanists in the last quarter of the fourteenth century. This was not a turning away from Petrarch – far from it. Rather, it was a development of his investigations into ancient culture that was to take men of letters in new directions. Petrarch himself, it might be said, had begun the change. From an early stage, he was profoundly attached to Cicero the philosopher, the high-minded guide to a moral life, which in turn derived from a life of contemplation. What a shock to Petrarch's psyche was his own discovery of Cicero's *Familiar Letters* in 1345, for these revealed the great philosopher's active involvement in the dirty business of politics:

Why did you choose to involve yourself in so many vain contentions? . . .
Why did you abandon the retirement proper to your age, profession and
fortune? . . . What tempted you to dealings that brought you to a death
unworthy of a philosopher?[31]

Yet had Cicero's death been 'unworthy', as Petrarch suggests? Cicero was
the victim of a judicial murder in 43 BC at the orders of Mark Antony
(supported by Octavian) for his invective *Philippics*: imitations of the Greek
orator Demosthenes (*c.*384–322 BC), who had spoken out against the
invader Philip of Macedon, the father of Alexander the Great. Was Cicero's
not the supreme sacrifice that the philosopher could make: to give up the
contemplative life and attempt to arrest the transition from free republic to
tyrannical empire, even at the cost of his own life? We must be cautious in
the face of the rhetoric here – both Petrarch's and Cicero's. Dante had
placed Cicero in hell for his silent approval of the murder of Caesar, so
exalting Cicero was another attempted put-down of Dante.[32] It was the
study of Roman history that led to the humanist experiment in deploying
the ancient skills of eloquent rhetoric in the service of the state.

In relation to more recent history, this was a crucial phase in the laicisation of the language of power, a secular challenge to the sermon, especially
in its moralising.[33] Coluccio Salutati (1331–1406) was a humanist *par excellence*. He was the enthusiastic pupil of Petrarch, and his collection of Latin
classics was probably the best in Europe. He sold some 800 works to
Niccolò Niccolì, thus making a vital contribution to the collection that
formed the basis of the library at San Marco. Immersing himself in his
collection made him aware of the diversity of ancient cultures. 'To
harmonise Aristotle with Cicero and Seneca, that is the Peripatetics with
the Stoics, is a great deal more difficult than you think.' Implicitly at least,
such comments created new agenda by pointing out the problems of reconciling the different schools of ancient thought with each other, never mind
lumping them all together and trying to render them compatible with
Christianity. That said, in Salutati's writings we also find some tension, at
times even conflict, between the values of antiquity and those of
Christianity. In reading Seneca's *Hercules furens*, he found an ancient hero
who went mad, killed his children – and subsequently became a god: how
could Seneca permit this? In considering that question, did Salutati know
that Seneca had taken the story from the drama of Euripides (480s–406
BC)? Did the Florentine admire Seneca's stoicism as a source of strength for
Christian martyrs? Or did he revile the Roman philosopher as the tutor of
the tyrannical Emperor Nero (AD 36–68)?[34]

Increasingly, humanists such as Salutati began to identify different concepts of time – which were profoundly to affect their view of history. The providential time of Christianity was essentially linear, running from Creation to Last Judgment. The antique notion of time was cyclical.[35] This raised some difficult questions, of which the most central and the most fundamental was: how did Christian Providence admit the exercise of free will? If there was a predetermined scheme of things, what influence, if any, did humans exercise on their own lives? This problem Salutati addressed in his *De fato et fortuna* (*c*.1396), though his guide on the operation of free will was Augustine. Salutati was more decisive in his defence of Latin poetry, pointing out that there were plenty of moral improprieties in the Bible – for example, the sins of Eve and of Cain, and the lasciviousness of the Song of Solomon – though the idea that everything in the Bible is justifiable is scarcely persuasive.[36]

Salutati was a meticulous scholar. Of the manuscript texts of the works of Petrarch and Boccaccio, he wrote that 'One can find scarcely a single manuscript of Petrarch or Boccaccio that has been accurately written (*vix enim invenitur iam ex Petrarce Boccacciúque libellis fideliter scriptus*)'. As Chancellor of Florence (1376–1406), he was not only 'the first prominent humanist to pursue a strictly lay career', he was the first to mobilise humanist rhetoric in an ideological cause.[37]

However, the struggle with Milan and the formulation of an ideology of republican liberty are closely associated with Salutati's pupil and deputy in the Chancery, Leonardo Bruni (*c*.1370–1444). His political rhetoric has tended to shout down his quieter role as a translator from Greek. He produced Latin versions of works by Plato, Aristotle, Thucydides (*c*.460–404 BC) and Plutarch (AD 46–120).[38] Such work was of enormous importance in increasing the absorbency of Florentine humanists to the Greek culture that deluged them later in the century. Yet his eloquence in using rhetoric disguised as history remains elegantly persuasive, and his role in presenting Florence's struggle with Milan as the struggle between liberty and tyranny is surely an oration on secular particular values that still rouses the spirit. Discussing the conflict in his *Panegyric on the City of Florence* (*c*.1401), he begins with a series of questions that can only be described as 'rhetorical':

> Can anyone of so absurd a mind or so deviant from truth be found who would not say that the whole of Italy would have come under the power of the Ligurian enemy [Visconti] unless this one city has, with its own forces and its own policy, resisted his power? For who was there in all Italy who had either power or energy to be matched with that enemy? Or who would have persevered against the attack of a man whose name brought terror to all mortals?

The might of Duke Gian Galeazzo Visconti (ruler of Milan 1385–1402) seemed increasingly unstoppable. His subtle deviousness seduced all his opponents into an inescapable web of 'divide and rule':

> He was present in all places, he pried into everything, he left nothing untried. And he brought friends to his cause: some with money, others with largesse, and still others with the semblance of his good offices or the promise of them. Having sown the seeds of discord among all the peoples of Italy, he set one against another and in those places in which they were worn down, he himself took possession, prevailing with his power.

Ironically, given the humanist predilection for the imitation of ancient Rome, Visconti's conquests sound similar to the construction of the Roman Empire in the Greek East in the second century BC.[39] Yet for Visconti, Florence was the one final obstacle. The power of Florentine rhetoric bears comparison with that of Winston Churchill as Nazi invasion threatened England.[40] This was the Florentines' finest hour. 'Florentine greatness of spirit could not be terrorised', and it was the Florentines who stemmed the tide of tyranny. The prosaic reality that Gian Galeazzo succumbed to plague while besieging the city of Florence, and that the Milanese army remained undefeated in the field – these matters are not worthy of mention. And the 'historical' sequence closes with another rhetorical outburst:

> O incredible magnificence and courage of Florence! O true Roman people and descendants of Romulus! Who would not now prize the Florentine name with the highest praise for its outstanding resilience and for the greatness of its history? For what could she do that might be greater, what could this city do more outstanding, or in what greater enterprise show that it had preserved the virtue of its ancestors than by its toil and resources to have liberated the whole of Italy from the danger of servitude?[41]

Bruni's *Panegyric* is a high point of Florentine civic humanism. It is a work that exemplifies the effort to turn the descriptive into the normative, to describe things in such a way that one can make them turn out that way, to intensify aspiration to such a degree that the ideal becomes attainable, and demonstrably so through illustration from history.

In Bruni's most polished rhetoric, we are carried along, even mesmerised. But sometimes the rhetorical fabric stretched and frayed. The imitation of the ancients was sometimes strained. Matteo Palmieri's *Vita civile* (1431–8) contains some splendid but almost incidental insights into the creative inter-action of humanism and the visual arts. But it is heavily derivative from

Cicero and Quintilian (*c*.AD 35–*c*.96) and boring.[42] In an invective against Antonio Loschi, the propagandist of Visconti, Salutati insisted on Florence's Roman origins, and invoked a quite vacuous parallel: 'It is our inheritance to have an unknown origin for our city, just like Rome, which is a very strong argument for its antiquity.'[43]

Such feeble contrivance made a poor case for the city of man. Much deeper and more serious currents can be found in the thought of another humanist who became chancellor of Florence, Poggio Bracciolini, for he presumed to take on the Augustinian heritage in open conflict. Poggio (1380–1459) was an avid researcher, constantly seeking out ancient texts. During the sessions of the council of the Church that met at Constance in 1415, he unearthed the architectural treatise of Vitruvius from the age of Augustus, and he found parts of the text of Quintilian's *Training in Oratory* in the monastery of St Gall. He was driven by the aspirations of Petrarch: 'there is in our hearts a longing for future centuries which compels us to seek eternal fame'.[44] When we first encountered Poggio in this book, he was contemplating the ruins of Rome with reference to the often cruel whim of Fortune (see above, Chapter 1). Even when he took up subjects that seemed to demand an overtly Christian conventionality in their treatment, such as 'the misery of the human condition', he made human affairs appear subject to a species of supernatural accident rather than divine providence.

Poggio produced a dialogue *On Avarice* (*De avaritia*, 1428) which is revealing. In a marvellous piece of presumptuous precocity, one of Poggio's participants attacks Augustine as the advocate of rural self-sufficiency, of the subsistence economy so antagonistic to the mercantile values of gain in towns. He opposes Augustine's 'world of farmers', with a tremendous invective. The rhetoric is worthy of Valla, the vision of Hobbes, and the intellectual seriousness of what Poggio says rules out the charges of both decadent materialism and speculative mischief. Indeed, what is there to life without cities in which people strive for gain? It is worth quoting a lengthy passage in order to illustrate this direct challenge of the city of man to the city of God:

> Suppose that no one did more than what was enough for himself and his family. See how there would be a confusion of all things, nothing more than what is enough for ourselves. The virtues most welcome to people, such as mercy and charity, would become useless, no one would be beneficent or liberal. Who would give to others who has no surplus to give? Who could be munificent who only owns as much as is sufficient for himself? Every magnificence of cities would be taken away, everything cultured or ornamental would disappear. No temples would be

built, no porticos, all the arts would cease, perturbation of our lives and of the state would follow, if everyone agreed to have only what were sufficient. But since we know that this appetite has been and is common to all ages, to all social groups and to all nations, that people want, even demand, more than enough for the circumstances of the future, and the buffets of fortune, to bring to the aid of their associates and friends, who will doubt that by this definition [i.e. Augustine's] everyone is to be called avaricious. But out of the avaricious are made villages, towns, cities, and if you believe that those who are avaricious should be ejected, you should add that cities should be uprooted and overturned. For this is what you [Augustine] say. For who would inhabit such places once the avaricious have been thrown out? We would be chased out, because there is no one amongst us, judged by your criterion, who does not come out as greedy and avaricious. According to your judgement, cities would have to stay empty and devoid of inhabitants. But why do I argue about individuals? Cities, states, provinces, kingdoms, what else are they, if you put your mind to it rightly, other than the public work-shop of avarice? . . . Desire for money has grown, so that avarice is not thought a vice but a virtue, and the wealthier a man becomes, the more he is honoured.[45]

In Poggio's case, it is as though the speculative abstraction had grown out of direct experience. At the Council of Constance, where he had found the opportunity to track down a large number of manuscripts of the work of classical authors, Poggio had been witness to the condemnation of Jerome of Prague (d. 1416), the follower of Jan Hus (Poggio's reaction to the condemnation of Hus is not recorded). Poggio's reflections show how troubled he was to see a good man and a great orator sentenced to death by burning at the stake. Did Jerome's judges know so much that they could be confident in condemning him?

I confess never to have seen anyone, especially on trial for his life, come closer to the eloquence of those ancients whom we so admire. It was a wondrous thing to see with what emphases, with what eloquence, what arguments, with what appearance, with what expression, with what steadfastness he replied to his adversaries, and in the end pleaded his case; so much so that it is to be regretted that so noble and excellent a spirit turned to heresy – if it is then true what they accuse him of. In fact, it is not within my capacities to judge a case so serious, and I defer for that reason to the decisions of people esteemed more expert.

Poggio concludes that 'if he acted as a heretic, and if he persisted in his own error, all the same, he died like a philosopher'.[46] The acknowledgements of the Church's authority in matters of Christian truth seem formulaic, and they fail to conceal Poggio's mental disquiet – a disquiet that also manifested itself in Boccaccio and in the visual arts (see below, Chapter 7). The paradox that Jerome used such eloquence to articulate what the Church deemed to be heresy was a source of unease. The condition of the Church may also have troubled him. Hus's judges had overridden an imperial safe-conduct in order to have him burnt. In the year of Jerome's death, Poggio was secretary to Pope John XXIII, an antipope from 1410 to 1415, who brought such ignominy to the name that it was expunged from the list of popes (and taken up again for a pontificate between 1958 and 1963). A pirate and *condottiere*, the antipope was accused of simony, perjury and sodomy, and deposed by the Council of Constance to make way for Martin V (*r.* 1417–31).

Poggio's admission of uncertainty is a rare manifestation amid the self-assurance of the civic humanists. With the establishment of the Medicean regime, the ideology of republican liberty became an inconvenience. The next generation of humanists reverted to the contemplative life, and sought to demonstrate the oneness of ancient wisdom and Christian truth – as Augustine would have wished.

Neo-neoplatonism

The subheading coins an awkward term, but a necessary one. Scholars who became interested and often immersed in the legacy of Plato exaggerated their own novelty as surely as did Petrarch or the civic humanists. 'Neo-neoplatonism' is intended to convey the fact that in many ways they were at a still further remove from Plato's works than were the authors of the early Christian era. Put more simply, the humanists were working with the Plato that Augustine wanted them to see. They appear to have found nothing new in Byzantine Neoplatonism, which Augustine (though not, of course, Plotinus) had scarcely touched. Were they perhaps conditioned by their familiarity with the Christianised Plato whom Augustine had passed on to the Middle Ages? On the odd occasion when any of them perceived the original Plato, they shied away, knowing they were looking at what was forbidden. For the light towards which Plato directs the soul, the oneness of the supreme good that is attainable through contemplation, is attainable without the Church's help. It is also a light that can blind and dazzle. As Plato himself had set out in *The Republic*, the quest for the sublime had a sinister side (see above, Forewords).

In a sense, Augustine had managed the shadows by insisting that they were shadows in which Christians could – and must – believe. They must not believe in the gods of the state, as the pagans had.[47] But were Christian shadows as illusory as those of the pagans? That painful possibility emerged only slowly, its realisation contorted with guilt. In the first place, the revival of Platonic learning voiced no such doubts. There was a single integrated truth in the cosmos that the philosopher could reach through his contemplation of the sublime. The mathematical and geometrical allusions that helped comprehension of this 'good' resonate with the vanishing point of artists, the infinity where parallel lines converge – and also where it is hard to tell the difference between everything and nothing:

> Since numerical unity is everywhere present in all numbers, and point in all lines, so too that divine Unity, remaining in itself indivisible, is equally present everywhere to all spirits and bodies, and equally links and connects the universe. And for this reason all things converge in a mutual convenience and to a single goal, being guided by a single principle. And as all bodies can be brought together in one single supreme body, which moves them all, so do all spirits to a single and supreme spirit which embraces everything.[48]

These are the words of Marsilio Ficino (1433–99), who greatly enlarged the audience for Plato's works by translating them from the original Greek into Latin. Yet he was still presenting Plato as Augustine thought fit. Ficino had wavered in his own faith, but ultimately learned obedience to the Church. The harmony of Platonism and Christianity carried Augustine's approval. Hence, Ficino was dependent on Plotinus. The intellect could aspire to the divine illumination. Moreover, Ficino introduces the disturbing image of Prometheus. According to Greek legend, Prometheus stole fire from heaven. As punishment, he was chained to a rock for eternity, a vulture devouring his liver – which always grew again. He had dared to take the divine light of reason from heaven, and he was punished for it for ever. Had he stolen the divine secret that there is no divinity (see below, Chapter 7)?

> Because of this very possession, on the highest peak of the mountain, that is, at the very height of contemplation, he is rightly judged most miserable of all, for he is made wretched by the continual gnawing of the most ravenous of vultures, that is, by the torment of inquiry.[49]

However, whether light and shade create reality or illusion is an unsettling question – which Plato had posed. In his commentary on Plato's *Symposium*, Ficino asked:

What is the value of that which you love, my friend? A surface captivates
you, a colour it is that has you rapt, or a certain reflection of lights and
the lightest shadow. Or a vain fantasy deceives you so that you love what
you dream rather than that you see.[50]

We are not quite in Macbeth's world of the 'walking shadow' where 'nothing is but what is not', but we are very close to Prospero's 'insubstantial
pageant' (see below, Chapter 9).

Along with Plato and Augustine, perhaps Ficino came to conclude that
for the vast majority of humans, illusions are more comfortable than realities. Such a conclusion is more ample and emphatic in the work of
Giovanni Pico della Mirandola (1463–94). He could be sure of Augustine's
approval. The principles of Pythagoras and Plato 'are so closely related to
the Christian faith that our Augustine gives immeasurable thanks to God
that the books of the Platonists came into his hands'.

It was possible, indeed natural, to mention Plato and Jerusalem, Bacchus
and Moses in the same breath, or to describe Job as a 'fugitive from the
gods'. The sum of all the world's religions seemed to express a common
truth, with 'many doctrines taken from the ancient theology of Hermes
Trismegistus, many from the principles of the Chaldeans and of
Pythagoras, and many from the more secret mysteries of the Hebrews'.
However, Pico was emphatic that the message was not for general transmission:

> But to reveal to the plebs the more secret mysteries, hidden within the
> shell of the law and the rough covering of words, to expose the supreme
> secrets of God, what was that if not to give the holy to dogs and cast
> pearls before swine? It was not therefore an act of human prudence, but
> of divine wisdom to conceal all that from the multitude, to communicate
> it to the initiate, among whom alone Paul says he pronounced words of
> wisdom.[51]

Plato had written in code.

While Ficino toyed only briefly with the ideas of the Dominican fire-
brand Girolamo Savonarola (1452–98), Pico was a strongly committed
enthusiast. It is an attractive speculation that perhaps such attraction
derived from the fact that Savonarola, the ordained Dominican, offered
rather more of a challenge to Augustine than all but a couple of lay humanists. As a prophet, he was presumptuous in predicting the work of God's
providence. More presumptuous still was his scheme to realise the city of
God in Florence, promising that 'the joy of the good citizens will be so great
that their happiness in this world will approach that of spiritual beatitude'.

His scheme also had a practical model in the Venetian Republic. However, while much attention has focused upon his design for a Greater Council on the Venetian model, rather less has been given to the idea that Florence would come under the patronage of St Mark, who, conveniently, was the patron of Savonarola's own convent. According to Donald Weinstein, Augustine would probably have regarded the Dominican as a Donatist heretic.[52]

Humanists of the Petrarchan, civic or Platonist persuasions – despite their protestations of piety – often strained to remain within a pattern of orthodox Christian belief. But ultimately they could only go as far as Augustine would allow. However, in two significant careers it is possible to discern more forthright dissent from Christianity – and even from religion in general. Wisely, neither of them took on Augustine in direct confrontation. Instead, they both used the devilish obliqueness of irony.

Anti-Christian humanism

> Talented, colourful, restless, a disdainful opponent of the temporal claims of the papacy and an acid critic of the pretensions of his own and past ages, Valla typifies the spirit of free inquiry and spiritual independence which many students find to be the essential quality of the Italian Renaissance.[53]

Jerrold Seigel's brilliant characterisation of Lorenzo Valla (1407–57) makes it all the more curious that this humanist has rarely received the attention that he unquestionably deserves, though this is more the case in Anglophone scholarship than in Italian. Scholars working in English do not seem to have added to the deft and incisive strokes of Mandell Creighton, who pointed out at the end of the nineteenth century that Valla was a pupil of Bruni, and an acerbic critic of Poggio: 'If Poggio is the most celebrated literary man of the Early Renaissance, Valla is undoubtedly the man of keenest mind.'[54] Valla's work communicates tremendous intellectual excitement, and he is a pivotal figure in understanding how the Renaissance influenced changes in religious life associated with the Reformation.[55]

In a certain intellectual mischief, and in a delight in the concealment that irony can provide, Valla also shares significant characteristics with Machiavelli. In the *Dialogue on Free Will* (*De libero arbitrio*) of 1440, for instance, he makes no effort to reconcile human freedom of action and divine providence. Like Machiavelli, he sets aside the workings of any divine plan:

So if it was possible for something to happen in another way than it was foreseen, providence is undermined, but if it is impossible, free will is undermined, a thing no less unworthy to God than if we should take away His providence.[56]

In a daring and dangerous discussion of pleasure (*De voluptate*, 1431) he again puts religion aside, referring his readers to Augustine. He writes a debate between the Stoic and Epicurean positions, with a Christian spokesman to adjudicate. This last sets out the Christian doctrine, but also praises the Epicurean (despite identifying him as an 'ironist') above Stoicism, even though Stoicism was far easier to reconcile with Christianity. In discussing whether humans naturally follow virtue or vice, Valla points to the sexual infidelities of Jupiter, and asserts that *voluptas* is a good. It is to be placed among Prudence, Continence, Justice and Modesty, 'not as a whore among good matrons, but as the lady of the house [*domina*] among handmaidens [*ancillae* – the role of the Virgin Mary]'. Wine is a gift of Nature – like speech – and that same Nature visits disasters upon human-kind. While the judgment is clear in identifying and contrasting the tran-sience of earthly pleasure and the eternal joy of the life to come, another dangerous possibility is taking shape: not all pleasure is sin, because not all sin is pleasure (see below, Chapter 7).[57]

Valla's discussion of the abstractions of value systems is complemented by his attacks on the institutional structures of the Church. Serving Alfonso the Magnanimous (king of Naples 1443–58) in his dispute with the papacy, Valla demolished any suggestion of the authenticity of the Donation of Constantine (*De falsa credita et ementita Constantini donatione*, 1440). This docu-ment purported to demonstrate that the bishop of Rome was superior to all other bishops in the Western empire, and to the emperor himself. In an extraordinary combination of meticulous scholarly detail and the most violent rhetorical polemic, Valla demonstrates that there is no historical foundation to the content of the Donation. The language is clumsy and anachronistic, for instance in describing imperial regalia and sleeping arrangements. The forger uses:

> 'concubitores' [bed-watchers] for 'contubernales' [companions or atten-dants]. 'Concubitores' are literally those who sleep together and have intercourse: certainly they must be understood to be whores. He adds those with whom he may sleep, I suppose, so that he may not be afraid of ghosts in the night.

Intriguingly, Valla attributes the work of falsification to the popes' capital sins, their pride and avarice, and unleashes an invective on aspects of the document's 'contradictions, impossibilities, stupidities, barbarisms and absurdities'. And he makes a thunderous criticism of clerical involvements in the affairs of this world: 'But I, if I believe anything, deem nothing more hateful to God and to the rest of humanity than such presumption of clergy in the secular sphere.'[58]

While Valla can readily be linked to Erasmus and Luther, the dangerous implications of what he was saying – which clearly separated religion from politics – find their most uncompromising expression in Machiavelli (1469–1527).

There was a clear, tough strand in ancient thought that acknowledged religion as the creation of the state. The Greek historian Polybius (*c.*200–*c.*118 BC) is unwavering in his analysis of the role of religion in the Roman constitution. This important passage in Book VI, Chapter 56 of his *Histories* is one which Machiavelli may have known:

> However, the sphere in which the Roman commonwealth seems to me to show its superiority most decisively is in that of religious belief. Here we find that the very phenomenon which among other peoples is regarded as a subject for reproach, namely superstition, is actually the element which holds the Roman state together. These matters are treated with such solemnity and introduced so frequently both into public and into private life that nothing could exceed them in importance. Many people may find this astonishing, but my own view is that the Romans have adopted these practices for the sake of the common people. This approach might not have been necessary had it ever been possible to form a state composed entirely of wise men.

Thus, he acknowledges the premise of Plato's *Republic* – 'if philosophers were kings . . .'. He then points out that since philosophers are not kings, a state religion is a necessity. Roman history appears to prove that the Plato who wrote *The Republic* must give place to the Plato who wrote *The Laws*:

> But as the masses are always fickle, filled with lawless desires, unreasoning anger and violent passions, they can openly be restrained by mysterious terrors or other dramatizations of the subject. For this reason I believe that the ancients were by no means acting foolishly or haphazardly when they introduced to the people various notions concerning the gods and belief in the punishments of Hades, but rather the moderns are foolish and take great risks in rejecting them.[59]

It is significant that Augustine has this possibility covered with the unique righteousness of Christianity:

> It was the business of the prudent and wise to make the people err in their true religion and make them not only worship demons, but even imitate them – whose chief desire is to deceive. For just as devils cannot possess anyone but those whom they have deceived; so also men who were princes, certainly not just men, but like devils themselves, taught the people in religion that the things that they knew to be false were true . . . And what weak and unlearned man can avoid the deception of the princes of states and of devils?[60]

But in an astonishing leap of the imagination, Machiavelli gets straight back to Polybius – and makes no exception of Christian states. One does not presume to say that Machiavelli had read Polybius specifically – though that remains a distinct and tantalising possibility.[61] However, at the very least he drew similar conclusions from a reading of ancient history – just as when observing his contemporaries he foreshadowed the conclusions of Shakespeare (see below, Chapter 9). In commenting on Livy, Machiavelli remarks:

> The rulers of a republic or a kingdom must, therefore, maintain the foundations of the religion that they hold; and, having done this, it will be easy for them to keep the state religious, and, as a consequence, good and united . . . And because this is the custom observed by wise men, there arose from it belief in miracles, which are revered even in false religions. For prudent men augment them, no matter their origin, and the authority of miracles increases anyone's faith in the rulers.

What is explosive here is that Machiavelli goes on – without saying so – to defy Augustine's moral distinction between pagan and Christian states. The Florentine identifies the papacy as a source of corruption but at the same time quite naturally compares Christ with the ancient Roman dictator Furius Camillus (445–365 BC) as the founder of a religion. Some Romans had heard a statue of Juno speak and 'their opinion and credulity were strongly encouraged by Camillus and the other rulers of the city'.

> If such a religion had been maintained among the rulers of the Respublica Cristiana as it had been instituted by its founder (*secondo che dal datore d'essa ne fu ordinato*), Christian states and republics would be more united and rather happier than they are.[62]

If we turn from the *Discourses* to *The Prince*, we find no shadows, but instead stark, challenging and intellectually exhausting juxtapositions that demonstrate that Christian virtues may not be appropriate to the ruler of a state. The terms are black and white. For a prince it might be sensible to be avaricious rather than generous, cruel rather than compassionate, deceitful rather than truthful, and so on. These are the characteristics of the instinctive ruler that demonstrate his *virtù*. What controversy that term has generated! This is unsurprising, for Machiavelli overturns both ancient and Christian notions of *virtus*. The Ciceronian quality of being a man (*vir*) gives way to the ruler who needs to be a hybrid animal who combines the strength of a lion with the cunning of a fox.[63] That is well known. It is rarely pointed out, however, that *virtus* was also the quality of Christ himself, the miraculous *virtus* that he sensed coming out of his robe when touched by the woman with the issue of blood in Mark 5:30, the quality that according to Luke 'cured all': 'quia virtus de illo exibat, et sanabat omnes' (Luke 6:19). Given Machiavelli's view that the fickleness of human nature makes man fallen and irredeemable, one is drawn to reflect that in Christ's passion a crowd had cried 'Hosanna!' on Sunday and 'Crucify him!' on Friday (John12:13; 19:15). Machiavelli's prince identified his power to a divine degree with Christ's – thus defying the Redeemer's strict injunction to 'render unto Caesar the things which be Caesar's, and unto God the things which be God's' (Luke 20:25). This was inadmissible, unthinkable, and *The Prince* was consigned to the *Index of Forbidden Books*, in that immense reappropriation of culture by the Church which flowed from the Council of Trent.

Ironically, the appeal of Renaissance culture broadened as a result of its fumigation at the hands of Catholic reformers: should we once again propose a 'Counter Renaissance' in tandem with a 'Counter Reformation'? The restored confidence of the Roman Church, its message unmistakable in the visual arts, found authoritative and authoritarian expression at the council (see below, Chapter 7). At that gathering in 1545, Diego Laínez, later to become Ignatius Loyola's successor as General of the Society of Jesus, destroyed any possibility of compromise regarding the real presence in the consecrated Host. He affirmed that this was a miracle performed in the hands of the priest and in the heart of the true believer. He concluded his oration with a quotation from Augustine:

> The things which you say are to be wondered at, the things which you say are new, the things which you say are false. We are amazed at the things which are to be wondered at, we are wary of the things which are new, we condemn the things which are false.[64]

Postscript

Augustine was at one and the same time both the custodian of the most influential and dangerous aspects of classical culture through his knowledge of Platonism, and the prophet of the Christian era through his conviction that Christianity was a clear progression from paganism. Put another way, he was acutely aware of the dangers of Platonism – the discovery of the ego and the triumph of pride – and interposed his own shadows between those aspects of Platonism and Christian posterity. Augustine is far more 'modern' – in the sense of being topical and having far more influence on the way we are now – than any Renaissance humanist. When Machiavelli set out his 'modern' vision of politics, pleading for the separation of religion from politics, few listened. Luther and Calvin quoted Augustine to demonstrate that religion and politics were one and the same. Our world may believe that such thinking is antiquated and ended with the Wars of Religion in the mid-seventeenth century, or at the very latest in the Enlightenment of the eighteenth century, which so derided superstitious belief. Yet, on a moment's reflection, in Latin America 'liberation theology' owes a vast debt to Augustinian notions of the justification for 'holy violence' that ideologues have deployed since the Crusades. The conflicts in Ireland, the Balkans, Chechnya and the Middle East, the global war with terrorism, all show that the mix of religion and politics is still tragically explosive.

In examining Augustine's enduring influence on the realisation of human experience, one's thoughts are drawn towards Renaissance art. Here again, we find those who thought they were Platonic puppet masters, with their cave walls and shadows. Here again, they flattered and flickered and then had to give way to the all-powerful, unitary vision of the Christian Church. The teaching of Augustine did not permit of alternative imaginations.

7 Space Travellers

Images for Christians

The previous chapter argued that Renaissance humanists, through their attempts to understand the classical age on its own terms, opened a new dimension of time to the imagination by their investigation of the pre-Christian past and its culture. Travel within and exploration of that new dimension were hampered by the constraints of Christianity as represented in particular and most significantly in the ideas of St Augustine. He had been determined that his vision of Christianity would stand between future generations and the ancient Pandora's box of Platonic mysteries. Inside Plato's cave, people chained in the dark, confronted by shadows and illusions, would only feel pain and blindness if they experienced the light of the real world outside. Augustine had an overpowering faith in the truth of Christianity, and it allowed no room for the kind of doubt that might set in if perceptions of space and time departed from his unitary vision. As he set out – with characteristic lack of compromise – in *On True Religion*:

> Accordingly, no one ought to have doubts about the existence of the truth, even if doubts arise for him from every possible quarter. Wherever this is seen, there is light that transcends space and time and all phantasms that spring from spatial and temporal things.[1]

Differently expressed, the Christian God was the source of both reason and authority, and for those wanting in reason, authority was the best guide. That authority would always steer the individual away from the contemplation of nature. As Ernst Cassirer put it, such contemplation was 'nothing but a danger to the one truly immediate relationship, the relationship of the soul to God'. He drives the point home with Augustine's admonition: 'Do not go out, return to your self, in the inner man lies the truth.'[2]

We have seen how humanist scholarship could challenge the value system that identified the Seven Capital Sins as wrong (see above, Chapter 6). This chapter deals with the visual arts, largely painting, and with the exploration of space which the artists of the Renaissance embarked upon. Although very few classical scholars were artists (Leon Battista Alberti was a notable exception), there are striking parallels between the visual arts and humanism in the questioning of traditional Christian values. For in the Platonic cave, control of what appeared to the eye was control of what entered the mind. Much the same can be said of Brunelleschi's exercise in optical illusion (see above, Forewords). The values of many Renaissance artists – indeed the whole notion of appealing to the 'bodily eyes' as an end in itself – were deeply incompatible with the values of Catholic Christianity as stated by St Augustine, its most significant and influential figure. Nonetheless it was possible for the two to reach an accommodation with each other – not precisely a synthesis, but an arrangement whereby certain elements of classical culture were absorbed into the Church's framework and others deemed unacceptable. That was not especially new: the magisterial synthesis of St Thomas Aquinas had accommodated the philosophy of the pagan Aristotle within Christian scholasticism in the thirteenth century.[3] However, the somewhat strained relationship between Renaissance humanism and the Christianity of Augustine was subjected to further pressure by developments in the visual arts.

How could the creation of images be reconciled with the Judaic strictures against images – expressed at the very outset of the Ten Commandments – in Exodus 20:3–6?

> Thou shalt have no other gods before me.
> Thou shalt not make unto thee any graven image, or any likeness of any thing that is in heaven above, or that is in the earth beneath, or that is in the water under the earth:
> Thou shalt not bow down thyself to them, nor serve them: for I the Lord thy God am a jealous God, visiting the iniquity of the fathers upon the children unto the third and fourth generation of them that hate me;
> And shewing mercy unto thousands of them that love me, and keep my commandments.

In a rationalisation which, as we shall see, foreshadows Ignatius Loyola, Augustine provides a clear answer: do not use bodily eyes, use the eyes of the mind. While Moses was away from the children of Israel, receiving the Ten Commandments from God, Exodus tells us that the Israelites began to worship a golden calf. This made Moses so angry that he broke the 'two tables of testimony, tables of stone, written with the finger of God'. Augustine commented:

They did not realise that God was present among them, but all their hope was placed in the presence of a man; and when they could not see the man with their eyes, they began to think that God was no longer there, since it was only through Moses that he had perfected such great things. They sought a man with their bodily eyes, since they had no eyes of the mind with which to see God in Moses.[4]

The further elaboration of such principles in the teachings of the Christian Church on images was the work of St Gregory the Great (c.540–605), who became the first monk to be elected pope, in 590; he was reluctant to abandon the contemplative life in order to take up the active life of the papal office. As pope, he reprimanded Serenus, the bishop of Marseilles, for his destruction of images in a church in his diocese. The cult of icons had come to the West at the turn of the sixth century, and the debate with Serenus in some ways anticipates the iconoclastic controversies of Byzantium.[5] While commending the destruction of idols, Gregory defended the use of pictures as a means of teaching the illiterate the truths of Scripture:

> We commend you indeed for your zeal against anything made with hands being an object of adoration; but we signify to you that you ought not to have broken these images. For pictorial representation is made use of in churches for this reason: that such as are ignorant of letters may at least read by looking at the walls [and seeing] what they cannot read in books.

Serenus's hostility to images compelled Gregory to restate and refine his position: 'For to adore a picture is one thing, but to learn through the story of a picture what is to be adored is another.'[6]

The doctrine was further developed in the late thirteenth century in the works of Gullielmus Durandus. In his *Rationale divinorum officorum*, he begins the chapter on pictures, images, curtains and ornaments by quoting Gregory the Great. Having examined scriptural references to idols, he adds: 'but blame there is none in a moderate use of pictures, to teach how ill is to be avoided and good followed'. Pictures, then, were to provide an unmistakable message of right and wrong: 'pictures are the letters of the laity'.[7] Not all members of the laity were illiterate, but by identifying the laity with illiteracy the passage expresses the clear assumption that literacy was a clerical monopoly. The next great restatement of these principles was to come at the Council of Trent in the mid-sixteenth century (see below). That followed the interlude of the Renaissance, in which the messages of pictures were pre-eminently mistakable, and the problems of distinguishing right from wrong became all the more disturbing.

Artistic calculation

That interlude, in the visual arts as in letters, owed much to the urban context of medieval Italy. For the distinctiveness of that context was that it contained a significant number of literate and numerate laymen who *de facto* challenged the clerical monopoly of learning to which Durandus had referred. Just as the merchant's legacy to humanism lay in his conquest of time through usurious gain, so his legacy to the arts was the conquest of that space that contained the known world's markets – one thinks of the travels of Marco Polo.[8] The connection between mercantile calculation and pictorial geometry, between merchandise and the artist's materials, can be grounded in the specific comparison of a late fourteenth-century merchant handbook with a more or less contemporary manual for painters. The works in question are the *Zibaldone da Canal*, whose author is anonymous, and the *Libro dell'arte* by Cennino Cennini.[9] The striking characteristics that the two works share are, first, a training in solving problems, and second, a training in the choice of materials. Thus, for example, in the *Zibaldone* we find:

> Make me this calculation: there is a barrel that has four stops. And by one of them it empties in a day, and by the second in two, and by the third in 3, and by the fourth in 4. I ask you to draw from all 4 of these stops at the same time; in how many days will that barrel be emptied and at what hour?

The answer is '12/25 of a day'. Sometimes the problems are less prosaic, and have a certain wit and imaginative sparkle that smack of the riddle or the fables of Aesop (who served the fabulously wealthy King Croesus of Lydia, and died around 561 BC). Perhaps one might connect the brainteasers of the *Zibaldone* with the short stories of the *novellisti* such as Boccaccio or those who followed him (see below, Chapter 8):

> Make me this calculation: there is a tower 50 *braccia* high [1 *braccio* was about 0.65 metres, or 23 inches] and at the foot is a serpent that wants to climb up it, and every day it climbs up ½ *braccio* and at night slips back ⅓ *braccio*. I ask you: in how many days will the serpent climb to the top of the tower?

There is a rough but charming sketch to accompany the text, and the answer is 300 days. There is also an illustration for a problem concerning a tower 40 *braccia* high:

> And at its foot is a cat that wants to climb it, and it climbs ¼ in the day

Plate 6 Couriers meeting. Sketch from the *Zibaldone da Canal.*

and at night falls back ¹/₅. And on top of the tower there is a mouse that wants to come down, and it descends ¹/₃ in the day and at night returns upwards ¹/₄.

They meet in 300 days. Another of these practical brain-teasers concerns calculations of time and space:

> Make me this calculation: from Venice to Rome is 200 miles. A courier is at Rome who wants to come to Venice, and he comes in 20 days to Venice. And a courier is in Venice who wants to go to Rome, and he goes from Venice to Rome in 30 days. In how many days will these couriers meet?
>
> This is your right rule: that we must multiply the journey times of the two together and say: 20 times 30 makes 600, and then say: 20 and 30 makes 50. Now divide 600 in 50 parts, and from that comes 12. And in 12 days they meet.
>
> Now you know that the one who comes from Rome to Venice comes 10 miles a day, and he had made 120 miles.
>
> And the one who goes from Venice to Rome goes 6²/₃ miles a day, had made 80 miles. And thus do all similar calculations.[10]

There is a sketch that shows the two couriers meeting and taking refreshment [Plate 6]. What is the impulse that drives our anonymous author to draw pictures as part of the text? It seems to come quite naturally and without pretension. The merchant's impulse to illustrate his book of problems may yet prove to have something in common with Botticelli's 93 drawings for Dante's *Commedia*. These testify to 'Botticelli's passion for literature and to his unmatched skill in translating words into poignant imagery', and date from around 1495.[11] Is such a handbook as the *Zibaldone* perhaps an example of the shift from a verbal culture to a visual one (see above, Chapter 1)?

Certainly, there is an important complementarity between the two handbooks. The style and tone of Cennini's advice to the aspiring painter are very similar. On the preparation of kid parchment:

> When you want to tint kid parchment, it is helpful first to soak it in spring or well water so that it becomes wet and soft. Then, fasten it with large nails, stretched over a board, like a drumskin, and apply the tints to it, much the same as said above, in due course . . .

There follows advice on various shades of tinting. Although Cennini almost certainly did not have an opposition to Augustine in mind, he urged the painter to be guided by 'the triumphal arch of copying from nature', and after the washes, if the artist should strive 'with delight and without hurry' the result will be that 'your shadows are smoky and delicately shaded'. The method of managing shadows is practical and material – shadow, colour, then highlights:

> When you have got this done, take a little white lead well worked with gum Arabic . . . A very little white lead is enough. Have some clear water in a little dish, and moisten this same brush of yours in it; and rub it over this ground white lead in the little dish, but especially if this has gone dry. Then put it on the back of your hand or your thumb, reshaping and pressing the brush, and getting the stuff off, almost clearing it. And begin rubbing the brush flat over and into the places where there are to be highlight and relief; and proceed to go over them many times with your brush, and guide it with feeling. Then, for the extremes of the reliefs, in the highest highlights, take a brush with a sharp point, and with the white lead touching up with the tip of this brush, heighten still further these high lights. Then go on to emphasise with a small brush, with clean ink, marking out the folds, the outlines, noses, eyes, and the hair of the heads and beards.

There is detailed and extensive information on how to waterproof a wall to protect frescoes.[12]

In the matter of colour sense, we can make concrete connections as well as noting similarities. In selecting spices, the merchant must pay particular attention to colour. Ginger should be white rather than dark inside, cloves 'ought to be black and red within, tending more toward black', mace 'big and bright red', cinnamon 'of a reddish colour', myrrh 'a reddish yellow colour inside', galbanum (a gum resin) 'tending in colour toward yellow'. Intriguingly, the author also offers advice on materials that painters might use. There is an obscure comment on the characteristics of white lead, while 'indigo from Baghdad' is a substance which 'ought to be violet and dark within'.[13]

What the merchant might purchase in the Levant, the painter might wish to buy from a local apothecary. Cennino says that in selecting red lac, 'take care to recognise the good kind'. Malachite comes from azurite: 'good in secco with tempera of egg yolk', 'this colour is of itself coarse by nature and looks like fine sand'. Of white lead, which the merchant might have supplied, 'if you wish to recognise the finest sort, always cut some of that on the top of the lump, which is in the shape of a cup'. 'The more you grind it', the painter is advised, 'the more perfect it will be'. Ultramarine requires precious lapis lazuli: 'take that which you see is fullest blue . . . but be careful that it is not the azurite stone'. It also needs pine resin, gum mastic and fresh wax. The best azurite comes from near the silver mines in Germany. An imitation can be made from a combination of two substances already noted in the *Zibaldone*: white lead and Baghdad indigo.[14]

Given such similarities, we may connect the merchant's eye for colour and shade (and his capacity to draw) with the changing perceptions of the spectrum itself. Here, perhaps Alberti's treatise *On Painting* (1436), important as it is, is less significant than Lorenzo Valla's characteristically energetic assault on the traditionalist view of the fourteenth-century jurist Bartolus of Sassoferrato (1314–57). According to Bartolus's *Treatise on Signs and Arms*, the spectrum begins with gold as the colour of the sun and goes on to 'sapphire-colour' as that of air, though he then makes white the noblest of colours, black the basest. Valla argues that the brightness of the sun is white, not gold. 'Why do we dye silk purple or white linen red, unless we find red more attractive than white?' he asks. He extols the blackness of Ethiopians, and points out that the Creator gave man a black pupil at the centre of the eye that observes creation.[15]

Valla's rhetoric, in putting forward an emphatically new way of perceiving the colours of nature, should not distract us from an examination of the continuing links between mercantile activity and artistic theory in the fifteenth century. Such links are exemplified in the life of Luca Pacioli (*c*.1445–1517). A Franciscan and a student of Plato, Pacioli was the author of the first treatise on double-entry book-keeping, published in Venice in

1494, an expression of the impulse to measure and quantify which, according to Alfred Crosby, was crucial to the world role of European 'capitalism'.[16] Pacioli's knowledge of the works of Plato led him to produce a work, *On Divine Proportion* (1509), moving from the arithmetic of the account book to the geometry of painters. He knew Alberti, and Leonardo provided some of his illustrations. [O.65]

Perhaps most significant of all, he was the friend of Piero della Francesca (1410/20–92). There are resonances between Pacioli's ideas on proportion and those that Piero expressed in his *On Perspective in Painting* and in his great pictures, such as *The Flagellation*, underpinned as it is with uncompromising geometrical precision. It gives pause for thought that Piero was also the author of *A Treatise on the Abacus*, an instrument of calculation more likely to figure in the education of the Renaissance artist than was Latin. Differently expressed, the connection between painting and mercantile activity is in many ways stronger than the connection between painting and humanistic thought.[17] As a visual impression, some of the points on the lines of Piero's systematised perspectival drawings resemble beads on the wire of the merchant's calculator. [Plate 7] However, Piero's sense of unwavering control and rational calculation is only one polarity of Renaissance image-making. Its opposite was abandonment to sensual – and sexual – pleasure.

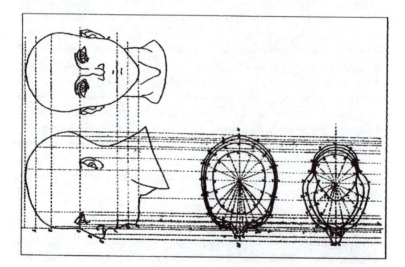

Plate 7   Piero della Francesca, *Diagram for foreshortening the head, c.*1480–90. In his *Of the perspective of painting.*

Grace, love – and blindness

As noted in the case of humanistic learning, so too in the visual arts, the recovery of pagan antiquity represented a challenge to the values that the Christian Church sought to inculcate in its members. Full-blooded, uninhibited indulgence in the rites of Bacchus was an overt celebration of gluttony, lechery and sloth. This is apparent from works such as Giovanni Bellini's *Feast of the Gods* (1514) in Ferrara. [Plate 8] The picture mocks its 'decidedly un-Olympian' gods. Neptune and Gaia, whose wedding is the cause for celebration, are drunk. The god Priapus was the ancient protector of gardens, and genitalia. Lest we should be in doubt as to the explicit nature of this role, he was sometimes distinguished in classical literature by the adjective 'phallus'. In this picture he attempts lewdly to molest the sleeping Vesta, protectress of virgins, and is prevented from doing so only by the braying of an ass, which frightens him off.[18] Bellini was about 80 years of age when he painted this, and he was evasive about accepting the commission from Isabella d'Este, suggesting that he may have been a pioneer in standing up to the demands of his patrons in defence of his own artistic tastes and convictions. As the humanist cardinal Pietro Bembo (1470–1547) tactfully explained to Isabella, Bellini

Plate 8 Giovanni Bellini, *Feast of the Gods*, 1514. Washington, DC, National Gallery.

does not like to be given many written details which cramp his style; his way of working, he says, is always to wander at will in his pictures, so that they can give satisfaction to himself as well as to the beholder.[19]

It is likely that Bellini's younger contemporary, Titian, made alterations to the older master's composition. Titian himself was to paint three works for the d'Este palace between 1518 and 1524. The first of them shows *Offerings to Venus* (1518–19): a throng of little Cupids gambols before a graven image of the goddess of love. [Plate 9] Many of them eat apples, some fly to pick them from the trees. There are plenty of references to apples in classical myth: the Apple of Discord that caused the Trojan War, the one that caused Atalanta to lose her race, the apples of the Hesperides that Hercules had to labour for – and Genesis does not specify that apples were the fruit of the tree of knowledge. But might one infer from this picture the innocence both of eating forbidden fruit and of the worship of original

Plate 9   Titian, *Offerings to Venus*, 1518–19. Madrid, Prado.

Plate 10   Titian, *Bacchus and Ariadne*, 1520–23. London, National Gallery.

sin? In the second of Titian's paintings for Ferrara, *Bacchus and Ariadne*, which dates from 1520–3, the distraught woman whom Theseus has abandoned encounters the god of wine and his drunken followers, some of whom carry the limbs of the animals they have torn apart. [Plate 10] In the third work, *Bacchanal of the Andrians* (1523–4), naked gods swill the fruit of the vine, consumption of which is the privilege of humans alone in all earthly creation and elevates them above the animal kingdom. In a perverse way, the wine that can reduce human beings to the senseless condition of a beast is also a mark of their special place in the scheme of creation. A beautiful nymph lies unconscious at the front, an ironic re-invention of the prostrate figure of drunken Silenus in the background. The innocent child urinating is part of the full-throttle orgy, a wild revelry which is nevertheless orchestrated by the master in the rhythms of the dance.[20] [Plate 11]

Animal pleasures are still more in evidence in the work of Piero di Cosimo (1462–1521), especially in *Battle of Lapiths and Centaurs*, about which

Plate 11 Titian, *Bacchanal of the Andrians*, 1523–4. Madrid, Prado.

we know little, except that it probably dates from the 1490s. However, this is another wedding feast – which the half-beast centaurs have disrupted – in which lewd bestiality entices, fascinates and seduces, and importunately removes the apparently secure barrier that separates pleasure from pain. [Plate 12]

In all these instances, nature itself can seem morally neutral, impassively cruel or even actively so. However, it may seem odd to locate so curious a figure as Piero di Cosimo within a broader tendency. Many contemporaries thought him quite mad. He was certainly perverse, being both recluse and showman. He loathed cultivation but loved nature in the wild. According to Vasari:

> He did not allow anyone to dig up or prune the fruit trees that grew in his garden, but indeed let vines grow and the shoots trail to the ground; no one ever lopped his fig trees or any others: on the contrary he was content to see everything wild, like his own nature, saying that one

Plate 12 Piero di Cosimo, *Battle of Lapiths and Centaurs*,1490s. London, National Gallery.

needed to leave nature's own things to her to care for, without doing anything more in the matter.

He was famous for his carnival floats, one of which was of 'strange and horrible, and unexpected novelty'. It was quite out of keeping with the spirit of carnival, not the least because its centrepiece was the chariot of Death, complete with actors costumed as skeletons. He did not like fire, even in cooking – he apparently lived off hard-boiled eggs that he cooked when he was making glue – and he was terrified of lightning. His patrons were not influential, though he produced a portrait of Cesare Borgia.[21] That is a connection that strengthens the identification of Piero as a true original, rather like Machiavelli, as opposed to a mere one-off eccentric. For him, it was a short step to identify the pagan gods as forces of nature. Moreover, exploiting antique myth, he explored the possibilities that humans developed from other forms of animal life. The implication that man was not made by God in the image of God is startlingly clear. As Erwin Panofsky brilliantly argued, Piero evokes 'an age older than Christianity', and, quite remarkably, he begins to develop an evolutionary vision of human society.[22] Fire – which caused the artist such terror – is crucial to the evolution, and the legends of Vulcan, the god of fire, and Prometheus, the human who dared to steal fire from heaven, figure prominently in the artist's work. [O.66; O.67] His scenes from what is known as *Human Life in the Stone Age* show half-beasts hunting. According to Panofsky, these scenes connect to other panels in New York and Oxford and form a series in which fire is decisive in enabling humans to separate their own existence from that of animals and to domesticate some creatures for their own purposes. [Plates 13, 14, and 15]

Piero appears to have been strongly influenced by a passage from Vitruvius Pollio, an architect from the first century AD known to us only by a remarkable treatise on his profession. Boccaccio had inserted the passage verbatim into his *Genealogy of the Gods* in the mid-fourteenth century. According to Vitruvius, the discovery of how to keep fire burning was the origin of society. Within its own terms of reference, the passage presents a thesis of natural evolution that is replicated in the paintings:

> Under men's ancient custom, they were born in woods and caves and groves, and they kept alive by eating raw food. Meanwhile, in a certain place, dense trees, swirling around in storms and winds, and rubbing branches one with another, sparked fire. Terrified by the flame, those who were around the place fled. When calm was restored, as they drew near, and noticed what a great comfort to their bodies was the warmth of the fire, they added wood, and, keeping it alive, they summoned some

Plate 13 Piero di Cosimo, *Human Life in the Stone Age: Hunting Scene*, 1490s. New York, Metropolitan Museum.

Plate 14 Piero di Cosimo, *Human Life in the Stone Age: Return from the Hunt*, 1490s. New York, Metropolitan Museum.

171

Plate 15 Piero di Cosimo, *Human Life in the Stone Age: Landscape with Animals*, 1490s. Oxford, Ashmolean.

of their fellows, and, gesticulating, they showed them the uses which they might have of it.

When they congregated, they made sounds which were the origins of speech, and 'because of the discovery of fire a beginning of human association was born among men'. The recognition of being set above the rest of creation led them to stop crawling and to walk erect, which in turn freed the use of their hands and 'some few imitating the nests and constructions of the swallows, made places of mud and twigs into which they might go'.[23] Boccaccio then rehearses formulaically the apologia and explanation that, of course, Vitruvius knew nothing of the Creation as set out in the Bible. Many faithful Christians may have taken the biblical story of the Garden of Eden as a metaphor or parable rather than as a literal account. Yet what Boccaccio transmits from Vitruvius is an intensely materialist concept of the cosmos, which derives from the Greek philosopher Epicurus (342–270 BC).

The revival of such ideas gave a physicality to grace and love, which was unsettling to Christian versions of such concepts as, in essence, divine gifts. For example, in Vasari's works grace is the supreme quality of a painting, as judged by the eye, which responds to 'a certain correct harmony in the proportions'. It is a natural quality, unforced and innate – not to be acquired through study.[24]

Manifestations of the new concepts of grace and love can be found in two of the most mysterious of Renaissance masterpieces. Some words of caution are necessary at this point. What is offered here is not 'the key to their meaning'. Rather, the point is that even when the interpretative possibilities are as diverse as they are in such cases, then in the representation of grace and love, what the observer may say need not be controversial.

Botticelli's *Primavera* (*c*.1478) has generated enormous debate,[25] yet the following observations seem to have gained general acceptance. [O.68] First, there is a Platonic progression from the darkness on the right of the picture to the light on the left. The presiding figure is Venus, and the Cupid above her aims (albeit blindly) toward the group of the Three Graces, interacting as love (*amor*), beauty (*pulchritudo*) and pleasure (*voluptas*). The narrative of the scene is contained within the rhythms of the seasons, without reference to the liturgical year of the Church. What we have here, then, are varieties of Grace and a goddess of love: grace and love without Christian connotations.

The painting by Titian that we know as *Sacred and Profane Love* (*c*.1514) did not originally have such a title, but it is a painting of twin Venuses. [O.69] At first glance, the clothed figure seems modest and restrained, the naked one beautiful but expressing her spirit through the glory of her body.

Yet it is the naked figure that is the more elevated, the clothed figure more earthbound, and it is the naked body that has shed the material constraints of clothing. It is as though the Cupid who stirs the water in the cistern on which they sit – itself decorated with a pagan bas relief of bestial love – is muddling our perceptions of which Venus is which.[26]

The erotic desire that physical beauty could excite at the prospect of pleasure was completely contrary to Christian ideals. For Augustine, the kind of sensual desire that could be provoked by what the eye saw was the enemy of chastity. As he put it in the *Rule* of his own religious order:

> You cannot say that your inner attitude is good if with your eyes you desire to possess a woman, for the eye is the herald of the heart. And if people allow their impure intentions to appear, albeit without words but just by looking at each other and finding pleasure in each other's passion, even though not in each other's arms, we cannot speak any longer of true chastity, which is precisely that of the heart.[27]

In contrast to Augustine's strictures, one should note the persistent intervention of Cupid in Renaissance representations of love. His innocence is decidedly compromised by his role as matchmaker, by his arrows of desire, and by the fact that he sometimes shoots blindfold. Love is blind. Cupid's name gives rise to the term *cupiditas* or 'inordinate desire', and his Greek name, Eros, to all that could be associated with the erotic.[28] [O.70]

By the end of the fifteenth century, a revolution had taken place with regard to the limits of what a painter might place in front of the eyes of his audience. It is vital to emphasise how limited the contemporary audience was. Paintings in a princely palace in Ferrara, or the less grand houses of Piero di Cosimo's patrons, such as Francesco Pugliese or Giovanni Vespucci, were intensely private possessions, not for general consumption. It was to be the Church's revived message that reached the unlettered masses. Yet, like the humanists, the artists of the Renaissance were happy to communicate to posterity – to us. That communication – limited, perhaps, but long-term, certainly – outweighed any considerations of instant celebrity. This is what made painting a liberal and noble pursuit.[29] Such considerations are far more important than notions of 'the rise of the artist' in terms of social status, because they were the preconditions of such a rise. Put another way, while Christian images had been – and were to become again – the books of the illiterate, the naturalising art of the Renaissance overtly offered the instantaneous gratification of the senses. It was precisely for this reason of the sheer speed of sensual response that no less a figure than Leonardo made painting superior to poetry:

Now, see what difference there is between hearing an extended account of something that pleases the eye and seeing it instantaneously, just as natural things are seen. Yet the works of the poets must be read over a long span of time. Often there are occasions when they are not understood and it is necessary to compose various commentaries, and very rarely do the commentators understand what was intended by the mind of the poet. And many authors do not read out more than a small part of their work through lack of time. But the work of the painter is instantaneously accessible to his spectators.[30]

Leonardo's infinite curiosity concerning the works of nature may have given him a greater sense of rational assurance with regard to the purpose of painting. Others, Botticelli among them, appear to have been troubled by the tensions between pagan and Christian themes in their work. Sandro Botticelli (c.1445–1510) was among the followers of Savonarola, and he may have sympathised with the preacher's condemnation of worldly things – including worldly pictures – to the bonfires of the vanities.[31]

However, there was to be a fleeting moment of synthesis in which the art of the High Renaissance achieved its supreme illusion: that Christianity and pagan philosophy were compatible, and comfortably so. In an important sense, that synthesis found a parallel in the work of Machiavelli, who saw a rapidly fading opportunity for the secular unification of Italy in a Medicean papacy that could link the power of Florence with that of Rome and extend throughout the peninsula to expel the barbarian invaders.[32] Machiavelli's reconciliation of the papacy with Italian secular politics is worth mentioning in that the work of synthesis in the visual arts was achieved at the same time under papal patronage.

Poignantly, this transitory moment is preserved in works of art that are timeless. In one of the papal apartments in the Vatican, the Stanza della Segnatura, Raphael worked for first Julius II and then Leo X between 1509 and 1511. Facing each other on opposite walls are two antithetical frescoes that seem as naturally harmonious in their humanity as a secular Monteverdi madrigal tune that sets sacred words. One scene, *The School of Athens*, represents pagan philosophy, the other, the *Disputa* or *Disputation concerning the Blessed Sacrament*, Christian theology. The former also includes a 'dispute' between the central figures of Plato and Aristotle. Plato points upward toward the heavens, Aristotle's palm extends towards a grasp of the earthly. Every figure in the crowded scene speaks of intellectual energy and inquiry: one, to the right, is too busy making his point even to sit down, and scribbles rapidly on a tablet balanced on his crossed knees as he stands on one leg and leans against a wall. To the fore is the geometer Euclid (*fl. c.*300

BC), and nearby the statuesque figure of Heraclitus contemplates – or at least darkly broods. Heraclitus (540–475 BC) was a Greek philosopher who foreshadowed the materialism of Epicurus and whose ideas offered a stark alternative to Christian cosmology. He believed everything to be in a permanent state of flux – nothing is born and nothing dies – and he wept at the folly and frailty of humanity. The identification between this scene and Raphael's own time is absolute. Plato appears to be a portrait of Leonardo, Heraclitus of Michelangelo. Euclid is the architect Donato Bramante (c.1444–1514), who built new streets in Rome for Julius II and in the tempietto at San Pietro in Montorio reused for the first time since antiquity the full Doric order. Raphael has included a self-portrait in a group to the right. The scene is contained within a great arching stoa, which is a miracle of perspective, both the architecture and its representation awesome in their evocation of the achievements of humankind. [O.42]

By contrast, the Christian *Disputa* takes place in the open air, directly beneath God's heaven. Nothing interferes with the translation of the celestial Word to earthly flesh, and all intellectual energy is focused on the miracle that brought the Son of God to live – and die – among men. The Fathers of the Church, the popes, the founders of religious orders, scholastics, and the lay poet Dante stand to either side of the altar, above which is the Redeemer with his stigmatised hands, flanked by the Virgin and the Baptist and by ranks of prophets and saints. God the Father connects the Word made flesh to the sublime, completing the Trinity amid the adoration of six weightless angels. [O.41] It is one of Raphael's supreme achievements that these two representations, one of classical philosophy, the other of Christian theology, should seem to be at one within the apartments of the pope.

Blind faith?

Michelangelo's work in the Vatican is more significant still, since it bears testimony not only to the great synthesis, but also to the recognition of its artificiality. The great project of the Sistine ceiling and its *ingegnere* tells us much about the religious ambiguities of the age (see above, Chapter 5). Like Botticelli, Michelangelo had been among the *piagnoni* who followed Savonarola. The ceiling is assured in its combination of ancient philosophy and Christian teaching. [O.56] The culminating image in the philosophical schema reverses the narrative. In the realm of pure spirit, God's first act is the separation of light from darkness. That first act in the creation of the world sets what is *chiaro* on one side and what is *scuro* on the other. It does not create a spectrum of colours, it creates a distinction in literally black and white terms. [O.8] That certainty of difference became muddled by the Fall.

In his later work, Michelangelo seems to want to return to the certainty of black and white, and his conclusion is inescapable: pagan and Christian philosophy cannot be seen as equal partners, and the former must be subordinated to the latter. It is misleading to characterise the transformation of Michelangelo's thinking as 'surrender'. It might be more accurate to say that in his later work, he chose to lose his single self in the infinity of Christ's love. Thus, in the *Last Judgment* (1541) it is Christ who opens graves and wakes their sleepers, Christ who lets them forth. [O.57] Michelangelo, himself known as 'il divino', the divine one, is no more than a self-portrait on the empty, flayed skin of St Bartholomew. [O.58] There is a still later self-portrait in the Vatican in his *Conversion of St Paul* (c.1550). Shown as Saul himself, there is no philosophical certainty for Michelangelo here: he is just a man grovelling toward faith to relieve his blindness, a blindness that only Christ's love can cure. [O.59]

In an important sense, Michelangelo's spirituality paves the way for the Council of Trent's pronunciation on images. In a dramatic and rock-like restatement of the principles of Augustine, of Gregory and of Durandus, in the 25th session of December 1563 the Council decreed on the 'legitimate use of images' and set down how idolatry was to be avoided. Images of Christ, the Virgin, and the other saints are due 'honour and veneration':

> not that any divinity, or virtue, is believed to be in them, on account of which they are to be worshipped; or that anything is to be asked of them; or, that trust is to be reposed in images, as was of old done by the Gentiles who placed their hope in idols, but because the honour which is shown them is referred to the prototypes which those images represent.

Gregory the Great's ideas on pictures as a means of instruction in the stories of the Scriptures are clearly re-invented:

> And the bishops shall carefully teach this, – that by means of the histories of the mysteries of our Redemption, portrayed by paintings or other representations, the people is instructed and confirmed in remembering, and continually revolving in mind the articles of faith.

There can also be no doubt as to how the unlettered are to use their eyes:

> And if at times, when expedient for the unlettered people [*indoitae plebi*]; it happen that the facts and narratives of sacred Scripture are portrayed

and represented; the people shall be taught, that not thereby is the Divinity represented, as though it could be seen by the eyes of the body, or be portrayed by colours or figures.[33]

As Augustine and, much later, Ignatius Loyola taught, the eyes of the body must be trained to defer to the eyes of the mind.

Yet again, one is prompted to query whether such teaching should be seen as a response to Protestantism, a 'Counter Reformation'. The Catholic revival was also an awakening to the dangers of a culture seduced by the fascinating tricks of pagan antiquity. One of the questions that might be said to have animated the revival is this: since God had begun the world through the separation of light from darkness, is it not presumptuous of his best-loved creature to toy with shadows?

The sense of space as an infinity could, after all, mean an infinity of nothing. Leonardo recognised this:

> This may be demonstrated by zero or nothing, that is to say, the tenth figure in arithmetic, which is represented by an '0', which is in itself nothing, but if it is placed after the unit it will make ten, and if you should put two after the unit it will make one hundred, and so on infinitely – the number to which it is joined always growing by ten times. But in themselves the noughts themselves do not have any value other than nought, and all the noughts in the universe are equal to a single nought with respect to substance and value.[34]

And if infinity is nothing, then there is nothing in it to see, and the quest for the sublime ends in blindness.[35] Leonardo began many projects, but completed only a handful, and may have felt acutely the tension between the infinity of everything and the infinity of nothing. The sense of blindness in the void was to find its most harrowing expression in *King Lear* (see below, Chapter 9).

The decrees of the Council of Trent are often portrayed as dogmatic and authoritarian – but were they not also a shield for the simple against the anxiety and pain that are the results of exposure to complexity and uncertainty? It is telling that the Catholic revival was to set down much deeper roots in broader society than the culture of the Italian Renaissance ever achieved. Perhaps this was because of the twin and parallel processes which the Catholic revival fostered in humanistic learning and the visual arts. Just as scholasticism reabsorbed humanism, so Renaissance art was accommodated anew within an ecclesiological framework.

This chapter has been largely concerned with painting, and the success of the Catholic revival in reaching out to the flock is evident in the pictorial images of the Redeemer, the Virgin, and saints which bombarded the eyes of Catholic churchgoers. However, two still grander examples suggest themselves, one in architecture, one in sculpture – both in Rome.

Julius II's project for the rebuilding of St Peter's was so vast in its conception that raising the funds to finance it strained every purse string, every sinew. Given the resistance of the monarchies of England, France and Spain to any suggestion that the pope had a right to tax their subjects on his own behalf, the burden fell on fragmented Germany. The sale of indulgences for the rebuilding programme notoriously prompted Luther's protest. This is both ironic and tragic, in that Julius's plans were at least as expressive of a religious renascence as they were of his own ego. Michelangelo's design for the new basilica and its square did not come to fruition in his own lifetime, yet the eventual construction surely displays every classical device, every expression of classical harmony, proportion and symmetry in the service of Holy Church. (Does not the classical Capitol of the secular state in Washington, D.C., resemble St Peter's?) Yet the new church is the concrete embodiment of that 'splendour of holiness' that was the watchword of the Catholic revival. [O.71]

The interior moved slowly to its final form in the seventeenth century. Another of the expressions of classical culture in the service of the Church was Gianlorenzo Bernini's (1598–1680) Baldacchino, its twisting columns imitating the imperial emblem of Rome.[36] Around 1650, Bernini completed a statue for the church of Santa Maria della Vittoria in Rome. This depicts the *Ecstasy of Santa Teresa*. [O.72; and cf. O.70] The Spanish mystic described in her spiritual autobiography a frequent heaven-sent vision in which an angel repeatedly pierced her heart with a lance representing the love of God:

> He was not tall, but short, and very beautiful, his face so aflame that he appeared to be one of the highest types of angel who seem to be all afire. . . . I saw a long golden spear in his hands and at the end of the iron tip there appeared a point of fire. This he seemed to put through my heart several times so that it penetrated to my entrails. When he withdrew it, I thought he was taking them with it and he left me all ablaze with a great love for God. So great was the pain that it made me give several moans; and so excessive was the sweetness caused by this very great pain that one cannot want it to stop, nor is the soul content.[37]

In the angel's small stature, in his smiling cherubic features, in the flame on the lance's point, and in the arrow with which Bernini replaces the lance, might one not discern a Cupid who has put his *cupiditas* in the service of the Christian God? Put another way, is *cupiditas* now the servant of *caritas*? Is erotic love now in thrall to spiritual love?[38] The repeated plunges that seem to draw out the saint's entrails, along with her apparent blindness in a pose that is suggestive of intercourse, convey a spiritual ecstasy inseparable from erotic climax. And still the statue remains reverent towards its subject and surroundings by placing the experience of the love of God on the highest imaginable spiritual plane.

Monuments to the power of the papacy in the capital of the popes themselves might be thought limited in their expression of how far the 'message' of the Catholic revival may have extended. It is revealing to reflect, however, on how far the revival was to penetrate the culture of the Italian state that was most resistant to papal claims.

Venice and the Catholic revival

At first sight, it seems odd to connect Venice with the changes that are identified with the revival of the Church of Rome, for both cultural and political reasons. In the works of Giovanni Bellini and Titian in Ferrara, as we have already seen, the colouristic tradition was readily associated with pagan sensuality (see above). We might add to the list at this point images of erotic coyness such as Titian's *Venus of Urbino*, or the sexual abandon of his *Danaë*, and the strangely matter-of-fact nudity of Giorgione's *Concert champêtre*. [O.73; O.74; O.75] In politics, the Republic consciously assumed the imperial and apostolic identities of Rome itself following the sack of 1527, after which Venice alone retained its independence of the invading powers (see above, Chapters 3, 5). Venice having withstood papal interdicts in 1482 and 1509, there was a further crisis in relations with the papacy in 1606. During the interdict of that year, the English ambassador, Sir Henry Wotton, wrote home that the Republic was on the brink of turning Protestant. He had even hired a Calvinist preacher to come from Geneva to hasten the event, and thought it likely that the Republic would join a European alliance of powers hostile to the papacy and the Spanish monarchy.

> The State useth me with much kindness, and I protest unto your Lordship [the earl of Salisbury] I think hereafter they will come nearer unto his Majesty [James I], not only in civil friendship, but even in religion. I have, upon the inclination of things that way, begun to take order for an Italian preacher from Geneva whatsoever it cost me, out of shame that in this kind, the disseminators of untruth do bear from us the praise of diligence.[39]

When the Roman Inquisition arrived in Venice in 1547, the state was careful to ensure its own representation on the tribunal and to link the investigation of suspected heresy to its own magistracy dealing with blasphemy.[40] Yet we should remember that in 1573 the painter Paolo Veronese was summoned to explain particular features of a Last Supper which seemed indecorous and forced to change the title of the piece (see above, Chapter 1). [O.76] There is further paradox in the career of Jacopo Tintoretto (1518–94). This most Venetian of masters appears never to have worked outside his native city. He painted few mythological or classical compositions relative to his vast output of pictures on religious subjects. Among the latter, he produced at least nine versions of the Last Supper, celebrating the miracle of transubstantiation. Significantly, the one in the church of San Marcuola (1547) shows the scene of the first celebration of the first host as contemporaneous with charitable works for the needy, in this case represented by a widow and her fatherless child. Thus, at one and the same time, Tintoretto celebrates the doctrine of the 'real presence' of Christ's body and blood in the wafer and wine and asserts the efficacy of good works. The patrons of the piece were the officers of San Marcuola's Confraternity of the Blessed Sacrament. [O.77] There is a similar formulation in the *Last Supper* that the artist painted for the church of San Polo.[41] [O.78] Tintoretto's oeuvre, so particularly Venetian in its attachments and resonances, yet so infused with the spirituality of the Catholicism emanating from Rome, illustrates a highly significant point. Venice was ostensibly resistant to Roman influence, and often outright hostile to it. Yet the city was penetrated to the core by the values of the Catholic revival – to the extent that any clear-cut classical Renaissance in the city is scarcely visible between the earlier traditions of the Gothic and the Byzantine and the later, yet precocious, manifestations of the Baroque.[42] But then the Venetian Republic, for all its apparent secularism, had inherited from Byzantium a political identity that was inseparable from religion. It may well be that the attractiveness of extending a religious and political message that the state could regulate outweighed even the Republic's suspicions of the Roman papacy.

The dispersal of shadows

That is a speculative point peculiar to the history of Venice. In more general terms, it is important to be aware of the attractiveness of revived doctrines that reached out, without condescension, to simple people and helped them to avoid complexity and pain – just as Augustine would have wished. Among the saints whose superhuman powers of charity and endurance came to be celebrated in pictures were those associated with the new religious orders, most notably the Society of Jesus, which was formally approved by the pope in 1540. Did the Society's founder, St Ignatius Loyola (1491–1556), ever visit the Sistine Chapel when he was in Rome? It is certainly possible, even likely, that he did. What might the eyes of his mind have made of the *Separation of Light from Darkness*? While any connection between Ignatius's thought and Michelangelo's fresco remains a matter of speculation, *The Spiritual Exercises* (first published in 1548) express a loudly harmonious conclusion – avoid shadows:

> If we wish to be sure that we are right in all things, we should always be ready to accept this principle: I will believe that the white that I see is black, if the hierarchical Church so defines it.[43]

This statement, in the clearly set down section of the *Exercises* dealing with 'Rules for Thinking within the Church', proclaimed that the management of shadows had passed back to the Church. The great experiment was over. Augustine would have been satisfied, but not surprised.

The coincidence of Ignatius's ideas with those of Augustine is captured in what a distinguished Jesuit scholar of our own time has to say about Augustine's views on the arts. In discussing Augustine's ideas on 'art and the Christian intelligence', Robert J. O'Connell cites a key passage from Augustine's *On True Religion*:

> Point me out one who sees, not one who merely cavils, and wants to appear to see what he does not see. Give me a man who can resist the carnal senses and the impressions which they impose on the mind; one who can resist human custom and human praise, who suffers the stings of conscience on his bed and restores his soul, who loves not external vanities nor seeks lies.

He continues: 'these imaginary things are false, and what is false cannot be known', and concludes: 'that is the true light which enables you to know that these things are not true'.[44] Father O'Connell's conclusion is unqualified – and devastating: 'Augustine has here signed the death warrant of all art'. He goes on:

> It is no small irony that the hand that signed was the one which wrote one of the Western world's greatest literary masterpieces, the *Confessions*. Incomparable triumph of human sensibility and imagination, its burden, when scrutinized in depth, is an uncompromising call for the utter annihilation of both.[45]

8   Soundscapes

New voices

Language, literature and music relate to humanism and the visual arts in many different ways. For instance, the humanist preoccupation with Latin, especially in the fifteenth century, was to stunt the development of a national Italian language. As for music, both Plato and Augustine thought it was something for the authorities to monitor and censor, something that should find expression only in prescribed forms. Plato was suspicious of the artist as a 'maker of phantoms', and in particular, he disapproved of allowing musicians 'to teach whatever rhythm or tune' they might choose. Augustine's *On Music* was his only venture into the field of aesthetics in all the vast corpus of his works. That tract was to prove a kind of prelude to *On True Religion*, which, as we saw in the previous chapter, dealt so crushing a blow to the artistic imagination. It seems to have been imagination that both Plato and Augustine hated because it was something that was essentially secular, and kept the soul below the level to which reason might hope to ascend. In music, as in the other arts, the imagination indulged *vanitas* and stalled a progression to *veritas*. In both notation and poetry, the mind was dealing with 'temporal measures'. Perhaps Augustine felt moved to write on music because music removed the distinction between matter and form, something particularly troubling to him given the 'symphonic' qualities of his later *Confessions*. As Walter Pater put it, 'all art aspires towards the condition of music'. The very abstraction of music – reflected in the problems of writing about it – was something of a challenge to the idea that only God can create something from nothing.[1]

Yet music was an integral part of Renaissance culture, and may have served to liberate creative energies from the strictures of Plato and Augustine. There are, for instance, many depictions of music and conversation in Renaissance pictures. The idea of musical accompaniment as a natural and integral part of life and especially of social intercourse is perhaps one of the most obviously 'modern' features of Renaissance cultures. Contemplating Lorenzo Costa's group of musicians singing and playing, or the angels in Piero's Nativity scene, can seem like turning on the radio, or sending in a request for a favourite piece of music. [O.79; O.80]

Baldassare Castiglione characterised his dialogue, *The Courtier*, as a 'portrait' which evokes conversation in a debate about the attributes of the perfect courtier. Among the most important of these are speaking properly and accomplished musicianship.[2] Indeed, an uncultivated man's incapacity to recognise a slide trombone is a source of ridicule:

> And when one of his friends asked him what sort of music pleased him most of all he had heard, he said: 'They were all good. But among the others, I saw someone playing a strange sort of trumpet which with every move he poked down his throat more than two palms' length, and then at once drew it out, and again poked it down; and you never saw a greater marvel.' Then everyone began to laugh, recognising the false thought of the man who had imagined that the musician was poking down his throat that part of the trumpet that hides itself as it re-enters.[3]

Famously, the chief characteristic of the courtier was *sprezzatura*, an ease, grace, effortlessness and lack of affectation in action and speech. The 'natural' character of the type of *conversazione* in which the courtier engaged – as Castiglione acknowledged – readily translated into paint, often with a musical theme: in Titian's *Concert* (1510–12), for instance. Sometimes, landscape merged with soundscape, for example in Giorgione's (or Titian's) *Pastoral Concert* (1510–12). [O.81; O.75] With a little variation and stretch, such a template could work with both allegorical and mythological subject matter. Titian depicted the *Three Ages of Man* (1512–13) with musical accompaniment from the pipes, and there are two very similar musical Venuses, one shown with an organist (1550), the other with a lutanist (1560), both in celebration of love, poetry and music, of the beauty of soul, body and sound. [O.82; O.83; O.84]

There was a parallel development in depictions of religious subjects. Traditionally, representations of the Madonna and Child with saints and sometimes donors had conformed to the rigid spatial definitions of the polyptych, a set of panels which made up the entire work (which was usually an altarpiece). However, in the course of the fifteenth century, and markedly in the sixteenth, the separate panels gave way to a unitary space in which landscape replaced gold background, and in a natural setting the holy figures related naturally to each other. This type of composition came to be known as the *sacra conversazione* (holy conversation). Giovanni Bellini painted many such pictures. Two especially fine examples, both of which include angels playing musical instruments, were for the churches of San Giobbe (1483/5) and San Zaccaria (1505) in Venice. Both are fascinating instances of tradition and innovation, since they feature, in oils, niches decorated with gold mosaic, which is more readily identified with the two-dimensional iconic style of Byzantium than with Western experiment with realism. Both pictures create an illusion of reality, apparently existing in chapels that extend the spectator's space within the church to a holy world that seems tangible as well as visible. [O.85; O.86]

While those examples may reflect the special significance of the Venetian contribution to Renaissance music, the question of sound could be taken as a barometer for the condition of the entire peninsula. In several imaginative and evocative essays, Peter Burke has explored the soundscapes of the Italian Renaissance. He refers to a wide range of evidence, including Inquisition and other court records, drama and literature, and relates these to a more general idea of behaviour as a species of intricately coded social performance. In pointing to the persistence of Latin, the flourishing slang of low life, new forms of politeness, and an increasing formality after 1500, his work provides a most helpful methodological guide.[4] An investigation into how people spoke and wrote, played and sang, produces some surprising harmonies where hitherto we have found only discord: the relationship within Renaissance culture of 'popular' and 'elite' elements, and the conflict between pagan and Christian beliefs. In particular, this chapter will emphasise two specific features of language and music in the context of the Renaissance. First comes the question of 'elite' and 'popular' culture. Again and again, we have remarked on the failure of cultural developments in the peninsula to set down social roots outside of a courtly or urban elite. Yet in song in particular, we find an interpenetration of the most refined culture of the social elite with the sounds of village and street. Second, previous chapters have pointed out a powerful tension between the exploration of classical culture and the fundamental tenets of the Christian faith. In music, language and literature we can identify an equality of co-existence between the sacred and the secular spheres, and an ease of passage in style and form from one to the other.

Devotional confraternities provide an example of how music harmonised the relationship between ordinary members of the laity and the art of the social elite and between the sacred and the profane. Some of these organisations were significant patrons of paintings. In Venice, such organisations were known as *scuole*. The Scuola Grande di San Giovanni Evangelista, for instance, commissioned an important cycle from masters such as Gentile Bellini and Vittore Carpaccio (*c*.1460/5–1523/6). Carpaccio also worked for the Slav confraternity, decorating their entire hall. In both cases, musicians are prominent. Carpaccio's St Augustine for the Scuola di San Giorgio degli Schiavoni has two visible pieces of polyphonic music in his study. [O.87] From the fourteenth century onwards, the rulebooks of confraternities are written in the local vernacular, not in

Latin. The regulations show particular concern that members should not use blasphemous language. In Venice, the lay brethren stipulate that their religious ceremonies are to be accompanied by organ music which the priests of the church in which they meet had to provide. Following the example of St Francis, of whom more in due course, some Florentine brotherhoods met to sing the praises of the Blessed Virgin in their own words, and such companies were known as *laudesi* from the 'lauds' to which they gave voice.[5]

However, it is equally important to acknowledge that the comfortable syntheses of learned and popular, and of sacred and profane, are both twisted by paradox. While the variety of linguistic and literary forms undoubtedly added immeasurably to the richness and variety of cultural expression, the failure of writers to establish a truly 'Italian' language was both a symptom and a cause of a more general failure to establish a truly 'national' Italian identity. Moreover, in both linguistic and musical development, Italy is not the source of originality, but is deeply indebted to outside influences. This is perhaps even more pertinent to music than to language, because one might argue that what composers achieved in Renaissance Italy is the foundation of both 'classical' and 'popular' music as we use those loose terms in our own times. Within the more limited scope of this book, it is in language and music that we can see new energies at their most dynamic at the end of the Renaissance. The process is one of 'shift' rather than 'decadence', and the voices to which we need to listen most closely are those of the celebrated scientist Galileo Galilei (1564–1642) and the innovatory composer Claudio Monteverdi (1567–1643).[6]

The obvious way of dealing with 'soundscapes' is to offer separate sections on first language and literature and then music. However, the interaction of words and music is so strong, and the legacy of that interaction so significant, that the structure of this chapter is a chronological treatment which follows the traditions of the literary canon: *Trecento* (the fourteenth century), *Quattrocento* (the fifteenth), *Cinquecento* (the sixteenth), and *il Primo Seicento* (the early seventeenth).[7] While the familiar theme of such a division is the *questione della lingua*, the problem of what constituted 'proper' or 'standard' Italian, the argument here is that a *questione della musica* should always hover nearby. In theatrical performance, speech was often close to song, and perhaps it was from this that opera was to develop. On the other hand, Cardinal Pietro Bembo's discourse on platonic love in *The Courtier* may be seen as a prose madrigal. Song in particular had its own eloquence, its own *sprezzatura*. As Giulio Caccini was to put it in a treatise published in 1614, *sprezzatura* is 'charm lent to a song'. Properly disposed notes make the song

pleasant, free and tuneful, just as in everyday speech eloquence and fa-
cility make pleasant and sweet the matters being spoken of. And to the
figures of speech and the rhetorical flourishes in such eloquence correspond the passaggi, tremolos and other such ornaments.[8]

To avoid becoming a chronological catalogue, the successive phases are
characterised in what should be readily recognisable Italian musical terminology. The fourteenth century is presented as an *intrata*, or 'entry', the
fifteenth as an *intermezzo* or 'interlude' dominated in its early stages by the
quest for eloquence in Latin. Then follows the sixteenth century, a period
of joyous creativity tinged with a nostalgia that becomes melancholy (*allegro
non troppo*), and finally come the brilliant inventions of Galileo and
Monteverdi which mark a close (*cadenza*). This heightens the paradox that
Italian terminology became the common language of the Western musical
tradition, despite the fact that Italians themselves could not agree on a
common language of everyday speech with each other. There are some
extended quotations in the original Italian throughout, particularly in verse
and song, in order to generate some sense of original sound; a translation is
always provided. But first we may reflect on the Renaissance characteristics
of modern Italian.

Regions, dialects and vernaculars

Today, Italy remains a country of immense regional diversity, and of fierce
local loyalties. Many Venetians would subscribe to the view that 'l'Africa
comincia a Roma' ('Africa begins at Rome'). Nor is that a piece of facetious
offhandedness. The most important political manifestation of such views is
the party Lega del Nord. This takes its name from the Lombard League of
the twelfth century (see above, Chapter 2) and sees the less prosperous and
more rural south as a burden on the north's economic performance. The
existence of the tiny sovereign Papal State in Vatican City in the centre of
the peninsula seems as anomalous to some Italians as its infinitely larger
predecessor did to Machiavelli five centuries ago. Moreover, within the 20
different administrative regions of Italy there remains a mutual suspicion
between town (*città*) and countryside (*contado*).

Perhaps the most obvious and sustained reminder of regional division
remains language. After a month spent learning Italian in Umbria, an
Anglophone native (such as the author) still finds considerable difficulty on
first arrival in Venice. The gravelly mumble of 'sottoportego' (also the name
for a type of street) takes a while to become recognisable as 'sotto il portico',

and there is only one *piazza* in Venice (at San Marco): all the other squares are confusingly known as *campi* or 'fields'. A prosperous businessman from the Marche operating in Venice would speak to a Venetian lawyer not in the cadences of his native speech but in the local Venetian dialect. The unsuspecting visitor to Venice may be asked for a version of 'they have tied up the cockerels' and offer 'hanno legato i galli' – which in Venetian dialect is 'iga' iega' i gai'.

While there is no clear consensus on what constitutes 'proper' Italian (as used to be the case, for example, with 'Oxford English'), the shrinkage of regionalism through modern communications and genuinely national media such as television (and to a lesser extent newspapers) does, however, enable us to use the term 'dialect' for the first time. A dialect is 'a variety of speech differing from the standard language'. The vernacular, on the other hand, is 'the native speech or language of a particular country or district'. Throughout the period with which we are concerned, there was no 'standard' Italian (just as there was no Italian standard in the sense of 'flag'). Indeed, throughout the period there was controversy, often heated, over the *questione della lingua*, the language question, with regard to what was most desirable in speech and in writing.

Intrata: *il Trecento* (Entry: the fourteenth century)

The recovery of Latin texts from the classical past seems an exciting and enriching phenomenon. Yet it was, at bottom, precisely the persistence of Latin usage, and the burden of Latin tradition, that made it so difficult for a truly 'Italian' language to emerge. Indeed, Latin remained the language of the Church and of academic dispute, as well as of the rediscovered classics from the ancient world, which remain so central to an understanding of what the Renaissance was about. That said, it is important to bear in mind that some significant Latin works survived in the medieval vernacular. Among these *volgarizzamenti*, we might point to Brunetto Latini's extracts from the works of Cicero, Bartolomeo da San Concordio's treatment of Sallust's *Catiline*, an anonymous work on Livy, translated into the ·'Deche', or 'Decades', Ovid's *Metamorphoses* translated by Arrigi Simontade, and an 'Italian' *Eneide* by Ciampolo di Meo degli Ugurgieri.[9] As early as 1300, Florentine, or at least Tuscan, was beginning to enjoy a certain predominance, and this may well reflect the city's economic power and the presence of its merchants and their commercial techniques and records throughout the peninsula and beyond. Certainly by the later fourteenth century, Florentine merchants such as Buonaccorso Pitti were combining autobiography, family history, advice book and diary in the consolidated form of their *ricordi*.[10]

However, it will not do to overemphasise the lay and secular characteristics of the various vernacular expressions of medieval 'Italian'. St Francis of Assisi made a crucial contribution to verse in Italian in his 'Cantico delle creature'. Celebrated for its references to 'Brother Sun' and 'Sister Moon', these must be related to praise for nature as a manifestation of God's work and God's love. It is also striking that the four elements which make up the world according to classical philosophy – air, water, fire and earth – are part of the Christian God's creation:

> Laudato si', mi Signore, per frate vento
> Et per aere et nubilo et sereno et onne tempo,
> Per lo quale a le tue creature dai sustentamento.
>
> Laudato si', mi Signore, per sor'aqua
> La quale è multo utile et humile et pretiosa et casta.
>
> Laudato si', mi Signore, per frate focu
> Per lo quale enallumini la nocte
> Et ello e bello et iocundo et robustoso et forte.
>
> Laudato si', mi Signore, per sora nostra matre terra,
> La quale ne sustenta et governa
> Et produce diversi fructi con coloriti fiori et herba.
>
> (Be praised, my Lord, for brother wind
> And for air, both cloudy and serene and in all weathers
> By which to your creatures you give sustenance.
>
> Be praised, my Lord, for sister water,
> Who is very useful and humble and precious and chaste.
>
> Be praised, my Lord, for brother fire,
> By which you illuminate the night,
> And he is handsome and joyful and vigorous and strong.
>
> Be praised, my Lord, for our sister mother earth,
> Who sustains and governs us
> And produces diverse fruits with coloured flowers and grass.)[11]

As already mentioned, one of the constraints on the development of a standard Italian language was the Latin heritage. It is intriguing to note, therefore, that among the Franciscans, the founder's expression of praise for God in a language of everyday life co-existed with one of the most memorable and enduringly influential of Latin rhymes. This was the 'Dies irae', the 'Day of Wrath', by Tomaso da Celano, Francis's first biographer, writing in the mid-thirteenth century. It is a text that became a part of the Requiem Mass, and its grim vision of the Day of Judgment seems a hundred years ahead of its time. The medieval plainsong tune was to inspire nineteenth-century composers such as Hector Berlioz and Franz Liszt:

> Dies irae, dies illa
> Solvet saeclum in favilla
> Teste David cum Sibilla
> Quantus tremor est futurus
> Quando iudex est venturus
> Cuncta stricte discussurus.
>
> (Day of wrath, that day,
> When the world dissolves in ashes
> As David bore witness with the Sybil
> What terror there will be
> When the judge will come
> To judge all things strictly.)

Innovation in Church Latin, no less than the burden of the classical Latin tradition, helped repress Italian as an alternative literary language. Perhaps it was this that made writers in the peninsula receptive to contemporary outside influence, most notably from France. The great troubadour poetry of the Middle Ages appears to have arrived in the peninsula by a circuitous route. In the best traditions of the wandering minstrel in the age of the crusades, Provençal French – perhaps en route to the Holy Land? – became for a time the literary language of the Venetians, for instance in the notable thirteenth-century chronicle by Martino da Canale, *Les estoires de Venise*. Even Marco Polo's (1254–1324) account of his travels appeared in a form of Franco-Venetian (which passed into Tuscan in the fifteenth century). At about the same time, seminal French influences arrived in Ferrara, and were to turn into the deep roots of an extraordinary literary culture from the late fifteenth century onwards.[12]

Whatever the uncertainties concerning the linguistic identity of Italian, there is no mistaking the towering formative influences of the fourteenth century: Dante Alighieri (1265–1321), Petrarch (Francesco Petrarca, 1304–74), and Giovanni Boccaccio (1313–75) – all of them Tuscans. Their critical fortunes dance around our central themes. Dante wrote a master-piece in the vernacular; Petrarch insisted on the superiority of classical Latin as a literary language; Boccaccio revered Petrarch, yet his most famous and enduring work was a vast collection of popular stories written in the language of everyday life. Thus, Latin traditions and French influences were compounded by what was to become a species of Tuscan linguistic imperialism. It seems significant that Dante discoursed on the characteristics and merits of literary Italian – in Latin. In his *De vulgari eloquentia* or *On Vernacular Eloquence* (probably 1303–4), he promotes Italian as a literary language, maintaining the mutual receptivity of the different regional vernaculars and their potential amalgamation into a 'courtly' Italian tongue. In *Il convivio* (*The Banquet*, 1304–8), he comments on his own poems of the 1290s, but seeks also to make available to a vernacular audience the Latin learning of contemporary universities. The *Commedia* itself we have already discussed; its literary greatness is unquestionable (see above, Chapter 2).[13] However, curiously and significantly, during the next three centuries it did not attract the kind of interest that Petrarch and Boccaccio were to excite.

The assessment of Petrarch's significance is a slippery task because of his own varying critical fortunes. Subsequent generations have taken to their hearts now his scholarship, now his poetry, now his Italian works, now those in Latin. This is partly the result of Petrarch's constant self-refashioning in his own lifetime, but it is also due to the extraordinary range of his literary activities. In the development of the Italian language, and in what was to pass from Italy to other places, it is appropriate to concentrate briefly on the sonnet, inseparable from the epithet 'Petrarchan' (save when Shakespearean). The curious mix of intense introspection and a desire to communicate what he found in himself to posterity may seem contradictory: why publicise what is so intensely private? One possible explanation – though he could never have admitted it, for it smacks of pride in the self and a lack of faith in Christian eternity – may be that fame in posterity offered the best chance of immortality. Certainly, a sense of the transience of human existence, and of the contrasting durability of the artistic masterpiece, foreshadow similar expressions in the sonnets of Shakespeare – especially in expressions of love which stand on the cusp between pleasure and pain:

> I do not find peace and I have not the arms for war
> And I fear, and I hope, and I burn and I am ice;
> And I fly above heaven, and lie on earth,
> And I grasp nothing and embrace the world. (*Canzone* 134)

> My love is as a fever, longing still
> For that which longer nurseth the disease,
> Feeding on that which doth preserve the ill
> Th'uncertain sickly appetite to please. (*Sonnet* 147)[14]

However, Petrarch seems to have doubted whether true eloquence could be achieved in the vernacular rather than (or as well as) in Latin. His stance was that Italian literature could only win its status in Latin. One wonders whether this was the result of Petrarch's inordinate personal vanity, and expressive of an envious petulance in not wishing to line up for comparison with Dante. Doubts about the potentialities of the vernacular persisted in the mind of Petrarch's follower and admirer Boccaccio. As discussed earlier (see above, Chapter 2), *Il Decamerone* owes little to Latin refinements. Rather, the raw energy and earthiness of the storytelling seem to derive from the vivid immediacy of its Florentine context. Boccaccio was the bastard son of a man who worked for the great banking company of the Bardi, and his illegitimacy may say something about the prominence of sexual peccadillo in the tales people tell. And the storytelling takes ten people's minds off the Black Death, which was ravaging the city at the time. Nevertheless, there are clear chivalric influences in many of the stories. Literary fantasy rather than social realism may explain why he transposed a story of courtly love to the world of Florentine weavers. Moreover, at the end of his life Boccaccio disowned the work. This was not necessarily an attack of Christian conscience, for he may have preferred to be remembered for the serious and subversive evolutionary theories of a still earlier work, the *Genealogia deorum* (see above, Chapter 7), but it is another example of hesitation by a great author in committing himself to the Italian vernacular. However, in the formation of literary Italian, Boccaccio may be credited with the rhyming scheme of the *ottava rima* (ABABABCC), which was to prove so significant a poetic vehicle, and he exerted an enormous influence on prose and on drama.[15]

Intermezzo: *il Quattrocento* (**Intermission: the fifteenth century**)

The 'civic' humanism of the early fifteenth century put Latin eloquence in the service of the state. This brought Latin back to life as the language of current affairs, but it was a setback for the vernacular as a vehicle for political, social and philosophical ideas. Moreover, it confined certain political offices to those who had the advantage of a Latin education. Valla had no time for the *volgare*. It is revealing that the most renowned of the civic humanists, Leonardo Bruni, thought only those with a command of refined Latin should represent the state. In a rhetorical duel with the historian Flavio Biondo (1392–1463), Bruni even enlisted some fairly specious historical argument. While Biondo put the case that Latin was a unitary language

for all Romans, Bruni took the view that the eloquent Latin that he used
was the language of the patrician ruling class of ancient Rome. The plebs,
on the other hand, had spoken a language akin to the uneducated vernacular Italian of his own day.[16] This proved to be a durable opinion which
generated a horror of the *volgare* as just that: 'vulgar'. So, for all the huff-
ing and puffing about republican liberty, those who articulated such an
ideology in Latin were, in a sense, appropriating freedom of political
expression from the very citizens who they expected to identify with the
state.

Paradoxically, it was a churchman who found an audience on the
wavelength of quotidian speech. One of the richest sources of everyday
language in the *Quattrocento* can be found in the sermons of San
Bernardino of Siena (1380–1444), which a notary jotted down as he
preached. As any preacher had to, he spoke to all ordinary people in a
language that they could easily comprehend. He gave practical advice to
women on family life (while Petrarch and Boccaccio, for instance, had
insisted on the superiority of the celibate state). What was more, he had
the capacity to break down some of the barriers that separated art and
philosophy from the populace at large. For instance, he warned women
of the dangers of cosmetics by reference to painting:

> Do not hate yourself, for you are hating your Maker . . . He has made
> [a woman] small, and you put stilts under her to make her seem tall;
> he has made her dark, and you paint and smear her to make her seem
> pale; He has made her yellow, and you paint her red. You are improv-
> ing on God, a good painter . . .

He could also present Neoplatonic ideas as common sense. Without the
love and care of a woman, a man was no more than an animal:

> He sleeps in a trough, and once he has put the sheet on it, he does not
> take it off again, until it is torn. The room where he eats has melon
> rinds, bones and bits of salad on the floor, without their ever being
> swept away. And the table? The cloth upon it is not changed until it is
> soaked. He rubs the plates a little, the dog licks them and washes them
> . . . Do you know how he lives? Like a brute beast . . . It is the woman
> who rules a house.

He sought to protect girls from incest or other abuse, and when it came
to choosing a husband, he argued that young women should at least be
allowed to express a preference. The relationship of mother and child was
sanctified in that of the Virgin and Christ, and to those who made Eve the
source of original sin, he said: 'Woman was the beginning of all good'.[17]

The world of San Bernardino was a celebration of the gift of life and the joy of living. It was a world away from the dreary pedantry of Latin speechmakers, but it was not a world away from great art. Renaissance art is at its most exhilarating when it is at its least exclusive. One of the most attractive features of life in Florence was that children were part of its soundscape, and it was their birthright to be happy. What a charming group Luca della Robbia (1400–82) depicts on the *cantoria* for the Duomo: children making music, dancing – and smiling. [O.88] This is entirely in keeping with the security afforded in the city's orphanage at the Innocenti, designed by Brunelleschi and decorated with roundels by Luca della Robbia's nephew Andrea (1434–1525), where abandoned children appear to have been well cared for. Here, and in the family, protective rituals prepared the young for this life, and for the next, which was never far away.[18] [O. 89]

Inclusiveness dominated the extraordinary interaction of popular and elite culture in the language and music of the fifteenth century, including a renewal of interest in the writing of short stories which the great Latin revival has tended to overshadow. As in the days of Boccaccio, intellectuals wrote about the foibles and follies of humanity with reference to everyday life as well as to the wisdom of the ancients, and their literary experiments seem a critical phase in the development of the drama. In a collection which Lauro Martines has assembled, a vernacular story by the Sienese author Gentile Sermini, writing around 1424, shows character sketches of peasants which call to mind the summaries of Tacitus, the historian of the first century AD, on the emperors of Rome. Another tale was from Antonio Manetti (1423–97), the biographer of Brunelleschi, who includes the great architect as well as the sculptor Donatello in *The Fat Woodcarver* (see below, Afterwords). Lorenzo de' Medici himself penned the story of a duped and jealous husband, *Giacoppo*, probably in the 1460s. Realism permeates popular story.[19]

Turning to poetry and song, Lorenzo also wrote a charming carnival song, fully attuned to the popular voice. Like the short stories and the romances, such poems represent a conscious attempt to give a decent language form to a popular culture. In this example, the refrain is a constant reminder of the joys and the transience of youth:

> Quant'è bella giovinezza
> Che si fugge tutta via
> Chi vuol esser lieto sia
> Di doman non c'è certezza.

Conventionally, this can be anglicised as:

> How lovely youth is
> That ever flies
> Let him be glad who will be
> There is no certainty in tomorrow.[20]

Unquestionably, however, what captures the spirit of the piece is one of Feste's songs in Shakespeare's *Twelfth Night*:

> What is love? 'Tis not hereafter,
> Present mirth hath present laughter:
>   What's to come is still unsure.
> In delay there lies no plenty,
> Then come kiss me sweet and twenty:
>   Youth's a stuff will not endure. (2.3.48–53)

Andrea Poliziano (1454–94), that interpreter of the most intricate and recondite of the Platonic mysteries, produced this extraordinary hymn to Bacchus, primitive in its drumming rhythm, animal even in some of its sounds:

> Ognun segua, Bacco, te!
> Bacco, Bacco, eù oé!
> Chi vuol bever, chi vuol bevere,
> Vegna a bever, vegna qui.
> Voi imbottate come pevere.
> Io vo' bever ancor mi.
> Gli è del vino ancor per ti.
> Lassa bever prima a me.
> Ognun segua, Bacco, te.
>
> Io ho voto già il mio corno:
> Dammi un po'il bottazo in qua.
> Questo monte gira intorno,
> E 'l cervello a spasso va.
> Ognun corra in qua e in là,
> Come vede fare a me;
> Ognun segua, Bacco, te.
>
> I'mi moro già di sonno.
> Son io ebra, o si o no?
> Star piu ritti i pié non ponno.
> Voi siet'ebrie, ch'io lo so.
> Ognun facci com'io fo:
> Ognun succi come me:
> Ognun segua, Bacco, te.

Ognun gridi Bacco Bacco
E pur cacci del vin giù:
Poi con suoni farem fiacco.
Bevi tu, e tu, e tu.
I' non posso ballar più.
Ognun gridi eù, oé; ognun segua, Bacco, te.
Bacco Bacco, eù oé!

No translation can capture the dizzy thumping of the repeated 'Bacco', but the poem has the following splendid English version by George Kay:

Let each one follow you, Bacchus! Bacchus, Bacchus, yuh yeh! Whoever wants to drink, whoever wants to drink, let him come and drink, let him come here. You swallow like big funnels. I want to drink, me as well. There is wine for you as well. Let me drink first. Let each one follow you, Bacchus.

I have already emptied my horn: give me the flask over here for a moment. This mountain is wheeling round, and my brain has gone for a spin. Everyone run here and there, as you see me doing; let each one follow you, Bacchus.

I am already dying of tiredness. Am I drunk, say yes or no? My feet cannot hold me upright any longer. You are drunk, that I know. Everyone do as I do: everyone swill like me: everyone follow you, Bacchus.

Everyone cry Bacchus, Bacchus, and still toss the wine back. Then with our noise, we'll break it all up. You drink, and you, and you. I can dance no longer. Everyone shout yuh yeh! Everyone follow you, Bacchus, Bacchus, Bacchus, yuh yeh![21]

Both Lorenzo and Poliziano would have found another contemporary song congenial to their taste. Popular in Florence, though written in street Flemish, its rhythms communicate its sauciness, even though the lyrics probably meant no more than 'Dum didi dum di dum didaa, / Dadada daa di dumdum daa' (and probably deserve no further elaboration than does the sound of someone casually whistling):

Rumfeltiere, rumfeldaer
Rumfelderan minduernit
Mimandiest miebetnit
Rumferdaran dieduernit
Anderduer rumpelnit
Mimdudiest iesteimit.

The translation is roughly:

> Don't knock at the door,
> Don't knock there at my door
> My husband hasn't gone to the mill
> So don't knock on the door;
> At the door don't knock, my husband is here now.[22]

But one is prompted to ask whether we would sit down to analyse rap lyrics in this way. As Aldous Huxley wrote of 'Ach, du lieber Augustin', 'by the very frankness of its cheerful imbecility, the thing disarms all criticism'.[23] In further examples of the dizzying mixture of classical and Christian, 'high' and 'low', sacred and profane, we find *sacre rappresentazioni* or holy dramas – which have a loose equivalence in English mystery plays. These include elements of classical triumphs in their tableaux, while Latin plays, which enjoyed a vogue at Ferrara, were performed with specially written elaborate musical and dance *intermezzi*: the *Menaechmi* of Plautus (active between about 205 and 184 BC) in 1486, his *Amphitryon* the following year, the *Andrea* of Terence (who wrote in the 160s BC) in 1491.[24]

Allegro non troppo: *il Cinquecento* (Merry not too much: the sixteenth century)

In the course of the sixteenth century, Italy enjoyed an astonishing and emphatic prominence in Europe in the printing of books. Aldus Manutius (1450?–1515) published the works of Dante and Petrarch edited by Pietro Bembo in Venice in 1501–2. Aldus, however, was not slavish toward Bembo. He felt that Greek was superior to Latin as a literary language, and he went ahead and offended purist sensibilities by including illustrations in his edition of that strange book attributed to Fra Francesco Colonna, the *Hypnerotomachia Polyphili* (1467 – published 1499).[25] Moreover, Aldus invented the elegant italic script, which, as a typeface, made possible the printing of much smaller books, easily handled as 'pocket editions'. Certainly, the printing press accelerated the spread of the Renaissance from Italy to other parts of Europe.[26]

One might anticipate that the new technology and Italy's prime place in its use might have had two consequences for the culture of the peninsula itself. First, one might assume that the spread of ideas in print might have consolidated a bridge between learned and popular culture. Second, it would seem logical to expect that the preparation and editing of texts would have promoted the standardisation of the Italian language. That, in fact, neither of these things came to pass is one of the most dramatic indications of the depth of political division in the peninsula. If anything, the *questione della lingua* produced perverse contraries to both the expectations sketched out above. First, literary circles remained intransigent to the popular voice and rigorously excluded the *volgare* as a vehicle for eloquence in writing. Second, the debate over what constituted 'correct' Italian mirrored exactly the petty bickerings of the various Italian states. Using the word 'common' to mean both 'shared' and 'vulgar', one could say that Italy had no common language because it had no common interest, and no common interest because it had no common language. There were endless debates about whether the vernaculars of the various regions should acknowledge the supremacy of the Florentine tongue. Moreover, there was controversy over whether the Tuscan model should be the literary language of the fourteenth century, or whether it should acknowledge the validity of linguistic innovation since that time. After the sack of Rome in 1527, only Venice retained its political independence, and then only barely. That simple fact gives the debates over language a surreal quality. Curiously, it was a Venetian, Cardinal Pietro Bembo, one of the participants in Castiglione's high-society dialogue, whose arguments carried the day. In his *Gli Asolani* (1505) and *Prose della volgar lingua* (1525), Bembo promoted the superiority of Tuscan, and asserted the supremacy of Petrarch and Boccaccio as literary models. Italian had to be 'courtly' in character. Any intrusion of the *volgare* into literary work was contemptible.[27]

The sterile bluster of these debates has half-drowned the melancholy voice of Machiavelli, who praised contemporary spoken Florentine rather than the archaic Tuscan of the fourteenth-century writers. He made his own contribution to the linguistic debate in a short dialogue (probably about 1515) which helps to explain the urgency of the message he passionately imparts by quoting Petrarch at the end of *Il Principe*:

> Then virtue against rage
> Will take up arms, and battle will be short,
> For all that ancient valour
> In the Italian heart is not yet dead.

But he knew only too well that the moment of opportunity was fleeting. That moment passed, and Italy fell under foreign dominion. The enormity of what was happening seems to have been wasted on many contemporaries. That at least saves us the task of rehearsing the learned variations on Bembo's themes from the dessicated classicism of Gian Giorgio Trissino (1478–1550) and a string of others. The opposition from Pietro Aretino (1492–1556) in the use of colloquialisms and obscenities in his dialogues

and plays is, however, worthy of mention.[28] Amid the undignified squab-
bles of parochial political entities and of self-appointed arbiters of literary
taste, the liberty of Italy itself, first articulated and defended in the twelfth
century, was lost.

The expressions of musical and literary greatness in the sixteenth
century demonstrate the connection between political division and cultural
vitality. Moreover, they pose fundamental questions about what defines an
'Italian' identity. The unique contribution of the Venetian Republic to
Renaissance music owed much to outside influence and to political independence. The first *maestro di capella* at San Marco, Adriaan Willaert
(*c*.1490–1562), appointed in 1527, was Flemish. The sack of Rome in that
year put the whole of the peninsula, with the exception of Venice, under
foreign rule. Subsequently, Venice's status as an apostolic city at the heart
of a politically independent Republic enabled it to assert an important
autonomy in music. It defended its own liturgical traditions, in particular,
against the conformity that the Tridentine Church sought to impose. This
independence in liturgical life made it easier for Andrea Gabrieli
(*c*.1520–86) and his nephew Giovanni (*c*.1555–1612) to borrow techniques
from composers elsewhere (notably the Franco-Flemish Orlando Lassus,
c.1530–94) and in turn develop them within the Venetian tradition. The
state maintained that tradition, especially at San Marco, and ostentatiously
so. It was the assurance of regular pay that was to draw Monteverdi to the
city as *maestro di capella* at St Mark's in 1613.

His great predecessor, Adriaan Willaert, had spent some time in Ferrara,
and the Estense court offers a fascinating example of how baffling it can be
to define what is Italian about the Italian Renaissance. The death of
Lorenzo the Magnificent in 1492 left Duke Ercole d'Este as the most
powerful of the Italian princes, and his court did nothing to understate that
status. However, it is difficult to see what, if anything, was indigenous in the
culture that thrived in Ferrara. The model of court life was Burgundian, the
literary inspiration was Carolingian and Arthurian epic: Roland and
Oliver, the Knights of the Round Table. The study of the classics existed
side by side with chivalric fantasy. Pisanello's studies of birds drawn from
the life demonstrate an unwavering observation of nature, and also the
importance of falconry in the life of the court (see above, Chapter 4).[29]
[O.27; O.28]

It is in literature that the Ferrarese influence was to be widest spread and
most enduring. Yet that literature reflects the escapism and fantasy of court
life, its remoteness from society at large, its reluctance to confront the realities of the peninsula's political crisis. Matteo Maria Boiardo (1441–94)
had experienced the realities of government at first hand, having been

appointed by Ercole d'Este to take charge of unruly Modena in 1480.[30] Yet his literary masterpiece, *Orlando Innamorato* (*Roland in Love*), was the first in a line of works celebrating the august and ancient roots of the d'Este dynasty. This mingles the epic story of Roland with the romance of courtly love by having Roland fall in love with a Saracen princess. The forces of the African king Agramante lay siege to Paris, only to be defeated by the Christian paladin Ruggiero, whose love for Bradamante is the origin of the Este dynasty. The action is contained in two books, the first concerned with the wanderings of the knights errant in the mythical East, the second a celebration of the chivalric ideal as embodied in the rulers of Ferrara. The stages of writing of the poem reflect the giddying change of perspective in Italy's affairs. The end of the Second Book alludes to the disruptions of the War of Ferrara (with the Republic of Venice) in 1482:

> Then with choice rhymes and better verses
> I'll tell of wars and love all afire.
> Times will not always be so strange,
> That they drag my mind from its place.
> But for the moment, my cantos are lost.
> And putting every thought into them is little help:
> Hearing Italy full of lament,
> Now no songs, but scarcely a sigh.

The poem first appeared in 1482 or 1483. The author extends his meditations on the condition of the peninsula at the beginning of a third book, which he never completed, appended to the first two in the edition of 1495. This begins with a celebration of restored peace, Italy a paradise for love. But by the last verse, the fantasy and derring-do of the age of Charles the Great of the Franks have been displaced by the realities of the invasion of Charles VIII of France.

> While I sing, O God, the Redeemer,
> I see Italy all aflame, and on fire
> Because of the Frenchmen, who with great valour
> Come to waste I know not what places.[31]

There were several attempts to produce an edition in standardised Tuscan in the course of the sixteenth century. The continuation, *Orlando Furioso*, by Ludovico Ariosto (1474–1533), was to earn greater fame.

As in Boiardo's work, so in Ariosto's, the chivalric elements are spiced with classical allusion: to Cupid, for instance, and indeed to fortune, over which virtue might triumph. There are elements too of a sensual rather than a gallant love.[32]

But the real fighting in the Italian peninsula had worn on and on and had become inescapable. The nostalgia for a golden age of chivalry seems quixotic *avant la lettre*. The terrible battles at Ravenna (1512) and Pavia (1525) – which are also mentioned in passing – were not chivalrous encounters but brutal, mercenary affairs involving gunfire and massed infantry, not the theatrical jousts of individual heroes. Firearms are beneath the dignity of a knight. Ariosto's Orlando disowns 'that torment . . . that they have said is like a thunderbolt in its every effect', and hurls it into the depths of the sea, along with the powder and shot: 'So that never again will a knight be burned, or a wicked man boast himself the equal of a good man thanks to you.' Unhappily, the 'abominable device' returned by magic into German hands, which prompts a further lamentation:

> How did you find, O wicked and ugly
> Invention, a place in the human heart?
> Because of you, the profession of arms is without honour;
> Because of you is [*sic*] valour and virtue razed
> That often the wicked seems better than the good:
> No more gallantry, no more daring
> Take the field to see which is beyond compare, because of you.
>
> Because of you lie buried – and will lie –
> So many lords and so many knights
> Before this war is finished
> You who have put to tears the world, but most of all Italy.[33]

Ariosto's final version of 1532 (revised to bring the language into line with Tuscan) was to exert a considerable pull on the European literary imagination, and some 25,000 copies sold in Italy in the sixteenth century.[34] The trilogy was completed by Torquato Tasso (1544–95). His *Jerusalemme liberata* (*Jerusalem Delivered*), completed in 1575, despite its crusading theme, does not embody a consistent Christian faith. It is unsurprising that Tasso operated under considerable pressure from ecclesiastical authorities and that later revisions reflect the demands of the Council of Trent for orthodoxy. His own attempts to harmonise Aristotelian poetical precept with the tenets of the Church did nothing for his peace of mind, and in the failure to achieve that synthesis 'he sums up and sets the seal on the work of the *Cinquecento*' in Italy itself, as well as providing lyrical inspiration for countless composers and writers. Among the first and foremost of these was Monteverdi, who set Canto 12, verses 52–68 to music as a drama, *Il Combattimento di Tancredi e Clorinda*, first performed in Venice at carnival time in 1624, his first experiment in the *stile concitato* – which agitated rather than soothed.[35]

As in poetry, so in dialogue and the drama, the principle to which writers adhered was one which we have already encountered in the visual arts: 'verisimilitude', or the appearance of reality, which returns us directly and firmly to the problems of Plato's cave.[36] Is *The Courtier* the transcript of a series of elegant conversations, or the play of shadows on the wall before the eyes of a captive readership? How cynical was the ideal? In the management of shadows and the manipulation of appearances, the distinction between reality and illusion can disappear altogether without the spectators knowing. The Sienese literary society of gl' Intronati produced a play called *Gl'Ingannati* (*The Deceived*), a plot full of mistaken identities which appears to have been the inspiration for *Twelfth Night*, in which Shakespeare's Clown reflects: 'To see this age! A sentence is but a chevril glove to a good wit – how quickly the wrong side may be turned outward!' (3.1.11–13). By the early seventeenth century, the fashioning of appearances became something of a cult: like Feste's 'chevril glove', how far the exterior revealed or concealed the interior was often impossible to say. The first troupe of actors to describe itself as the *commedia dell'arte* was recorded in 1545. Harlequin, Punch, Pantaloon, braggarts and bawds: stereotypes in masks. The process of acting out a part or watching other people act out a part was not just the experience of the theatre, but of life itself. And how could one tell when a person was not acting? Again we find ourselves chasing shadows. Perhaps a wariness of the fashioning of appearances helps to explain why *The Courtier* as well as *The Prince* appeared on the Church's *Index of Prohibited Books*.

Cadenza: *il Primo Seicento* (Close: the early seventeenth century)

My character is such that, like a chameleon, I imitate the behaviour of those amongst whom I find myself. Thus, if I am amongst people who are reserved and gloomy I become, despite myself, unfriendly. I respond openly and freely to people who are cheerful and uninhibited. I am compelled to wear a mask. Perhaps there is nobody who can survive in Italy without one.

Paolo Sarpi (1552–1623) gained a reputation throughout Europe as the defender of Venice's cause in its dispute with the papacy in the early seventeenth century (see above, Chapter 7). Disputes about whether or not the Republic's courts had jurisdiction over secular offences committed by the clergy resulted in the pope issuing an interdict, which included the excommunication of the Doge and Senate, in 1606. Sarpi championed the rights of the sovereign secular state. Although he himself was a friar, he had something of the Renaissance polymath about him: historian, philosopher, jurist, and in his optical theories perhaps the precursor of William Harvey. He can also be regarded as 'the great unmasker', ripping off the plausible disguises of others.[37] Or might we refashion the list a little? Outwardly a Servite friar, inwardly perhaps an atheist, formally official historiographer of the Venetian Republic, informally the Republic's chief propagandist, a rhetorician without rhetoric, apparent victim of the Jesuits, yet sworn enemy of what the Society of Jesus stood for, rational scientific observer, architect of the political cover-up . . . one could no doubt extend the list. How many masks did Sarpi need? The irony of the 'perhaps' in the final sentence of his quoted above is that he assumes that everyone he meets may be playing the same game.[38]

Again using an example from Ferrara to reinforce a point made in relation to Venice, Sarpi's legitimisation of masquerading among other masqueraders finds some justification in the work of Tasso, who acknowledged that in his own times 'dissimulation is one of the greatest virtues'.[39] This sentiment was echoed by a minor Ferrarese author by the name of Torquato Accetto. In 1641, he published a short pamphlet entitled *Della dissimulazione onesta* (*On Honest Dissimulation*), which was at one with a whole body of writings making its subject a virtue. Thus, in marvellous hypocritical twist, dissimulation was to be distinguished from simulation since the former 'simulates what is not', the latter 'dissimulates what is'. Dissimulation, in keeping with the Platonic theme, was 'a veil made of honest shadows and violent respects which serves not to form falsehood but to give respite to the truth'.[40] Such definitions appear in the *Oxford English Dictionary* as attributed to Richard Steele (1672–1729), though a quotation from William Cowper (1731–1800) is still more telling: 'Smooth Dissimulation, skilled to grace / A devil's purpose with an angel's face'.

In his quest for scientific truth, Galileo Galilei (1564–1642) seems far ahead of his time. However, the dialogue form in which he expounded his most controversial theories was, by 1600, rather outmoded. As Virginia Cox has shown, the openness of the dialogue and the whole notion of the free exchange of ideas had given way to the didactic 'closed book', which set down solid, unquestionable truths for the reader to absorb.[41] It was the absence of certainty as to where scientific investigation might lead that raised the suspicions of the ecclesiastical authorities – but not necessarily on religious grounds. Galileo's work and writings began a new era in the history of science. However, he is also a figure who brings the Italian Renaissance to a climax. He was a unique stylist, who demonstrated an uncompromising commitment to writing in Italian rather than Latin. This came in part from his attention to the concrete and the practical. In discussing mathematical theory, his analogy recalls the medieval merchant's handbook:

> It would indeed be news to me if bookkeeping in abstract numbers did not correspond to concrete coins of gold and silver or to merchandise. Just as an accountant who wants his calculations to deal with sugar, silk and wool, must discount boxes, bales, and packings, so the philosopher-geometer, when he wants to recognise in the concrete those effects which he has proved in the abstract, must deduct the material hindrances; and if he is able to do that, I assure you that material things are in no less agreement than arithmetical computations.[42]

Moreover, somewhat in the manner of St Francis (at least in his *Cantico delle creature*), Galileo saw no contradiction between nature and the Bible, he merely felt (as did many very traditionalist churchmen) that the Scriptures should only be invoked in matters of salvation.[43] Like Leonardo, he also seems to have recognised that infinity could be an infinity of nothing, which came home to him powerfully during his last years, when he was completely blind:

> Alas, your friend and servant Galileo has for the last month been irremediably blind, so that this heaven, this earth, this universe which I, by my remarkable discoveries and clear demonstrations had enlarged a hundred times beyond what has been believed by wise men of past ages, for me is from this time forth shrunk into so small a space as to be filled by my own sensations.[44]

His trial before the Inquisition, which began in 1633, is often taken to be the confrontation of free scientific inquiry with ecclesiastical dogma. However, it is important to remember that Galileo never turned his back on the Church, and always asserted the zeal of his religious beliefs. It is an irony that his true revolution was not to separate science from religion, but to separate science from ancient philosophy, particularly that of Aristotle, but also that of Plato. In this, Galileo was building on a 'growing interest in first-hand observation' that questioned previously accepted authority. Alessandro Piccolomini, bishop of Siena, was selective in his acceptance of Aristotle's ideas, writing in 1558 that 'reason and demonstration' might show differently. Yet departure from traditional authority still required lengthy justification, as in the case of Galileo's predecessor in Padua, Giacomo Zabarella.[45] This may help us understand Galileo's insistence on the compatibility of his new ideas with religious orthodoxy. The fact that his philosopher critics and opponents were often churchmen has tended to deflect attention from the main point. Galileo's work opens a new age because he does not take for granted the authority of the classics, not because he rejects the authority of the Scriptures.

Galileo's last and most controversial book compared the Aristotelian and Copernican world systems. He presented the discussion as a dialogue. That same dialogue form had served the scientist's father, Vincenzo, admirably in the elaboration of his musical theories (and Galileo was to use notational tempi to illustrate and calibrate some of his experiments with time and motion).[46] It is perhaps in the glories of seventeenth-century music that we can see some of the tensions in Renaissance culture begin to ease, especially in the work of Claudio Monteverdi (1567–1643), the composer of the earliest operas that have more than a historical interest and reach an audience beyond academic musicologists. The tune of one of his madrigals could serve as a setting for a risqué lyric or for a sacred text. Moreover, in the music drama that was to become opera, there was a way in which the problem of verisimilitude, of what constituted illusion and reality, could also be resolved. Opera is perhaps the most artificial of all artistic expression in the Western tradition. People do not sing their thoughts and feelings to each other in the routine exchanges of everyday life. Entering into the world of operatic action demands a conscious and collective 'suspension of disbelief'. Opera is not an illusion of what might really happen, and its invention represented something of a truce in the battle between a version of truth based on constant questioning, and another based on unquestioning constancy, between artistic inquisitiveness and ecclesiastical inquisition. In this way, the role of music in the liturgy of the Tridentine Church was a more than ample pay-off for any flirtations with non-Christian forms (popular madrigals) and themes (classical tragedy). The *ritornello* of an opera could become a strictly instrumental part of the mass, the motet 'Nigra sum' combined 'secular vocal artistry with religious fervour'.[47] The trumpet fanfare near the beginning of Monteverdi's *Vespers of 1610* transposes readily to the overture of the opera *L'incoronazione di Poppaea*. That opera has been described as the first in which characters appear 'as they are in real truth rather than imagined' – which makes one think that Machiavelli, who said exactly the same of his intentions in *The Prince*, would have enjoyed the piece had he lived to see it performed for the first time in 1643.[48] He would also have enjoyed the irony that such sentiments were no longer subject to censure. In the longer term, too, Giuseppe Verdi, that entrenched enemy of the papacy, was to write a Requiem Mass in 1873 which is often seen as his finest opera – and which includes a terrifying setting of Tomaso da Celano's mid-thirteenth-century 'Dies irae' (see above).

That link to a much later era is intended to convey the idea that in the course of the early seventeenth century, the cultural energies of Italy had found new forms of expression within the peninsula itself. But a little before then, the cultures of Italy had not only germinated and cross-fertilised with others elsewhere in Europe, they had also flowered.

9 Legacies

The Renaissance in Europe

The previous chapter argued that in the early seventeenth century, science and music, as represented by Galileo and Monteverdi respectively, assumed a new prominence, and the elements of Renaissance culture began to adjust to a new balance. First, in different ways but with similar results, vernacular culture was shedding its sense of inferiority to learned culture. Second, in music positively and in science somewhat painfully, there was a new awareness of the differences between the secular and the spiritual spheres. Third, spectacularly in science, more gradually in music, there was a sense of a new experimental creativity that was no longer in thrall to the authority of the classics and the Scriptures. These developments link the Renaissance with broader movements in Europe, notably the scientific revolution of the seventeenth century and beyond that the Enlightenment in the eighteenth. However, the contact between Italy and Europe was a continuum from the fourteenth century, not the export of some sort of finished product after 1600: consider the influence of Boccaccio's *Decameron* on Geoffrey Chaucer's *Canterbury Tales*.[1] In the fifteenth, there was plenty of contact between the cities of the peninsula and Flanders, between its courts and that of Burgundy. Around 1500, Erasmus's collaboration with Aldus Manutius helped make Italian humanism a European phenomenon; later in the century the classical revival in Italy animated the rational spirit of free inquiry in the *Essais* of Michel de Montaigne (1533–92), including the anthropocentric motto he borrowed from the Roman playwright Terence, writing in the 160s BC: 'Homo sum: humani nil alienum puto' ('I am a man. I consider nothing human to be alien to me'), which was painted on a beam of his ceiling. In the seventeenth, one may explore the connections between Galileo and the German mathematician and astronomer Johannes Kepler (1571–1630), and Kenneth Clark famously connected the work of the great Dutch painter Rembrandt van Rijn (1606–69) with the Italian Renaissance.[2] More generally, one could indeed see the tolerant, republican and prosperous United Provinces as the economic and cultural heirs of the Italian city-states. The music of the Italian Baroque was to make a significant impression on both Handel (1685–1759) and J. S. Bach (1685–1750).

There is a splendid array of reading on the Renaissance as a European phenomenon which it would be churlish to attempt to summarise here (see the Bibliography). Furthermore, a general survey of what Europe learned and selected from the Italian Renaissance carries the burden of a historiographical tendency that sees Italy in 'decline' in the seventeenth century – which in turn makes other places somehow more interesting. At bottom, the manifestations of the decline of Italy in existing historical writing are economic and cultural, with Italy at the geographical centre of the Mediterranean world when the future lay with the Atlantic economies. Economic decline was, it is alleged, compounded by cultural malaise represented by the bigoted repressiveness of political and religious authorities (see above, Chapters 1 and 2). Meanwhile the pressure of the 'Counter Reformation' was stifling free inquiry and insisting on a saccharin art that served the Church's purposes.

These characterisations have survived doggedly, but they are far from unquestionable. The seventeenth century was a period of stagnation and decline for nearly all of Europe's economies with the exception of those of England and the United Provinces. However, England's trade with Italy only achieved a surplus in the late eighteenth century, by which time the Dutch 'golden age' was on the wane.[3] While there is no doubting the tolerant and open character of Dutch society, there were many absolutist and authoritarian tendencies in other societies, and the latter were by no means invariably Catholic: Sweden, Brandenburg and England, for instance.[4] Most important, this book has argued throughout that the idea of the 'Counter Reformation' as forcing an end to the Renaissance is a misleading oversimplification. Some of the most profound achievements of the Renaissance raised doubts about institutional religion that often generated pain and sorrow. Disquiet within the Church concerning such ideas as being undesirable for general consumption (see above, Chapters 6 and 7), rather than being thoughtless and instinctive repression, was symptomatic of a pastoral concern for the broader society that much of the Renaissance had passed by – and often ignored.

In the light of those considerations, what follows is a different and perhaps unconventional exercise. It sets aside some of the stereotypical assumptions and concentrates instead on the ambiguous and anxious legacy of the Renaissance in the work of William Shakespeare (1564–1616). In an important sense, this brings the book full circle. It is in part a tribute to Aldous Huxley, whose very last essay was on religion in the age of Shakespeare. It is also an acknowledgement of the enormous impact that Shakespearean criticism has had on the historian's understanding of the Renaissance, particularly Stephen Greenblatt's discussions of 'self-fashioning' (see above,

Forewords). It also seeks to show how the preoccupations of the writers and artists who have appeared in previous chapters found a broader audience, literally as well as figuratively. That the greatest writer in the English language should present the ideas of the Renaissance to a popular audience is one of the most emphatic ways of demonstrating how the Renaissance became a general phenomenon. Its richness and depth continue to deserve our attention as a source of delight in what humanity can achieve, and as a source of understanding as to why we have become what we are.[5] But the limitations of the exercise must also be clear. This is not an attempt to reinterpret the whole of Shakespeare's work, merely to relate some Shakespearean themes to some Renaissance themes.

As Ben Jonson (1572–1637) tells us, Shakespeare himself had 'small Latin, and less Greek', and we are not dealing with a 'humanist' in the conventional and technical sense. Shakespeare was not a member of an intellectual circle, still less of an academic one. Moreover, he wrote for a general and popular audience in the commercial theatre in a comprehensible vernacular. (Even now, computers underline his abbreviations to ''tis' and ''em' as 'incorrect'.) Shakespeare himself, his sources, their translations and the nature of his literary genius do not concern us here and need not intrude excessively on the discussion.[6] Instead, what follows is an examination of the intricate mental circuitry that connects, say, the meditations of Leonardo with an unlettered carpenter or cobbler in the audience for *King Lear*. What one hopes to demonstrate is that Shakespeare's plays tell us an enormous amount (hitherto rather neglected) about the recognition and reception of the Italian Renaissance in Shakespeare's London, the fastest growing metropolis of the age.[7] Shakespeare was not a passive conductor in the process of transmission. Within that mental circuitry there were many wires to clip and others to solder in, producing any number of electric charges, puffs of obscuring smoke and long silences. But above all he made the Renaissance electrically topical. Performances did not attempt authenticity. Shakespeare's noble Romans wore doublet and hose, plus the occasional mantle, 'plucked Casca by the sleeve', asked 'What is't o'clock?' and made their perorations from a 'pulpit', using the audience as the equivalent of 'film extras' in the crowd scenes, and so involving them in the action on stage. When Macbeth referred to his 'hangman's hands', he evoked not blood on his fingers, but the whole forearm of the public executioner, who showed his 'skill' by disembowelling the condemned and ripping out the heart still beating. If such a spectacle was part of public 'entertainment', how did *Macbeth* attract some of the same audience?

Four centuries on, the corpus of Shakespeare's works forms an emphatic reminder of some of the fundamental and enduring features of the Italian

Renaissance. The Renaissance began with a revival of interest in the ancient world: Shakespeare wrote a few plays based on classical sources and set in antiquity. The recovery of the culture of the pagan world of the Greeks and the Romans raised all kinds of questions about the mainsprings of human thought and action in the Christian Middle Ages: Shakespeare wrote a number of plays on the earlier history of England. The application of knowledge of the ancient past to contemporary society and to the natural world produced some disturbing uncertainties about Christian morality and Christian cosmology: Shakespeare was an acute observer of the world around him and in the tragedies portrayed a world full of religious uncertainty. There is no suggestion that Shakespeare's beliefs can be tracked down as Catholic, Anglican, atheist or agnostic. He would almost certainly not have wished the censor to know. Indeed, one wonders whether any writer has ever proved so apparently respectful of the censor while dodging him. This is part of the rhetorical double helix. For instance, are the scheming bishops at the start of *Henry V* – planning how to buy off the king – a throwback to the bad old days of popish rule, or are they a recognisable contemporary type?[8]

A significant question here is how far the impact of the religious upheavals of the Reformation might have cut Shakespeare off from the Renaissance. In answer to that, one might point to the role of Renaissance culture in promoting reform of the Church, to Erasmus's debt to Lorenzo Valla, and to the application of source criticism not just to classical works, but also to the text of the Bible.[9] Moreover, there is a persuasive sense in which it is the very uncertainty of religious identity in Shakespeare's England that may have raised doubts about religion in general, and this certainly coincides with some of the deepest philosophical concerns of the Renaissance. Even the sketchiest of historical outlines shows the bewildering switch from one 'true' confession to another. The Anglican Church of Henry VIII (r. 1509–47) was schismatic Catholic, Edward VI (r. 1547–53) seemed to veer towards a thoroughgoing Calvinism, Mary (r. 1553–8) returned the Anglican Church to a strict Roman allegiance, and it is uncertain as to when Elizabeth I's (r. 1558–1603) England became 'Protestant', as James I's (r. 1603–25) search for a Catholic match for his sons seemed to bear out. Yet for all the unease and anxieties, we should also recall the joy of discovery in the Renaissance. Ambiguity does not necessarily mean unrelieved depression: one of Shakespeare's last plays, and certainly his last truly great play, *The Tempest* (1613), can be seen as a celebration of all that the Renaissance achieved – and it bids farewell to that achievement.

The validity of the exercise is something that Shakespeare's many specifically Italian settings and Italian sources might confirm.[10] Venice is the setting for Shylock (1600) and part of *Othello* (1603–4), Verona for *Romeo and Juliet* (1597) and *Two Gentlemen* (1590–1?), Padua for *The Taming of the Shrew* (1592), Florence for the wars in *All's Well that Ends Well* (1602–6). Syracuse is an important backdrop for *The Comedy of Errors* (1594), Messina for *Much Ado* (1598), Naples and Milan for *The Tempest*. Milan's identification as a port does not say much for Shakespeare's geography, but then in *The Winter's Tale* (1611) 'our ship hath touched upon the deserts of Bohemia' (3.3.1–2) as well as Sicily. Recent research has also suggested strong links between the emergent drama of the *commedia dell'arte* in Italy and the form and structure of *The Merry Wives of Windsor* (1597) – which transferred back into an Italian masterpiece as Verdi's last and only comic opera, *Falstaff* (first performed in 1893).[11]

Shakespeare's work underscores one of the central arguments of the previous chapter. The contrast between the astonishing enrichment of the English vernacular in Shakespeare's time and the stunting of Italian provides food for thought as to what the Italian *volgare* might have become had it not been deemed 'vulgar'. Some estimates suggest that between 1500 and 1650, 10,000 new words entered the English vocabulary.[12] Discussion refers frequently to a champion of a national Italian language and a national Italian identity: Niccolò Machiavelli (1469–1527). There is no point in attempting to prove that Shakespeare read *The Prince*, but his view of the world and of humanity's place in it shows many similarities to that of Machiavelli. While Machiavelli was a great political thinker, he was also a great dramatist of human affairs (and a considerable author of stage drama) in his own right. Similarly, Shakespeare was not only a great dramatist, he was also a great (and neglected) guide to the psychology of power. And we find in both of them a mastery of rhetoric that is wary of rhetoric, rejecting both the high-blown idealism of classical virtue and the morality of the more recent Christian era, since neither value system is reflected in observable human behaviour. More expansively, both of them ask questions central to the subject of this book. What is sincerity? What is acting? Who is acting what? How can one tell whether someone is wearing a mask? What is the audience seeing: objects or shadows? What is the difference between appearance and reality? These are recurrent questions that are posed in plays with a classical setting, in the history cycle, and in those portraying contemporary life.

Shakespeare and antiquity

Shakespeare's source for the greatest epic of antiquity, the Trojan Wars, reached him via a roundabout route. *Troilus and Cressida* (1601–2) is based on *Troilus and Creseyde* by Chaucer, who in turn was writing under the Italianate influence of Boccaccio's stories. Unlike the *Iliad* of Homer, written between 750 and 700 BC (many of whose *dramatis personae* appear in the play), this is no epic of love and heroism, but a seamy tale of sex and violence. As Thersites, a marvellous development of the character in Book 2 of the *Iliad*, puts it: 'Lechery! Lechery! Still wars and lechery! Nothing else holds fashion' (5.3.193–4), and in referring to the abduction of Helen and its consequences, 'all the argument is a whore and a cuckold' (2.3.74–5). The great Achilles is the 'idol of idiot worshippers' (5.1.7), whose gang of Myrmidons mug Hector as he disarms. Achilles immediately creates his own legend of this brutal and seedy killing: 'On Myrmidons, and cry you all amain / Achilles hath the mighty Hector slain!' (5.9.13–14). Agamemnon is unrecognisable to the Trojan Aeneas as a 'King of Men'. Thersites taunts the lumbering Ajax as having 'no more brain than I have in mine elbows' (2.1.46); and as for Agamemnon's brother, Thersites would rather be a bug on a syphilitic: 'I care not to be the louse of a lazar, so I were not Menelaus' (5.1.65).

The play is wanting in action and is enervatingly static. Yet how many of Shakespeare's audience would have known of or experienced the impossibly long and boring sieges of the wars in the Netherlands, where relief from the dreariness of the camp at a local brothel might result in the French disease, so gratingly anachronistic in the story, so fiercely topical for the spectators, right down to Pandarus's parting reference to a Southwark brothel? And there are no gods. How many of the audience might have questioned whether those Dutch wars were really a conflict between different versions of the Christian truth?

What of ancient Rome? Again there is no rhetorical idealisation. In *Coriolanus* (1608), Shakespeare follows both Plutarch (AD 46–120) and Livy (50 BC–AD 17).[13] The mob demands bread, and within the body politic which is to supply it, the Senators are the 'good belly' – not, be it noted, the brain or heart – which distributes corn. The tribunes of the people are disreputable backroom fixers. The tragedy of the eponymous hero is that he is incapable of dissimulation. That in itself is not a principled choice. When it behoves him to flatter the mob for the consulship, he cannot do it. He insists that he will not blandish: 'Would you have me / False to my nature? Rather say I play / The man I am' (3.2.14–16). What the mob sees is what Coriolanus is: an unattractively arrogant killing machine, and as a consequence 'the beast with many heads butts me away' (4.1.1–2). Finally, at the head of an army of Rome's Volscian enemies, he lays down his life, but there is a tremendous ambiguity as to whether this is in the name of the

Roman state or whether it is because he remains in thrall to the wishes of his formidable mother.

In *Julius Caesar* (1599) Brutus shares a similar fatal flaw. Caesar's apparently regal ambition troubles him and it shows: 'Tell me, good Brutus, can you see your face?' asks Cassius (1.2.50). By contrast, Brutus is shocked by the arrival at his house of the conspirators, whose faces are concealed by their hats and cloaks (not togas). The 'dangerous brow' (2.1.78) of conspiracy, he muses, must hide in 'smiles and affability' (2.1.82). His conventional classical *virtus*, passed from the ancient world to the Renaissance by the writings of Cicero in particular, fails to prevent him from making some critical errors of judgement. He discounts trying to enlist Cicero, the finest orator of the day, and ignores the advice of Cassius that Mark Antony should also die. Compounding that mistake, Antony seizes the Machiavellian opportunity to speak, which Brutus insists on offering, and sways the mob against the conspirators. Opportunism is, indeed, foreign to Brutus's nature, which makes his last and fatal error of judgement all the more ironic, especially since his terms are startlingly similar to those of Machiavelli. When Cassius urges delay in engaging the armies of Antony and Octavius in order to wear them out with a longer march, Brutus is insistent on taking the battle to them:

> There is a tide in the affairs of men
> Which, taken at the flood, leads on to fortune;
> Omitted, all the voyage of their life
> Is bound in shallows and in miseries.
> On such a full sea are we now afloat
> And we must take the current when it serves
> Or lose our ventures. (4.3. 217–23)

Machiavelli had a similar view of fortune, but fortune favoured those whose instinctive *virtù* led them to seize the *occasione* which presented itself. Brutus, on the other hand, had misread the signs. Machiavelli, having asserted that 'fortune is arbiter of our actions, but that also she leaves the other half or so of them to us', continues:

> I compare her [Fortune] to one of those destructive rivers which, when they are angered, make the plains into lakes, tear down trees and buildings, take earth from one place and put it in another: everyone flees before them, everybody gives way to their impetus, without being able anywhere to stand in the way.

Rather than opposing the flood, one must learn to channel it. This is how fortune can be mastered, 'because fortune is a woman and if she is to be submissive it is necessary to beat and coerce her'.[14] Furthermore, that notable omission of any place for divine providence in the scheme of things gives pause for thought. The action of *Julius Caesar* – and the complicated consequences of that action – examines the question of tyrannicide in a non-Christian world, but, as mentioned above, that action unfolded through actors wearing contemporary dress. At the time when the play was written and performed, the sole justification for assassinating a prince was on the grounds that his or her religious policies went against the conscience and convictions of his or her subjects. That in turn imperilled their chance of salvation and made removing such a prince a religious obligation.[15] Shakespeare's audience was left with the question, 'What if tyrannicide has nothing to do with religion but is a matter of secular power politics?' When Shakespeare presents the mainsprings of political behaviour in the Christian era, is there any difference? That question is subtly reinforced by the action of a play set in the penumbra between the ancient world and the Middle Ages, *Pericles, Prince of Tyre* (1607–8). In this, the leading character follows a route around the Levant very similar to the wanderings of St Paul. Yet the miraculous return to life of one of the female characters has no relation to Christian belief: on the contrary, it is due to the intervention of the pagan goddess Diana, whose cult at Ephesus so exercised St Paul in his epistle to the citizens of that place. Shakespeare's principal source is John Gower's *Confessio amantis*, written in the late fourteenth century, in turn deriving from a romance by Apollonius of Tyre, the earliest manuscript dating from the ninth century AD. The point is not to overrate Shakespeare's originality in using a pagan miracle, but to ask why he chose to follow his source so closely.[16]

Shakespeare and the Middle Ages

When Shakespeare staged the politics of medieval England, those politics were untouched by Christian piety. Appearances are all. In *Richard II* (1597), the king only becomes a 'glistering Phaeton' when he has ceased to be in political control, and his Christ-like passion begins only when he is uncrowned. He thus gives place to Henry Bolingbroke, whose capacity for ingratiation, his 'courtship of the common people', Richard finds enviable. The future usurper goes into exile 'with the craft of smiles':

> Off goes his bonnet to an oyster-wench,
> A brace of draymen bid God speed him well,
> And had the tribute of his supple knee (1.4.31–4)

With Laurence Olivier's portrayal of Henry V as the hero of English nationalism now less vivid than when the film was made in 1944, opinion has found a much more Machiavellian side to Prince Hal's nature. In his very first soliloquy, in *Henry IV, Part I* (1598), having seen Falstaff and his rowdy mates depart, Hal clinically and cynically sets out for the audience how he will fashion himself into a king, and shows himself to be his father's son:

> I know you all, and will a while uphold
> The unyok'd humour of your idleness
> Yet herein will I imitate the sun
> Who doth permit the base contagious clouds
> To smother up his beauty from the world
> That, when he please again to be himself
> Being wanted he may be more wonder'd at
> By breaking through the foul and ugly mists
> Of vapours that did seem to strangle him. (1.2.190–8)

As a narrative, the cycle of history plays culminates in the rise and fall of Richard of Gloucester, by his own account a Machevil beyond compare. This too is a fascinating anachronism, since the historical action of the cycle written in the 1590s ends at Bosworth Field in 1485, when Machiavelli would have been an unheard of 16-year-old, and 28 years before he wrote *The Prince*.

> Why, I can smile, and murder whiles I smile
> And cry 'Content!', to that which grieves my heart
> And wet my cheeks with artificial tears
> And frame my face to all occasions.
> I'll drown more sailors than the mermaid shall,
> I'll slay more gazers than the basilisk
> I'll play the orator as well as Nestor
> Deceive more slyly than Ulysses could
> And like a Sinon, take another Troy.
> I can add colours to the chameleon
> Change shapes with Protheus for advantages
> And set the murtherous Machevil to school.
> Can I do this, and cannot get a crown?
> Tut, were it farther off, I'll pluck it down.

That speech often appears in performance at the start of *Richard III* (1597), but it is in fact from that great neglected masterpiece, the third part of *Henry VI* (3.2.182–95). In the portrayal of Henry VI himself in all three of the plays that bear his name (Part 1, 1592, Part 2, 1594, Part 3, 1595) we find a paradigmatic opposite to the Machiavellian Richard. The pious Henry, the only conventional Christian in the entire cycle, is completely out of place in the world of power politics. Worse, his piety is inimical to the stability of the state and generates civil war. His assertion of obedience to divine providence on hearing news of the loss of France is 'Cold news, Lord Somerset, but God's will be done' and merely isolates him further in the midst of the feudal gangsters who surround him (*2 Henry VI* 3.1.86). In Part 2, Henry's belief in miracles is exposed as gullibility as Gloucester (one of the few characters of high principle) demonstrates that the blind man could see all along, and that the 'cripple' will jump and run if he is flogged (*2 Henry VI* 2.1). Henry's clear preference for prayer over politics is merely confirmed by his tiger-hided wife, Queen Margaret, who sneers at the king's devotion to his rosary to her lover, Suffolk: 'all his mind is bent to holiness; To number Ave-Maries on his beads' (*2 Henry VI* 1.3.56). As Machiavelli had quoted Cosimo de' Medici as saying, 'states are not held with paternosters in hand'.[17]

There is a case for saying that Henry is far more isolated as a Christian than is Richard as a Machevil. In a way, through his confiding in his audience, Richard can seem the only honest character. In the rest of the cycle, characters such as Northumberland, Cardinal Beaufort, the man of the Church who dies 'blaspheming God and cursing men on earth', Suffolk, 'wind-changing Warwick' (the Kingmaker), or Buckingham display no hint of scruple or conscience, and the latter comes to 'false, fleeting perjur'd Clarence' only just before his death. The politics of the history cycle are godless. The audience again faces an implicit but deeply troubling question. If history shows that there is no evidence of divine providence as operative in political life, where else in existence can we find its manifestations? Part of the answer may lie in other plays, not least because the boundary between history and tragedy in contemporary classification was so mobile.

Shakespeare and his contemporaries

Like Machiavelli, Shakespeare depicts a wide variety of political situations which nevertheless retain a fundamental consistency of vision. This is partly because what Machiavelli had predicted in the early sixteenth century had emphatically come to pass by its end. The prince was in the ascendant. The princely court had become the central institution of the state. However, while Machiavelli had warned princes to avoid flatterers, Castiglione had written them a handbook. In *King Lear*, Kent, banished for speaking the

truth to the king, returns in disguise to serve his old master and ends up in
the stocks for assaulting Oswald, Goneril's upstart lackey. As night draws in,
he reflects on those courtly creatures who owed their very existence to the
whim of their princely masters:

> Such smiling rogues as these,
> Like rats oft bite the holy cords atwain
> Which are too intrince t'unloose; smooth every passion
> That in the natures of their lords rebel,
> Being oil to fire, snow to their colder moods,
> Renege, affirm and turn their halcyon beaks
> With every gale and vary of their masters,
> Knowing naught, like dogs, but following. (2.2.71–8)

Such a creature is central to that enigmatic comedy *All's Well that Ends Well*
(1602–4), which derives from one of Boccaccio's stories in the *Decameron*
(3.9). The anti-hero Bertram is the perfect snob, and looks down upon the
affection of Helena as someone beneath his social station. His mentor is the
dreadful Parolles, a braggart and a coward who is never the less *au fait* with
the latest court fashions. Appearances are literally everything, but as the
wise old Lafew recognises, there is nothing behind the façade. The fancy
lace that Parolles sports is transparent: 'so, my good window of lattice,
fare thee well; thy casement I need not open, for I look through thee'
(2.3.212–14), and 'the soul of this man is his clothes' (2.5.43–4).

As for Machiavelli, so for Shakespeare, the bleak view of human nature
as manifested in political life extends into an equally bleak view of the
cosmos itself, with life on earth – as for Piero di Cosimo and Boccaccio (see
above, Chapter 7) – subject to the rhythms of nature, which is often cruelly
regardless of human arrangements.[18]

This is especially vivid in three of the great Shakespearean tragedies,
Macbeth (1606), *King Lear* (1605) and *Hamlet* (1599). They are treated below
in that order, which is the reverse of their appearance. There is no point in
attempting to trace some kind of philosophical development in the works.
The precise dating of the plays is so controversial that such an exercise
would be foredoomed. Furthermore, the demands of subject and staging
are so different in each case as to make it impossible to turn three such
diverse works into some sort of unfolding philosophical treatise. These
masterpieces represent experiments with and explorations of different
cosmological possibilities, asking the same question, 'What is it that governs
human existence?', and presenting three very different answers. What a
shock to the contemporary psyche the whole notion of tragedy must have
been, especially because 'tragedies' and 'histories' were so readily inter-

changeable.[19] One can 'suspend one's disbelief' in order to enter into the action of a masterpiece of tragedy. One cannot do that with historical events – however loosely interpreted – that are documented as having happened, personalities known to have existed. Here we have a revived classical form, one of the most significant and enduring legacies of ancient Greece, the antithesis of the medieval 'morality play' (elements of which Shakespeare also weaves in): no happy ending, no hopeful message, no moralising, and an inscrutable fate which governs the destinies of the gods themselves.

The deeply disturbing possibility in *Macbeth* is that Providence itself might be malign. Macbeth is led into temptation, and nothing delivers him from evil. The witches' prophecies for Macbeth himself perversely prove to be predictions 'That palter with us in a double sense, / That keep the word of promise to our ear / And break it to our hope' (5.9.20–2). Macbeth, like Coriolanus and Brutus, is a failed Machevil, as his wife recognises when urging him to learn the art of dissimulation:

> Your face, my thane, is as a book, where men
> May read strange matters. To beguile the time,
> Look like the time; bear welcome in your eye,
> Your hand, your tongue: look like th'innocent flower,
> But be the serpent under't. (1.5.62–6)

But Macbeth botches his opportunities, his explanation of why he murdered King Duncan's grooms convinces no-one, and Lady Macbeth has to pretend to faint to take attention away from him. Fleance escapes his murderous designs, and so does Macduff. Having recognised 'Time, thou anticipat'st my dread exploits' (4.1.144), Macbeth then indulges in the 'cruelty used badly' against which Machiavelli had so firmly cautioned. The pointless murders of Macduff's wife and son serve only to expose Macbeth's tyranny and isolate him within the dark night of his own soul. Moral numbness had already taken over: 'I am in blood stepp'd in so far, that, should I wade no more, / Returning were as tedious as go o'er' (3.4.135–7). He is entirely alone. When his wife kills herself, he has 'supp'd full with horrors' (5.5.13), and his despair becomes careless – just as his world is godless:

> Life's but a walking shadow; a poor player
> That struts and frets his hour upon the stage
> And then is heard no more: it is a tale
> Told by an idiot, full of sound and fury, signifying
>   nothing. (5.5.25–8)

That sense of nothingness, of illusion and shadows, is still bleaker in *King Lear* because it is compounded by a Leitmotif of the illusions of sight. There are no witches in the play, it is Nature that presides over humanity. 'Nature', however, lacks any unitary integrity and appears in several allusive forms. 'Thou Nature art my goddess', as the villain Edmund proclaims (1.2.1). 'Hear, Nature, hear, dear goddess hear!' (1.4.268) cries Lear as he calls down its curses on his own daughter, Goneril, urging that Nature destroy its own processes in his child in the grim phrase, 'Dry up in her the organs of increase' (1.4.271). Man is never very far from the state of nature, and clothes – not values – are all that keep him from it. When Lear then confronts the elements himself, he makes one of the play's few remotely Christian references (to church steeples), but only to suggest that nature's power can overwhelm any human institution.

> Blow, winds and crack your cheeks!
> Rage! Blow! You cataracts and hurricanoes spout
> Till you have drenched our steeples, drowned the cocks
> You sulphurous and thought-executing fires
> Vaunt-couriers of oak-cleaving thunderbolts
> Singe my white head! And thou, all-shaking thunder
> Strike flat the thick rotundity o' the world
> Crack nature's moulds, all germens spill at once
> That make ingrateful man. (3.2.1–10)

Leonardo's mysterious anatomisations of Nature's own turbines and vortices crowd into the mind. [Plate 16] So too do the sentiments of his late notebooks. Writing on 'the cruelty of man', Leonardo too seeks to 'crack nature's moulds':

> O Earth! What delays thee to open and hurl them [men] headlong into the deep fissures of thy huge abysses and caverns, and no longer to display in the sight of heaven so savage and ruthless a monster?[20]

When Lear encounters Gloucester's son Edgar, who feigns to be a lunatic vagrant, he sees 'the thing itself', and the stage instruction has him 'tearing at his clothes':

> Is man no more than this? Consider him well. Thou ow'st the worm no silk, the beast no hide, the sheep no wool, the cat no perfume. Ha! Here's three on's us are sophisticated; thou art the thing itself. Unaccommodated man is no more but such a poor, bare, forked animal as thou art. Off, off, you lendings: come, unbutton here. (3.4.101–7)

Away from his court, Lear reflects on the false insulation that it had provided (in a passage that has one of the most lyrical rhythms imaginable for unscanned prose):

Plate 16 Leonardo, *Cloudburst*, after 1512. Windsor, Royal Library.

They flattered me like a dog and told me I had the white hairs in my beard ere the black ones were there. To say 'ay' and 'no' to everything that I said 'ay' and 'no' to was no good divinity. When the rain came to wet me once and the wind to make me chatter, when the thunder would not peace at my bidding, there I found 'em, there I smelt 'em out. Go to. They are not men o' their words: they told me I was everything, and 'tis a lie: I am not ague proof. (4.6.96–104)

Why is nature so unforgiving that there is no love, even from a man's own children? 'Is there any cause in nature that makes these hard hearts?' (3.6.74–5). True understanding of the world is realised when a man who is mad talks to a man who is blind. When the eyeless Gloucester protests that he cannot see what Lear is pointing to, the king whose wits have turned replies, 'What? Art mad? A man may see how this world goes with no eyes.' Again, there is the question of clothing as a protective disguise:

> Through tattered clothes small vices do appear;
> Robes and furr'd gowns hide all. Plate sin with gold,
> And the strong lance of justice hurtless breaks;
> Arm it in rags, a pygmy's straw doth pierce it.

In his parting advice to the blind man, Lear returns to the theme of seeming and seeing: 'Get thee glass eyes, / And like a scurvy politician seem / To see the things thou dost not' (see the whole sequence poised between comedy and tragedy at 4.6.143–68).

Is there any other work of art that looks so steadfastly into the void? The use of the words 'nothing' and 'never' strengthens the play's unwavering tragedy. When Cordelia refuses to flatter her father as her sisters have done, by replying 'nothing', Lear replies, with Epicurean materialism, 'Nothing will come of nothing. Speak again' (1.1.89–90). Even as Lear rages against the elements, he seems to recognise the futility of his words: 'I will say nothing' (3.2.38). As in the cases of Leonardo and the blind Galileo, the expanded infinity that the Renaissance had discovered could be an infinity of nothing. And then there is what may be the most difficult line that Shakespeare ever wrote for an actor to deliver, the fivefold repetition landing like hammer blows on every human hope. As Lear clasps Cordelia's corpse, the awful realisation dawns that she will 'come no more': 'Never, never, never, never, never' (5.3.307). Yet – impossibly – the tragedy deepens. In his final deranged hallucination Lear sees a feather move and points to it as a sign that Cordelia is still breathing. Does he die happy because he is deceived? Does nature taunt us all the way to the grave?

What happens in the grave – which itself raises doubts about what might lie beyond – is the subject of the most famous scene in the most famous play ever written. Hamlet evokes all pictures of men and women holding or contemplating skulls, and any man in black holding and contemplating a skull immediately evokes Hamlet. The religious world of the play is remarkably confused. The source for the play dates the action to the eleventh century, but the intrigues of the court, the poison and the duel all evoke the contemporary world. So too does Hamlet's vehement response to his mother about his appearance: 'Seems, madam? Nay, it is. I know not "seems"' (1.2.76). On similar grounds, but somewhat in the manner of San Bernardino, he objects to women painting their faces: 'God hath given you one face, and you make yourselves another' (3.1.150). Hamlet has studied at Wittenberg, the birthplace of the Reform. But Protestantism repudiated belief in Purgatory as Catholic superstition. That in turn would mean that the ghost of Hamlet's father could not have come from Purgatory, but is rather an evil spirit from hell. Its call for Hamlet to revenge his father's murder leaves no room for God's justice – or indeed God's mercy. Then again, the funeral of Ophelia is Catholic, despite the priest's reluctance to bury her in hallowed ground because of her suspected suicide.

It is the reflections of Hamlet as he looks at Ophelia's grave before the arrival of the funeral cortège that occupy us here. For in this most celebrated scene, Shakespeare – like Machiavelli – has a character reject both the religious beliefs of the Christian era and the rhetoric that glorifies the ancient world: human existence merely follows Nature's cycle. Earlier speeches have already prefigured these sentiments. Most famously, Hamlet has posed the question as to whether suicide might be a legitimate expression of free will. While everyone knows the line 'To be, or not to be, that is the question', the most disturbing idea for Christian believers is that we are only afraid of the afterlife because we do not know what will happen to us in it:

> The undiscovered country, from whose bourn
> No traveller returns, puzzles the will,
> And makes us rather bear those ills we have
> Than fly to others that we know not of? (3.1.79–82)

He is more blunt about the way the grave is simply part of the natural cycle – the food chain even – after he has killed Polonius. When asked the whereabouts of the body, Hamlet replies: 'At supper', and then moves from the single example, via the political world, to a broader cosmology:

> Not where he eats, but where a is eaten. A certain convocation of politic worms are e'en at him. Your worm is your only emperor for diet: we fat all creatures else to fat us, and we fat ourselves for maggots. (4.3.19–23)

We are all 'the quintessence of dust' (2.2.316). In the graveyard, Hamlet's expression is at once more concentrated and more expansive. In Michael Almereyda's excellent film, the whole sequence before the funeral procession's entry is omitted. But for an understanding of the Renaissance, the scene is fundamental, central and quintessential. Moreover, it is worth remarking that the ideas find expression in dialogue form, not in soliloquy. In a few lines, we move from what becomes of the corpse after a Christian burial to what became of the most famous figures from antiquity, from the court jester Yorick, whom he knew, to Alexander the Great and Julius Caesar. There is reference neither to Christian eternity, nor to eternal fame:

> *Hamlet*. To what base uses we may return, Horatio! Why, may not imagination trace the noble dust of Alexander till a find it stopping a bunghole?

Horatio. 'Twere to consider too curiously to consider so.

Hamlet. No faith, not a jot, but to follow him thither with modesty
enough, and likelihood to lead it. Alexander died, Alexander was
buried, Alexander returneth to dust, the dust is earth, of earth we
make loam, and why of that loam whereto he was converted might
they not stop a beer-barrel?
Imperious Caesar, dead and turn'd to clay,
Might stop a hole to keep the wind away.
O that that earth which kept the world in awe
Should patch a hole t'expel the winter's flaw. (5.1.197–209)

The entry of the funeral procession follows immediately. Soon afterwards,
Hamlet's dilemmas seem to reach something of a resolution. Despite his
own – and Horatio's – unease about the duel with Laertes, he leaves
matters to Providence, and in mentioning a sparrow, refers to the Bible
(Matthew 10:29). Yet he seems to have found psychological calm, almost a
oneness with the natural cycle, in fatalism:

There's special providence in the fall of a sparrow. If it be now, 'tis not
to come; if it be to come, it will not be now; if it be not now, yet it will
come. (5.2.215–18)

The greatest of revenge tragedies fulfils what the ghost of Hamlet's father
had urged – vengeance of a father's murder – but it comes at the cost of his
son's life (and many others).

However, the very genre that takes justice out of God's hands and gives
it to man has certain formal and dramatic constraints that would be
misleadingly melancholy as representative of what the Renaissance
expressed through Shakespeare to a wider audience, including us.
Shakespeare's last great play sublimates revenge itself into something which
art, the highest of human faculties, can master. The play, *The Tempest*, is the
supreme expression of the joy of the Renaissance in exploring and expressing the potentialities of humanity.

Prospero, once duke of Milan, had been the victim of court intrigue. His
own brother, Antonio, conspired to usurp his office, and only the kindness
of 'an honest old councellor', Gonzalo, had enabled Prospero to escape,
along with his daughter, Miranda, some provisions and some books.
Washed ashore on an enchanted isle, Prospero translates his learning into
power over the monster of the place, Caliban, and through the spirit Ariel
over the forces of nature. Twelve years later, the conspirators are aboard
ship and come within the scope of Prospero's powers, enabling him to take
an elaborate revenge. The stage action, uniquely in Shakespeare, is

contained within the passage of a few hours. It is worth reflecting on how much human ingenuity and imagination can be concentrated in so short a time.

Having raised a fearful storm, to Miranda's consternation, Prospero (who, unlike Lear, knows the cause of thunder) reassures her that 'there's no harm done' (1.2.13), and proceeds to explain how she and he came to the island. His description of how he was usurped remains among the most succinct summaries of the politics of the Renaissance court. He had given his brother Antonio the 'manage of my state' and devoted himself to study, but Antonio:

> Being once perfected how to grant suits,
> How to deny them, who t'advance, and who
> To trash for over-topping, new created
> The creatures that were mine . . . (1.2.79–82)

In acknowledging why he had lost his state, Prospero touches on a central and recognisable tension in Renaissance culture. In trying to play the 'universal man', the multi-talented individual, he had lost the balance between the contemplative life and the active. He had immersed himself in 'the liberal arts'. Thus he was 'neglecting worldly ends, all dedicated / To closeness and the bettering of my mind' (1.2.90–1), and 'my library / was dukedom large enough' (1.2.109–10). Again with marvellous art, Shakespeare presents Prospero's return to the active life through a piece of Machiavellian opportunism. An *occasione* has presented itself. The reflexive verb form is inescapable. What power has provided this opportunity for revenge baffles even the Renaissance magus himself. There is no single controlling force. When Miranda asks 'How came we ashore?', Prospero's unqualified reply is 'By Providence divine' (1.2.159). When she asks his reason 'for raising this sea storm', he presents a quite different causality:

> Know thus far forth.
> By accident most strange, bountiful Fortune,
> (Now my dear lady) hath mine enemies
> Brought to this shore; and by my prescience
> I find my zenith doth depend upon
> A most auspicious star, whose influence
> If now I court not, but omit, my fortunes
> Will ever after droop. (1.2.18–84)

Thus, divine Providence has offered rescue, then accident, and Fortune (a woman again) has provided an opportunity that Prospero must seize or else languish. As the day unfolds, so revenge gives way to resolution. Prospero's art thwarts Caliban's 'foul conspiracy' with the drunken butler Stefano and the jester Trinculo. Antonio, 'whom to call brother would infect my mouth', and the scheming courtier Sebastian, who had plotted the death of Alonso, king of Naples, are constantly watched by Ariel, and for all their machinations have no secrecy whatsoever. 'The good Gonzalo' muses on the golden age and the innocence of the state of nature, though we all know there is no going back to it. Nevertheless, in an enchanted island, in such a place, then state, society, civilisation itself seem a diseased sophistication, which the sneering interruptions of the conspiring courtiers confirm:

> *Gonzalo.* I' th' commonwealth I would by contraries
> Execute all things; for no kind of traffic
> Would I admit; no name of magistrate;
> Letters should not be known, riches, poverty,
> And use of service, none; contract, succession,
> Bourn, bound of land, tilth, vineyard, none;
> No use of metal, corn, or wine, or oil;
> No occupation; all men idle, all;
> And women too, but innocent and pure,
> No sovereignty; –
> *Sebastian.* Yet he would be king on't.
> *Antonio.* The latter end of his commonwealth forgets the beginning.
> *Gonzalo.* All things in common Nature should produce
> Without sweat or endeavour: treason, felony,
> Sword, pike, knife, gun, or need of any engine,
> Would I not have; but Nature should bring forth,
> Of its own kind, all foison, all abundance,
> To feed my innocent people. (2.1.144–61)

While the play is incomparable testimony to the poetic imagination, it nevertheless related closely to matters of topicality and moment as Europe moved to the brink of the last and worst of its religious conflicts, the Thirty Years War. The Emperor Rudolf II (*r.* 1576–1612), who was deposed in favour of his brother for devoting himself to study and neglecting affairs of state, may have been the model for Prospero, and the succession of the more militantly Catholic Matthias (*r.* 1612–19) brought war a step closer.[21] In 1613, the play was performed as one of many celebrations of the marriage of King James's daughter Elizabeth to Frederick of the Palatinate, the masque for Ferdinand and Miranda's wedding assuming a special prominence for the royal couple. Frederick was a militant Calvinist, whose election to the kingdom of Bohemia in 1618 was finally to precipitate the war. The wedding celebrations themselves took on an illusory quality. Sir

Henry Wotton wryly remarked that he had read an account of the festivities that greeted Frederick and Elizabeth in Heidelberg – some days before they had left Dover, 'so nimble an age it is'.[22] Despite Elizabeth's pleading both to the king and to her brother Charles, James refused to intervene in Europe, which was to alienate Protestant opinion in his own monarchy. At the end of conflict in Europe and in the Stuart monarchy, Thomas Hobbes (1588–1679) was to envision the need for a sovereign Leviathan state that ran completely counter to what Gonzalo idealised in the state of Nature. For Hobbes, without the state the life of man would be 'solitary, poor, nasty, brutish and short'. To think otherwise was an illusion.[23]

So, while *The Tempest* is often interpreted as a deeply personal statement, there is also a sense in which its joy in formal resolution and its poetic completeness mark the end of an era, and precede the onset of a new and darker age. 1613, the year of its first performance, was also the year that the Globe was destroyed by fire, which brings our story to a close.

> Our revels now are ended. These our actors,
> As I foretold you were all spirits, and
> Are melted into air, into thin air:
> And, like the baseless fabric of this vision
> The cloud-capp'd towers, the gorgeous palaces,
> The solemn temples, the great globe itself,
> Yea, all which it inherit, shall dissolve,
> And like this insubstantial pageant faded
> Leave not a wrack behind. We are such stuff
> As dreams are made on; and our little life
> Is rounded with a sleep. (4.1.148–58)

Prospero's giving up his magical powers is sometimes seen as Shakespeare's farewell to the theatre, his farewell to writing. That may be the case, but it does not preclude the idea that Prospero's decision to return to society is an expression of a need for companionship, and we might also see it as a confession that the universal man of the Renaissance is not, after all, self-sufficient. There is another world beyond the imaginative self. However exhilarating the achievements of the individual, he or she surely does not wish to live and die according to Richard of Gloucester's principle, 'I am myself alone'. It is preferable to turn one's back on power over nature itself:

> I have bedimm'd
> The noontide sun, call'd forth the mutinous
> winds,

> And 'twixt the green sea and the azur'd vault
> Set roaring war: to the dread rattling thunder
> Have I given fire and rifted Jove's stout oak
> With his own bolt; the strong-bas'd promontory
> Have I made shake, and by the spurs pluck'd up
> The pine and cedar: graves at my command
> Have wak'd their sleepers op'd and let 'em
>   forth,
> By my so potent Art. But this rough magic
> I here abjure; and when I have required
> Some heavenly music, – which even now I do, –
> To work mine end upon their senses, that
> This airy charm is for, I'll break my staff,
> Bury it certain fathoms in the earth,
> And deeper than did ever plummet sound
> I'll drown my book. (5.1.41–57)

The Epilogue spoken by Prospero at the very end of *The Tempest* finds a strange parallel in Machiavelli. The Florentine's last work had none of the ruthless, thrusting individualism of *The Prince*. No: it was an *Exhortation to Penitence*, and it was addressed to members of that institutionalisation of the bonds of Christian love, a devotional confraternity. Like St Francis, Machiavelli (how often do we see those two names together?) celebrates Nature as God's gift to man and man's not being in the state of Nature as the earthly manifestation of God's divine grace. The natural evolution celebrated by Vitruvius, Boccaccio and Piero di Cosimo (see above, Chapter 7) becomes in the work of Machiavelli – of all people – part of the divine plan:

> Think then how all the things made and created were made and created for the benefit of man.
>   . . . and man is created only for the benefit and honour of God. To man He gave speech so that he could praise Him; He gave him sight not turned to the earth like the other animals but to the sky so that he could constantly see Him, gave him hands so that he could build temples, make sacrifices in His honour, gave him reason and intellect that he might speculate and know the greatness of God . . .[24]

If there is any point to life – and for Macbeth and Lear there is not – then it derives from an acknowledgement of dependence on others, on human association in the bonds of love.

Some of our other principals may now take their bow. It is an attractive coincidence that Aldous Huxley's most famous book, *Brave New World*

(1932), takes a phrase from *The Tempest* for its ironic title. His last novel (1962) is a truly utopian vision of a state governed by reason and love: its title is *Island*. And let us permit Augustine a final intrusion. For those bonds of love that Lear and Macbeth lost were bonds that perhaps St Augustine never found, and the place of Christian love or *caritas* in his thinking is unusually unsteady. Augustine's *caritas* is disciplined and didactic, a means of helping fellow-pilgrims to the City of God, but not of much help for life on earth, where humans are only 'souls using bodies'. This may be a reflection of Augustine's incapacity to talk to others as equals. Indeed, he could be vehemently hostile about the role of *caritas* during earthly life: 'If we are ablaze with love for eternity we shall hate temporal relationships.' Is this really compatible with Christ's urgent and repeated commandment to his disciples at the Last Supper?

> A new commandment I give unto you, That ye love one another; as I have loved you, that ye also love one another . . . This is my commandment, That ye love one another, as I have loved you . . . These things I command you, that ye love one another (John 13:34; 15.12, 17)

Perhaps Augustine's failure of accommodation between his Platonism and Christ's new, precious and final command to his disciples is reflected in the description of his *Confessions* as both 'Odyssey' and 'pilgrimage'.[25]

By contrast, but yet with a similar symmetry, Shakespeare imbues the relationships in this life with their own eternity. The epilogue to *The Tempest*, spoken by Prospero, has a rich concerto of religious rhythms and resonances forming an essential *sottofondo* for the voice of humanity talking to other humans. The 'deceiver' is 'pardon'd' as though in a mystery play, while 'prayer', 'mercy' and 'indulgence' are all necessary to ward off 'despair', the hopelessness of being without God and entirely alone. With *The Tempest*, Renaissance man has reached the end of his lonely journey, unsure as to whether it has been an odyssey in classical style, or a Christian pilgrimage, but now certain of his need of others:

> Now my charms are all o'erthrown
> And what strength I have's mine own
> Which is most faint. Now 'tis true
> I must be here confined by you
> Or sent to Naples. Let me not
> Since I have my dukedom got
> And pardon'd the deceiver dwell
> In this bare island by your spell
> But release me from my bands

With the help of your good hands
Gentle breath of yours my sails
Must fill or else my project fails
Which was to please. Now I want
Spirits t'enforce, art t'enchant
And my ending is despair
Unless I be relieved by prayer
Which pierceth so that it assaults
Mercy itself, and cures all faults
As you from crimes would pardon'd be
Let your indulgence set me free.

Afterwords

La Novella del Grasso

Before asking the audience to release him, Prospero had responded to Ariel's pleas that the magus should restore the senses of those who were under his spell. Even the spirit had begun to pity their afflictions, since they were now penitent. Prospero sets aside his angry vengeance, and gently promises that 'they shall be themselves'. The idea that 'the rarer action is / In virtue than in vengeance' is entirely in keeping with the resolution of the plot (*The Tempest* 5.1.17–32). Yet in Prospero's very act of laying aside his power is a reminder of a darker side of the Renaissance.[1] For, if it was possible to construct an identity, it was also possible to deconstruct the same. At the end of the introduction to this book, there was some discussion of an example of how the Florentine architect Filippo Brunelleschi displayed his virtuosity by an illusion that seemed inseparable from its surrounding reality (see above, Forewords). The biographer who supplied that anecdote, Antonio Manetti, was the author of a separate story about Brunelleschi. It seems fitting to add a short codicil by way of conclusion to take us back to the theme of how the outstanding figures of the Renaissance shifted around the building blocks of reality. While we often marvel at how this reflected changing perceptions of the world, and all the horizons that it opened up, there was also the possibility of changing how people saw themselves, muddling their sense of reality and illusion and generating mistaken identities. Manetti's *La Novella del Grasso* (*The Story of the Fat Woodcarver*), from the 1480s, is a tale of rather dubious hilarity and it describes something more unsettling and puzzling than a mere prank.[2] However, since it may be no more than a story, and we will never be sure that it 'really happened', perhaps we should take it in the spirit of fiction. More conventional documentary sources reveal that Brunelleschi was an irritable sort, impatient of others. Piqued by Ghiberti's being paired with him in the construction of the dome, for instance, Brunelleschi was, at the most difficult stage of the construction, absent, feigning illness. The purpose, it would appear, was to emphasise that Ghiberti's skills were inferior to his own, and that the project could not proceed without Brunelleschi himself.[3] There are similar themes of short temper, play-acting and stage management in the story.

The woodcarver in question, called Manetto, was skilled at his trade, and kept company with Brunelleschi and a wider circle that included Donatello. His failure to attend a supper, according to the story, led Brunelleschi's *ingegno* to devise an elaborate and cruel revenge: ' "I have thought that we would make him believe that he had become somebody else, and that he was no longer Fatso the Woodcarver." '[4] So it is that Brunelleschi arranges for people in the street to address the man as Matteo – another individual known to the circle of friends, though not part of it. Filippo then pretends to be the Grasso, occupying his house – which stood near the cathedral, where Brunelleschi had set up that picture of his that was indistinguishable from reality. In a brilliant impersonation of Grasso's voice, he apparently then berates the woodcarver's mother – fashioning himself to be someone he is not. So convincing is Brunelleschi's mimicry that Manetto is convinced he has heard himself. As part of the joke, he is then arrested for debt as Matteo, and imprisoned as Matteo, until he no longer knows who he is. He even asks another member of the circle, Giovanni Rucellai, who comes to the jail and pretends not to recognise him, to bring Manetto the woodcarver to visit him. When he is released, he is released by the intervention of Matteo's brothers, and resolves from now on to be Matteo. His 'brothers' drug his wine during dinner (the potion was supplied by Brunelleschi). They then take him to his workshop, leave him on his bed with his feet where his head should have been, and reverse the position of all the tools of his trade. When he awakes he finds that the 'brothers' are at his door, inquiring about their brother Matteo, who, they say, thinks he is a woodcarver called Grasso. Matteo then materialises to explain his absence and is impatient of all the interest in his affairs. There is much laughter at the eventual *dénouement* when all is revealed – all, that is, except Brunelleschi's role as puppet master. As Grasso leaves to work in Hungary, he hears people talking and laughing about what has happened to him: the story had spread from the prison. He makes his fortune in the service of King Sigismund. When he returns to Florence, he tells the whole story to Brunelleschi, in great mirth, 'for most of the funny things had happened, so to say, in the mind of Grasso'.[5] The architect in turn related it on a number of occasions, so the author tells us, to, among others, Michelozzo and Lucca della Robbia, and it is from their accounts of what Brunelleschi told them that Manetti has pieced together his own account.

   It is a long tale, and the fact that this reader finds it tiresome is no doubt reflected in the summary. Unlike many Renaissance stories – of Boccaccio, say, or Salernitano – it does not offer a moral. Grasso is not a hypocritical priest, or an avaricious merchant: he has merely crossed Brunelleschi, whose revenge is tart. The story celebrates the architect's capacity to manipulate reality in such a way as to deprive an individual of his identity until he does not know who he is and no-one – apparently – can tell him. The characterisation of new identities in the Renaissance – traditionally 'the discovery of the individual', more recently the construction of individuality through 'self-fashioning' – tells us much about the great bursts of egotism to which the rich and dynamic cultures of Italy owed so much. In a European context, too, stories of mistaken identity can generate great good cheer. We have mentioned the connection between *Twelfth Night* and *Gl'Ingannati* (see above, Chapter 8), and there is more comedy over mistaken identities in *A Comedy of Errors*, *A Midsummer Night's Dream* and *All's Well that Ends Well*.

However, the delight in imitating reality through illusion depended on an assurance that a lost self could be restored. If self-doubt set in on self-fashioning, indeed if there were ever uncertainty about the difference between illusion and reality and who – or what – controlled it, then wit, reason, memory, *ingegno*, power itself counted for nothing in the face of despair and madness. Are we reminded of the moment when Richard II changes his identity from king to subject? In his grief, he shatters the image of his crownless head in a mirror on the floor. He tells his usurping successor, about to become Henry IV rather than Bolingbroke, 'my sorrow hath destroyed my face'. With menacing reassurance, Henry replies: 'The shadow of your sorrow hath destroy'd / The shadow of your face'. Richard gives the Neoplatonic dichotomy of shadow and substance an ingenious twist, and retorts that, on the contrary, the grief that he shows is as nothing to the grief that he feels.

> And these external manners of lament
> Are merely shadows to the unseen grief
> That swells with silence in the tortur'd soul.
> There lies the substance. (*Richard II*, 4.1.291–9)

Does the *Tale of the Fat Woodcarver* remind us of another moment of seeming hilarity, when it takes a fool to remind a man closer to madness than he knows that he has lost his own self and has become an image fluttering on the wall of a cave?

> *Lear:* . . . Who is it that can tell me who I am?
> *Fool:* Lear's shadow. (1.4.221–2)[6]

All's well that ends well . . .?

This book has sought to present the diversity of the phenomenon conventionally known as the Italian Renaissance, the diversity of achievements, of locations in time and space, of participants and audiences – and the large and significant parts of Italy and its societies that took no important part in it. Yet there remain some abiding themes, even though they do not necessarily unify the subject. In Italy after about 1300, drawing on the remnants of the classical world in Rome and elsewhere, and also on the commercial legacies of some of Italy's great medieval cities, a number of lay people (almost invariably men) developed and presented new ways of looking at the world and of humanity's place within it. They did so with a view to their contemporary patrons (and rarely to a broader society), and with a view to posterity. In that promotion of earthly memory, which they themselves learned from the ruined monuments and fragmentary texts of the ancients, some of them, wittingly and unwittingly, willingly and less willingly, began to call into question the monopoly of eternity represented by the city of the Christian God. This was not, in any consistent way, a process of liberation. All too frequently, the presentation of alternative realities became confused with the substitution of alternative illusions. Delight in surpassing reality generated anxieties that only faith – often blind faith – could assuage. Yet in wrestling with history, and looking to posterity, the phenomenon that began in Italy constantly excites questions about the location and identity of every generation. Paradoxically, we might see the manifestations of the Renaissance as forming a 'middle age' in the history of the classical tradition, standing between pagan antiquity and the Enlightenment. However, intertwining with that classical tradition was another, that of Christianity, in its predominant shaping of the European world after the fall of the Roman Empire in the West at the end of the fifth century AD. That Christian tradition reasserted itself again in the wars that followed the break-up of the Western Church after 1500 and that lasted until the middle of the seventeenth century. Neither 'Renaissance' nor even 'Enlightenment' opened an irreversible way to 'modernity'. Who knows? Might future generations rediscover the Renaissance anew and see the 'post-modern' world as the new 'Dark Ages'? Such speculation takes us all too close to the stereotypes and clichés that this book has sought to question, and must draw this interpretation to an end. The preceding chapters have, I hope, offered some stimulus to further reading and further thought on the significance of parts of Italy and their 'Renaissances', on their meanings for the way we are now, and, more generally, on how fragile is our understanding of the complexities of cultures.

Notes

Forewords

1. Jacob Burckhardt, *The Civilization of the Renaissance in Italy*, trans. S.G.C. Middlemore (London, 1945); see also the valuable Introduction by Peter Burke in the edition ed. Peter and Linda Murray (Harmondsworth, Middx, 1990), which, maddeningly, lacks illustrations; John Hale, *The Civilization of Europe in the Renaissance* (London, 1993).

2. See for example Peter Nichols, *Italia, Italia* (London, 1973); Luigi Barzini, *The Italians* (London, 1966).

3. Erwin Panofsky, *Renaissance and Renascences in Western Art* (Stockholm, 1960, then New York, 1969); cf. Charles Homer Haskins, *The Renaissance of the Twelfth Century* (Cambridge, Mass., 1927).

4. 'Conxolus', in Huxley, *Along the Road* (London, 1925), pp.166–76, and 'The Best Picture', ibid., pp.177–89; Piero della Francesca, *Resurrection*, *c*.1460. Sansepolcro, Museo Civico; 'Popular Music', *Along the Road*, p.246.

5. *Show Magazine* (1964), reprinted in *Aldous Huxley, A Memorial Volume* (London, 1965), pp.165–75.

6. At Eton, Huxley taught one Eric Blair, who, having changed his name to George Orwell, wrote an essay called 'Politics and the English Language' in *Inside the Whale* (London, 1962), pp.143–58, of which Huxley would surely have approved; the collection also includes a brilliant essay on the stature of Shakespeare, 'Lear, Tolstoy and the Fool', pp.101–20. On Huxley at Eton, see Sybille Bedford, *Aldous Huxley. A Biography*, vol.1, pp.85–92.

7. Plato, *The Republic*, in *Great Dialogues of Plato*, trans. W.H.D. Rouse, ed. Eric H. Warmington and Philip G. Rouse (New York, 1956), p.314.

8. Ibid., pp.312–16.

9. Figure 2 from John White, *The Birth and Rebirth of Pictorial Space*, 3rd edn (London, 1987), p.115.

10. Figure 3 from Ross King, *Brunelleschi's Dome. The Story of the Great Cathedral in Florence* (London, 2001), p.37.

11. Antonio Manetti, *Vita di Filippo Brunelleschi*, ed. Domenico de Robertis, intro. and notes by Giuliano Tanturli (Milan, 1976), pp.58–9.

Chapter 1. Deconstructions

1. 'De fortunae varietate urbis Romae, et de ruina eiusdem, descriptio', in 'De miseria humanae conditionis', Book 2, in *Opera omnia* (Basel, 1538; facs. edn, ed. R. Fubini, 4 vols., Turin, 1964), vol.1, p.132; cf. James Bruce Ross and Mary Martin McLaughlin (eds.), *The Portable Renaissance Reader* (Harmondsworth, Middx, 1977), pp.380–1.

2. Machiavelli, *Discorsi sopra la Prima Deca di Tito Livio*, I.2; cf. *Discourses on Livy*, trans. Julia Conaway Bondanella and Peter Bondanella (Oxford, 1997), p.17.

3. Peter Burke, *The Renaissance Sense of the Past* (London, 1969).

4. Letter to Iacopo Pizzinga (1372), in *Opere latine minori*, ed. Francesco Massera (Bari, 1928), p.195; cf. *Renaissance Reader*, ed. Ross and McLaughlin, pp.124–5.

5. Gerhard Ladner, 'Homo viator', *Speculum*, 42 (1967), pp.233–57.

6. Denys Hay and John Law, *Italy in the Age of the Renaissance, 1380–1530* (London, 1989); John Stephens, *The Italian Renaissance* (London, 1990).

7. Hay and Law, *Renaissance*; John Larner, *Italy in the Age of Dante and Petrarch, 1218–1380* (London, 1980).

8. Rosario Villari (ed.), *Baroque Personae*, trans. Lydia Cochrane (Chicago, 1995).

9. Quoted in T.H. Mommsen, 'Petrarch's Conception of the "Dark Ages" ', *Speculum*, 17 (1942), pp.232, 239, 241.

10. Ioannes Saresberiensis, *Policraticus I–IV*, ed. K.S.B. Keats-Rohan, *Corpus Christianorum* CXVIII (Turnhout, 1993), pp.231–2; cf. John of Salisbury, *Policraticus. The Statesman's Book*, abr. and ed. Murray F. Markland (New York, 1979), pp.44–5; Philippe de Commynes, *Memoirs. The Reign of Louis XI*, trans. Michael Jones (Harmondsworth, Middx, 1972), p.270; Denys Hay, *The Italian Renaissance in its Historical Background* (Cambridge, 1970), p.197; Quentin Skinner, *The Foundations of Modern Political Thought*, 2 vols. (Cambridge, 1978), vol.2.

11. Marc Bloch, *Feudal Society*, 2 vols., trans. L.A. Manyon (London, 1965); Georges Duby, *The Three Orders: Feudal Society Imagined*, trans. Arthur Goldhammer (Chicago, 1980).

12. Walter Ullmann, *Medieval Foundations of Renaissance Humanism* (London, 1977), pp.vii, 11, 196.

13. Iris Origo, *Tribune of Rome. A Life of Cola di Rienzo* (London, 1938), p.127; Ronald G. Musto, *Apocalypse in Rome. Cola di Rienzo and the Politics of the New Age* (Berkeley and Los Angeles, 2003).

14. R.W. Southern, *Scholastic Humanism and the Unification of Europe*, vol.1, *Foundations* (Oxford, 1995), p.8.

15. Peter Burke, *The European Renaissance: Centres and Peripheries* (Oxford, 1998), pp.91–2.

16. Geoffrey Barraclough, 'Medium Aevum: Some Reflections on Medieval History and on the Term "Middle Ages" ', in his *History in a Changing World* (Oxford, 1955), p.63; see also E. F. Jacob, ' "Middle Ages" and "Renaissance" ', in his *Essays in the Conciliar Epoch*, 2nd edn (Manchester, 1953), pp.170–84.

17. Paul O. Kristeller, *Medieval Aspects of Renaissance Learning* (New York, 1992), pp.57–60, 63.

18. Wallace K. Ferguson, *The Renaissance in Historical Thought. Five Centuries of Interpretation* (Cambridge, Mass., 1948), p.155.

19. Augusto Campana, 'The Origins of the Word "Humanist" ', *Journal of the Warburg and Courtauld Institutes*, 9 (1946), p.66.

20. Kristeller, *Aspects*, pp.96–9; George Holmes, *The Florentine Enlightenment, 1400–1450* (Oxford, 1969), p.19; Nicolai Rubinstein, 'An Unknown Letter by Jacopo di Poggio Bracciolini on Discoveries of Classical Texts', *Italia Medioevale e Umanistica*, 1 (1958), pp.383–400.

21. Cecilia M. Ady, 'Morals and Manners of the *Quattrocento*', in George Holmes (ed.), *Art and Politics in Renaissance Italy* (Oxford, 1993), pp.1–18.

22. Denys Hay, *The Medieval Centuries* (London, 1964) first appeared as *From Roman Empire to Renaissance Europe* (London, 1953); see Preface to the Second Edition, p.vii.

23. Trevor Dean, 'The Courts', in Julius Kirshner (ed.), *The Origins of the State in Italy, 1300–1600* (Chicago, 1995), p.151.

24. Lauro Martines, *Power and Imagination. City-States in Renaissance Italy* (New York, 1980), p.192.

25. Cecil Grayson, 'Dante and the Renaissance', in C.P. Brand et al. (eds.), *Italian Studies presented to E.R. Vincent* (London, 1962), p.65; Hans Baron, *The Crisis of the Early Italian Renaissance. Civic Humanism and Republican Liberty in an Age of Classicism and Tyranny*, 1 vol. edn (Princeton, NJ, 1966), pp.331, 531–2 n.82.

26. E.H. Gombrich, 'The Early Medici as Patrons of Art', in E.F. Jacob (ed.), *Italian Renaissance Studies* (London, 1960), p.279; Holmes, *Enlightenment*, p.2; Mommsen, ' "Dark Ages" ', p.237; Martines, *Power and Imagination*, p.206.

27. Johan Huizinga, 'The Problem of the Renaissance', in his *Men and Ideas*, trans. James S. Holmes and Hans von Marle (New York, 1970), pp.271–8; William Manchester, *A World Lit Only by Fire. The Medieval World and the Renaissance* (London, 1993), pp.26, 95.

28. Alfred von Martin, *Sociology of the Renaissance*, trans. W.L. Luetkens (New York, 1963); Frederic Antal, *Florentine Painting and its Social*

Background (London, 1948); Richard A. Goldthwaite, *Wealth and the Demand for Art in Italy, 1300–1600* (Baltimore, Md., 1993).

29. Lisa Jardine, *Worldly Goods. A New History of the Renaissance* (London, 1996) has strong claims to be the worst book on the Renaissance.

30. Jacob Burckhardt, *Reflections on History*, trans. M.D. Hottinger (Indianapolis, Ind., 1979); Ferguson, *Historical Thought*, pp.180, 184.

31. Peter Burke, *Culture and Society in Renaissance Italy, 1420–1540* (London, 1972), pp.150, 188; Andrew Martindale, *The Rise of the Artist* (London, 1972).

32. Anthony Blunt, *Artistic Theory in Italy, 1450–1600* (Oxford, 1962), pp.115–17.

33. Diana Norman, 'The Art of Knowledge', in eadem (ed.), *Siena, Florence and Padua. Art, Society and Religion, 1280–1400*, 2 vols. (New Haven, Conn., 1995), vol.2, p.217.

34. George Holmes, *Renaissance* (London, 1996), p.7; cf. Martin Kemp, *The Science of Art* (New Haven, Conn., 1990); see also J.V. Field, *The Invention of Infinity. Mathematics and Art in the Renaissance* (Oxford, 1997), and Aldous Huxley, 'Literature and Examinations', in his *The Olive Tree* (London, 1936), pp.108–16.

35. Sergio Bertelli (ed.), *Italian Renaissance Courts*, trans. Mary Fitton and Geoffrey Culverwell (London, 1986), p.142; Christopher Black, 'The High Renaissance', in *Cultural Atlas of the Renaissance* (New York, 1993), p.82.

36. A. Richard Turner, *Inventing Leonardo* (London, 1993), p.55.

37. Giorgio Vasari, *Le vite dei più eccellenti pittori, scultori ed architetti*, ed. G. Sansoni, 9 vols. (Florence, 1906); see *Lives of the Artists*, ed. George Bull, 2 vols. (Harmondsworth, Middx, 1987), vol. 1, pp.15, 455; Ferguson, *Historical Thought*, pp.62–3.

38. Millard Meiss, *Painting in Florence and Siena after the Black Death* (Princeton, NJ, 1951); Edgar Wind, *Pagan Mysteries in the Renaissance* (London, 1958); Holmes, *Enlightenment*; John White, *The Birth and Rebirth of Pictorial Space*, 3rd edn (London, 1987), esp. p.66.

39. Bram Kempers, *Painting, Power and Patronage*, trans. Beverley Jackson (London, 1992), p.179; Charles Harrison, 'Giotto and the "Rise of Painting" ' in Norman, *Siena, Florence and Padua*, vol. 1, p.89; Catherine King, 'The Trecento: New Ideas, New Evidence', ibid., p.222.

40. Richard Mackenney, 'Venice', in Roy Porter and Mikulas Teich (eds.), *The Renaissance in National Context* (Cambridge, 1992), pp.53–67.

41. Kempers, *Painting*, p.10; John Ruskin, *The Stones of Venice*, 3 vols. (e.g.

London, 1907); Richard Goy, *The House of Gold* (Cambridge, 1992); idem, *Venice. The City and its Architecture* (London, 2000).

42. John Pope-Hennesy, *Essays on Italian Sculpture* (London, 1968), p.208.

43. Clark concluded, acerbically, that Berenson 'was perched on the pinnacle of a mountain of corruption': see Kenneth Clark, *Another Part of the Wood* (New York, 1974), pp.115–17; see also Patricia Rubin, 'Portrait of a Lady: Isabella Stewart Gardner, Bernard Berenson and the Market for Renaissance Art in America', *Apollo* (September 2000), pp.37–44. I am grateful to Michael Bury for this reference.

44. Peter Burke, 'Conspicuous Consumption in Seventeenth-Century Italy', in his *The Historical Anthropology of Early Modern Italy: Essays on Perception and Communication* (Cambridge, 1987), pp.132–49.

45. Mary Hollingsworth, *Patronage in Renaissance Italy* (London, 1994), pp.38, 75.

46. Stephen Greenblatt, *Renaissance Self-Fashioning. From More to Shakespeare* (Chicago, 1984). See pp.1–10 for the origins of the concept. On Bloch and Febvre, see in particular Peter Burke, *The French Historical Revolution* (Oxford, 1989), Part One.

47. Hans Baron, 'Burckhardt's *Civilization of the Renaissance* a Century after its Publication', *Renaissance News*, 13 (1960), pp.207–22; Ivan Gaskell, 'History of Images', in Peter Burke (ed.), *New Perspectives on Historical Writing* (Oxford, 1991), pp.168–92.

48. Marvin Becker, 'An Essay on the Quest for Identity in the Early Italian Renaissance', in J.G. Rowe and W.H. Stockdale (eds.), *'Florilegium Historiale'. Essays Presented to Wallace K. Ferguson* (Toronto, 1971), pp.296–308; idem, 'Aspects of Lay Piety in Early Renaissance Florence', in Charles Trinkaus and Heiko A. Oberman (eds.), *The Pursuit of Holiness in Late Medieval and Renaissance Religion* (Leyden, 1974), pp.177–98; Richard Goldthwaite, *Private Wealth in Renaissance Florence. A Study of Four Families* (Princeton, NJ, 1968); F.W. Kent, *Household and Lineage in Renaissance Florence* (Princeton, NJ, 1977); John M. Najemy, *Corporatism and Consensus in Florentine Electoral Politics, 1280–1400* (Chapel Hill, NC, 1982); Denis Romano, *Patricians and Popolani. The Social Foundations of the Venetian Renaissance State* (Baltimore, Md., 1987); Samuel K. Cohn, *The Laboring Classes in Renaissance Florence* (New York, 1980); idem, *The Cult of Remembrance and the Black Death* (Baltimore, Md., 1982); John Henderson, *Piety and Charity in Late Medieval Florence* (Oxford, 1994); Ronald Weissman, *Ritual Brotherhood in Renaissance Florence, 1200–1600* (New York, 1980); Brian Pullan, *Rich and Poor in Renaissance Venice* (Oxford, 1971); Richard Mackenney, *Tradesmen and Traders. The World of the Guilds in Venice and Europe, c.1250–c.1650* (London, 1987).

49. Goldthwaite, *Private Wealth*, p.253; Becker, 'Quest for Identity', p.306.

50. Vasari, *Lives*, vol.1, pp.106, 134; Richard Goldthwaite, *The Building of Renaissance Florence* (Baltimore, Md., 1980).

51. Ferguson, *Historical Thought*, p.94; Burke, *Culture and Society*, p.206; Lauro Martines, *The Social World of the Florentine Humanists* (London, 1963), p.90; Anthony Molho, 'Politics and the Ruling Class in Early Renaissance Florence', *Nuova Rivista Storica*, 52 (1968), pp.401–20.

52. Martines, *Power and Imagination*, p.217.

53. Kenneth Clark, *Civilisation* (London, 1968), p.112.

54. Baldassare Castiglione, *The Book of the Courtier*, trans. George Bull (Harmondsworth, Middx, 1967), p.310; Bertelli, *Courts*, p.75; Hollingsworth, *Renaissance*, p.210.

55. Ady, 'Morals and Manners'; Richard Mackenney, *Sixteenth Century Europe. Expansion and Conflict* (London, 1993), pp.219–42; David Abulafia (ed.), *The French Descent into Renaissance Italy, 1494–5* (Aldershot, Hants., 1995); John Henderson et al., *The Great Pox* (New Haven, Conn., 1997); *Courtier*, p.90.

56. Jacob Burckhardt, *The Civilization of the Renaissance in Italy*, trans. S.G.C. Middlemore (London, 1945), pp.240, 241.

57. Joan Kelly, 'Did Women have a Renaissance?', in Benjamin Kohl and Alison Andrews Smith (eds.), *Major Problems in the History of the Italian Renaissance* (Lexington, Mass., 1995), pp.15–26; Samuel Cohn, 'The Social History of Women in the Renaissance', in his *Women in the Streets* (Baltimore, Md., 1996), pp.16–38; Paola Tinagli, *Women in Renaissance Art* (Manchester, 1997); Catherine E. King, *Renaissance Women Patrons* (Manchester, 1998).

58. Burke, *Culture and Society*, pp.293–302.

59. Cohn, 'Women in the Streets'; Richard Mackenney, 'Continuity and Change in the Scuole Piccole of Venice, *c*.1250–1600', *Renaissance Studies*, 8 (1994), pp.393–4; *idem*, 'The Guilds of Venice, *c*.1200–*c*.1700: State and Society in the *longue durée*', *Studi Veneziani* n.s.34 (1997), pp.15–43; Stanley Chojnacki, *Women and Men in Renaissance Venice* (Baltimore, Md., 2000); Margaret F. Rosenthal, *The Honest Courtesan* (Chicago, 1992).

60. Loren Partridge, *The Renaissance in Rome* (London, 1996), pp.103–4.

61. Ibid., p.121.

62. Ibid., pp.135–6. For a fascinating interpretation of the Virgin's centrality to Renaissance cultures, see Pier Paolo Pasolini's film of selected stories from Boccaccio, *Decamerone* (1970).

63. Barraclough, *History in a Changing World*; Francis Haskell, *History and its Images* (New Haven, Conn., 1993), p.201; Evelyn Welch, *Art and Society*

in Italy, 1350–1500 (London, 1997), p.9; Ferguson, *Historical Thought*; Lionel Gossman, *Basel in the Age of Burckhardt* (Chicago, 2000).

64. Turner, *Leonardo*, pp.76, 86, 180; Peter Burke, *The Fortunes of the Courtier* (Oxford, 1995), pp.131, 136–7.

Chapter 2. Reconstructions

1. R-H. Bautier, *The Economic Development of Medieval Europe*, trans. Heather Karolyi (London, 1971); Robert S. Lopez, *The Commercial Revolution of the Middle Ages* (Cambridge, 1976); for Italy, Daniel Waley, *The Italian City-Republics* (London, 1969), pp.14–16; Lopez, 'Still Another Renaissance?', *American Historical Review*, 57 (1951–2), pp.1–21.

2. R.W. Southern, *The Making of the Middle Ages* (London, 1967); Robert Bartlett, *The Making of Europe* (London, 1993).

3. Marc Bloch, *Feudal Society*, trans. L.A. Manyon, 2 vols. (London, 1965); Georges Duby, *The Three Orders. Feudal Society Imagined*, trans. Arthur Goldhammer (Chicago, 1980); Jonathan Riley-Smith, *What were the Crusades?* (London, 1977).

4. Jacob Burckhardt, *The Civilization of the Renaissance in Italy*, trans. S.G.C. Middlemore (London, 1945), pp.2–3; Steven Runciman, *The Sicilian Vespers* (Harmondsworth, Middx, 1960); Peter Partner, *The Lands of St Peter. The Papal State in the Middle Ages and the Early Renaissance* (London, 1972), pp.229–65.

5. John Larner, *The Lords of Romagna* (London, 1965), pp.45, 53, 91.

6. Philip Jones, 'Communes and Despots', *Transactions of the Royal Historical Society*, 15 (1965), pp.71–95; *idem, The Italian City-State* (Oxford, 1997).

7. Ottonis Episcopi Frisingensis et Rahewini, *Gesta Frederici seu rectius Cronica*, ed. Adolf Schmidt, intro. Franz-Josef Schmale (Berlin, 1965), II.14, pp.308–10; cf. Otto of Freising, *The Deeds of Frederick Barbarossa*, trans. Christopher Mierow (New York, 1966), p.128; Giorgio Falco, *The Holy Roman Republic*, trans. K.V. Kent (London, 1964).

8. Enrico Fiumi, 'Fioritura e decadenza dell'economia fiorentina', *Archivio Storico Italiano*, 115 (1957), pp.385–439.

9. Gino Luzzatto, *Breve storia economica dell'Italia medievale* (Turin, 1973).

10. Quentin Skinner, *The Foundations of Modern Political Thought*, 2 vols. (Cambridge, 1978), vol.1.

11. Donald E. Queller, *The Fourth Crusade* (Philadelphia, Pa., 1977).

12. Waley, *City-Republics*.

13. Moses I. Finley (ed.), *Slavery in Classical Antiquity* (Cambridge, 1960); Iris Origo, 'The Domestic Enemy: Eastern Slaves in Tuscany in the

Fourteenth and Fifteenth Centuries', *Speculum*, 30 (1955), pp.321–66; Gene Brucker (ed.), *The Society of Renaissance Florence* (New York, 1971), pp.222–8; John Larner, *Culture and Society in Italy, 1290–1420* (London, 1971), pp.28, 86–7; Fiumi, 'Fioritura'; Richard Goldthwaite, *Private Wealth in Renaissance Florence* (Princeton, NJ, 1968); Iris Origo, *The Merchant of Prato* (Harmondsworth, Middx, 1963); Florence de Roover, 'Andrea Banchi', *Studies in Medieval and Renaissance History*, 3 (1966), pp.231–85; Frederic C. Lane, *Andrea Barbarigo, Merchant of Venice, 1418–1449* (Baltimore, Md., 1944); C.T. Davis, 'Education in Dante's Florence', *Speculum*, 40 (1965), pp.415–35.

14. Tim Benton, 'The Three Cities Compared: Urbanism', in Diana Norman (ed.), *Siena, Florence and Padua. Art, Society and Religion, 1280–1400*, 2 vols. (New Haven, Conn., and London, 1995), vol.2, p.24; David Thomson, *Renaissance Architecture. Critics. Patrons. Luxury* (Manchester, 1993), pp.175–8.

15. Jacques Le Goff, *Medieval Civilization*, trans. Julia Barrow (Oxford, 1988), pp.165–6, 175, 180.

16. Armando Sapori, *The Italian Merchant in the Middle Ages*, trans. P.A. Kennen (New York, 1970); J.T. Noonan, *The Scholastic Analysis of Usury* (Cambridge, Mass., 1957); Jacques Le Goff, 'Merchant's Time and Church's Time in the Middle Ages', in his *Time, Work and Culture in the Middle Ages*, trans. Arthur Goldhammer (Chicago, 1980), pp.29–42; the quotation from canon law is cited and discussed in Lester K. Little, *Religious Poverty and the Profit Economy in Medieval Europe* (London, 1979), p.38.

17. Pierre Francastel, 'L'art italien et le role personnel de Saint François', *Annales* (1956), pp.481–9; Alastair Smart, *The Dawn of Italian Painting* (London, 1978) p.6; Little, *Religious Poverty*, pp.146–73.

18. Brian Pullan, *A History of Early Renaissance Italy* (London, 1973), pp.305–40; Iris Origo, *The World of San Bernardino* (London, 1963).

19. Quoted in George Holmes, *Florence, Rome and the Origins of the Renaissance* (Oxford, 1986), p.58.

20. Ibid. has successive chapters on 'the model of St Francis of Assisi' and 'lay thought in Florence'.

21. John Henderson, *Piety and Charity in Late Medieval Florence* (Oxford, 1994), pp.21, 254, 323, 414.

22. Marvin Becker, 'Dante and Co. as Political Men', *Speculum*, 41 (1966), p.675; Randolph Starn, *Contrary Commonwealths* (Berkeley, Cal., 1982); Johan Huizinga, 'Renaissance and Realism', in his *Men and Ideas*, trans. James S. Holmes and Hans van Marle (New York, 1959), pp.275, 278.

23. Holmes, *Origins*, p.89; see also *idem, Dante* (Oxford, 1980).

24. Holmes, *Origins*; J.K. Hyde, *Society and Politics in Medieval Italy* (London, 1973); Robert Brentano, *Rome before Avignon* (London, 1974); Pullan, *Early Renaissance*, pp.49–59; Yves Renouard, *The Avignon Papacy*, trans. Dennis Bethell (London, 1970); Walter Ullmann, *A Short History of the Papacy in the Middle Ages* (London, 1972), pp.279–305; idem, *The Origins of the Great Schism* (London, 1948).

25. Lauro Martines (ed.), *Violence and Civil Disorder in Italian Cities, 1200–1500* (Berkeley, Cal., 1978); Jones, *City-State*, e.g. pp.42, 66.

26. Quoted in Iris Origo, *Tribune of Rome* (London, 1938), pp.149–50.

27. Marvin Becker, 'A Study in Political Failure: The Florentine Magnates, 1280–1343', *Medieval Studies*, 27 (1965), esp. pp.247, 248, 252, 256; W.M. Bowsky, 'The Anatomy of Rebellion', in Martines, *Violence*, pp.229–72.

28. See Little, *Religious Poverty*; Jacques Le Goff, *Your Money or Your Life*, trans. Patricia Ranum (New York, 1988); and the older studies by J.T. Noonan, *The Scholastic Analysis of Usury* (Cambridge, Mass., 1957); and B.N. Nelson, *The Idea of Usury: From Tribal Brotherhood to Universal Otherhood* (Princeton, NJ, 1949).

29. Marvin Becker, 'Church and State in Renaissance Florence', *Speculum*, 37 (1962), pp.9, 14; Raymond de Roover, *The Rise and Decline of the Medici Bank, 1397–1494* (Cambridge, Mass., 1963), p.12; W.M. Bowsky, *A Medieval Italian Commune: Siena under the Nine, 1287–1355* (Berkeley, Cal., 1981).

30. Armando Sapori, *La crisi delle compagnie mercantili dei Bardi e dei Peruzzi* (Florence, 1926).

31. Larner, *Culture and Society*, p.245; Andrew Martindale, *The Rise of the Artist* (London, 1972), pp.121–2.

32. Millard Meiss, *Painting in Florence and Siena after the Black Death* (Princeton, NJ, 1951); Larner, *Culture and Society*, pp.142–4; John White, *The Birth and Rebirth of Pictorial Space*, 3rd edn (London, 1987).

33. Samuel K. Cohn, *The Cult of Remembrance and the Black Death* (Baltimore, Md., 1992); see also his *The Black Death Transformed. Disease and Culture in Early Renaissance Europe* (London, 2002).

34. Larner, *Culture and Society*, p.142.

35. Quoted in Bram Kempers, *Painting, Power and Patronage*, trans. Beverley Jackson (London, 1992), p.166.

36. F. Petrarca, *Le familiari*, vol.2, ed. Vittorio Rossi (Florence, 1934), Book 8, no.7, p.176; vol.4, ed. Umberto Bosco (Florence, 1940), Book 24, no.1, p.220; cf. *Letters from Petrarch*, ed. Morris Bishop (Bloomington, Ind., 1966), pp.73–4.

37. *Le familiari*, vol.4, ed. Umberto Bosco (Florence, 1940), Book 24, no.1, p.220; cf. *Letters from Petrarch*, ed. Bishop, p.200.

38. *Decameron*, First Day, Preface to the first story; see also John Larner, 'The Artists and Intellectuals in the Fourteenth Century', *History*, 54 (1969), pp.15–30.

39. *Cronaca fiorentina*, in *Rerum Italicarum Scriptores*, vol.30 (Città di Castello, 1903), p.634; translation in Henderson, *Piety and Charity*, p.299.

40. V.I. Rutenburg, *Popolo e movimenti popolari nell'Italia medioevale*, trans. G. Borchini (Bologna, 1971); N. Rodolico, *I Ciompi* (Florence, 1945); *Il tumulto dei Ciompi* (Florence, 1981); Raymond de Roover, 'Labour Conditions in Florence', in Nicolai Rubinstein (ed.), *Florentine Studies* (London, 1968), pp.277–313; Marvin Becker and Gene Brucker, 'The Arti Minori in Florentine Politics, 1342–1378', *Medieval Studies*, 18 (1956), pp.246–308; John M. Najemy, *Corporatism and Consensus in Florentine Electoral Politics, 1280–1400* (Chapel Hill, NC, 1982); C.M. de la Roncière, *Prix et salaires à Florence au 14e siècle* (Rome, 1982); Hidetoshi Hoshino, *L'industria della lana a Firenze* (Florence, 1981).

41. Hans Baron, *The Crisis of the Early Italian Renaissance*, one vol. edn (Princeton, NJ, 1966).

42. B. L. Ullmann, *The Humanism of Coluccio Salutati* (Padua, 1963), esp. p.14.

43. J.R. Hale, *Florence and the Medici.The Pattern of Control* (London, 1977).

44. Frederick Hartt, 'Art and Freedom in '400 Florence', in L.F. Sandler (ed.), *Essays in Memory of K. Leymann* (New York, 1964), pp.114–30.

45. Larner, *Culture and Society*, p.100.

46. George Holmes, *The Florentine Enlightenment* (London, 1969), pp.202–41.

47. Lauro Martines, *The Social World of the Florentine Humanists* (London, 1963).

48. Holmes, *Enlightenment*, pp.68–76, 243–7, 260; see also Hale, *Florence and the Medici*; Nicolai Rubinstein, *The Government of Florence under the Medici, 1434–1494* (Oxford, 1966); Dale Kent, *The Rise of the Medici* (Oxford, 1978).

49. E. B. Fryde, 'Lorenzo de' Medici', in A.G. Dickens (ed.), *The Courts of Europe* (London, 1977), pp.77–98; Alison Cole, *Art of the Italian Renaissance Courts* (London, 1995).

50. Geoffrey Parker, *The Military Revolution, 1500–1800* (Cambridge, 1986).

51. Michael Mallett, *Mercenaries and their Masters* (London, 1974); J.R. Hale, *Artists and Warfare in the Italian Renaissance* (New Haven, Conn., 1990).

52. Richard Mackenney, *Sixteenth Century Europe* (London, 1993), pp.219–42.

53. See, however, the notable studies in Marjorie Reeves (ed.), *Prophetic Rome in the High Renaissance Period* (Oxford, 1992); Stephen Bowd, *Reform before the Reformation* (Leyden, 2002).

54. Lauro Martines, *Power and Imagination. City-States in Renaissance Italy* (New York, 1980), pp.334–5.

55. Pullan, *Early Renaissance Italy*, pp.30–40; Origo, *San Bernardino*; Donald

Weinstein, *Savonarola and Florence. Prophecy and Patriotism in the Renaissance* (Princeton, NJ, 1970); Robert S. Lopez, *The Three Ages of the Italian Renaissance* (Charlottesville, Va., 1970), p.38.

Chapter 3. Contexts I: Cities

1. Bram Kempers, *Painting, Power and Patronage*, trans. Beverley Jackson (London, 1992), p.306.
2. Christopher Black, 'The High Renaissance', in *Cultural Atlas of the Renaissance* (New York, 1993), pp.76–99.
3. Erwin Panofsky, *Renaissance and Renascences in Western Art* (New York, 1969).
4. J.G.A. Pocock, *The Machiavellian Moment* (Princeton, NJ, 1975).
5. Kenneth Clark, *Civilisation* (London, 1969), p.117.
6. Robert Brentano, *Rome before Avignon* (London, 1964), pp.15, 83.
7. John White, *The Birth and Rebirth of Pictorial Space*, 3rd edn (London, 1987), pp.48–52; Alastair Smart, *The Dawn of Italian Painting* (London, 1978), pp.21–3.
8. Brentano, *Rome*, pp.66–7.
9. Iris Origo, *Tribune of Rome* (London, 1938).
10. Peter Partner, *The Lands of St Peter* (London, 1972), pp.333–4; Origo, *Tribune*; John Law, *The Lords of Renaissance Italy* (London, 1981).
11. Loren Partridge, *The Renaissance in Rome* (London, 1996), p.24.
12. Walter Ullmann, *A Short History of the Papacy in the Middle Ages* (London, 1972).
13. John F. d'Amico, *Renaissance Humanism in Papal Rome* (Baltimore, Md., 1983), pp.58, 16.
14. Ibid., pp.123, 31, 124–5; Partridge, *Rome*, p.36.
15. H.A. Enno van Gelder, *The Two Reformations in the Sixteenth Century* (The Hague, 1964); A.G. Dickens, *The German Nation and Martin Luther* (London, 1976).
16. D'Amico, *Rome*, pp.56, 143.
17. Partridge, *Rome*, p.54.
18. W.M. Bowsky, *A Medieval Italian Commune: Siena under the Nine, 1287–1355* (Berkeley, Cal., 1981); Brian Pullan, *A History of Early Renaissance Italy* (Harmondsworth, Middx, 1973). See also Daniel Waley, *Siena and the Sienese in the Thirteenth Century* (Cambridge, 1991); Helene Wieruszovski, 'Art and the Commune in the Age of Dante', *Speculum*, 19 (1944), pp.14–33; Nicolai Rubinstein, 'Political Ideas in Sienese Art', *Journal of the Warburg and Courtauld Institutes*, 21 (1958), pp.179–207.

19. Waley, *Siena*, p.77.

20. Ibid., pp.127–54.

21. Agnolo di Tura, 'Cronaca Senese', in L. Muratori (ed.), *Rerum Italicarum Scriptores* vol.XV, pt vi (Bologna, 1931–7), p.313; also quoted in Bowsky, *Siena*, p.284.

22. Bowsky, *Siena*; Rubinstein, 'Sienese Art'.

23. White, *Birth and Rebirth*, pp.78–9; Smart, *Dawn*, p.106; Kempers, *Painting*, p.141.

24. Quotation from Kempers, *Painting*, p.115; White, *Birth and Rebirth*, p.84.

25. Bowsky, *Siena*, p.285.

26. Kempers, *Painting*, p.158.

27. Ibid., pp.158–9; Judith Hook, 'Fortifications and the End of the Sienese State', *History*, 62 (1977), pp.372–87.

28. Jacob Burckhardt, *The Civilization of the Renaissance in Italy*, trans. S.G.C. Middlemore (London, 1945), p.40.

29. George Holmes, *The Florentine Enlightenment* (London, 1969).

30. Daniel Waley, *The Italian City-Republics* (London, 1969), p.36 on the expanding city walls.

31. Hidetoshi Hoshino, *L'industria della lana a Firenze* (Florence, 1981).

32. Francesco Guicciardini, *Storie Fiorentine, dal 1378 al 1509*, ed. Roberto Palmarocchi (Bari, 1931), pp.4–5; cf. *The History of Florence*, trans. Mario Domandi (New York, 1970), p.5.

33. Nicolai Rubinstein, *The Government of Florence under the Medici, 1434–1494* (Oxford, 1966); see also the brilliant summary in J.R. Hale, *Florence and the Medici. The Pattern of Control* (London, 1977), pp.15–20.

34. A. Richard Turner, *The Renaissance in Florence* (London, 1997), p.9.

35. Richard Krautheimer, *Lorenzo Ghiberti* (Princeton, NJ, 1956), doc.52, p.372; cf. D.S. Chambers (ed.), *Patrons and Artists in the Italian Renaissance* (London, 1970), p.48.

36. Leonardo Bruni, 'Laudatio Florentinae Urbis', in Hans Baron, *From Petrarch to Leonardo Bruni. Studies in Humanistic Literature* (Chicago, 1968), pp.234–5; cf. 'Panegyric to the City of Florence', in Benjamin Kohl and Ronald G. Witt (eds.), *The Earthly Republic* (Manchester, 1978), p.138.

37. John Larner, *The Lords of Romagna* (London, 1965), p.129.

38. For Florentine history after 1500, see John Stephens, *The Last Florentine Republic* (Oxford, 1983); Humphrey Butters, *Governors and Government in Early Sixteenth-Century Florence* (Oxford, 1985); Eric Cochrane, *Florence in the Forgotten Centuries, 1527–1800* (Chicago, 1973).

39. Felix Gilbert, *Machiavelli and Guicciardini. Politics and History in Sixteenth-Century Florence* (Princeton, NJ, 1973).

40. Holmes, *Enlightenment*, p.176; Richard Mackenney, 'Venice', in Roy Porter and Mikulas Teich (eds.), *The Renaissance in National Context* (Cambridge, 1992), pp.53–67.

41. For a narrative, see Frederic C. Lane, *Venice. A Maritime Republic* (Baltimore, Md., 1975); on art and politics, Patricia Fortini Brown, *The Renaissance in Venice* (London, 1997); and for the period after 1380, David Chambers, *The Imperial Age of Venice, 1380–1580* (London, 1970).

42. Chambers, *Imperial Age*.

43. Sally McKee, *Uncommon Dominion: Venetian Crete and the Myth of Ethnic Purity* (Philadelphia, Pa., 2000).

44. Brian Pullan (ed.), *Crisis and Change in the Venetian Economy* (London, 1969); Richard Mackenney, *Tradesmen and Traders. The World of the Guilds in Venice and Europe, c.1250–c.1650* (London, 1987); Richard Rapp, *Industry and Economic Decline in Seventeenth-Century Venice* (Cambridge, Mass., 1974).

45. Giorgio Vasari, *Le opere di Giorgio Vasari*, ed. G. Milanesi, 9 vols. (Florence, 1906), vol.2, p.413; cf. *Lives of the Artists*, ed. and trans. George Bull, 2 vols. (Harmondsworth, Middx, 1987), vol.1, pp.182–3.

46. J.K. Hyde, *Padua in the Age of Dante* (Manchester, 1966), p.309.

47. *The Defender of Peace*, trans. and intro. Alan Gewirth (New York, 1967), p.126.

48. Gordon Leff, *The Dissolution of the Medieval Outlook* (New York, 1976), pp.137–8.

49. David Herlihy, *Pisa in the Early Renaissance* (New Haven, Conn., 1958).

50. Stephen Epstein, *Genoa and the Genoese, 958–1528* (Chapel Hill, NC, 1996); Jacques Heers, *Gênes au quinzième siècle* (Paris, 1961); Fernand Braudel, *The Perspective of the World*, trans. Siân Reynolds (London, 1984), pp.157–74; Mary Hollingsworth, *Patronage in Sixteenth-century Italy* (London, 1996), pp.235–7.

51. Robert S. Lopez, 'Hard Times and Investment in Culture', in William Werkmeister (ed.), *The Renaissance. Six Essays* (New York, 1962), pp.29–54.

52. On the momentous consequences of the discovery, see Frederic C. Lane, 'The Economic Meaning of the Invention of the Compass', in his *Venice and History* (Baltimore, Md., 1966), pp.331–44.

53. References to Amalfi in works on medieval Italy are quite sparse, but for succinct summaries, see Barbara M. Kreutz, *Before the Normans:*

Southern Italy in the 9th and 10th Centuries (Philadelphia, Pa., 1996), pp.87–93; J.K. Hyde, *Society and Politics in Medieval Italy. The Evolution of the Civil Life, 1000–1350* (London, 1973), pp.35–7; Robert S. Lopez, *The Commercial Revolution of the Middle Ages, 950–1350* (Cambridge, 1976), pp.64–5. For specialised comparisons of the maritime republics, see Ottavio Banti (ed.), *Amalfi–Genova–Pisa–Venezia. La cattedrale e la città nel Medioevo. Aspetti religiosi, istituzionali e urbanistici* (Pisa, 1993).

54. By contrast to such dark shadows, Burckhardt's Teutonic contemporaries found the Amalfi coast charming. The garden at Ravello was to provide Richard Wagner (1813–83) with his inspiration for the garden of Klingsor and its flower maidens in his last opera, *Parsifal.* Writing the opera had taken 17 years, and having seen the Villa Rufolo, the composer wrote in the visitors' book (26 May 1880) in calm ecstasy, 'The enchanted garden of Klingsor has been found'. On Wagner at Ravello, see John Deathridge and Carl Dahlhaus, *The New Grove Wagner* (London, 1984), p.64.

Chapter 4. Contexts II: Courts

1. J.A. Symonds, *The Age of the Despots*, in *Renaissance in Italy*, 7 vols. (London, 1904), vol.1, pp.84–5.

2. Ibid., p.87

3. Ibid., p.89.

4. John Larner, *The Lords of Romagna* (London, 1965), p.200.

5. P.J. Jones, 'Communes and Despots', *Transactions of the Royal Historical Society*, 15 (1965), pp.71–95; *idem, The Italian City-State. From Commune to Signoria* (Oxford, 1997).

6. Brian Pullan, *A History of Early Renaissance Italy* (London, 1973), p.301.

7. Larner, *Romagna*, p.154; Pierangelo Schiera, 'Legitimacy, Discipline, and Institutions: Three Necessary Conditions for the Birth of the Modern State', in Julius Kirshner (ed.), *The Origins of the State in Italy, 1300–1600* (Chicago, 1995), p.22.

8. John Law, *The Lords of Renaissance Italy* (London, 1981); Denys Hay and John Law, *Italy in the Age of the Renaissance* (London, 1989), pp.47–74.

9. Elena Fasano Guarini, 'Center and Periphery', in Kirshner, *Origins*, p.82; Larner, *Romagna*, pp.18, 81, 154.

10. Bram Kempers, *Painting, Power and Patronage*, trans. Beverley Jackson (London, 1992), pp.103, 151; Peter Partner, *The Lands of St. Peter* (London, 1972), pp.308, 382; P.J. Jones, *The Malatesta of Rimini and the Papal State* (Cambridge, 1974), pp.89, 113; Larner, *Romagna*, p.90.

11. J.R. Hale, *Florence and the Medici. The Pattern of Control* (London, 1977); Frederic C. Lane, *Venice. A Maritime Republic* (Baltimore, Md., 1975), p.252.

12. Kenneth Clark, *Civilisation* (London, 1969), p.112.

13. Paula Clarke, 'A Sienese Note on 1466', in Peter Denley and Caroline Elam (eds.), *Florence and Italy. Renaissance Studies in Honour of Nicolai Rubinstein* (London, 1988), p.51, n.2.

14. Francesco Guicciardini, *Storie fiorentine dal 1378 al 1509*, ed. Roberto Palmarocchi (Bari, 1931), pp.4–5; cf. *The History of Florence*, ed. and trans. Mario Domandi (New York, 1970), pp.5–6.

15. Quoted in Hale, *Medici*, p.61.

16. 'The Pazzi Conspiracy', in Benjamin Kohl and Ronald G. Witt (eds.), *The Earthly Republic* (Manchester, 1978), p.314.

17. E.H. Gombrich, 'The Early Medici as Patrons of the Arts', in E.F. Jacob (ed.), *Renaissance Studies* (London, 1960), pp.279–311; E.B. Fryde, 'Lorenzo de' Medici', in A.G. Dickens (ed.), *The Courts of Europe* (London, 1977), pp.77–98.

18. A. Richard Turner, *The Renaissance in Florence* (London, 1997), p.150.

19. Kempers, *Painting*, pp.277–8.

20. Eric Cochrane, *Florence in the Forgotten Centuries, 1527–1800* (Chicago, 1973).

21. Law, *Lords*, p.18; Werner L. Gundersheimer, *Ferrara. The Style of a Renaissance Despotism* (Princeton, NJ, 1973); Denis Tuohy, *Herculean Ferrara* (Cambridge, 1996); David Chambers and Trevor Dean, *Clean Hands and Rough Justice* (Ann Arbor, Mich., 1997).

22. Alison Cole, *Art of the Italian Renaissance Courts* (London, 1995), p.119.

23. Luke Syson and Dillian Gordon, *Pisanello. Painter to the Renaissance Court* (London, 2001); Tuohy, *Ferrara*, p.184; William F. Prizer, 'North Italian Courts, 1460–1540', in Iain Fenlon (ed.), *The Renaissance Man and Music*, vol. 2 (London, 1989), p.149.

24. Quoted in David Thomson, *Renaissance Architecture. Critics. Patrons. Luxury* (Manchester, 1993), p.18.

25. Vespasiano da Bisticci, *Vite di uomini illustri del XV secolo*, ed. Paolo d'Ancona and Erhard Aeschlimann (Milan, 1951), pp.191–225; cf. *Renaissance Princes, Popes and Prelates*, trans. William George and Emily Waters, intro. Myron P. Gilmore (New York, 1963), pp.83–114.

26. Cole, *Courts*, pp.67–92; Kempers, *Painting*, p.227.

27. *Il libro del cortegiano*, I. ii; cf. *The Courtier*, trans. George Bull (Harmondsworth, Middx, 1967), pp.40–1.

28. David Chambers and Jane Martineau (eds.), *Splendours of the Gonzaga* (London, 1981); Cole, *Courts*, pp.143–70.

29. Caroline Elam, 'Mantegna at Mantua', in Chambers and Martineau, *Splendours*, pp.15–27; Mary Hollingsworth, *Patronage in Renaissance Italy* (London, 1994), p.223.

30. Hollingsworth, *Renaissance Italy*, pp.167–73.

31. Gregory Lubkin, *A Renaissance Court. Milan under Galeazzo Maria Sforza* (Berkeley and Los Angeles, 1994), pp.247–8.

32. Evelyn Welch, *Art and Authority in Renaissance Milan* (New Haven, Conn., 1995); Cole, *Courts*, pp.93–118.

33. Kempers, *Painting*, p.150; Alan Ryder, *The Kingdom of Naples under Alfonso the Magnanimous* (Oxford, 1976), esp. pp.54, 90.

34. Cole, *Courts*, pp.45–66.

35. Jerry H. Bentley, *Politics and Culture in Renaissance Naples* (Princeton, NJ, 1987).

36. Benjamin G. Kohl, *Padua under the Carrara, 1318–1405* (Baltimore, Md., 1998).

37. Symonds, *Despots*, p.83.

38. Diana Norman, 'The Three Cities Compared: Patrons, Politics and Art', in eadem (ed.), *Siena, Florence and Padua. Art, Society and Religion, 1280–1400*, 2 vols. (New Haven, Conn., 1995), vol.1, p.21.

39. J.K.Hyde, *Padua in the Age of Dante* (Manchester, 1966); Margaret Plant, 'Patronage in the Circle of the Carrara Family: Padua, 1337–1405', in F.W. Kent and Patricia Simons (eds.), *Patronage, Art and Society in Renaissance Italy* (Oxford, 1987), p.194.

40. Plant, 'Patronage', p.199.

41. Kempers, *Painting*, pp.26, 29; Pullan, *Early Renaissance Italy*, pp.26–48.

42. Roberto Bizzocchi, 'Church, Religion, and State in the Early Modern Period', in Kirshner, *Origins*, pp.155–6.

43. Walter Ullmann, *A Short History of the Medieval Papacy* (London, 1972); idem, *Origins of the Great Schism* (London, 1948); Michael Wilkes, *The Problem of Sovereignty in the Late Middle Ages* (London, 1964); J.N. Figgis, *From Gerson to Grotius*, 2nd edn (Cambridge, 1931); E.F. Jacob, *Essays in the Conciliar Epoch*, 2nd edn (Manchester, 1953); George Holmes, *Europe: Hierarchy and Revolt, 1320–1450* (London, 1975); Paolo Prodi, *The Papal Prince*, trans. Susan Haskins (Cambridge, 1987).

44. Bizzocchi, 'Church', p.154; Denys Hay, *The Church in Italy in the Fifteenth Century* (Cambridge, 1977).

45. Jones, *Malatesta*, p.42.

46. Smart, *Dawn*, pp.89–97.

47. Michael Levey, *Early Renaissance* (Harmondsworth, Middx, 1967), p.24.

48. Vespasiano, *Princes, Popes and Prelates*, p.19.

49. Donald R. Weinstein, *Savonarola and Florence. Prophecy and Patriotism in the Renaissance* (Princeton, NJ, 1970).
50. Christine Shaw, *Julius II. The Warrior Pope* (Oxford, 1993).
51. Kempers, *Painting*, pp.254–65.
52. Ullmann, *Short History*, pp.21, 318.

Chapter 5. Sponsors

1. Charles Harrison, 'Giotto and the "Rise of Painting" ', in Diana Norman (ed.), *Siena, Florence and Padua. Art, Society and Religion, 1280–1400*, 2 vols. (New Haven, Conn., 1995), vol.1, p.76; *eadem*, 'The Arena Chapel: Patronage and Authorship', ibid., vol.2, pp.86–7, 83.
2. Diana Norman,' "The Glorious Deeds of the Commune": Civic Patronage of Art', in *eadem, Siena, Florence and Padua*, vol.1, p.138; William Hood, *Fra Angelico at San Marco* (New Haven, Conn., 1993), p.250; cf. Dale Kent, *Cosimo de' Medici and the Florentine Renaissance* (New Haven, Conn., 2000), p.153; Bram Kempers, *Painting, Power and Patronage*, trans. Beverley Jackson (London, 1992), p.317.
3. Kempers, *Painting*, p.318.
4. Peter Burke, *Culture and Society in Renaissance Italy, 1420–1540* (London, 1972), pp.109–10.
5. E.H. Gombrich, 'The Early Medici as Patrons of the Arts', in E.F. Jacob (ed.), *Renaissance Studies* (London, 1960), p.308; Thomas Tuohy, *Herculean Ferrara* (Cambridge, 1996).
6. Giovanni Gaye (ed.), *Carteggio inedito d'artisti*, 3 vols. (Florence, 1839–40), vol.2, p.191; cf. D.S. Chambers (ed.), *Patrons and Artists in the Italian Renaissance* (London, 1970), p.96.
7. John Stephens, *The Italian Renaissance. The Origins of Intellectual and Artistic Change before the Reformation* (London, 1990), p.67.
8. F.W. Kent and Patricia Simons, 'Renaissance Patronage: An Introductory Essay', in *eidem* (eds.), *Patronage, Art and Society in Renaissance Italy* (Oxford, 1987), p.2.
9. David Thomson, *Renaissance Architecture. Patrons. Critics. Luxury* (Manchester, 1993), p.25.
10. Chambers, *Patrons and Artists*; Mary Hollingsworth, *Patronage in Renaissance Italy* (London, 1994), p.54; Kempers, *Painting*, p.188.
11. Rona Goffen (ed.), *Masaccio's* Trinity (Cambridge, 1998); Evelyn Welch, *Art and Society in Italy, 1350–1500* (Oxford, 1997), p.11; Tuohy, *Ferrara*, p.34.
12. Hollingsworth, *Renaissance Italy*, pp.38, 69, 92.

13. Colin Cunningham, 'For the Honour and Beauty of the City: The Design of Town Halls', in Norman, *Siena, Florence and Padua*, vol.2, p.31 – a list that omits Venice.

14. Thomson, *Architecture*, pp.9–16.

15. Ibid., p.194.

16. Welch, *Art and Society*, p.108.

17. The arguments of Gene Brucker are summarised by Ronald Weissman, 'Taking Patronage Seriously', in Kent and Simons, *Patronage*, pp.28–9, 37.

18. Lauro Martines, *The Social World of the Florentine Humanists* (London, 1963); see also Lily Ross Taylor, *Party Politics in the Age of Caesar* (Berkeley, Cal., 1971).

19. Robert Gaston, 'Liturgy and Patronage in San Lorenzo, Florence, 1350–1650', in Kent and Simons, *Patronage*, pp.121–2, 126–7.

20. Diana Webb, *Patrons and Defenders. The Patron Saints in the Italian City-States* (New York, 1996).

21. Hood, *Fra Angelico*, pp.242–4.

22. Jacques Le Goff, *Your Money or your Life: Economy and Religion in the Middle Ages*, trans. Patricia Ranum (New York, 1988), pp.17–32, quotation on p.17; Lester K. Little, *Religious Economy and the Profit Economy in Medieval Europe* (London, 1978), pp.179–83; see also the older works of John T. Noonan, *The Scholastic Analysis of Usury* (Cambridge, Mass., 1957), and of B.N. Nelson, 'The Usurer and the Merchant Prince: Italian Businessmen and the Ecclesiastical Law of Restitution', *Journal of Economic History*, 7 (1947), *Supplement* 7.

23. Vespasiano da Bisticci, *Vite di uomini illustri del xv secolo*, ed. Paolo d'Ancona and Erhard Aeschlimann (Milan, 1951), pp.422–3; cf. *Renaissance Princes, Popes and Prelates*, trans. William George and Emily Waters, intro. Myron P. Gilmore (New York, 1963), pp.221, 224, 227.

24. Thomson, *Renaissance Architecture*, p.11.

25. James Stubblebine (ed.), *Giotto: The Arena Chapel Frescoes* (New York, 1969), p.72.

26. Ibid., p.111.

27. See also Matthew 21:12–13; Luke 19:45–6; John 2:14–17.

28. Lester K. Little, 'Pride goes before Avarice: Social Change and the Vices in Latin Christendom', *American Historical Review*, 76 (1971), pp.27–9.

29. Chambers, *Patrons and Artists*, pp.43, 46.

30. A. Richard Turner, *The Renaissance in Florence* (London, 1997), p.51.

31. Turner, *Renaissance Florence*, p.41; Chambers, *Patrons and Artists*, pp.39–41.

32. Vespasiano, *Vita di Cosimo de' Medici* in *Vite di uomini illustri*, p.410; cf. *Princes, Popes and Prelates*, p.218.

33. Hood, *Fra Angelico*, pp.18, 21, 116.

34. Ibid., pp.30, 252.

35. Ibid., pp.249–50.

36. Kent, *Cosimo de' Medici*, pp.153–4.

37. *Vita di Cosimo*, pp. 411–14; cf. *Princes, Popes and Prelates*, pp.219–21.

38. *Vita di Nicolao Nicoli*, pp.440–2; cf. *Princes, Popes and Prelates*, pp. 400–2.

39. B.L. Ullmann and Philip A. Stadter, *The Public Library of Renaissance Florence* (Padua, 1972), pp.7, 219.

40. Andrew Martindale, *The Rise of the Artist* (London, 1972).

41. Charles Seymour, Jr. (ed.), *Michelangelo: The Sistine Chapel Ceiling* (New York, 1972), p.106.

42. Michelangelo Buonarotti, *Rime*, ed. Enzo Noé Girardi (Bari, 1960), pp.4–5; cf. Seymour, *Michelangelo*, p.110.

43. Seymour, *Michelangelo*, pp.69–70.

44. Mary Hollingsworth, *Patronage in Sixteenth Century Italy* (London, 1996), pp.1–44.

45. Kenneth Clark, *Civilisation* (London, 1969), p.168.

46. Deborah Howard, *Jacopo Sansovino* (New Haven, Conn., 1975).

47. Pietro Aretino, *Il Primo Libro delle Lettere*, ed. Fausto Niccolini (Bari, 1913), p.27; cf. *Selected Letters*, ed. and trans. George Bull (Harmondsworth, Middx, 1976), p.66.

48. *Il Primo Libro*, p.256; cf. *Selected Letters*, p.117.

49. Quoted in Bernard Berenson, *Lorenzo Lotto* (London, 1956), p.128.

50. Carlo Ridolfi, *The Life of Titian*, ed. and trans. Julia Conaway Bondanella, Peter Bondanella et al. (Philadelphia, Pa., 1996), p.95.

51. Norbert Huse and Wolfgang Wolters, *The Art of Renaissance Venice*, trans. Edmund Jephcott (Chicago, 1990), p.303.

52. Patricia Fortini Brown, *The Renaissance in Venice* (London, 1997), p.67.

53. Richard Mackenney, 'Public and Private in Renaissance Venice', *Renaissance Studies*, 12 (1998), pp.109–30; Huse and Wolters, *Renaissance Venice*, pp.297–314.

Chapter 6. Time Travellers

1. John of Salisbury, *Metalogicon*, ed. C.C.J. Webb (Oxford, 1929), Book 3, ch.4, p.136.

2. R.W. Southern, *The Making of the Middle Ages* (London, 1953),

pp.63–7; Petrarch's letter is in Ernst Cassirer et al. (eds.), *The Renaissance Philosophy of Man* (Chicago, 1948), p.142.

3. *Purgatorio*, canti 4–26; R.W.B. Lewis, *Dante* (London, 2001), pp.132–44.

4. Thomas Aquinas, *Summa Theologica*, Latin text and English translations, 61 vols. (London and New York, 1964–81), II(i), quaestio 84, articles 1–4, vol. 26, pp.61–79.

5. For an illustration, see Millard Meiss, *Painting in Florence and Siena after the Black Death* (Princeton, NJ, 1951), Pl.71.

6. See for example the women on sex-strike in Aristophanes' *Lysistrata*; *The Poems of Catullus*, trans. Peter Whigham (Harmondsworth, Middx, 1966), no.32, p.89; Ovid, *Elegies*, Bk.3, no.6, trans. Christopher Marlowe, in *Ovid in English*, ed. Christopher Martin (London, 1998), p.112.

7. *Enneads* VI.ix.9, trans. A.H. Armstrong, in *Plotinus*, 7 vols. (Cambridge, Mass., and London, 1888), vol.6, p.337, also quoted in part in Edgar Wind, *Pagan Mysteries in the Renaissance* (London, 1958), p.59.

8. Peter Brown, *Religion and Society in the Age of St Augustine* (London, 1972), quotation from p.30, also pp.25, 45; Augustine, *The City of God against the Pagans*, ed. and trans. R.W. Dyson (Cambridge, 1998).

9. E.g. Kenneth Clark, *Civilisation* (London, 1969), p.92; Nicholas Mann, *Petrarch* (Oxford, 1984), p.113.

10. Petrarch, *De sui ipsius et multorum ignorantia*, ed. P. de Nolhac and L. Dorez (Paris, 1906), p.24.

11. Ibid., p.44.

12. Ibid., p.63.

13. Ibid., p.75.

14. Ibid., p.69; cf. Petrarch, *On his own Ignorance*, in Cassirer et al., *Renaissance Philosophy*, pp.57, 79, 99, 111, 105.

15. Petrarca, *Secretum*, ed. Enrico Carrara, in Petrarca, *Prose* (Milan–Naples, 1955), pp.21–215, p.56.

16. Ibid., p.86.

17. Ibid., p.94.

18. Ibid., p.98.

19. Ibid., p.160.

20. Ibid., pp.195–6.

21. Ibid., p.198.

22. Ibid., pp.203, 213; cf. *Petrarch's Secret, or, The Soul's Conflict with Passion. Three Dialogues between himself and St. Augustine*, trans. William Draper (Westport, Conn., 1978), pp.35, 65, 73, 77, 137, 172, 173, 176, 179, 190; Charles Trinkaus, *The Poet as Philosopher. Petrarch and*

the Formation of Renaissance Consciousness (New Haven, Conn., 1979); Kenelm Foster, *Petrarch. Poet and Humanist* (Edinburgh, 1984), pp.172ff.

23. Petrarca, *Le familiari*, vol.1, ed. Vittorio Rossi, *Edizione Nazionale delle Opere di Francesco Petrarca*, vol.10 (Florence, 1933), pp.157, 159; cf. *The Ascent of Mount Ventoux*, in Cassirer et al., *Renaissance Philosophy*, pp.41, 44.

24. Albert Rabil, 'Petrarch, Augustine and the Classical Christian Tradition', in *idem* (ed.), *Renaissance Humanism: Foundations, Forms and Legacies*, vol.1, *Humanism in Italy* (Philadelphia, Pa., 1988), p.107.

25. Quoted in Aldo S. Bernardo, 'Petrarch, Dante and the Medieval Tradition', in Rabil, *Renaissance Humanism*, vol.1, p.127.

26. Rabil, 'Petrarch', p.95.

27. Peter Brown, *Augustine of Hippo. A Biography* (London, 1967), pp.299–312.

28. Translated from the Latin:

Inclytorum Pisanorum scripturus historiam
Antiquorum Romanorum renovo memoriam
Nam extendit modo Pisa laudem admirabilem
Quam olim recepit Roma vincendo Carthaginem

cited in Hans Baron, *In Search of Florentine Civic Humanism*, 2 vols. (Princeton, NJ, 1988), vol.1, p.47, n.4.

29. Hans Baron, *The Crisis of the Early Italian Renaissance*, 1 vol. edn (Princeton, NJ, 1966).

30. Quentin Skinner, *The Foundations of Modern Political Thought*, 2 vols. (Cambridge, 1978), vol.1, pp.28–48.

31. Quoted in Maristella Lorch, 'Petrarch, Cicero and the Classical Pagan Tradition', in Rabil, *Renaissance Humanism*, vol. 1, p.90.

32. On Cicero in his own time, see Ronald Syme, *The Roman Revolution* (Oxford, 1939), pp.135–48; on Dante's (and Shakespeare's) depictions of Brutus and Cassius, see J.B. Morrall, *Political Thought in Medieval Times*, 2nd edn (New York, 1962), p.136.

33. See Bruni quoted in Jerrold Seigel, *Rhetoric and Philosophy in Renaissance Humanism. The Use of Eloquence and Wisdom, Petrarch to Valla* (Princeton, NJ, 1968), pp.107–8.

34. Charles L. Stinger, 'Humanism in Florence', in Rabil, *Renaissance Humanism*, vol.1, p.180; quotation from Seigel, *Rhetoric*, p.105; B.L. Ullmann, *The Humanism of Coluccio Salutati* (Padua, 1963), pp.22–4.

35. Jacques Le Goff, *Medieval Civilization*, trans. Julia Barrow (Oxford, 1988), p.165; G.W. Trompf, *The Idea of Historical Recurrence in Western*

Thought from Antiquity to the Reformation (Berkeley, Cal., 1979): I am most grateful to Peter Burke for this reference.

36. Ullmann, *Salutati*, pp.30–2, 60–2.

37. Quoted in Ullmann, *Salutati*, p.104; Stinger, 'Humanism', pp.181–3.

38. Stinger, 'Humanism', p.187.

39. R.M. Errington, *The Dawn of Empire* (London, 1971).

40. It is possible that there is a link rather than a mere parallel here. Churchill was familiar with Macaulay's work, especially his *Lays of Ancient Rome*. Macaulay drew inspiration from Livy and wrote essays on Dante, Petrarch and Machiavelli.

41. Quotations from 'Laudatio Florentinae Urbis', in Hans Baron, *From Petrarch to Leonardo Bruni. Studies in Humanistic and Political Literature* (Chicago, 1968), pp.256–8; cf. 'Panegyric to the City of Florence', in Benjamin Kohl and Ronald G. Witt (eds.), *The Earthly Republic* (Manchester, 1978), pp.166–8.

42. George Holmes, *The Florentine Enlightenment* (London, 1969) pp.150–2.

43. 'Invectivum in Antonium Luschum Vicentinum', in *Prosatori Latini del Quattrocento*, ed. Eugenio Garin (Milan and Naples, 1952), p.18; cf. Stefano Ugo Baldassarri and Arielle Saiber (eds.), *Images of Quattrocento Florence* (New Haven, Conn., 2000), p.9.

44. Stinger, 'Humanism', pp.185–6; quotation from Albert Rabil, 'The Significance of Civic Humanism in the Interpretation of the Italian Renaissance', in *idem*, *Renaissance Humanism*, vol. 1, p.143.

45. Peter Brown, *Augustine of Hippo* (London, 1967), p.20; Poggio, 'De Avaritia', in *Prosatori Latini*, pp.266, 268; cf. 'On Avarice', in Kohl and Witt, *Earthly Republic*, pp.260–1.

46. Letter to Leonardo Bruni, 1416, in *Prosatori Latini*, pp.230, 238; cf. James Bruce Ross and Mary Martin McLaughlin (eds.), *The Portable Renaissance Reader* (London, 1977), pp.615–16, 622–3; see also R.R. Betts, 'Jerome of Prague', in his *Essays in Czech History* (London, 1969), pp.195–235.

47. Benjamin Farrington, *Science and Politics in the Ancient World* (London, 1939).

48. Marsilio Ficino, *Argumentum in Platonicam Theologiam* quoted in Eugenio Garin, *L'umanesimo italiano: filosofia e vita civile nel Rinascimento* (Bari, 1952), p.126; cf. *Italian Humanism. Philosophy and Civic Life in the Renaissance*, trans. P. Munz (Oxford, 1965), p.97. Now see also *Platonic Theology*, vol.1, Books I–IV, ed. James Hankins, trans. Michael J.B. Allen with John Warden (Cambridge, Mass., 2001).

49. *Epistolae*, Book 2, no.1, in *Opera Omnia*, facs. edn, 2 vols. (Turin, 1962), vol.1, pp.681, 710; cf. 'Five Questions Concerning the Mind', in Cassirer et al., *Renaissance Philosophy*, pp.207–8.

50. *In convivium Platonis amore commentarium*, in *Opera Omnia*, vol.2, p.350; cf. Kenneth R. Bartlett (ed.), *The Civilization of the Italian Renaissance* (Lexington, Mass., 1992), p.122; cf. Plato, *The Symposium*, trans. W. Hamilton (Harmondsworth, Middx, 1951), pp.79–95, where the female philosopher Diotima is lecturing Socrates.

51. Giovanni Pico della Mirandola, *De hominis dignitate. Heptaplus. De ente et uno*, ed. Eugenio Garin (Florence, 1942), pp.160, 144, 156; cf. 'On the Dignity of Man', in Cassirer et al., *Renaissance Philosophy*, pp.252, 254, 245, 250.

52. Baldassari and Saiber, *Quattrocento*, p.262; Donald R. Weinstein, *Savonarola and Florence. Prophecy and Patriotism in the Renaissance* (Princeton, NJ, 1970), pp.174, 195. In strongly Judaic tradition, Donatists believed in the idea of a chosen people set apart by ritual purity. For Augustine, such ideas were too defensive, since his own vision of the Church was militantly expansionist. See Brown, *Augustine of Hippo*, pp.216–20. On Savonarola's vision of a chosen people, see Lorenzo Polizzotto, *The Elect Nation. The Savonarolan Movement in Florence, 1494–1545* (Oxford, 1994).

53. Seigel, *Rhetoric*, p.137.

54. Mandell Creighton, *A History of the Papacy from the Great Schism to the Sack of Rome*, 6 vols. (London and New York, 1897), vol.3, pp.170–3, quotation from p.170.

55. H.A. Enno van Gelder, *The Two Reformations in the Sixteenth Century* (The Hague, 1964), pp.14, 28, 123, 132.

56. Lorenzo Valla, 'De Libero Arbitrio', in *Opera Omnia*, facs. edn, fwd by Eugenio Garin, 2 vols. (Turin, 1962), vol.1, pp.1001, 1004; cf. 'Dialogue on Free Will', in Cassirer et al., *Renaissance Philosophy*, pp.160, 168.

57. Lorenzo Valla, 'De voluptate', in *Scritti filosofici e religiosi*, ed. and trans. Giorgio Radetti (Florence, n.d.), pp.3, 6, 16–17; *Opera omnia*, vol.2, pp.912, 903, 921; cf. 'Of the True and False Good', in Peter Elmer, Nick Webb and Roberta Wood (eds.), *The Renaissance in Europe: An Anthology* (New Haven, Conn., 2000), pp.73–87.

58. Lorenzo Valla, 'De falso credita et ementita Constantini donationem Declamatio', in *Opera Omnia*, vol.1, pp.761–95, quotation from p.763; cf. 'Treatise on the Donation of Constantine', in Elmer et al., *Anthology*, pp.26, 23, 24, 27.

59. Polybius, *The Rise of the Roman Empire*, trans. Ian Scott-Kilvert (Harmondsworth, Middx, 1979), p.349; see also Farrington, *Science and Politics*.

60. Latin text from Augustine, *Civitas Dei*, IV.32, in *Works*, ed. and trans. William Green, 7 vols. (London and Cambridge, Mass., 1963), vol.2, p.122; Augustine here argues against Varro (116–28 BC), who was a great historian but whose works are lost: he evidently enjoyed common ground with Polybius.

61. On the possibility of Machiavelli's acquaintance with these ideas, see J.H. Hexter, 'Seyssel, Machiavelli, and Polybius VI: The Mystery of the Missing Translation', *Studies in the Renaissance*, 3 (1956), pp.75–96.

62. Machiavelli, *Discorsi*, I.xii. 2–3; cf. *Discourses on Livy*, trans. Julia Conaway Bonadella and Peter Bonadella (Oxford, 1997), p.54.

63. *The Prince*, trans. George Bull (Harmondsworth, Middx, 1961), p.99.

64. Richard Mackenney, *Sixteenth Century Europe* (London, 1993), p.189, quoting *Jacobi Laynez Disputationes Tridentinae*, ed. Hartmahnn Grisar, 2 vols. (Innsbruck, 1886), vol.2, p.192.

Chapter 7. Space Travellers

1. Augustine, *On True Religion*, trans. H.S. Burleigh, in *Augustine's Early Writings* (London, 1953), xxix, 73, p.263.

2. Quoted in Ernst Cassirer, *The Individual and the Cosmos in Renaissance Philosophy*, trans. Mario Domandi (Oxford, 1963), p.144.

3. See for example David Knowles, *The Evolution of Medieval Thought* (London, 1962), pp.257–8, 264–5.

4. Augustine, *Sermons*, vol.III/1, 4:12, p.192, in *The Works of St Augustine. A Translation for the 21st Century*, ed. John E. Robelle, OSA, 3 vols. in 13 (New York, 1991–5).

5. See Patricia Karlin-Hayter, 'Iconoclasm', in Cyril Mango (ed.), *The Oxford History of Byzantium* (Oxford, 2002), pp.153–62.

6. Gregory I, *The Book of Pastoral Rule and Selected Epistles*, trans. with intro. notes and indices by James Barmby, *A Select Library of Nicene and Post-Nicene Fathers of the Christian Church*, 2nd ser., vol. xiii, ii (Grand Rapids, Mich., 1956), Epistle CV, p.23, Epistle XIII, p.53.

7. William Durandus, *The Symbolism of Churches and Church Ornaments*, trans./intro. John Mason Neale and Benjamin Webb (London, 1906), pp.44–5.

8. John Larner, *Marco Polo and the Discovery of the World* (London, 1992).

9. *Zibaldone da Canal. Manoscritto mercantile del sec. xiv*, ed. Alfredo Stussi (Venice, 1967); cf. *Merchant Culture in Fourteenth Century Venice. The Zibaldone da Canal*, trans. with intro. and notes by John E. Dotson, *Medieval and Renaissance Texts and Studies*, vol.98 (Binghamton, NY, 1994); Cennino d'Andrea Cennini, *Il libro dell'arte*, ed. Franco Brunello (Vicenza, 1971); cf. *The Craftsman's Handbook*, trans. Daniel V. Thompson, Jr. (New Haven, Conn., 1933). See also Michael Baxandall, *Painting and Experience in Fifteenth-Century Italy. A Primer in the Social History of Pictorial Style* (Oxford, 1972), pp.86–108.

10. *Zibaldone*, pp.25, 26, 29; cf. *Merchant Culture*, pp.51, 54, 62.

11. See the explanatory marginal note to Vasari's Life of Botticelli in Giorgio Vasari, *The Great Masters*, trans. Gaston de Vere, ed. Michael Sonino (New York, 1986), p.70; the quotation is the very last part of Michael Amy's entry 'Botticelli, Sandro', in *Encyclopedia of the Renaissance* (New York, 1999), vol.1, p.265.

12. *Libro dell'arte*, pp.19, 31–2, 192–6; cf. *Handbook*, pp.10, 18, 119–22.

13. *Zibaldone*, pp.75–8; cf. *Merchant Culture*, pp.129–30.

14. *Libro dell'arte*, pp.45, 55–6, 61, 62–3; cf. *Handbook*, pp. 26, 31, 34, 35–6.

15. For the Latin text, see Leon Battista Alberti, *On Painting and on Sculpture*, ed. and trans. Cecil Grayson (London, 1972); the trans. is also published in *On Painting*, intro. and notes by Martin Kemp (Harmondsworth, Middx, 1991); Michael Baxandall, *Giotto and the Orators. Humanist Observers of Painting in Italy and the Discovery of Pictorial Composition, 1350–1450* (Oxford, 1971), pp.115–16.

16. Alfred Crosby, *The Measure of Reality. Quantification and Western Society, 1250–1600* (Cambridge, 1997), esp. pp.211–34: Pacioli's portrait by Jacopo de' Barbari appears on the cover. For some case histories connecting exploration, art and commerce, see Pamela H. Smith and Paula Findlen (eds.), *Merchants and Marvels. Commerce, Science and Art in Early Modern Europe* (London, 2002).

17. Francis Ames-Lewis, *The Intellectual Life of the Early Renaissance Artist* (New Haven, Conn., 2000), pp.18–19, 27.

18. Edgar Wind, *Bellini's Feast of the Gods* (Cambridge, Mass., 1948).

19. D.S. Chambers (ed.), *Patrons and Artists in the Italian Renaissance* (London, 1970), pp.131–33, quotation p.131.

20. On these pictures and their interrelationship, wonderfully evoked in the exhibition at the National Gallery in London in 2003, see the catalogue by David Jaffé et al. (eds.), *Titian* (London, 2003), pp.100–12.

21. Giorgio Vasari, *Le Opere*, ed. G. Milanesi, 9 vols. (Florence, 1906), vol.4, pp.133–4, 135, 142, 143; cf. *Lives of the Artists*, 2 vols., ed. and trans. George Bull (Harmondsworth, Middx, 1987), vol.2, pp.107, 109, 114.

22. Erwin Panofsky, *Studies in Iconology* (New York, 1972), p.67.

23. Boccaccio, *Genealogia deorum gentilium*, ed. Vincenzo Romano, 2 vols. (Bari, 1951), vol.2, p.624; see also Panofsky, *Iconology*, p.39.

24. Quoted in Anthony Blunt, *Artistic Theory in Italy, 1450–1600* (Oxford, 1962), p.93.

25. E.H. Gombrich, 'Botticelli's Mythologies: A Study of the Neo-

Platonic Symbolism of his Circle', *Symbolic Images*, in *Gombrich on the Renaissance*, 4 vols. (London, 1985), vol.2, pp.31–81.

26. Panofsky, *Iconology*, p.52; David Rosand, *Titian* (New York, 1978), p.80.

27. *The Rule of St Augustine: Masculine and Feminine Version*, intro. and commentary by Tarsicius J. van Bavel, trans. Raymond Canning (London, 1984), p.16.

28. Panofsky, *Iconology*, pp.95–128.

29. Ames-Lewis, *Intellectual Life*.

30. Leonardo, *On Painting*, ed. Martin Kemp, sel. and trans. *idem* and Margaret Walker (New Haven, Conn., 1989), p.23.

31. Roberto Ridolfi, *The Life of Girolamo Savonarola*, trans. Cecil Grayson (London, 1959), p.213.

32. Machiavelli, *The Prince*, trans. George Bull (Harmondsworth, Middx, 1961), pp.133–7.

33. *Canons and Decrees of the Sacred and Oecumenical Council of Trent*, trans. J. Waterworth (London, 1848), Session 25, pp.234–5.

34. Leonardo, *On Painting*, p.14.

35. Edgar Wind, *Pagan Mysteries in the Renaissance* (London, 1958), p.57.

36. Charles Avery, *Bernini. Genius of the Baroque* (London, 1997), pp.94–100.

37. Santa Teresa de Jesus, *Libro della vida*, ed. Otger Steggink (Madrid, 1986), cap.29, para.13, p.384; cf. *Life of Saint Teresa of Avila by herself*, trans. J.M. Cohen (Harmondsworth, Middx, 1957), p.210; also quoted in Avery, *Bernini*, p.145.

38. Panofsky, *Iconology*, p.100.

39. *The Life and Letters of Sir Henry Wotton*, ed. Logan Pearsall Smith, 2 vols. (Oxford, 1907), vol.1, pp.350–1.

40. Brian Pullan, *The Inquisition of Venice and the Jews of Europe* (Oxford, 1983), pp.26–44.

41. Paul Hills, 'Piety and Patronage in Cinquecento Venice', *Art History*, 6 (1983), pp.30–43.

42. Richard Mackenney, 'Venice', in Roy Porter and Mikulas Teich (eds.), *The Renaissance in National Context* (Cambridge, 1992), pp.53–67.

43. Ignatius Loyola, *The Spiritual Exercises*, trans. Anthony Mottola (New York, 1989), p.141.

44. Augustine, *On True Religion*, pp.257–8; Robert J. O'Connell, SJ, *Art and the Christian Intelligence in St Augustine* (Oxford, 1978), p.89.

45. O'Connell, *Art*, p.90.

Chapter 8. Soundscapes

1. E.H. Gombrich, *Art and Illusion*, 5th edn (London, 1977), pp.107–8; Robert J. O'Connell, SJ, *Art and the Christian Intelligence in St Augustine* (Oxford, 1978), pp.58, 62, 71–2, 80, 91; also Augustine, *On Music*, trans. Robert Catesby Taliaferro, in *The Fathers of the Church*, vol.4 (Washington, DC, 1947), pp.151–379; Walter Pater, *The Renaissance. Studies in Art and Poetry*, 4th edn (London, 1893), p.140.

2. David Rosand, 'The Portrait, the Courtier and Death', in Robert W. Hanning and David Rosand (eds.), *Castiglione. The Ideal and the Real in Renaissance Culture* (New Haven, Conn., 1983), pp.69–90.

3. *Il libro del Cortegiano*, ed. Ettore Bonora, 2nd edn (Milan, 1976), p.162; cf. *The Book of the Courtier*, trans. George Bull (Harmondsworth, Middx, 1967), p.163.

4. Peter Burke, *The Historical Anthropology of Early Modern Italy* (Cambridge, 1987), esp. Part III; *idem*, *The Art of Conversation* (Oxford, 1993), pp.66–88.

5. Richard Mackenney, *Tradesmen and Traders. The World of the Guilds in Venice and Europe, c.1250–c.1650* (London, 1987); Ronald Weissman, *Ritual Brotherhood in Renaissance Florence, 1200–1600* (New York, 1982); John Henderson, *Piety and Charity in Late Medieval Florence* (Oxford, 1994).

6. Helmut Koenigsberger, 'Decadence or Shift?', in his *Estates and Revolutions* (Ithaca, NY, 1971) pp.278–98.

7. C.P. Brand and Lino Pertile (eds.), *The Cambridge History of Italian Literature* (Cambridge, 1996).

8. Giulio Caccini, *Le nuove musiche e nuova maniera di scriverle* (1614), ed. H. Wiley Hitchcock (Madison, Wisc., 1970), p.45n.; quoted in James Haar, 'The Courtier as Musician', in Hanning and Rosand, *Castiglione*, p.170.

9. *Volgarizzamenti del Due e Trecento*, ed. Cesare Segrè (Turin, 1953).

10. *Two Memoirs of Renaissance Florence. The Diaries of Buonaccorso Pitti and Gregorio Dati*, trans. Julia Martines, ed. Gene Brucker (New York, 1967); Robert Hall, *The Italian Questione della Lingua* (Chapel Hill, NC, 1942), p.51.

11. *The Penguin Book of Italian Verse*, ed. George Kay (Harmondsworth, Middx, 1965), pp.1–3.

12. Brand and Pertile, *History*, pp.32–3; C.P. Brand, *Ludovico Ariosto. A Preface to the 'Orlando Furioso'* (Edinburgh, 1974), p.1. For an evocation of this linguistic pot pourri, one might listen to the babblings of the half-witted hunchback, Salvatore, in *The Name of the Rose* (dir. Jean-Jacques Annaud, 1986).

13. George Holmes, *Dante* (Oxford, 1980), pp.16–18, 28–30.

14. See Leonard Forster, *The Icy Fire. Five Studies in European Petrarchism* (Cambridge, 1969), esp. p.56.

15. Brand and Pertile, *History*, pp.74–92.

16. Hall, *Questione,* p.13.

17. Iris Origo, *The World of San Bernardino* (London, 1963), pp.43–76, quotations from pp. 50, 58.

18. Philip Gavitt, *Charity and Children in Renaissance Florence* (Ann Arbor, Mich., 1990); Louis Haas, *The Renaissance Man and his Children* (New York, 1998).

19. Lauro Martines (ed.), *An Italian Renaissance Sextet*, trans. Murtha Baca (New York, 1994), pp.40, 126, 173, 176, 198–9.

20. *Italian Verse*, pp.142–5.

21. Ibid., pp.147–8.

22. Sleeve notes in *Music and Art in Renaissance Florence* (London, 1999).

23. 'Popular Music', in Aldous Huxley, *Along the Road* (London, 1925), p.246.

24. Gustav Reese, *Music in the Renaissance* (London, 1954), p.567; Brand, *Ariosto*, p.31.

25. Carlo Dionisotti, *Gli umanisti e il volgare fra '400 e '500* (Florence, 1968), pp.1–5; Anthony Blunt, *Artistic Theory in Italy, 1450–1600* (Oxford, 1962), pp.39–43; see also the recent translation (with reproductions of the original woodcuts) by Joscelyn Godwin (London, 1999), and *idem, The Pagan Dream of the Renaissance* (London, 2002), pp. 21–38.

26. Martin Lowry, *The World of Aldus Manutius* (Oxford, 1979); Paul Grendler, *The Roman Inquisition and the Venetian Press* (Princeton, NJ, 1977).

27. Hall, *Questione.*

28. Burke, *Anthropology*, p.93.

29. Luke Syson and Dillian Gordon, *Pisanello. Painter to the Renaissance Court* (London, 2000).

30. David Chambers and Trevor Dean, *Clean Hands and Rough Justice* (Ann Arbor, Mich., 1997).

31. Matteo Maria Boiardo, *Orlando Innamorato. Amorum Libri*, ed. Aldo Scaglione, 2 vols. (Turin, 1966), vol.2, Book II, Canto 31, v.49, p.497; Book III, Canto 9, v.26, p.625; cf. the first two books of *Orlando Innamorato*, trans. with intro. and notes Charles Stanley Ross (Oxford, 1995).

32. Brand, *Ariosto*, p.55.

33. Ludovico Ariosto, *Orlando Furioso*, ed. Mario Apollonio and Pio Fontana (2nd edn, Brescia, 1968), Canto 9, stanze 88, 90, p.207; Canto

11, stanze 26, 27, p.240; cf. trans. and intro. Guido Waldman (Oxford, 1983), pp.91–2, 109.

34. Brand, *Ariosto*, pp.171, 184.

35. *Jerusalem Delivered*, trans. and ed. Ralph Nash (Detroit, Mich., 1987); C.P. Brand, *Torquato Tasso. A Study of the Poet and his Contribution to English Literature* (Cambridge, 1965), p.133; Gerald Abraham (ed.), *The Age of Humanism, 1540–1630, New Oxford History of Music*, 4 (Oxford, 1968), p.834.

36. J.R. Woodhouse, *Castiglione. A Reassessment of* The Courtier (Edinburgh, 1978), p.108.

37. Peter Burke, 'The Great Unmasker: Paolo Sarpi, 1552–1623', *History Today*, 15 (1965), p.430.

38. David Wootton, *Paolo Sarpi. Between Renaissance and Enlightenment* (Cambridge, 1983), quotation p.119.

39. Woodhouse, *Courtier*, p.151.

40. Translation in Brendan Dooley (ed.), *Italy and the Baroque: Selected Readings* (New York and London, 1995), p.372; see also Salvatore S. Nigro, 'The Secretary', in Rosario Villari (ed.), *Baroque Personae*, trans. Lydia G. Cochrane (Chicago, 1995), p.94.

41. Victoria Cox, *The Renaissance Dialogue. Literary Dialogue in its Social and Political Contexts, Castiglione to Galileo* (Cambridge, 1992), esp. pp.60–72.

42. *Dialogue Concerning the Two Chief World Systems*, trans. Stillman Drake, foreword by Albert Einstein (Berkeley and Los Angeles, 1953), pp.207–8.

43. Stillman Drake, *Galileo* (Oxford, 1980), p.58.

44. Quoted ibid., p.85.

45. Peter Laven, *Renaissance Italy, 1464–1534* (London, 1966), p.177.

46. Drake, *Galileo*, pp.23, 39.

47. Reese, *Music*, pp.562–8.

48. Donald McLeod, 'Composer of the Week: Monteverdi', BBC Radio 3, 2 February 2001.

Chapter 9. Legacies

1. Michael Levey, *Early Renaissance* (Harmondsworth, Middx, 1967), p.24.

2. Kenneth Clark, *Rembrandt and the Italian Renaissance* (London, 1966).

3. Gigliola Pagano de Divitiis, *English Merchants in Seventeenth-Century Italy* (Cambridge, 1998), pp.126–30.

4. Perry Anderson, *Lineages of the Absolutist State* (London, 1973).

5. 'The Renaissance figure with the greatest influence in the popular

imagination of the English-speaking world has been William Shakespeare', Paul F. Grendler and Stephen Wagley, entry 'Renaissance: the Renaissance in Popular Imagination' in *Encyclopedia of the Renaissance*, ed. Paul F. Grendler, 6 vols. (New York, 1999), vol.5, p.271.

6. Jonathan Bate, *The Genius of Shakespeare* (London, 1997).

7. *The Norton Shakespeare*, ed. Stephen Greenblatt et al. (New York, 1997).

8. Ibid., pp.37–9.

9. H.A. Enno van Gelder, *The Two Reformations in the Sixteenth Century* (The Hague, 1964).

10. M. Marrapodi et al. (eds.), *Shakespeare's Italy* (Manchester, 1993).

11. *The Merry Wives of Windsor*, ed. Giorgio Melchiori (London, 2000), pp.9–18.

12. On the growth of the vernacular, see Michael Mangan, *A Preface to Shakespeare's Tragedies* (London, 1991), esp. pp.31–42; data from p.36.

13. *Coriolanus*, ed. Philip Brocklebank (London, 1976), p.29; *Shakespeare's Plutarch*, ed. T.J.B. Spencer (London, 1964), pp.303–4.

14. Machiavelli, *Il Principe*, ed. Luigi Rosso (Florence, n.d.), pp.188–9; cf. *The Prince*, trans. George Bull (Harmondsworth, Middx, 1961), pp.130, 133.

15. Steve Sohmer, *Shakespeare's Mystery Play* (Manchester, 1999); Roland Mousnier, *The Assassination of Henri IV*, trans. Joan Spencer (London, 1973); Quentin Skinner, *The Foundations of Modern Political Thought*, 2 vols. (Cambridge, 1978), vol.2, pp.189–348.

16. *Pericles*, ed. F.D. Hoeniger (London, 1963), pp.xiii–xix.

17. Quoted in Sebastian de Grazia, *Machiavelli in Hell* (London, 1996), p.224, from *Istorie fiorentine*, 7.6.

18. John F. Danby, *Shakespeare's Doctrine of Nature* (London, 1948); Thomas McAlindon, *Shakespeare's Tragic Cosmos* (Cambridge, 1991).

19. According to the First Folio, *King Lear* was a 'true chronicle history'.

20. *The Notebooks of Leonardo da Vinci*, arranged, rendered into English and introduced by Edward MacCurdy, 2 vols. (London, 1938), vol.2, p.457.

21. R.J.W. Evans, *Rudolf II and his World* (Oxford, 1973).

22. *The Life and Letters of Sir Henry Wotton*, ed. Logan Pearsall Smith, 2 vols. (Oxford, 1907), vol.2, p.22.

23. Thomas Hobbes, *Leviathan* (1651), pt 13, ch.51.

24. 'Discorso morale', in *Opere di Niccolò Machiavelli*, 10 vols. (Milan, 1804–5), vol.10, pp.390–1; cf. *Exhortation to Penitence*, in *The Prince. A Revised Translation. Backgrounds. Interpretations. Marginalia*, trans. and ed. Robert M. Adams, 2nd edn (New York and London, 1992), p.120; also quoted in De Grazia, *Machiavelli*, p.73, who dates it to 1525–7, ibid., p.24.

25. *De moribus ecclesiae*, I, 52, quoted in Robert J. O'Connell, SJ, *Art and the Christian Intelligence in St Augustine* (Oxford, 1978), p.61; Augustine, *On True Religion*, trans. H.S. Burleigh, in *Augustine's Early Writings* (London, 1953), p.89, quoted in O'Connell, *Art and the Christian Intelligence*, p.89; on the *Confessions* as pilgrimage, ibid., p.33, and as odyssey, *idem*, *St Augustine's* Confessions. *The Odyssey of the Soul* (Cambridge, Mass., 1969).

Afterwords

1. See the important collection of essays, Robert S. Kinsman (ed.), *The Darker Vision of the Renaissance. Beyond the Fields of Reason* (Los Angeles, 1974).

2. Antonio Manetti, *Vita di Filippo Brunelleschi, preceduta da La Novella del Grasso*, ed. Domenico de Robertis, intro. and notes by Giuliano Tanturli (Milan, 1976), pp.1–44; and see the translation by Murtha Baca, *The Fat Woodcarver*, followed by the essay 'Who does he think he is?' by Lauro Martines, in Martines (ed.), *An Italian Renaissance Sextet* (New York, 1994), pp.171–242.

3. See Ross King, *Brunelleschi's Dome. The Building of the Great Cathedral in Florence* (London, 2001), pp.79–82.

4. *Novella*, p.5.

5. Ibid., p.43; cf Martines, *Sextet*, p.211.

6. See the important and extensive footnotes in the Arden 3rd series, *King Richard II*, ed. Charles R. Forker (London, 2002), pp.292–3, and *King Lear*, ed. R.A. Foakes (London, 1997), pp.204–5.

Other works of art referred to in the text

O.1   Leonardo, *Man in Circle and Square*. *c*.1485–90. Venice, Accademia.

O.2   Escher, *Autre monde*. 1947. Amsterdam, Stedelijk Museum.

O.3   Leonardo, *Youth costumed for the Festa del Paradiso*. 1511–13? Windsor, Royal Library.

O.4   Titian, *Presentation of the Virgin*. 1534–8. Venice, Accademia.

O.5   Botticelli, Venus, det. from the *Birth of Venus*. *c*.1485. Florence, Uffizi.

O.6   Botticelli, Virgin Mary, det. from *Madonna of the Pomegranate*. *c*.1482. Florence, Uffizi.

O.7   Michelangelo, *Pietà*. 1497–1500. Rome, St Peter's.

O.8   Michelangelo, *Separation of Light from Dark*, from Sistine ceiling. 1508–12. Rome, Sistine Chapel.

O.9   Michelangelo, Mother Church, from *Last Judgment*. 1541. Rome, Sistine Chapel.

O.10   Michelangelo, *Creation of Eve*, from Sistine ceiling. 1508–12. Rome, Sistine Chapel, with plan of ceiling.

O.11   Basilica of St Francis, Assisi.

O.12   Giovanni del Biondo, *St Sebastian*. After 1348. Florence, Museo dell'Opera del Duomo.

O.13   Michelangelo, *Sketch of Fortifications*. 1528. Florence, Casa Buonarotti.

O.14   Uccello, *Route of San Romano*. *c*.1451. London, National Gallery.

O.15   San Clemente, Rome, apse.

O.16   Cavallini, apostles, det. from *Last Judgment*. 1290–1300. Santa Cecilia, Rome.

O.17   Raphael, *The Pantheon*. After 1515. Florence, Uffizi.

O.18   Heemskerck, *St Peter's under Construction*. 1535–6. Berlin, Kupferstich-kabinett.

O.19   Duccio, *Maestà*. 1308–11. Siena, Museo dell'Opera del Duomo.

O.20   Simone Martini, *Guidoriccio da Fogliano*. 1328. Siena, Palazzo Pubblico.

O.21   Ambrogio Lorenzetti, *Allegory of Good and Bad Government*. 1337–9. Siena, Palazzo Pubblico.

O.22   Ambrogio Lorenzetti, *Purification of the Virgin*. 1342. Florence, Uffizi.

O.23   Leonardo, *Bernardo di Bandino Baroncelli on the Gallows*. 1479. Bayonne, Musée Bonnat.

O.24   Medici Palace courtyard, Florence (Michelozzo).

O.25 Palace of Urbino courtyard (Laurana).

O.26 Benozzo Gozzoli, Lorenzo 'il Magnifico', from *Journey of the Magi*. *c*.1459. Florence, Palazzo Medici.

O.27 Pisanello, *Vision of St Eustace*. *c*.1438–42. London, National Gallery.

O.28 Pisanello, *Bird Studies: Wryneck and Two Goldfinches*. 1434–5. Paris, Louvre.

O.29 Justus of Ghent/Berruguete, *Federico da Montefeltro in his Study*. 1476–7. Urbino, Galleria Nazionale delle Marche.

O.30 Piero della Francesca, *Federico da Montefeltro and his Wife Battista Sforza*. *c*.1472. Florence, Uffizi.

O.31 Piero della Francesca, *Flagellation* (and perspective plan). *c*.1460. Urbino, Galleria Nazionale delle Marche.

O.32 Mantegna, det. from *Triumph of Caesar*. 1480–95. London, Hampton Court.

O.33 Mantegna, *Camera degli Sposi*. 1474. Mantua, Ducal Palace.

O.34 Leonardo, *Drawing for the Sforza Monument*. Windsor, Royal Library.

O.35 Leonardo, *War Machines*. 1485–8. London, British Museum.

O.36 Donatello, *Gattamelata*, 1443–53. Padua, San Lorenzo.

O.37 Alberti, *Tempio Malatestiano/Church of San Francesco*. 1446–55. Rimini.

O.38 Simone Martini, *Annunciation*. 1333. Florence, Uffizi.

O.39 Botticelli, *Temptation of Christ*. 1481–2. Rome, Sistine Chapel.

O.40 Perugino, *Christ's Charge to Peter*. 1481–2. Rome, Sistine Chapel.

O.41 Raphael, *Disputa*. 1509–11. Rome, Vatican Stanze.

O.42 Raphael, *School of Athens*. 1509–11. Rome, Vatican Stanze.

O.43 Raphael, *Mass at Bolsena*. 1511–14. Rome, Vatican Stanze.

O.44 Raphael, *Expulsion of Heliodorus*. 1511–14. Rome, Vatican Stanze.

O.45 Raphael, *Liberation of St Peter*. 1511–12. Rome, Vatican Stanze.

O.46 Raphael, *Leo I and Attila*. *c*.1513. Rome, Vatican Stanze.

O.47 Titian, *Paul III and his Grandsons*. 1546. Naples, Museo Nazionale.

O.48 Piero della Francesca, *Sigismondo Malatesta and his Patron Saint*. 1451. Rimini, San Francesco.

O.49 Giotto, *The Kiss of Judas*. *c*.1306. Padua, Scrovegni Chapel.

O.50 Giotto, *Last Judgment*. *c*.1306. Padua, Scrovegni Chapel.

O.51 Ghiberti, *St Matthew*. 1418. Florence, Orsanmichele.

O.52 Ghiberti, *St Stephen*. 1427. Florence, Orsanmichele.

O.53 Donatello, *St Mark*. 1411–13. Florence, Orsanmichele.

O.54 Donatello, *St George*. 1416–20. Florence, Orsanmichele.

O.55 Brunelleschi/Ghiberti, models for *Sacrifice of Isaac*. 1401–2. Florence, Bargello.

O.56 Michelangelo, *Sistine Ceiling*. 1508–12. Rome, Sistine Chapel.

O.57 Michelangelo, *Last Judgment*. 1541. Rome, Sistine Chapel.

O.58 Michelangelo, St Bartholomew, det. from *Last Judgment*. Rome, Sistine Chapel.

O.59 Michelangelo, St Paul, from *Conversion of St Paul*. *c*.1550. Rome, Vatican.

O.60 Titian, *Doge Andrea Gritti*. After 1533. Washington, DC, National Gallery.

O.61 Plan of Piazza San Marco, Venice, before and after Sansovino.

O.62 Piazzetta from San Giorgio Maggiore, Venice.

O.63 Tintoretto, *Paradiso*. 1588–92. Venice, Ducal Palace.

O.64 Giovanni del Biondo, Pride, Avarice and Vainglory, from *St John the Evangelist*. After 1348. Florence, Uffizi.

O.65 Jacopo de' Barbari, *Luca Pacioli*. 1495. Naples, Museo Nazionale di Capodimonte.

O.66 Piero di Cosimo, *Vulcan and Aeolus as Teachers of Mankind*. 1490s. Ottawa, Canada, National Gallery.

O.67 Piero di Cosimo, *The Myth of Prometheus*. *c*.1510? Strasbourg Museum.

O.68 Botticelli, *Primavera*. *c*.1478. Florence, Uffizi.

O.69 Titian, *Sacred and Profane Love*. *c*.1514. Rome, Galleria Borghese.

O.70 Piero della Francesca, *Cupid*. ?1454–66? Arezzo, San Francesco.

O.71 Aerial view of St Peter's, Rome.

O.72 Bernini, *Ecstasy of Santa Teresa*. 1650. Rome, Santa Maria della Vittoria.

O.73 Titian, *Venus of Urbino*. 1538. Florence, Uffizi.

O.74 Titian, *Danaë*. 1545–6. Naples, Gallerie Nazionali di Capodimonte.

O.75 Giorgione, *Concert champêtre*. 1509–10. Paris, Louvre.

O.76. Veronese, *Banquet in the House of Levi*. 1573. Venice, Accademia.

O.77 Tintoretto, *Last Supper*. 1547. Venice, San Marcuola.

O.78 Tintoretto, *Last Supper*. 1565–70. Venice, San Polo.

O.79 Lorenzo Costa, *Concert*. *c*.1500. London, National Gallery.

O.80 Piero della Francesca, *Nativity*. 1470s. London, National Gallery.

O.81 Titian, *Concert*. 1510–12. Florence, Pitti Palace.

O.82 Titian, *Three Ages of Man*. *c*.1512–13. Edinburgh, National Gallery.

O.83 Titian, *Venus with Lutanist*. *c*.1550. Cambridge, Fitzwilliam Museum.

O.84 Titian, *Venus with Organist*. *c*.1560. Berlin-Dahlem, Staatliche Gemäldegälerie.

O.85 Giovanni Bellini, *Sacra conversazione*. 1505. Venice, San Zaccaria.

O.86 Giovanni Bellini, *Sacra conversazione* (San Giobbe altarpiece). 1483–5. Venice, Accademia.

O.87 Carpaccio, *St Augustine in his Study*. 1507–9. Venice, Scuola di San Giorgio degli Schiavoni.

O.88 Luca della Robbia, *Cantoria*. 1430s. Florence, Museo dell'Opera del Duomo.

O.89 Andrea della Robbia, *Puttino*. 1463–6. Florence, Ospedale degli Innocenti.

Bibliography

The reading listed here does not pretend or attempt to be comprehensive. These are books and essays that the author has found most useful. Other, more specialist, works are occasionally listed in the footnotes. The subdivisions are intentionally loose, and the bare alphabetical ordering (in all but the first entry) is an attempt to provide clarity and ease of reference, in preference to the discursive but often impenetrable bibliographies of many other general books. The list is almost entirely confined to works in English, but includes a large proportion of primary and secondary sources in translation. I have only included works on individual artists when these are directly referred to in the text and notes. I devoutly hope that the large number of books listed under 'Reference' does something to compensate for these deficiencies. I make no apologies for making it clear that in order to understand the Renaissance, it is essential to acquire some knowledge of the classical and medieval eras that preceded it.

Introductory

Burckhardt, Jacob, *The Civilization of the Renaissance in Italy*, trans. S.G.C. Middlemore (London, 1945), also with introduction by Peter Burke, but minus illustrations (Harmondsworth, Middx, 1990). For Burckhardt's broader mental world, see his *Reflections on History*, trans. M.D. Hottinger (Indianapolis, Ind., 1979); and for the context in which he worked, see Gossman, Lionel, *Basel in the Age of Burckhardt* (Chicago, 2000). Among other general surveys see:

Brown, Alison, *The Renaissance* (London, 1988)

Burke, Peter, *The Renaissance* (London, 1964)

Burke, Peter, *The Renaissance Sense of the Past* (London, 1969)

Clark, Kenneth, *Civilisation* (London, 1969)

Hay, Denys, *The Italian Renaissance in its Historical Background* (Cambridge, 1972)

Hay, Denys, *The Renaissance* (London, 1963)

Hole, Robert, *The Italian Renaissance* (London, 1998)

Huizinga, Johan, *Men and Ideas*, trans. James S. Holmes and Hans van Marle (New York, 1959)

Kohl, Benjamin F. and Andrews Smith, Alison (eds.), *Major Problems in the History of the Italian Renaissance* (Lexington, Mass., 1995)

Ferguson, Wallace K., *The Renaissance* (New York, 1940)

Ferguson, Wallace K., *The Renaissance in Historical Thought* (Cambridge, Mass., 1948)

Lopez, Robert S., *The Three Ages of the Italian Renaissance* (Charlottesville, Va., 1970)

Martines, Lauro, *Power and Imagination. City-States in Renaissance Italy* (New York, 1980)

Pater, Walter, *The Renaissance*, 5th edn (London, 1901)

Stephens, John, *The Italian Renaissance. The Origins of Intellectual and Artistic Change before the Reformation* (London, 1989)

Symonds, John Addington, *Renaissance in Italy*, 7 vols. (London, 1904)

Aldous Huxley and cultural history

Grey Eminence (London, 1941)
The Devils of Loudon (London, 1952)
Along the Road (London, 1925)
Music at Night (London, 1931)
The Olive Tree (London, 1936)
Themes and Variations (London, 1950)

Reference

Attwater, Donald (ed.), *A Dictionary of Saints* (Harmondsworth, Middx, 1965)

Burns, J.H. and Goldie, Mark (eds.), *The Cambridge History of Political Thought, 1450–1750* (Cambridge, 1991)

Encyclopedia of the Renaissance, ed. Paul F. Grendler, 6 vols. (New York, 1999)

Fifty Key Classical Authors, ed. Alison Sharrock and Rhiannon Ash (London, 2002)

Fifty Key Medieval Thinkers, ed. G.R. Evans (London, 2002)

Hale, J.R. (ed.), *Dictionary of the Italian Renaissance* (London, 1981)

Hall, James, *Hall's Dictionary of Subjects and Symbols in Art* (London, 1974)

Kelly, J.N.D. (ed.), *The Oxford Dictionary of Popes* (Oxford, 1986)

Murray, Peter and Linda, *A Dictionary of Art and Artists*, 3rd edn (London, 1972)

Black, Christopher, *Early Modern Italy. A Social History* (London, 2001)

Cochrane, Eric, *Italy, 1530–1630* (London, 1988)

Hanlon, Gregory, *Early Modern Italy, 1550–1800* (London, 2000)
Hay, Denys, and Law, John, *Italy in the Age of the Renaissance, 1380–1530* (London, 1989)
Larner, John, *Italy in the Age of Dante and Petrarch, 1216–1380* (London, 1980)
Laven, Peter, *Renaissance Italy, 1464–1534* (London, 1966)
Pullan, Brian, *A History of Early Renaissance Italy* (Harmondsworth, Middx, 1973)
Schmitt, Charles B. and Skinner, Quentin (eds.), *The Cambridge History of Renaissance Philosophy* (Cambridge, 1988)

Ancient history

Boardman, John, Griffin, Jasper and Murray, Oswyn (eds.), *The Oxford History of the Classical World* (Oxford, 1986)
Dodds, E.R., *The Greeks and the Irrational* (Berkeley and Los Angeles, 1951)
Errington, R.M., *The Dawn of Empire* (London, 1971)
Syme, Ronald, *The Roman Revolution* (Oxford, 1939)

Plato's influence

The Republic, in *Great Dialogues of Plato*, ed. W.H.D. Rouse (New York, 1956)
The Laws, trans. Trevor J. Saunders (Harmondsworth, Middx, 1970)
Cassirer, Ernst, *The Myth of the State* (New Haven, Conn., 1946)
Farrington, Benjamin, *Science and Politics in the Ancient World* (London, 1939)
Popper, Karl, *The Open Society and its Enemies*, 2 vols., 2nd edn (London, 1950), vol. 1, *The Spell of Plato*
Taylor, Charles, *Sources of the Self* (London, 1989)

Augustine and his legacy

Confessions, trans. R.S. Pine-Coffin (Harmondsworth, Middx, 1961)
The City of God against the Pagans, ed. and trans. R.W. Dyson (Cambridge, 1998)
Brown, Peter, *Augustine of Hippo* (London, 1967)
Brown, Peter, *Religion and Society in the Age of St Augustine* (London, 1972)
Brown, Peter, *The World of Late Antiquity* (London, 1971)
O'Connell, Robert J., SJ, *Art and the Christian Intelligence in St. Augustine* (Oxford, 1978)

O'Connell, Robert J., SJ, *Augustine's* Confessions: *The Odyssey of the Soul* (Cambridge, Mass., 1969)
Wills, Garry, *Saint Augustine* (New York, 1999)

The Middle Ages

Bartlett, Robert, *The Making of Europe* (London, 1993)
Brooke, Christopher, *The Twelfth Century Renaissance* (London, 1969)
Brown, Peter, *The Rise of Western Christendom* (Oxford, 1999)
Duby, Georges, *The Three Orders. Feudal Society Imagined*, trans. Arthur Goldhammer (Chicago, 1980)
Haskins, Charles Homer, *The Renaissance of the Twelfth Century* (Cleveland, Ohio, 1958)
Leff, Gordon, *The Dissolution of the Medieval Outlook* (New York, 1976)
Le Goff, Jacques, *Medieval Civilization*, trans. Julia Barrow (Oxford, 1988)
Le Goff, Jacques, *Time, Work and Culture in the Middle Ages*, trans. Arthur Goldhammer (Chicago, 1980)
Le Goff, Jacques, *Your Money or Your Life*, trans. Patricia Ranum (New York, 1988)
Mâle, Émile, *The Gothic Image*, trans. Dora Nussey (New York, 1958)
Southern, R.W., *The Making of the Middle Ages* (London, 1953)
Ullmann, Walter, *A Short History of the Medieval Papacy* (London, 1972)
Ullmann, Walter, *Medieval Foundations of Renaissance Humanism* (London, 1977)

The Italian Middle Ages

Bec, Christian, *Les marchands écrivains* (Paris and The Hague, 1967)
Hyde, J.K., *Society and Politics in Medieval Italy. The Evolution of the Civic Life, 1000–1300* (London, 1973)
Jones, Philip, *The Italian City-State in the Middle Ages* (Oxford, 1997)
Little, Lester K., *Religious Poverty and the Profit Economy in Medieval Europe* (London, 1978)
Origo, Iris, *The Merchant of Prato* (London, 1963)
Runciman, Stephen, *The Sicilian Vespers* (Harmondsworth, Middx, 1960)
Sapori, Armando, *The Italian Merchant in the Middle Ages*, trans. P.A. Kennen (New York, 1960)
Waley, Daniel P., *The Italian City-Republics* (London, 1969)

Sources I: Collections of documents, technical treatises

Alberti, Leon Battista, *On Painting*, trans. Cecil Grayson, intro. Martin Kemp (London, 1991)

Alberti, Leon Battista, *On Painting and On Sculpture*, trans. Cecil Grayson (London, 1972)

Baldassari, Stefano Ugo and Staiber, Ariella (eds.), *Images of Quattrocento Florence* (New Haven, Conn., 2000)

Bartlett, Kenneth R. (ed.), *The Civilisation of the Italian Renaissance* (Lexington, Mass., 1992)

Brucker, Gene (ed.), *The Society of Renaissance Florence* (New York, 1971)

Brucker, Gene (ed.), *Two Memoirs of Renaissance Florence*, trans. Julia Martines (New York, 1967)

Cennini, Cennino, *The Craftsman's Handbook*, trans. Daniel V. Thompson, Jr (New York, 1954)

Chambers, D.S. (ed.), *Patrons and Artists in the Italian Renaissance* (London, 1970)

Dionisotti, Carlo and Grayson, Cecil (eds.), *Early Italian Texts*, 2nd edn (Oxford, 1965)

Holt, Elizabeth (ed.), *A Documentary History of Art, vol.1, The Middle Ages and the Renaissance* (New York, 1957)

Leonardo da Vinci, *Leonardo on Painting*, sel. and trans. Martin Kemp and Margaret Walker (New Haven, Conn., 1989)

Leonardo da Vinci, *The Notebooks of Leonardo da Vinci*, ed. Edward MacCurdy, 2 vols. (London, 1954)

Merchant Culture in Fourteenth Century Venice: The Zibaldone da Canal, ed. and trans. John E. Dotson (Binghamton, NY, 1994)

Sources II: Literary works

Aretino, Pietro, *Selected Letters*, ed. and trans. George Bull (Harmondsworth, Middx, 1976)

Ariosto, Lodovico, *Orlando Furioso*, trans. and ed. Guido Waldman (Oxford, 1983)

Boccaccio, Giovanni, *The Decameron*, 2 vols., trans. J.M. Rigg (London, 1968)

Boccaccio, Giovanni, *Famous Women*, ed. and trans. Virginia Brown (Cambridge, Mass., 2001)

Boiardo, Matteo Maria, *Orlando Innamorato*, ed. and trans. Charles S. Ross (Oxford, 1995)

Bruni, Leonardo, *History of the Florentine People*, vol.1, ed. and trans. James Hankins (Cambridge, Mass., 2001)

Cassirer, Ernst, Kristeller, Paul Oskar and Randall, John Herman, Jr (eds.), *The Renaissance Philosophy of Man* (Chicago, 1948)

Castiglione, Baldassare, *The Book of the Courtier*, trans. George Bull (Harmondsworth, Middx, 1967)

Cellini, Benvenuto, *The Life of Benvenuto Cellini, Written by Himself*, trans. J.A. Symonds, intro. and illus. John Pope-Hennesy (London, 1949)

Colonna, Francesco, *Hypnerotomachia Polifili* (1499), trans. Joscelyn Godwin (with reproductions of original woodcuts) (London, 1999)

Condivi, Ascanio, *The Life of Michelangelo*, 2nd edn, trans. Alice Sedgwick Wohl, ed. Helmut Wohl (Philadelphia, Penn., 1999)

Dante Alighieri, *The Divine Comedy*, 3 vols., trans. Charles S. Singleton (Princeton, NJ, 1970)

Ficino, Marsilio, *Meditations on the Soul. Selected Letters*, trans. members of the Language Department of the School of Economic Science, London (Rochester, Vt., 1996)

Ficino, Marsilio, *Platonic Theology*, vol. 1, trans. Michael J.B. Allen, ed. James Hankins (Cambridge, Mass., 2001)

Five Italian Renaissance Comedies, ed. Bruce Penman (Harmondsworth, Middx, 1978)

Fonte, Moderata, *The Worth of Women*, ed. and trans. Virginia Cox (Chicago, 1997)

Galilei, Galileo, *Dialogue Concerning the Two Chief World Systems*, ed. and trans. Stilman Drake, forewd. Albert Einstein (Berkeley and Los Angeles, 1953)

Galilei, Galileo, *Discoveries and Opinions of Galileo*, ed. and trans. Stilman Drake (New York, 1957)

Guicciardini, Francesco, *Dialogue on the Government of Florence*, ed. and trans. Alison Brown (Cambridge, 1994)

Guicciardini, Francesco, *The History of Florence*, ed. and trans. Mario Domandi (New York, 1970)

Guicciardini, Francesco, *The History of Italy*, trans. and ed. Sydney Alexander (Princeton, NJ, 1969)

Guicciardini, Francesco, *Maxims and Reflections of a Renaissance Statesman*, trans. Mario Domandi, intro. Nicolai Rubinstein (New York, 1965)

Kohl, Benjamin G. and Witt, Ronald (eds.), *The Earthly Republic* (Manchester, 1978)

Kraye, Jill (ed.), *Cambridge Translations of Renaissance Philosophical Texts*, 2 vols. (Cambridge, 1997)

Loyola, Ignatius, *The Spiritual Exercises of St Ignatius*, trans. Anthony Mottola, intro. Robert J. Gleason, SJ (New York, 1964)

Machiavelli, Niccolò, *Discourses on Livy*, ed. and trans. Julia Conaway Bondanella and Peter Bondanella (Oxford, 1997)

Machiavelli, Niccolò, *The Florentine History*, ed. and trans. W.K. Marriott (London, 1909)

Machiavelli, Niccolò, *The Portable Machiavelli*, ed. and trans. Peter Bondanella and Mark Musa (New York, 1979)

Machiavelli, Niccolò, *The Prince*, trans. George Bull (Harmondsworth, Middx, 1961)

Martines, Lauro (ed.), *An Italian Renaissance Sextet*, trans. Murtha Baca (New York, 1994)

Michelangelo Buonarotti, *Complete Poems and Selected Letters*, trans. Creighton Gilbert, ed. Robert N. Linscott (New York, 1970)

Petrarch, *Petrarch's Secret, or, The Soul's Conflict with Passion. Three Dialogues between Himself and St. Augustine*, trans. William H. Draper (Westpoint, Conn., 1978)

Petrarch, *Selections from The Canzoniere and Other Works*, ed. and trans. Mark Musa (Oxford, 1985)

Petrarch, *Selected Sonnets, Odes and Letters*, ed. Thomas G. Bergin (Wheeling, Ill., 1966)

Ridolfi, Carlo, *The Life of Titian*, ed. and trans. Julia Conaway Bondanella, Peter Bondanella et al. (Philadelphia, Penn., 1966)

Strozzi, Barbara, *Selected Letters*, ed. and trans. Heather Gregory (Berkeley and Los Angeles, 1997)

Tasso, Torquato, *Jerusalem Delivered*, trans. and ed. Ralph Nash (Detroit, Mich., 1986)

Vasari, Giorgio, *Lives of the Artists*, ed. and trans. George Bull, 2 vols. (Harmondsworth, Middx, 1987)

Vasari, Giorgio, *The Great Masters*, ed. Michael Sonino, trans. Gaston de Vere (New York, 1986)

Vespasiano da Bisticci, *Renaissance Princes, Popes and Prelates*, trans. William George and Emily Waters, intro. Myron P. Gilmore (New York, 1963)

Woodward, W.H. (ed.), *Vittorino da Feltre and Other Humanist Educators* (Cambridge, 1897)

Cities

Bowsky, William M., *A Medieval Italian Commune: Siena under the Nine, 1287–1355* (Berkeley and Los Angeles, 1981)

Brucker, Gene, *Renaissance Florence* (New York, 1969)

Butters, Humphrey, *Government and Governed in Early Sixteenth Century Florence* (Oxford, 1985)

Chambers, David S., *The Imperial Age of Venice, 1380–1580* (London, 1970)

Cochrane, Eric, *Florence in the Forgotten Centuries, 1527–1800* (Chicago, 1973)

Epstein, Stephen, *Genoa and the Genoese, 958–1528* (Chapel Hill, NC, 1996)

Fortini Brown, Patricia, *The Renaissance in Venice* (London, 1997)

Goldthwaite, Richard, *The Building of Renaissance Florence* (Baltimore, Md., 1980)

Hale, J.R., *Florence and the Medici. The Pattern of Control* (London, 1977)

Herlihy, David, *Pisa in the Early Renaissance* (New Haven, Conn., 1958)

Holmes, George, *The Florentine Enlightenment* (London, 1969)

Holmes, George, *Florence, Rome and the Origins of the Renaissance* (Oxford, 1986)

Hyde, J.K., *Padua in the Age of Dante* (Manchester, 1966)

Krautheimer, Richard, *Rome. Profile of a City, 312–1308* (Princeton, NJ, 1980)

Lane, Frederic C., *Venice: A Maritime Republic* (Baltimore, Md., 1975)

Martinelli, Giuseppe (ed.), *The World of Renaissance Florence*, trans. Walter Darwell (London, 1968)

Origo, Iris, *Tribune of Rome* (London, 1938)

Partner, Peter, *Renaissance Rome, 1500–59* (Berkeley and Los Angeles, 1976)

Partridge, Loren, *The Renaissance in Rome* (London, 1996)

Ramsey, P.A. (ed.), *Rome in the Renaissance. The City and the Myth* (Binghamton, NY, 1982)

Rubinstein, Nicolai, *The Government of Florence under the Medici, 1434–1494* (Oxford, 1966)

Rubinstein, Nicolai (ed.), *Florentine Studies* (London, 1968)

Stephens, John, *The Fall of the Florentine Republic, 1512–1530* (Oxford, 1983)

Stinger, Charles L., *The Renaissance in Rome* (Bloomington, Ind., 1985)

Turner, A. Richard, *The Renaissance in Florence* (London, 1997)

Waley, Daniel P., *Siena and the Sienese in the Thirteenth Century* (Cambridge, 1991)

Wolters, Wolfgang and Hulse, Norbert, *The Art of Renaissance Venice*, trans. Edmund Jephcott (Chicago, 1990)

Signori and courts

Abulafia, David (ed.), *The French Descent into Renaissance Italy* (Aldershot, Hants., 1995)

Bentley, Jerry H., *Politics and Culture in Renaissance Naples* (Princeton, NJ, 1987).

Bertelli, Sergio (ed.), *Italian Renaissance Courts*, trans. Mary Fitton and Geoffrey Culverwell (London, 1986)

Chambers, D.S. and Dean, Trevor, *Clean Hands and Rough Justice* (Ann Arbor, Mich., 1997)

Chambers, David and Martineau, Jane (eds.), *Splendours of the Gonzaga* (London, 1981)

Cole, Alison, *Art of the Italian Renaissance Courts* (London, 1995)

Gundersheimer, Werner L., *Ferrara: The Style of a Renaissance Despotism* (Princeton, NJ, 1973)

Jones, Philip, *The Malatesta of Rimini and the Papal State* (Cambridge, 1974)

Kohl, Benjamin F., *Padua under the Carrara, 1318–1405* (Baltimore, Md., 1998)

Larner, John, *The Lords of Romagna* (London, 1965)

Law, John, *The Lords of Renaissance Italy* (London, 1981)

Lubkin, Gregory, *A Renaissance Court: Milan under Galeazzo Maria Sforza* (Berkeley and Los Angeles, 1994)

Mallett, Michael, *Mercenaries and their Masters* (Oxford, 1974)

Ryder, A.J., *The Kingdom of Naples under Alfonso the Magnanimous. The Making of a Modern State* (Oxford, 1976)

Syson, Luke, and Gordon, Dillian, *Pisanello. Painter to the Renaissance Court* (London, 2000)

Tuohy, Thomas, *Herculean Ferrara* (Cambridge, 1996)

Welch, Evelyn, *Art and Power in Milan under the Sforza* (New Haven, Conn., 1995)

Patronage, art and society

Burke, Peter, *Culture and Society in Renaissance Italy, 1420–1540* (London, 1972)

Dean, Trevor, and Lowe, K.J.P. (eds.), *Marriage in Italy, 1300–1650* (Cambridge, 1998)

Goffen, Rona, *Piety and Patronage in Renaissance Venice* (New Haven, Conn., 1986)

Goffen, Rona (ed.), *Masaccio's* Trinity (Cambridge, 1998)

Goldthwaite, Richard, *Wealth and the Demand for Art in Italy, 1300–1600* (Baltimore, Md., 1993)

Hollingsworth, Mary, *Patronage in Renaissance Italy* (London, 1994)

Hollingsworth, Mary, *Patronage in Sixteenth Century Italy* (London, 1996)

Howard, Deborah, *Jacopo Sansovino* (New Haven, Conn., 1975)

Kempers, Bram, *Painting, Power and Patronage*, trans. Beverley Jackson (London, 1992)

Kent, Dale, *Cosimo de' Medici and the Florentine Renaissance* (New Haven, Conn., 2000)

Kent, F.W. and Simons, Patricia (eds.), *Patronage, Art and Society in Renaissance Italy* (Oxford, 1987)

King, Catherine E., *Renaissance Women Patrons* (Manchester, 1998)

Larner, John, *Culture and Society in Italy, 1290–1420* (London, 1971)

Martin, Alfred von, *Sociology of the Renaissance*, trans. W. Luetkens, intro. Wallace K. Ferguson (New York, 1963)

Martindale, Andrew, *The Rise of the Artist* (London, 1972)

Norman, Diana (ed.), *Siena, Florence and Padua. Art, Society and Religion, 1280–1400*, 2 vols. (New Haven, Conn., 1995)

Seymour, Charles (ed.), *Michelangelo: The Sistine Chapel Ceiling* (New York, 1972)

Stubblebine, James (ed.), *Giotto: The Arena Chapel* (New York, 1969)

Thomson, David, *Renaissance Architecture: Critics. Patrons. Luxury* (Manchester, 1993)

Religious and social life

Black, Christopher, *Italian Confraternities in the Sixteenth Century* (Cambridge, 1989)

Bowd, Stephen, *Reform before the Reformation* (Leyden, 2002)

Cohn, Samuel K., *The Cult of Remembrance and the Black Death* (Baltimore, Md., 1992)

Cohn, Samuel K., *Women in the Streets* (Baltimore, Md., 1996)

Gavitt, Philip, *Charity and Children in Renaissance Florence* (Ann Arbor, Mich., 1990)

Goldthwaite, Richard, *Private Wealth in Renaissance Florence* (Princeton, NJ, 1968)

Haas, Louis, *The Renaissance Man and his Children* (New York, 1998)

Hay, Denys, *The Church in Italy in the Fifteenth Century* (Cambridge, 1977)

Henderson, John, *Piety and Charity in Late Medieval Florence* (Oxford, 1994)

Niccoli, Ottavia, *Prophecy and People in Renaissance Italy*, trans. Lydia G. Cochrane (Princeton, NJ, 1990)

Origo, Iris, *The World of San Bernardino* (London, 1963)

Polizzotto, Lorenzo, *The Elect Nation. The Savonarolan Movement in Florence, 1494–1545* (Oxford, 1994)

Pullan, Brian, *Rich and Poor in Renaissance Venice* (Oxford, 1971)

Ridolfi, Roberto, *The Life of Savonarola*, trans. Cecil Grayson (London, 1959)

Rosenthal, Margaret, *The Honest Courtesan* (Chicago, 1992)

Terpstra, Nicholas, *Lay Confraternities and Civic Religion in Renaissance Bologna* (Cambridge, 1995)

Terpstra, Nicholas (ed.), *The Politics of Ritual Kinship* (Cambridge, 2000)

Tinagli, Paola, *Women in Renaissance Art* (Manchester, 1997)

Trexler, Richard C., *Public Life in Renaissance Florence* (New York, 1980)

Verdon, Timothy and Henderson, John (eds.), *Christianity and the Renaissance* (Syracuse, NY, 1990)

Weinstein, Donald R., *Savonarola and Florence: Prophecy and Patriotism in the Renaissance* (Princeton, NJ, 1970)

Humanism, literature and music

Abraham, Gerald (ed.), *The Age of Humanism, 1540–1630* (London, 1968)

Baron, Hans, *In Search of Florentine Civic Humanism*, 2 vols. (Princeton, NJ, 1988)

Baron, Hans, *The Crisis of the Early Italian Renaissance*, 1 vol. edn (Princeton, NJ, 1966)

Bernardo, Aldo S. (ed.), *Francesco Petrarca, Citizen of the World* (Albany, NY, 1980)

Burke, Peter, *The Art of Conversation* (Oxford, 1993)

Burke, Peter, *The Fortunes of the Courtier* (Oxford, 1995)

Burke, Peter, *The Historical Anthropology of Early Modern Italy* (Cambridge, 1987)

D'Amico, John F., *Renaissance Humanism in Papal Rome* (Baltimore, Md., 1983)

D'Entrèves, A.P., *Dante as a Political Thinker* (Oxford, 1952)

Drake, Stillman, *Galileo* (Oxford, 1980)

Fenlon, Iain (ed.), *The Renaissance Man and Music*, vol. 2 (London, 1989)

Garin, Eugenio, *Italian Humanism: Philosophy and Civic Life in the Renaissance*, trans. P. Munz (Oxford, 1965)

Geanakoplos, Deno J., *Greek Scholars in Venice: Studies in the Dissemination of Greek Learning from Byzantium to the West* (Cambridge, Mass., 1962)

Godman, Peter, *From Poliziano to Machiavelli* (Princeton, NJ, 1998)

Holmes, George, *Dante* (Oxford, 1980)

Hughes, Dom Anselm and Abraham, Gerald (eds.), *Ars Nova and the Renaissance, 1300–1540* (Oxford, 1960)

Kraye, Jill (ed.), *The Cambridge Companion to Renaissance Humanism* (Cambridge, 1996)

Kristeller, Paul O., *Eight Philosophers of the Italian Renaissance* (Stanford, Cal., 1964)

Kristeller, Paul O., *Medieval Aspects of Renaissance Learning* (Columbia, NY, 1992)

Kristeller, Paul O., *Renaissance Thought* (New York, 1961)

Kristeller, Paul O., *Renaissance Thought and the Arts* (Princeton, NJ, 1965)

Lewis, R.W.B., *Dante* (London, 2001)

Mann, Nicholas, *Petrarch* (Oxford, 1984)

Martines, Lauro, *The Social World of the Florentine Humanists* (London, 1963)

O'Malley, J.W., Izbicki, T.M. and Christiansen, Gerald (eds.), *Humanity and Divinity in Renaissance and Reformation. Essays in Honor of Charles Trinkaus* (Leyden, 1993)

Rabil, Albert (ed.), *Renaissance Humanism. Foundations, Forms and Legacies*, 2 vols. (Philadelphia, Penn., 1988)

Reese, Gustav, *Music in the Renaissance* (London, 1954)

Seigel, Jerrold, *Rhetoric and Philosophy in Renaissance Humanism. The Use of Eloquence and Wisdom, Petrarch to Valla* (Princeton, NJ, 1968)

Tambling, Jeremy (ed.), *Dante* (London, 1999)

Trinkaus, Charles, *In Our Image and Likeness*, 2 vols. (London, 1970)

Trinkaus, Charles, *The Poet as Philosopher. Petrarch and the Formation of Renaissance Consciousness* (New Haven, Conn., and London, 1979)

Ullmann, B.L., *The Humanism of Coluccio Salutati* (Padua, 1963)

Ullmann, B.L. and Stadter, Philip A., *The Public Library of Renaissance Florence. Niccolò Niccoli, Cosimo de' Medici and the Library of San Marco* (Padua, 1972)

Weiss, Roberto, *The Renaissance Discovery of Classical Antiquity* (Oxford, 1969)

Whitfield, J.H., *Petrarch and the Renascence* (Oxford, 1943)

Wilkins, E.H., *Studies in the Life and Work of Petrarch* (Cambridge, Mass., 1955)

Witt, Ronald G., *Coluccio Salutati and his Public Letters* (Geneva, 1976)

Machiavelli

Anglo, Sydney, *Machiavelli* (London, 1969)

Bock, Gisella, Skinner, Quentin and Viroli, Maurizio (eds.), *Machiavelli and Republicanism* (Cambridge, 1990)

Chabod, Federico, *Machiavelli and the Renaissance*, trans. David Moore, intro. A.P. D'Entrèves (Cambridge, Mass., 1958)

De Grazia, Sebastian, *Machiavelli in Hell* (London, 1996)

Donaldson, Stephen, *Machiavelli and Mystery of State* (Cambridge, 1988)

Gilbert, Felix, *Machiavelli and Guicciardini* (Princeton, NJ, 1965)

Hale, J.R., *Machiavelli and Renaissance Italy* (London, 1961)

Parel, Anthony, *The Machiavellian Cosmos* (New Haven, Conn., 1992)

Skinner, Quentin, *Machiavelli* (Oxford, 1981)

Sullivan, Vicky (ed.), *The Comedy and Tragedy of Machiavelli* (New Haven, Conn., 2000)

Viroli, Maurizio, *Machiavelli* (Oxford, 1998)

Viroli, Maurizio, *Niccolo's Smile*, trans. Antony Shugaar (New York, 2001)

Artistic development

Ames-Lewis, Francis, *The Intellectual Life of the Early Renaissance Artist* (New Haven, Conn., 2000)

Avery, Charles, *Bernini: Genius of the Baroque* (London, 1997)

Avery, Charles, *Florentine Renaissance Sculpture* (London, 1970)

Baxandall, Michael, *Giotto and the Orators* (Oxford, 1971)

Baxandall, Michael, *Painting and Experience in Fifteenth Century Italy* (Oxford, 1972)

Berenson, Bernard, *Lorenzo Lotto* (London, 1956)

Blunt, Anthony, *Artistic Theory in Italy, 1450–1650* (Oxford, 1962)

Boucher, Bruce, *Italian Baroque Sculpture* (London, 1998)

Clark, Kenneth, and Finn, David, *The Florence Baptistery Doors* (London, 1980)

Edgerton, Samuel Y., *The Renaissance Rediscovery of Linear Perspective* (New York, 1975)

Field, J.V., *The Invention of Infinity* (Oxford, 1997)

Gombrich, E.H., *Art and Illusion*, 5th edn (London, 1977)

Gombrich, E.H., *Gombrich on the Renaissance*, 4 vols. (London, 1986)

Gombrich, E.H., *Ideals and Idols* (London, 1979)

Hale, J.R., *Artists and Warfare in the Renaissance* (New Haven, Conn., 1990)

Haskell, Francis, *History and its Images* (New Haven, Conn., 1993)

Hood, William, *Fra Angelico at San Marco* (New Haven, Conn., 1993)

Kemp, Martin, *Behind the Picture* (New Haven, Conn., 1997)

Kemp, Martin, *The Science of Art* (New Haven, Conn., 1990)

Levey, Michael, *Early Renaissance* (Harmondsworth, Middx, 1967)

Levey, Michael, *High Renaissance* (Harmondsworth, Middx, 1975)

Meiss, Millard, *Painting in Florence and Siena after the Black Death* (Princeton, NJ, 1951)

Millon, Henry A. (ed.), *Italian Renaissance Architecture. From Brunelleschi to Michelangelo* (London, 1996)

Murray, Peter, *The Architecture of the Italian Renaissance*, 3rd edn (London, 1986)

Murray, Peter and Linda, *The Art of the Renaissance* (London, 1963)

Olson, Roberta J.M., *Italian Renaissance Sculpture* (London, 1992)

Panofsky, Erwin, *Renaissance and Renascences in Western Art* (New York, 1969)

Panofsky, Erwin, *Studies in Iconology* (New York, 1962)

Pope-Hennesy, John, *Essays on Italian Sculpture* (London, 1968)
Pope-Hennesy, John, *Italian Gothic Sculpture* (London, 1955)
Pope-Hennesy, John, *Italian Renaissance Sculpture*, 4th edn (London, 1996)
Pope-Hennesy, John, *Italian Renaissance and Baroque Sculpture*, 4th edn (London, 1996)
Seznec, Jean, *The Survival of the Pagan Gods*, trans. Barbara F. Sessions (Princeton, NJ, 1981)
Smart, Alistair, *The Dawn of Italian Painting* (London, 1978)
Thomas, Anabel, *The Painter's Practice in Renaissance Tuscany* (Cambridge, 1995)
Turner, A. Richard, *Inventing Leonardo* (London, 1995)
Welch, Evelyn, *Art and Society in Italy, 1350–1500* (London, 1997)
White, John, *The Birth and Rebirth of Pictorial Space*, 3rd edn (London, 1987)
Wind, Edgar, *Pagan Mysteries in the Renaissance* (London, 1958)
Wittkower, Rudolph, *Architectural Principles in the Age of Humanism* (New York, 1965)
Wittkower, Rudolph and Margaret, *Born under Saturn. The Character and Conduct of Artists. A Documented History from Antiquity to the French Revolution* (London, 1963)

Some collections of essays

Black, Robert (ed.), *Renaissance Thought. A Reader* (London, 2001)
Brown, Alison (ed.), *Languages and Images of Renaissance Italy* (Oxford, 1995)
Cochrane, Eric (ed.), *The Late Italian Renaissance* (London, 1970)
Denley, Peter and Elam, Caroline (eds.), *Florence and Italy. Renaissance Studies in Honour of Nicolai Rubinstein* (London, 1988)
Findlen, Paula et al., *Beyond Florence* (Stanford, Cal., 2003)
Holmes, George (ed.), *Art and Politics in Renaissance Italy* (Oxford, 1993)
Jacob, E.F. (ed.), *Italian Renaissance Studies* (London, 1960)
Kinsman, Robert S. (ed.), *The Darker Vision of the Renaissance: Beyond the Fields of Reason* (Berkeley and Los Angeles, 1974)
Kirshner, Julius (ed.), *The Origins of the State in Italy, 1300–1600* (Chicago, 1995)
Kristeller, Paul O. and Wiener, Philip P. (eds.), *Renaissance Essays* (New York, 1968)
The Renaissance: Six Essays (New York, 1962)
Werkmeister, William H., *Facets of the Renaissance* (New York, 1959)

The Renaissance in Europe

Aston, Margaret, *Panorama of the Renaissance* (London, 1996)

Bouwsma, William J., *The Waning of the Renaissance, 1550–1640* (New Haven, Conn., 2000)

Burke, Peter, *The Renaissance* (London, 1987)

Burke, Peter, *The European Renaissance* (Oxford, 1998)

Crosby, Alfred J., *The Measure of Reality* (Cambridge, 1997)

Cultural Atlas of the Renaissance (New York, 1993)

Elmer, Peter, Webb, Nick and Wood, Roberta (eds.), *The Renaissance in Europe. An Anthology* (New Haven, Conn., 2000)

Enno van Gelder, H.A., *The Two Reformations in the Sixteenth Century* (Paris and The Hague, 1964)

Goodman, Anthony and MacKay, Angus (eds.), *The Impact of Humanism on Western Europe* (London, 1990)

Greeenblatt, Stephen, *Renaissance Self-Fashioning* (Chicago, 1984)

Hale, John, *The Civilization of Europe in the Renaissance* (London, 1993)

Hay, Denys (ed.), *The Age of the Renaissance* (London, 1967)

Mackenney, Richard, *Sixteenth Century Europe* (London, 1993)

Martin, John Jeffries (ed.), *The Renaissance. Italy and Abroad* (London and New York, 2003)

Nauert, Charles, *Humanism and the Culture of Renaissance Europe* (Cambridge, 1995)

Porter, Roy and Teich, Mikulas (eds.), *The Renaissance in National Context* (Cambridge, 1992)

Rabb, Theodore K., *Renaissance Lives. Portraits of an Age* (New York, 1993)

Shakespeare, William, *The Norton Shakespeare*, ed. Stephen Greenblatt et al. (New York, 1997)

Villari, Rosario (ed.), *Baroque Personae*, trans. Lydia G. Cochrane (Chicago, 1995)

Weiss, Roberto, *The Spread of Italian Humanism* (London, 1964)

Whitlock, Keith (ed.), *The Renaissance in Europe: A Reader* (New Haven, Conn., 2000)

Yates, Frances, *Collected Essays*, 3 vols. (London, 1982–4)

Index

abacus, 162 *see also* merchants, mercantile activity

Accetto, Torquato, 17th-cent. Ferrarese author, 202

Acciaiuoli, Florentine banking company, 66

accountancy *see* book-keeping, double entry

Achilles, ancient Greek hero of the Trojan Wars, 132

active life (*negotium*), 51, 59, 139–40, 157, 223 *see also* civic humanism

Aeschylus, ancient Greek playwright (525–456 BC), 120

Aesop, Greek philosopher and story-teller (*d.* 561 BC), 158

Agnadello, battle of (1509), 71, 75, 123

Agrippa, Marcus, Roman commander and builder of the Pantheon (63–12 BC), 60

Alberti, Leon Battista, Florentine humanist and architect, 'Renaissance man' (1404–72), 29, 50, 80, 112, 115, 156, 161, 162

Albizzi, Florentine family, 50

Alexander III, pope (*r.* 1159–81), 126

Alexander III of Macedon, 'the Great', emperor (355–323 BC), 141, 221

Alexander VI, pope (*r.* 1492–1503), 62, 101 *see also* Borgia family

Alidosi family, 79

Alfonso I of Aragon, 'the Magnanimous' (*r.* 1443–58), 36, 93–4, 150

Alighieri, Dante *see* Dante Alighieri

Almereyda, Michael, American film director of *Hamlet*, 221

Alps, 138

Altichiero, 14th-cent. painter, 95

Amalfi, 74, 75–6

'Ambrosian Republic', Milan (1447–50), 92 *see also* Milan, city of, duchy of

America, United States of, 57–8

amor, 172 *see also* Three Graces

Amsterdam, 54, 55

Anagni, 99

Anaxagoras, ancient Greek materialist philosopher (500–428 BC), 43

Ancient Greece, 38, 50, 138 *see also* Athens; Greek; Sparta

Ancient Rome, 15, 18, 20, 57, 103, 110, 138, 192, 211; imitation of, 49, 140, 143, 144; influence in Florence, 67, 69 *see also* Rome

Ancient world, antiquity, 14–17, 90, 98, 101, 120, 128, 133, 163–7

Angelico, Fra *see* Fra Angelico

anger, 131, 132 *see also* Seven Capital Sins; Seven Deadly Sins

Anguissola, Sophonisba (*c.*1532–1625), Cremonese painter, 31

Anjou, Angevins, 35, 36, 77 *see also* Robert of Anjou

Antonello da Messina, Sicilian painter (*c.*1430–79), 86–7

Apollonius of Tyre, tale of, 213 *see also*, Gower, John

appearance, appearances *see* reality and illusion

Apple of Discord, 164

Apples of the Hesperides, 164

Aquinas, St Thomas, medieval scholastic philosopher (1224/5–74), 20, 43, 129, 130–1, 156

Arabs, Arabic learning, 129, 135

Aragon, Aragonese, 36, 77

Arena Chapel *see* Padua, Scrovegni Chapel

Aretino, Pietro, bawdy vernacular writer (1492–1556), 71, 124, 197; works on the *Index*, 54 *see also* Gritti, Andrea; Sansovino, Jacopo; Titian

Ariadne, daughter of Minos, king of Crete, abandoned by the hero Theseus, 165

Arienti, Giovanni Sabadino degli, late